THROUGH THE PALE DOOR

THROUGH
THE
PALE DOOR

A Guide to and through the American Gothic

Frederick S. Frank

Bibliographies and Indexes in American Literature,
Number 11

GREENWOOD PRESS
New York • Westport, Connecticut • London

Library of Congress Cataloging-in-Publication Data

Frank, Frederick S.
    Through the pale door : a guide to and through the American gothic
/ Frederick S. Frank.
        p. cm.—(Bibliographies and indexes in American literature, ISSN 0742-6860
; no. 11)
    Includes bibliographical references.
    ISBN 0-313-25900-3 (lib. bdg. : alk. paper)
    1. Gothic revival (Literature)—United States—Bibliography.
2. Horror tales, American—Bibliography. 3. American literature—
Bibliography. I. Title. II. Series.
Z1231.G66F7   1990
[PS374.G68]
016.813'08729—dc20   90-31733

British Library Cataloguing in Publication Data is available.

Library of Congress Catalog Card Number: 90-31733
ISBN: 0-313-25900-3
ISSN: 0742-6860

First published in 1990

Greenwood Press, 88 Post Road West, Westport, CT 06881
An imprint of Greenwood Publishing Group, Inc.

Printed in the United States of America

The paper used in this book complies with the
Permanent Paper Standard issued by the National
Information Standards Organization (Z39.48-1984).

10 9 8 7 6 5 4 3 2 1

"While, like a rapid ghastly river,
Through the pale door;
A hideous throng rush out forever,
And laugh—but smile no more."

Edgar Allan Poe

Contents

Introduction

THROUGH THE PALE DOOR is a selective bibliographical census of American Gothic literature from its origins in the dark visions of Charles Brockden Brown at the end of the Eighteenth Century to its proliferation in the works of the masters of modern American horror, H.P. Lovecraft, Shirley Jackson, Joyce Carol Oates, and Stephen King. The book's aim is to conduct the reader on a bibliographical excursion spanning two centuries of intense and unique fascination with horror in its manifold forms and thereby to provide some explanation for the broadly used but still elusive term American Gothic. The 509 entries not only summarize the energy and depth of the American Gothic vision, they also attest to the unity of mood and theme that marks the American Gothic movement. What lies beyond the pale door might well be considered the collective unconscious of the American experience, the nightmares, fears, monsters and demonic anti-myths of American life that lurk below the optimism and confidence that have characterized our culture.

While the American Gothic drew extensively upon the technology and structure of the English Gothic novel, a genre which reached its popular apex just as American literature was beginning, our Gothic would rapidly diverge from the European model just as our country had broken away from England. Individual potential for evil in a new society of uncertainties would determine the primal American Gothic themes that have fascinated our writers over the years. In its obsession with family disintegration, incest, murder, racial and sexual violence, and contamination of the landscape, the American Gothic spirit was driven by what Herman Melville called in his review of Hawthorne's Mosses from an Old Manse "the power of blackness." Terror of self, psychic and social disorder, ontological conflicts and dilemmas, a terrible sense of loneliness and homelessness, and spiritual stagnation and entrapment have been the motivating themes of American Gothicism from Charles Brockden Brown's Wieland (1798) to Stephen King's Carrie. The thematic continuity is described by Louis Gross in Redefining the American Gothic: From Wieland to The Day of the Dead (1989) as a "long line of Gothic texts which show the land, people, and institutions of this country as participants in the nightmare of history. The vision of a world of darkness, terror, oppression, and perversity, seemingly so alien from the rational bias of the founding fathers, is as persuasive in our national consciousness as its daylight opposite." Beginning with the early Gothicism of Brown, developing and deepening in the work of the nineteenth century masterbuilders of American Gothic, Poe, Hawthorne, James, and Bierce, and perhaps climaxing in the mechanized and domestic supernaturalism of Stephen King, the American Gothic has sought to confront its readers with the spectres and monsters at large in our culture. As Anthony Magistrale has recently pointed out in Landscape of Fear: Stephen King's American Gothic (1988), our Gothic impulse even in the crude forms of the horror comic or the dime novel "has less to do with prehistoric creatures roaming the night or vampires cruising for nourishment. Rather, the deepest terrors are sociopolitical in nature reflecting our worst fears about vulnerable western institutions,--our governmental bureaucracies, our school systems, our communities, our familial relationships." One might add that in its later stages, the American Gothic has acknowledged the creeping Atomic shadow and recorded the distresses of feminine identity among other Gothic aspects of the haunted society.

Yet, a serious critical consideration of the American Gothic's modes and meanings has only recently come into its own and the definitive book on the unique and special character of our Gothic still remains to be written. Until quite late in the Twentieth Century, it was critically fashionable to dismiss the tendency toward Gothicism as a stylistic debility or concession to cheap sensationalism. Even one of the greatest of our Gothic writers, Edgar Allan Poe, was often censured for his use of the tawdry contraptions of horror or his derivative Germanism. Poe both defended and defined his profounder versions of the Gothic in the famous injunction, "My terror is not of Germany, but of the soul," a remark which might stand as a motto for American Gothic endeavor. Other nineteenth century American Gothicists had to endure, sometimes posthumously, the official critical opinion that the Gothic was an inferior genre incapable of high seriousness and appealing only to readers of questionable tastes. Such critical prejudices against Gothic fiction, however, did not prevent the Gothic from generating a huge readership in American households. The queen of the tea table romancers, Mrs. E.D.E.N. Southworth, outsold all of her male rivals and offered the public a steady flow of sentimental and domestic Gothics. Cooper and Irving turned to the example of the Gothic in creating their own American versions of history and comedy. The brilliant fantasist Fitz-James O'Brien and the historical novelist of the antebellum south William Gilmore Simms attracted large audiences often using Gothic characters and techniques to allure their readers. Hawthorne's editor friend, Charles Wilkins Webber, relocated the Gothic to the frontier in his western tales of terror. And the redoubtable Ned Buntline (Edward Zane Carroll Judson) made Gothic episodes and personages almost a compulsory element of that primitive precursor of paperback horror, the nickel and dime novel. Still, a conspiracy of silence reigned among the literary historians and remained in force until the 1920's. Not only was no critical effort made to define the American Gothic or to distinguish it from the English parent form, but any Gothic tendency in American literature was viewed as simply incompatible with the proper code of realism, an exclusive doctrine of American letters militantly preached by Vernon Parrington in his encyclical Main Currents in American Thought (1927-1930).

But despite the monolithic position of Parrington, the critical climate was changing. The British critic and first literary historian of the Gothic, Edith Birkhead, had dared to include a chapter entitled "American Tales of Terror" (Chapter XI) in her landmark survey, The Tale of Terror: A Study of the Gothic Romance (1921) and the Finnish student of the Gothic, Eino Railo, extended her general commentary by introducing American Gothic examples into his thematically organized history of the Gothic, The Haunted Castle: A Study of the Elements of English Romanticism (1927).

Ironically, the first recognition of a separate American Gothic convention
had come from abroad, not from the ranks of American critics. In 1926, the
republication of Charles Brockden Brown's Wieland (1798) as a genuine
specimen of the American variety of Gothic romance was undertaken by Fred
Lewis Pattee. Pattee's preface to the novel was a first glimpse through
the pale door, for it stimulated the search for the American Gothic and
made a whole generation of new critics aware of the significant role of
Gothicism in shaping our literature. Pattee viewed Wieland as an American
tragedy rendered in Gothic terms, a pessimistic parable and dark response
to the Edenic promises of the new world. On the popular front, Pattee's
work was supplemented by the eminent supernaturalist Howard Phillips Lovecraft, whose unpretentious monograph, Supernatural Horror in Literature
(1927), would brilliantly clarify the relationship between American Gothic
themes and the powerful roots of the Gothic story in timeless cosmic dread
and the metaphysical fear of both the unknown and the unknowable. Writing
on Poe, Lovecraft suggested that it was Poe who internalized the Gothic
with "a master's vision of the terror that stalks about and within us.
Penetrating to every festering horror in the gaily painted mockery called
existence, and in the solemn masquerade called human thought and feeling,
that vision had the power to project itself till there bloomed in the
sterile America of the thirties and forties such a moon-nourished garden
of gorgeous poison fungi as not even the nether slopes of Saturn might
boast."

In the work of Pattee and Lovecraft, the forbidden counter-myth of
America as fallen Eden, a mythic environment where apprehension and anxiety overshadowed the brighter hopes and expectations of Americans for
themselves and for their new country, was given original critical sanc-
tion. The new world was also a Gothic world, an atmosphere full of unidentified disaster and mysterious catastrophe, a place where appearances de-
ceive, ideals become dangerously delusive or empty, and where the most
malevolent passions can overwhelm reason. As Ann Tracy has expressed it,
in The Gothic Novel, 1790-1830, "The Gothic world is quintessentially the
fallen world, the vision of fallen man, living in fear and alienation,
haunted by images of his mythic expulsion, by its repercussions, and by an
awareness of his unavoidable wretchedness. Tempters, natural and supernatural, assault in impenetrable disguises, precipitating ruin and damnation. Nobody is entirely safe; nothing is secure."

The image of America as an unsafe civilization, a new version of the
original haunted castle of the European Gothic, became the foundation for
fresh perspectives on the American Gothic. Frontier and forest, city and
town, family home and newly built house, lose their pastoral quality or
abandon their symbolism of security, purity, and stability to assume the
horrific dimensions traditionally depicted in the Gothic as closed and
corruptive space, a chamber of horrors or a subterranean enclosure which
affords no return to light.

The exposure of the American experience as a ruined Eden or fallen
world opened for future critics the prospective of America not as a transcendental sanctuary but as a Gothic landscape. Soon, that landscape was
being explored by critics and cultural historians of every sort in quest
of a satisfactory set of criteria for defining the American Gothic. In the
late 1940's and early 1950's, the influential Edmund Wilson appraised the
cultural appropriateness of Gothic materials to the mental terrors and
moral horrors of American life in Classics and Commercials: A Literary
Chronicle of the Forties (1951), and to the dismay of formalist academi-
cians, American Gothic subjects were beginning to seep into the university
curriculum. Numerous concentrated studies of individual Gothic authors
such as George Snell's "Charles Brockden Brown: Apocalypicalist," published in The University of Kansas City Review in 1944 often provided the
occasion for attempts at definition of the American Gothic form. In com-

menting on America's first Gothic writer, Snell also sought to explicate the American Gothic itself as when he wrote of Brown: "He was the shaper of a tradition that affected writers greater than he and which continues today to fructify some of our most serious fiction. In Brown we discover foreshadowed all the demonic, macabre, or apocalyptic idiosyncracies of what, to employ an inexact but useful term, amounts to a school in the American novel. A beginning had been made; the shape of American fiction had been set in at least one of its characteristic channels." Whether the critic was examining the Gothic from a Marxist, a Freudian, or later a feminist perspective, the quest for the American Gothic after the 1940's and 1950's assumed an enduring and unbroken bloodline from America's first Gothic writer to the masters of modern horror. Furthermore, it was becoming apparent that the social and psychological motives that had called the American Gothic into existence at the end of the Eighteenth Century remained equally active in the Twentieth Century and accounted for the popularity of the Gothic impulse in contemporary American fiction.

Two books appearing in the early 1960's offered challenging answers to the rise and persistence of an American Gothic tradition. Leslie Fiedler's Love and Death in the American Novel (1960) posited an answer to the question of American Gothicism in a Freudian context, arguing forcibly that the Gothic was the inevitable expression of "the failure of the American fictionist to deal with adult heterosexual love and his consequent obsession with death, incest, and innocent homosexuality. American Gothic identified evil with the id and was therefore conservative at its deepest level of implication, whatever the intent of its authors." The Freudian framework was again brought to bear on the question in Irving Malin's New American Gothic (1962), an analysis of the neo-Gothic symbolism and technique of Flannery O'Connor, James Purdy, J.D. Salinger, Truman Capote, John Hawkes, and Carson Mc Cullers. With their grotesque gallery of characters, narcissistic or Faustian isolation, hostility to community, and substitution of violent sexuality for love, these modern Gothic writers shared a vision of demonic chaos in which, according to Malin's definition, "order often breaks down, chronology is confused, identity is blurred, sex is twisted, and the buried life erupts." If not entirely conclusive, these general speculative responses to the problem of American Gothicism showed that American horror was a distinct and important mode worthy of further inquiry and research.

By the end of the 1960's as the renaissance in Gothic criticism was entering its major phase, the critical hypotheses of Fiedler and Malin were being applied to the entire range of American writers, and, with some extremely insightful results. It was now clear that the American tale of terror did differ fundamentally from the English tradition which it had inherited and exploited. While the English Gothic was a fashion, a short-lived mania, and a group style devoted to the peculiar pleasure generated by fantasies of horror, grotesque thrill, and supernatural shock, the American Gothic would go deeper even in its popular variety. While the English Gothic had dealt with physical terror and social horror, the American Gothic would concentrate on mental terror and moral horror. Such concentration rendered the American Gothic a medium of conceptions as well as contraptions and made it a vehicle for ideas, particularly problems of self. Although there was much technical correspondence or similarity between the two national Gothics, there was almost no ideological resemblance. Thus, while it was closely related in form and technique to English Gothicism, American Gothic was far apart from the English model in theme and idea.

Throughout the 1970's and on into the 1980's, several excellent doctoral dissertations provided some refined answers to the definition of an American Gothic. Richard S. Dimaggio's "The Tradition of the American Gothic Novel" (Arizona, 1976) judged the form to be "a novel of ideas as

well as intense emotions." Stephen T. Ryan, in "Chaotic Slumber: Pica-
resque and Gothic in Contemporary American Novels" (Utah, 1976) traced the
Gothic vein in the works of John Hawkes, Joyce Carol Oates, and Walker
Percy and found it to be reflective of "the breakdown of order in the
modern world." Examining the presence of the Gothic in the writings of
Washington Irving, Robert Montgomery Bird, William Gilmore Simms, George
Lippard, and several other pre-Civil War writers, Jo Anne Yates in
"American Gothic: Sources of Terror in American Fiction Before the Civil
War" (North Carolina, 1980) reached the provocative conclusion that "The
American experience forced writers again and again to turn inward into the
mind and heart rather than outwards toward society. If writers were to
find terror in the new world, which many did, they were forced to find it
not in outmoded social systems but within man himself." To a large extent,
the mysterious American landscape, particularly the western wilderness,
had supplanted the darkened abbey or sullen castle of European Gothic fiction. In "America's Gothic Landscape" (New York University, 1980), Amy
Tucker proposed a sociopolitical reading of American Gothicism, arguing
that "Writers on this side of the Atlantic frequently used the Gothic as a
way of looking at their homeland. The American landscape in their fiction
not only projects the protagonists' inward exploration but illuminates the
dark regions of the American psyche itself by allegorizing the guilty history of the country's settlement." Perhaps the most sophisticated analysis
of the inner significance of the American Gothic mode was made by Gary Lee
Green in his "The Language of Nightmare: A Theory of American Gothic Fiction" (Oklahoma, 1985). The Gothic was an inevitable reaction and intense
response to those native sources of fear and anxiety bred by a terror of
the unknown self. For Green, the American Gothic spoke "a language of
negativity" and projected "the fear that self-autonomy is merely a lin-
guistic construct, a fear based on the self's relation to an environment
which appears to prohibit a coherent sense of identity."
   The search for the American Gothic was certainly broadened and
sharpened by doctoral writing on the subject. In the 1980's, critical en-
dorsement of the importance of Gothicism to the American imagination came
from many quarters. Both the academy and advocates of popular culture contributed book-length studies to the field although the absence of one
single selective bibliographical survey of the primary sources of American
Gothicism was still a gap in the scholarship. Donald Ringe's American
Gothic: Imagination and Reason in Nineteenth Century Fiction (1982)
scorned the Freudian approach to place our Gothic within a restrictive
historicist framework. According to Ringe's thesis, the Gothic exerted its
main influence during the first four decades of the Nineteenth Century,
culminating in the achievements of Poe, Hawthorne, and Melville. His conclusion, that "the American Gothic reached its peak in their work" in the
mid-century and declined into an insignificant role thereafter is a point
worth debating. In The Delights of Terror: An Aesthetics of the Tale of
Terror (1987), Terry Heller takes exception to Ringe's notion of the American Gothic as a temporary force in our literature which subsided after
the 1850's. Heller begins with Charles Brockden Brown and carries the
search for the American Gothic through the works of Faulkner and the mod-
erns. This eclectic reading of the survival and importance of the Gothic
in American literature continues to have its impact on the critical study
of many authors not normally associated with the Gothic. For example,
James K. Morris's doctoral dissertation, "Stephen Crane and the Gothic
Tradition" (Mississippi, 1983), Susan J. Rosowski's article, "Willa Cather's American Gothic" in The Great Plains Quarterly (1984), and Ruth D.
Weston's doctoral investigation "Nothing So Mundane as Ghosts: Eudora Welty and the Gothic" (Tulsa, 1984) demonstrate this modern trend in American
Gothic criticism. The trend continues as seen in Kathy Anne Fedorko's re-
cent dissertation, "Edith Wharton's Haunted House: The Gothic in her Fic-

tion" (Rutgers, 1988), while the union of Gothic criticism and the American black experience as evidenced by Joseph Bodziock's essay "Richard Wright and Afro-American Gothic" in Richard Wright: Myths and Realities (Garland, 1988) is equally indicative of the wider view scholars are now taking toward traditionally non-Gothic writers.

Finally, Stephen King's perceptive thesaurus of popular horror, Danse Macabre (1981), and his foreword to his own collection of Gothic tales, Night Shift (1978), can both stand as exercises in definition from the insider's point of view. King conceives of the American Gothic as an internal mood as much as it is an external literary mode with the entrapped or enclosed characters "turning inward instead of growing outward. The new American Gothic provides a closed loop of character, and in what might be termed a psychological pathetic fallacy, the physical surroundings often mimic the inward-turning of the characters themselves." The best scholarly book on the American Gothic in the 1980's (cited above) is Louis S. Gross's Redefining the American Gothic: From Wieland to Day of the Dead (1988). The book combines the previous research and criticism with its own acute readings of American Gothic texts over two centuries of Gothic activity and arrives at a kind of grand synthesis of the various critical positions, the macro-politics, the cultural psychology, the national and personal iconography of the American Gothic.

Yet, the finest and most sensitive interpretation of the American Gothic mood comes not from a critic or scholar of the form but from a nineteenth century poet who knew at firsthand the pleasures and the torments of the Gothic vision and who led a Gothic life. The recurrent elements of the American Gothic experience converge to a radiant point in Emily Dickinson's poem "One Need Not Be A Chamber To Be Haunted." For her, the "superior spectre," the internal monster, the unholiest ghost of all stalking through the castle of the American mind, is ourselves.

> One need not be a chamber to be haunted.
> One need not be a house;
> The brain has corridors surpassing
> Material place.
>
> Far safer, of a midnight meeting
> External ghost,
> Than an interior confronting
> That whiter host.
>
> Far safer through an abbey gallop,
> The stones achase,
> Than, moonless, one's own self encounter
> In lonesome place.
>
> Ourself, behind ourself concealed,
> Should startle most;
> Assassin hid in our apartment,
> Be horror's least.
>
> The prudent carries a revolver,
> He bolts the door,
> O'erlooking a superior spectre
> More near.

THE USE AND ORGANIZATION OF THE BIBLIOGRAPHY

THROUGH THE PALE DOOR selects, classifies, and comments on 509 specimens

of American Gothicism. It is a bibliography of primary materials and sources covering a diverse array of Gothicism over two centuries of American
literature. The user will quickly discern various categories of Gothic
fiction among the entries. Along with formal or traditional examples of
the Gothic novel, there are Gothic plays, tales of spiritualism, vampirism, and werewolfery, nickel and dime Gothics, and that most preeminent
contribution to the international Gothic canon, the American Gothic short
story. Survivals, revivals, and imitations are noted by means of the cross
references. Use of the book in conjunction with the critical studies of
American Gothicism cited above should validate the premise that the American Gothic is a unity and an entity, not a disparate movement of isolated
parts.

THROUGH THE PALE DOOR does not replace the prior bibliographies in
the field, but it does strive to be more comprehensive and focal in scope
than earlier compilations. It goes beyond, for example, one of the earliest inventories of American Gothic fiction, Sister Mary Mauritia Redden's
The Gothic Fiction in the American Magazines, 1765-1800 (1939) and is more
directive and concentrated than such recent horror bibliographies and
guides as E.F. Bleiler's The Guide to the Supernatural in Fiction. A Full
Description of 1,775 Books from 1750 to 1960 (1983) and his Supernatural
Fiction Writers (1985) or Frank N. Magill's Survey of Modern Fantasy Literature (1983). These are superlative bibliographical gatherings but not
exclusively centered on American Gothic materials.

In selecting the titles for inclusion, I was guided and informed by
the work of Kay J. Mussell. Her bibliographical essays in Women's Gothic
and Romantic Fiction: A Reference Guide (1981) and her piece on "Gothic
Novels" in Handbook of American Popular Literature (1988) proved indispen-
sable. My own chapter on the early Gothic in Horror Literature: A Reader's
Guide (1990), under the general editorship of Neil Barron and forthcoming
from Garland Publishing, gave me initial contact with some of the more obscure Gothic titles which I decided to include as illustrative of nineteenth century Gothic trends. When published in 1990, the Barron Guide
should be an intellectual asset to any scholar seeking the sources of
American Gothicism. Although title accessibility was something of a consideration in the construction, I wanted above all to choose systematic examples that would confirm the vigorous presence of the Gothic spirit in
American letters during every age and stage of our history, thus leaving
no doubt about the masterworks of the American Gothic or the deep impression that Gothicism made even on non-Gothic authors.

The entry format is uniform throughout the bibliography and consists
of four elements. Publication data shows the original or first edition of
the work in book form with serial or periodical publication occasionally
noted. Titles are organized alphabetically by author, then by date of publication in cases where more than one title by that author is listed, thus
enabling the user to track an author's Gothic career or chronology. Anonymous titles are integrated alphabetically by title, but pseudonymous titles (e.g., Mark Twain, "The Golden Arm") are located under the author's
true or legal name (q.v., Samuel Langhorne Clemens), not the nom de plume.
Reprintings are shown where modern or obtainable reissues or reprintings
exist, either singly or as parts of anthologies or collections, with this
category omitted where no reprintings or second editions are available.
The critical sources heading assembles the most pertinent and useful criticism of the work and author for the inspection of the user. In most
cases, full bibliographical information is furnished, but where a frequently consulted research source such as Henri Petter's The Early American Novel or Donald Ringe's The American Gothic is cited, the title is
shortened to avoid bibliographical redundancy. Journal titles are given in
full rather than by acronym, and doctoral dissertations are cited with
their abstract information to permit the researcher instantaneous access

to the vital contents of the dissertation and the means of acquiring the entire dissertation if necessary. The critical synopses vary in length and detail with some emphasis on those aspects of plot, character, and setting which imbue the work with its Americanized Gothic properties. Without creating an inextricable web of cross references, these devices direct the user to related or similar works, to parallel motifs, settings, style, character, and traits in common.

The two appendixes and three indexes speak for themselves and are particularly designed to assist the user who is engaged on a specialized research project in American Gothicism. Consulted more generally, they should also enhance the investigator's passage through the American Gothic maze. All numerical references are to entry numbers, never to page numbers. Appendix One, Annual Chronology of American Gothics, is a year-by-year register of Gothic fiction over two centuries. Appendix Two, Bibliography of Critical Sources, is a three-part assemblage of books and articles essential to an understanding of the history of the Gothic in America. Bibliographical data that does not appear in full in this introduction or in the individual entries can be obtained from these listings. It should be stressed that this secondary bibliography is highly selective and should be supplemented by the various pieces of criticism mentioned under research sources in the individual entries.

Two of the three indexes that conclude THROUGH THE PALE DOOR require no elaboration. Index One, Author and Critic Index, and Index Two, Title Index, enable the user to reach a topic, subject, or title rapidly and efficiently or to collect a larger body of information or to locate a specific piece of criticism when only the author's or critic's name is known and used as a starting point. The third index, Gothic Themes, Motifs, Events, Character Names, and Settings, has been prepared to guide the researcher to explicit instances of how and where the Gothic operates in American literature, but the index is certainly not exhaustive and admittedly some of the subject areas do overlap. Partial and incomplete, the index can still function as a locator by directing those users with special interests, such as the presence of the Wandering Jew figure in American literature or the substitution of an American locale or building for its forerunner in English Gothicism to specific instances of these. What emerged for the bibliographer during the making of the index was conclusive proof of just how super-saturated our Gothic movement is with the traditional paraphernalia of horror and what ingenious modifications our writers have accomplished in installing the devices of the Gothic to accommodate native themes and settings.

Users wishing to pursue the spirit of the American Gothic beyond the limits of THROUGH THE PALE DOOR are urged to plan a research visit to two peerless libraries, The American Antiquarian Society in Worcester, Massachusetts, and the Alderman Library of the University of Virginia which offers the Gothic quester a unique experience with its splendid Sadleir-Black and Barrett Collections.

ACKNOWLEDGMENTS

Unlike the traditional Gothic victim, I have not been forced to grope my way alone inside the dark corridors of the American Gothic. Fortunately, I received able intellectual assistance and gracious emotional support from several generous friends, colleagues, and institutions. Without their contributions of time, knowledge, and (yes) money, the pale door of this study would have remained forever sealed. I do not thank these individuals and institutions in any particular order since I wish to have it understood each contribution to the research and writing of this book was of equal and inestimable value to me. I therefore express my gratitude to all of the following: Dr. Sir Devendra P. Varma of Dalhousie University for his encouragement in all of my Gothic projects over the years; my colleagues at Allegheny College, Professor Bruce L. Clayton of the Department of History and Provost Andrew T. Ford, who looked after my financial and intellectual needs from their listening posts on the Faculty Development Committee; the Faculty Development Committee of Allegheny College for the bestowal of sabbatic leave and an additional research grant; my patient and scrupulous editor at the Greenwood Press, Marilyn Brownstein; my old teacher, Dr. Walter E. Bezanson, whose graduate seminar in Poe, Hawthorne, and Melville in the Rutgers University graduate school was certainly the genesis of my Gothic passions; Mildred Abraham, Dr. Richard Lindemann, and the entire staff of the Rare Book Department of the Alderman Library, University of Virginia; Joann D. Chaison, Head of Readers' Services at the American Antiquarian Society, Worcester, Massachusetts; Neil Barron, author of the internationally acclaimed Anatomy of Wonder; the always-cooperative staff of the Pelletier Library of Allegheny College whose professional help is always there when I need it; the staff of the Meadville Public Library whose expertise at tracking down obscure Gothics was vastly useful; and my dear and devoted wife, Nancy, whose brains, imagination, and unusual skills as my eternal research assistant should be the envy of every scholar.

GOTHIC AUTHORS
AND WORKS

001. Adelio. A Journey to Philadelphia; or, Memoirs of Charles Coleman
      Saunders. Hartford, CT: Lincoln & Gleason, 1804.

      REPRINT EDITION: New York, AMS Press, 1978.
      RESEARCH SOURCES: Petter, Henri, The Early American Novel, pp.324-
      325; Ringe, Donald, American Gothic, p.80.

      CRITICAL SYNOPSIS: Although the novel contains no supernatural el-
      ements, it offers those properties, characters, and events soon to
      be associated with a distinctive strain of American Gothic. The
      pseudonymous Adelio also seems well-versed in the Gothicism of
      Charles Brockden Brown, particularly his Arthur Mervyn (see 064)
      since the altruistic but naive hero, Charles Coleman Saunders, un-
      dergoes the ordeal of loss of innocence in the labyrinthine
      streets of the perilous city. An endangered maiden, Emilia, and a
      reasonably competent villain, Carnell, fill out the Gothic cast. A
      fourth character, Susan, seems to be a suicide early in the novel
      when she plunges into the Susquehannah River, but will be resur-
      rected on the final pages to avert the unjust execution of Saun-
      ders for a murder which never occurred. Homicide, suicide, secret
      threats, abduction, a sensational murder trial, and a last moment
      release at the place of execution for the falsely accused hero
      produce plenty of physical horror. But the higher horror is in the
      psychological and introspective mode, the hero's mounting aware-
      ness of the self's capacity for moral evil despite his American
      self. The journey from farm to city is an American Gothic meta-
      phor for the journey inward to the heart of darkness. Saunders's
      confrontation with the spectral figure at his brother's bedside
      early in the novel is a confrontation with the Gothic self and a
      repetitive crisis in the American Gothic experience when the young
      hero is forced into a meeting with an unknown side of his own be-
      ing. The theme of self-encounter is reenforced by the dark bond
      that forms between Saunders and the criminal, Carnell, who, like
      Welbeck in Arthur Mervyn, or the fatherly fiend of fire and night
      in Hawthorne's "My Kinsman, Major Molineux" (see 202), becomes a
      demonic father figure in the education of young Saunders.

002. Adventures in a Castle, An Original Story. Written by a Citizen of
      Philadelphia. Harrisburg, PA: J. Elder, 1806.

RESEARCH SOURCES: Petter, Henri, The Early American Novel, pp. 308-309; Ringe, Donald, American Gothic, p.80.

CRITICAL SYNOPSIS: Clearly deriving from the English Gothic models of Mrs. Ann Radcliffe and "Monk" Lewis, this anonymous Gothic specimen also reflects the ghastly pace of the shorter Gothic chapbooks and bluebooks. The plotting, setting, and characterization are wholesale imitations of one standard and popular form of the English Gothic novel begun by Walpole in his Castle of Otranto (1764) and extended by Clara Reeve in her Old English Baron (17-77). A domestic struggle for ownership of the castle between good and evil relatives forms the core of this type of Gothic romance. Here, this basic Gothic storyline is not adapted to the American setting in any way. The novel is a pure facsimile of English Goth-ic fiction and is "American" only by way of authorship and place of publication. The period of action is fifteenth century France. The two decent brothers, Louis and Henri Boileau, are the heredi-tary victims of their nefarious uncle, the Count of Vauban, who would deprive them of their family legacy by any means he can de-vise. Within the walls of the old castle are to be found all of the customary Gothic appliances and staff: a sealed chamber from which Henri mysteriously disappears only to reappear when the vil-lain must be exposed and overthrown; a gang of cutthroats command-ed by the resourceful villain, Vauban; a maiden in need of rescue, Antoinette of Alençon; sinister noises and ghostly glidings; men-acing architecture which makes the interior of the castle seem al-most alive; and a fiery climax which disposes of the villain and his plans for power. American Gothic imports of this type often indulged in supernatural sensation for its own sake at the expense of the theme of genealogical purification which is secondary to the horrid "adventures in a castle." As it evolves, American Goth-ic retains the notion of enclosure, but replaces the haunted cas-tle with the haunted house or forest. Going deeper than such Euro-pean Gothic prototypes, the true American Gothic also goes beyond external thrill and is in some ways a redefining of the tradition-al responses to terror and horror.

003. Aiken, Conrad. "Silent Snow, Secret Snow." Among the Lost People. New York: Scribner's, 1934.

REPRINT EDITION: Great Tales of Terror and the Supernatural, eds. Herbert A. Wise and Phyllis Fraser, New York, Modern Library, 19-44.
RESEARCH SOURCE: Hoffmann, Frederick J., Conrad Aiken. New York, Twayne, 1969, pp.40-41.

CRITICAL SYNOPSIS: The story is a case study of the joys and ter-rors of the insular life, the onset of madness, and the rejection of reality culminated by the living burial fantasy of "silent snow, secret snow." The narrator, the twelve year old Paul Hasle-man, shows the unbearable strain of trying to lead a double exist-ence as he recedes into insanity. Withdrawing from home, school, and parents, and the cares of growing up, "he did in a sense cease to see, or to see the obvious external world, and substituted for this vision the vision of snow." The story's climax is marked by a fantasy of live burial as "white darkness" fills Paul's room and he chooses madness and oblivion over life and adulthood with the outcry, "Mother! Mother! Go away! I hate you." The boy's retreat into the white infinitude carries reminders of the mysterious cli-max of Poe's Narrative of Arthur Gordon Pym (see 378) where another suicidal hero embraces the great white death at the ends of the earth. There are also echoes of Andersen's famous fairytale "The Snow Queen" as well as Hans Castorp's self-consuming dream experience in the "Snow" chapter of Thomas Mann's The Magic Mountain (1922).

004.   Albee, Edward. Who's Afraid of Virginia Woolf? New York: Atheneum, 1962.

REPRINT EDITION: New York, New American Library, 1983.
RESEARCH SOURCES: Harris, Wendell V., "Morality, Absurdity, and Albee," Southwest Review 49 (1964): 249-256; Roy, Emil, "Who's Afraid of Virginia Woolf? and the Tradition," Bucknell Review 13 (1965): 27-36; Witherington, Paul, "Albee's Gothic: The Resonance of Cliché," Comparative Drama 4 (1970): 151-165.

CRITICAL SYNOPSIS: Deadly games of talk and internecine verbal slaughter mark this domestic drama of death which sees Albee transform the American dream into the American nightmare. Two academic couples, George and Martha and Nick and Honey, torment one another in a play saturated with gestures and references to death. Comments Paul Witherington, "Routine is upset, roles are inverted, clichés come to life and a black mass celebrates the exorcism of rationality." Previous Gothic families had often engaged in physical malice, deceit and torture, while the family seat crumbles to ruins. Albee's Gothic family is thrown together in a ramshackle faculty house following another routine and boring faculty party in New Carthage where the characters proceed to abuse, humiliate, and betray one another in a "total war" of the generations, the sexes, and the spirit. Like a Gothic melodrama or a Strindberg play with its lethal sado-masochistic tensions, the drunken evening encloses all of the characters and compels each to commit verbal suicide or homicide. We have the verbal murder of Martha's fictional child by George, the exposure of Honey's infertility, the eruption of Nick's crude sexual longings, and the dismantling of George's self-respect in the mockery of his unpublished novel about parricide. The evening of verbal terror and malicious assault burns itself to ashes to become the dismal morning of Martha's admission that she is indeed "afraid of Virginia Woolf," her childless and suicidal predecessor. An unbearable situation of enclosure and the threat of evil emanating from close relatives relate Albee's Gothic family to early Gothic families in the rise of an American Gothic such as the Wielands in Charles Brockden Brown's novel of 1798, Wieland; or, The Transformation (see 063).

005.   _____. Tiny Alice. New York: Atheneum, 1965.

REPRINT EDITION: The Plays, New York, Atheneum/Macmillan, 1981.
RESEARCH SOURCES: Ballew, Leighton M., "Who's Afraid of Tiny Alice?" Georgia Review 20 (1966): 292-299; Witherington, Paul, "Albee's Gothic: The Resonance of Cliché," Comparative Drama 4 (1970): 151-165.

CRITICAL SYNOPSIS: The fact that Albee's cryptic, allegorical drama takes place within a castle should establish its affinity with traditional Gothic locales. The cast also has the insularity associated with Gothic families who are victimized by the castle and by one another. The characters also resemble the figures in a medieval mystery play even though Albee's message is the direct opposite of religious truth and directed at the meaninglessness of all relationships. Tiny Alice is Miss Alice, the wealthiest woman in the world and the proprietress of a grand castle. Other characters are her lawyer, butler, the cardinal, and a character very appropriate to Gothic mystery, Brother Julian, a lay brother who enters the castle on a special mission to negotiate a two billion dollar donation for the cardinal and is seduced by Alice, then murdered. The strange relationship between Brother Julian and Alice forms the psychological core of the Gothic drama. Albee's heavily Gothic play infuriated the reviewers, perhaps because they failed to see it as a piece of Gothic stagecraft and violent psychodrama. Writing in the New York Review of Books, Philip Roth certainly missed the point when he wrote: "The world of Tiny Alice is mysterious because Albee cannot get it to cohere." But the horrible disintegration of human relationships and values is precisely the Gothic effect that Albee sought to evoke.

006. Alcott, Louisa May. "Pauline's Passion and Punishment." Frank Leslie's Illustrated Newspaper, January 3, January 10, 1863.

REPRINT EDITION: Behind a Mask: The Unknown Thrillers of Louisa May Alcott, ed. Madeleine B. Stern, New York, William Morrow, 19-75.
RESEARCH SOURCE: Rostenberg, Leona, "Some Anonymous and Pseudonymous Thrillers of Louis M. Alcott," Papers of the Bibliographical Society of America 37 (1943): 131-140.

CRITICAL SYNOPSIS: Adulated by generations of readers for her juvenile classic Little Women (1868), Louisa May Alcott was also the clandestine writer of several highly Gothic thrillers published as sensation fiction in various magazines under the pseudonym A.M. Barnard. A shocker in four chapters, "Pauline's Passion and Punishment" is a tale of frustrated passion and the elaborate revenge of a woman possessed. Courted, loved, then jilted by Gilbert Redmond, Pauline Valery vows retaliation, "a subtler vengeance than men can conceive [in the] tournament so often held between man and woman where the hardest heart is the winner of the prize." She enlists the aid of the Cuban, Manuel, to carry forth her scheme of humiliation. But even the willing Manuel is appalled at the demonic transformation in the once-delicate Pauline and "stood aghast at the baleful spirit which had enslaved this woman--one human soul rebelling against providence to become the nemesis of another." A dropped glove becomes the symbol of Pauline's rejection of Redmond's appeal for forgiveness, a glove which is then struggled over on a ledge by Redmond and Manuel until there is heard a "heavy plunge into the black pool below." Pauline's passion has pushed the punishment beyond lethal limits and she realizes too late that revenge, like lust, is an appetite without satisfaction. The tale closes bleakly not with a moral but with a psychological axiom: "With that moment of impotent horror, remorse, and woe, Pauline's long punishment began."

007. _____. "A Whisper in the Dark." Frank Leslie's Illustrated Newspaper, June 6, June 13, 1863.

REPRINT EDITION: Plots and Counterplots: More Unknown Thrillers of Louisa May Alcott, ed. Madeleine B. Stern, New York, William Morrow, 1976.

CRITICAL SYNOPSIS: A quintessential Gothic tale published anonymously and later acknowledged, Alcott's work can be compared favorably with the best maiden-centered Gothics of Mrs. Radcliffe or even the Gothic endeavors of the Brontes. Madeleine Stern adds that "With an unusual last will and testament, a large measure of maternal love, and a house of horrors for a background, 'A Whisper in the Dark' becomes not only an engrossing gruesome Gothic but an interesting foray into the disorders of the mind." The story line follows classic Gothic story patterns. A lecherous uncle attempts to drive his seventeen-year-old heiress niece, Sybil, insane using mind control, a ferocious guardian hound, a sealed room in a remote mansion on the moors, and even a sinister Spaniard (Dr. Karnac) to unhinge her wits and thereby seize her fortune. Sybil's mind runs the gamut of Gothic emotions while her body trembles with the orthodox terrors of enclosure: "The house was so well guarded that I soon relinquished all hope of escape and listlessly amused myself by roaming through the unfurnished rooms and echoing halls." But she manages to escape back into the safe world of courtship, self-control, and marriage when a stupendous chemical explosion resulting from some obscene experiment ignites the house and her tormentors. If escape from the Gothic building signifies a change in identity, then Alcott's presentation of the escape heightens the symbolism of such an egress. Sybil's resistance to panic and endurance during her incarceration are actually metaphors of woman's determination to be free from the subordinate roles superimposed upon her by an avaricious male society. One might say that although the Gothic matter is quite ordinary and typical, Alcott's manner of handling these materials extracts their maximum symbolic potential.

008. _____. "A Marble Woman; or, The Mysterious Model." The Flag of Our Union, May 20, May 27, June 3, June 10, 1865.

REPRINT EDITION: Plots and Counterplots: More Unknown Thrillers of Louisa May Alcott, ed. Madeleine B. Stern, New York, William Morrow, 1976.
RESEARCH SOURCES: Douglas, Ann, "Mysteries of Louisa May Alcott," New York Review of Books, September 28, 1978, pp.60-63; Stern, Madeleine B., "Introduction," Plots and Counterplots, pp.7-25.

CRITICAL SYNOPSIS: The tale reveals the deeply Gothic preoccupations of Louisa May Alcott's pseudonymous thrillers. There are also some visible parallels with Poe's "The Oval Portrait" (see 387) and Hawthorne's "The Birthmark" (see 190) as well as Henry James's supernatural statue story, "The Last of the Valerii" (see 238). The artist's reduction of his human subjects to mere material and the demonic potential of the artist as destroyer are concerns for Alcott as much as for Hawthorne. What is unique and unexpected is her candid introduction of the incest motif and the opium experience to accompany the stereotypical Gothic situation of a persecuted maiden menaced by a fiend. The menaced maiden is the twelve-year-old Cecilia Bazil Stein whose dying mother has consigned her to the care of her previous lover, the sculptor Bazil Yorke. Yorke's turret studio becomes a chamber of horrors for his virgin ward as he seeks total domination over her to avenge himself upon the mother. Also, to counter his pedophiliac longings, he would transform his human model into an object of cold, cadaverous beauty. By plying her with laudanum, he "marblelizes" the warm and pliant young woman until he has changed her into a marble beauty of "deathlike immobility." "I can mold the child as I will," he exults, "and make the daughter pay the mother's debt." But her addiction to the drug and her pitiable condition of death-

in-life finally arouse Yorke's sympathy and he reconverts her from
marble to flesh in a storm scene which resembles the awakening of
the lovers in Alcott's "Perilous Play" (see 010). The higher moral
indicates that the artist should use his special powers to give
life, not to take it.

009. _____. "The Abbot's Ghost; or, Maurice Treherne's Temptation."
The Flag of Our Union, January 5, January 12, January 19, January
26, 1867.

REPRINT EDITION: Behind a Mask: The Unknown Thrillers of Louisa
May Alcott, ed. Madeleine B. Stern, New York, William Morrow, 19-
75.
RESEARCH SOURCE: Stern, Madeleine B., "Introduction," Behind a
Mask, pp.vii-xxxiii.

CRITICAL SYNOPSIS: A Gothic novella in eight chapters and a capable facsimile of any of Mrs. Radcliffe's novels of suspense, slowly mounting terror, and eventual happy marriage for the confined
heroines. Madeleine Sterne writes that "The plot, revolving prin-
cipally about the sudden cure of the crippled Maurice Treherne and
ending with a triple wedding in the Abbey, is basically a love
story narrated against a strongly Gothic background." This is
true, but there is also plenty of Gothic activity in the foreground as Alcott demonstrates her technical acquaintance with the
methods of the mistress of the English Gothic school. Many of the
special effects and terror scenes derive directly from Mrs. Radcliffe's books, especially The Mysteries of Udolpho (1794). The
curse of Abbot Boniface, which hangs over the present owners of
the Abbey, the Treherne family; the violent death of Sir Jasper,
who mocks the Abbot's ghost, then is killed in a fall from his
horse; and the stupendous atmosphere of doom, gloom, and impending
death are all orthodox Gothic details according to the formula.
But in the management of spectres, Alcott showed herself to be a
firstrate Gothic stylist. When the menaced maiden, Edith Snowdon,
and her companion, Octavia, finally meet the Abbot's ghost, the
scene generates all the frisson of Mrs. Radcliffe herself: "Eight
narrow Gothic windows pierced either wall of the North gallery. As
Octavia cried out, all looked and distinctly saw a tall, dark figure moving noiselessly across the second bar of light far down
the hall. Nothing human ever wore a look like that of the ghastly,
hollow-eyed, pale-lipped countenance below the hood. All saw it
and held their breath as it slowly raised a shadowy arm and pointed a shriveled finger at Sir Jasper." This is a Gothic type
scene, to be sure, but composed with the conviction of a writer
whose pseudonymous indulgence in Gothic fancies goes beyond mere
historical interest.

010. _____. "Perilous Play." Frank Leslie's Chimney Corner, February
3, 1869.

REPRINT EDITIONS: The Evil Image: Two Centuries of Gothic Short
Fiction and Poetry, eds. Patricia L. Skarda and Nora Crow Jaffe,
New York, New American Library, 1981; Plots and Counterplots: More
Unknown Thrillers of Louisa May Alcott, ed. Madeleine B. Stern,
New York, William Morrow, 1976.
RESEARCH SOURCE: Stern, Madeleine B., "Louisa M. Alcott: An Ap-
praisal," New England Quarterly 12 (1949): 494-496.

CRITICAL SYNOPSIS: "Perilous Play" is a euphemism for indulgence in hashish in this supercharged sexual fantasy. Two inhibited and repressed young people, the frigid Rose St. Just and the shy Mark Done, eat hashish while on an outing with their friends and become sexually alive during a stormy midnight boatride. Both in style and explicit sexual content, this is a daring story which sees the release of two passionate selves from the prison of domestic propriety. The drug experience elevates Rose into a warm and sensuous woman and gives Mark the courage to express his hidden passion. The play may be perilous, but two "lonely statues" are granted a heightened aliveness. "We have been near death together, let us share life together," Mark tells Rose, before speaking the subversive moral, "Heaven bless hashish if its dreams end like this!"

011. Aldrich, Thomas Bailey. The Stillwater Tragedy. Boston: Houghton, Mifflin, 1880.

REPRINT EDITION: Chicago, Americans in Fiction Series, 1968.
RESEARCH SOURCES: Cowie, Alexander, Rise of the American Novel, pp.586-589; Samuels, Charles E., Thomas Bailey Aldrich, New York, Twayne, 1965; Wagenknecht, Edward, Cavalcade of the American Novel, p.466.

CRITICAL SYNOPSIS: More mystery than tragedy, the story concerns the brutal murder of the miser, Lemuel Shackford, owner of an iron works and marble yard in the New England Village of Stillwater. His nephew, Richard Shackford, is implicated in the deed by circumstantial evidence and also tormented by guilt even though he had no direct part in his uncle's death. The novel's Gothicism lies in the Hawthornesque vein of secret guilt that haunts the interior of Richard's character since he had both willed and desired his uncle's death. The persistent detective, Edward Taggett, is an interesting successor to Poe's Monsieur Dupin in that his methods of investigation rest upon scientific skepticism rather than "ratiocination."

012. Alexander, Sigmund B. "A Modern Mephistopheles." Ten of Us. Original Stories and Sketches. Boston: Laughton, Macdonald, 1887.

CRITICAL SYNOPSIS: Concerns the theme of sinister reincarnation. Other tales by Alexander with occasional Gothic moments are "A Dual Life" and "The Living Dead."

013. Allston, Washington. Monaldi: A Tale. Boston: Little, Brown, 1841.

REPRINT EDITION: ed. Nathalia Wright, New York, Scholars' Facsimiles & Reprints, 1967.
RESEARCH SOURCES: Hunter, Doreen, "America's First Romantics: Richard Henry Dana, Sr. and Washington Allston," New England Quarterly 45 (1972): 3-30; Ringe, Donald A., "Early American Gothic: Brown, Dana, and Allston," American Transcendental Quarterly 19 (1973): 3-8; Welsh, John R., "Washington Allston, Cosmopolite and Early Romantic, Georgia Review 21 (1967): 491-502.

CRITICAL SYNOPSIS: Allston's Gothic novel of passion, jealousy, insanity, and betrayal has serious qualities and genuine psychological depth. It explores the hazards of the imaginative life lived too intensely and moves toward a high minded order of American Gothic in its portrait of the artist as madman. Alston was a painter, a romantic theorist, and an explorer of the hazards of the artistic life, all of which figure into the violent fabric of Monaldi. Aspects of the plot and the handling of character suggest Allston's debt to the English Gothic school and specifically to such writers as Charlotte Dacre ("Rosa Matilda") whose work The Passions (1811) gave expression to an important theme which reappears in Monaldi: the mind's constant vulnerability to its own repressed forces. Allston's Gothic passions operate in a lurid, Italianate atmosphere of revenge, deceit, and erotic villainy. The shy painter-hero, Monaldi, attends an art seminary in Bologna. Accompanying him is the bold criminal, Maldura, whose evil nature shortly manifests itself when both men fall in love with Rosalia Landi and Maldura schemes to keep her from Monaldi at any price. Moving with Iago-like precision, he hires a libertine, Fialto, to pretend a seduction of Rosalia. Monaldi succumbs to the ruse, stabs his beloved and goes mad. But she recovers and seeks out the insane Monaldi to reveal Maldura's plot and consecrate her love for him. Monaldi, however, is convinced that Rosalia is a spectre come back from the dead to torment him, a Gothic delusion brought on by excesses of imagination and his incurable madness. Yet, his insanity heightens his talents as a painter and he creates a nightmarish painting of ghastly power and fatal beauty, but this act of artistic creation destroys Monaldi. According to Allston's retelling of the Gothic fable, the imagination can become a demon far more appalling than any external ghost.

014. Anderson, Sherwood. Winesburg, Ohio. New York: B.W. Huebsch, 1919.

REPRINT EDITION: intro. Malcolm Cowley, New York, Viking Press, 1965.
RESEARCH SOURCES: Baldanza, Frank, "Northern Gothic," Southern Review, 10 (1974): 566-582; Malin, Irving, New American Gothic, p.6.

CRITICAL SYNOPSIS: The twenty-one stories are preceded and framed by "The Book of the Grotesque," which defines the prisons of the mind and soul to which the various characters are condemned. Illusion, disillusion, psychic isolation, and primal loneliness are the psychological dungeons into which the Winesburg characters are cast. They are grotesques and they remain grotesques despite brief moments of aliveness because they are victims of their dreams and self-deceptions. This is Anderson's Gothic principle of characterization whereby "the moment one of the people took one of the truths to himself, called it his truth, and tried to live by it, he became a grotesque and the truth he embraced became a falsehood." Four story-portraits in particular convert traditional Gothic motifs or events into American Gothic themes. "Hands," Wing Biddlebaum's story, adapts the Gothic episode of flight and pursuit to the retreat into self. Part Four of "Godliness," which is subtitled "Terror," is David Hardy's story of his coming to manhood through a violent deed when he strikes his spiritual father, Jesse Bentley, with a stone from his sling. Alice Hindman, the heroine of "Adventure," tears off her clothes and runs naked through the streets of Winesburg only to collide with the terrible truth "that many people must live and die alone, even in Winesburg." "Death" concerns Doctor Reefy and Elizabeth Willard and contains a corpse vigil during which George Willard is seized by a mad desire "to lift the sheet from the body of his mother and look at the face." This is a moment of pure terror, but it is by no means a unique moment in Anderson's American Gothic album.

015. Armstrong, Mary Frances Morgan. A Haunted House. New York: Hampton Tract Committee by G.P. Putnam's Sons, 1879.

CRITICAL SYNOPSIS: Published as "Sanitary Series Number 5." The haunted house novel with a Victorian moral attached was a common form of American Gothic in the 1870's and 1880's. This is a ghost story with a moral since it concerns purity of character through patient endeavor. To believe in spirits is to acknowledge the separate afterlife of the soul itself.

016. Arthur, Timothy Shay. The Angel and the Demon: A Tale of Modern Spiritualism. Philadelphia: J.W. Bradley, 1858.

RESEARCH SOURCES: Davis, David Brion. Homicide in American Fiction, 1798-1860, Ithaca, NY, Cornell UP, pp.43-44; Kerr, Howard, Mediums, and Spirit-Rappers, and Roaring Radicals: Spiritualism in American Literature, 1850-1900, Urbana, IL, Illinois UP, 1972.

Critical Synopsis: The popular author of temperance tracts and tales who is still remembered for his Ten Nights in a Barroom and What I Saw There (1854) also wrote an American Gothic novel about two opposite governesses, the angelic governess, Miss Florence Harper, and her demonic counterpart, Mrs. Jeckyl. To their care are consigned the children of Mrs. Edward Dainty, Agnes, Madeline, and George. In the contest of the two governesses for the souls of the children, Shay propounded a double moral, intending to show that "the wrong done to childhood is, too often, wrong done for the whole life" and to expose the perils of spiritualism and mesmerism in the lives of innocent victims. The particular form of Mrs. Jeckyl's demonism consists in her secret affiliation with "a nest of pseudo-spiritualists" who have singled out Madeline for transformation into a child-medium to be used in their occult rituals and seances. A typical Gothic crisis in Chapter 9, "The Shadow of Evil," finds Madeline in a catatonic trance and Mrs. Jeckyl exulting in "a potency of will almost irresistible." Other "insane orgies of mesmerism run mad...table-tippings, wrappings, writings, and all sorts of diablerie" precede Madeline's mysterious removal from the household. The novel concludes with the recovery of Madeline, the reinstatement of the angelic governess, and the exposure of Mrs. Jeckyl's sinister spiritualist circle. Having alarmed his readers with the near victory of evil, Shay restored them to the desired moral satisfaction by seeing to the overthrow of the demon governess. "Mrs. Jeckyl vanished," moralized the author, "like an evil spirit when the sun rays of truth stream down through the rifted clouds of error. The shadow of her presence had left a blight on the earth; but warm sunshine and gentle dews made the soil fruitful again. And so good triumphed." Novels and tales about the sinister activities of spiritualist cults and circles form almost a distinctive category of American Gothicism. Shay's grim tale of children psychically enslaved should be compared with Garland's similar treatment in The Tyranny of the Dark (see 150).

017. Atherton, Gertrude. "The Bell in the Fog." The Bell in the Fog, and Other Stories. New York: Harper, 1905.

REPRINT EDITION: New York, Irvington Publishers, 1972.
RESEARCH SOURCE: Mc Clure, Charlotte S., "Gertrude Atherton (1857-1948)," American Literary Realism, 1870-1910 9 (1976): 95-101.

CRITICAL SYNOPSIS: Two Gothic qualities pervade this short story:

the artist as violator of the private psyche and the imagination as invader of the natural order of things. Some parallels can be drawn with Poe's "The Oval Portrait" (see 387) and Hawthorne's "The Birthmark" (see 190). The narrative is restricted to the gathering guilty consciousness of Ralph Orth, an American writer who has taken up residence in an English country mansion. He becomes infatuated with a portrait of a young woman and decides to create a life for her by writing a novel about her. Following the book's publication, he has a shocking encounter with Blanche Root, the lady in the portrait come to life, a passionate projection of Orth's own sexual desires. The beautiful Blanche of the portrait had been a suicide; the projected Blanche of Orth's artistic imagination, like Georgiana in "The Birthmark," becomes the victim of the artist's demonic compulsion to reshape nature and alter reality.

018. _____. "The Dead and the Countess." The Bell in the Fog, and Other Stories. New York: Harper, 1905.

REPRINT EDITION: New York, Irvington Publishers, 1972.
RESEARCH SOURCE: Holt, Marilyn J., "Gertrude Atherton," Supernatural Fiction Writers, pp.777-781.

CRITICAL SYNOPSIS: Best remembered as a Californian regionalist, Gertrude Atherton also wrote several genuinely Gothic tales. These were collected under the solemn title, The Bell in the Fog, which by itself suggests a familiar Gothic acoustic, the dismal pealing of a "surly, sullen bell" or death knell. The story exploits the motif of the restless and vocal corpse, a supernatural idea inherited from Poe and previous Gothic writers. Buried in a Brittany graveyard near the railroad line to Paris, the countess cries to her husband from her grave as she seeks final rest or release as the train bearing the Count roars past the graveyard. But by providing no horrible reunion between the living and the dead as does Poe in the cadaverous meeting of Roderick and Madeline in "The Fall of the House of Usher" (see 379), Atherton mismanages one of the primary requirements of the successful Gothic tale, a climactic moment when the supernatural world triumphs over the natural world typically in the form of a regenerated body returning to claim its lost love.

019. _____. "Death and the Woman." The Bell in the Fog, and Other Stories. New York: Harper, 1905.

REPRINT EDITION: New York, Irvington Publishers, 1972.
RESEARCH SOURCE: Holt, Marilyn J., "Gertrude Atherton," Supernatural Fiction Writers, pp.777-781.

CRITICAL SYNOPSIS: The tale dramatizes Emily Dickinson's lines concerning death's courtship, "Because I could not stop for death, He kindly stopped for me." A sudden shift from the natural to the supernatural at the end of the story is also skillfully managed. The situation is a death vigil as the woman literally stands guard at her moribund husband's bedside to prevent the approach of death. She expects a ghastly Gothic phantom but when death enters the room in physical form he proves to be an ordinary gentleman with no fearsome features at all. Death is as natural and as commonplace as life itself and this unadorned truth appears to shock the woman into suicide although the psychological ambiguities of her meeting with death allow other readings. On the morning after

death's visitation, the bodies of the husband and wife are found in contented embrace. For sheer suggestive power, this story is one of Atherton's best Gothic pieces.

020. _____. "The Striding Place." The Bell in the Fog, and Other Stories. New York: Harper, 1905.

REPRINT EDITION: New York, Irvington Publishers, 1972.
RESEARCH SOURCE: McClure, Charlotte S., Gertrude Atherton, Boston, Twayne, 1979.

CRITICAL SYNOPSIS: Usually considered Atherton's masterpiece in the craft of supernatural horror, the tale indulges in an array of stunning and grotesque effects. These include the refusal of the body to release the soul after death; the cadaverous hand appearing from the water and "shaking savagely in the face of that force which leaves its creatures to immutable law"; the delayed revelation of an animated corpse which, when finally exposed, has no face. These Gothic details and others converge to yield Atherton's most Biercian story, a merciless denial of the peaceful rest of death. The title refers to a lethal area or a death zone into which Wyatt Gifford has strayed by night. His friend, Weigall, seeks for Gifford within the striding place. He sees a hand rising from the river, rushes to rescue the drowning Gifford, and discovers to his horror that the body is Gifford's but the face is missing. Weigell's night journey to save his friend from the striding place drives him insane instead.

021. Austin, William. "Peter Rugg, The Missing Man." New England Galaxy, September 10, 1824, September 1, 1826, January 19, 1827.

REPRINT EDITION: More Great Ghost Stories, ed. Dale Harrison, London, Herbert Jenkins, 1932.
RESEARCH SOURCES: Levin, Harry, The Power of Blackness: Poe, Hawthorne, Melville. New York, Vintage Books, 1960, pp.3-5; Young, Philip, "The Story of the Missing Man," Directions in Literary Criticism: Contemporary Approaches to Literature, eds. Stanley Weintraub and Philip Young, University Park, Pennsylvania State UP, 1973, pp.143-159.

CRITICAL SYNOPSIS: The classic situation of entrapment in the early English Gothic tale is incarceration within a haunted castle or ruined abbey. In this New Englandized version of the Flying Dutchman story, Austin's Peter Rugg, the involuntary voyager, is displaced forever in time. Elements of the folk story of the perpetual traveller who can never go home again, of the legendry of the Wandering Jew, also a familiar character in Gothic novels, and the Biblical Cain figure are to be found in the predicament of Peter Rugg. While enroute to his home in Boston, Rugg is caught in a storm and invited to take shelter for the night by Mr. Cutter. Rugg's arrogant reply denotes his breaking of "the magnetic chain of humanity" and condemns him to homelessness and the damnation of eternal life, a fate which had already been allotted to Maturin's Gothic hero-villain, Melmoth, in Melmoth the Wanderer (1820). "I will see home tonight, in spite of the last tempest, or may I never see home," shouts Rugg in defiance of both nature and the human community. Self-damned by his proud rejection of human sympathy he must travel the roads around Boston in a cycle of hopelessness. Austin's blending of folklore material with the Gothic situation of horrible entrapment impressed Hawthorne who gave homage to the story by introducing Rugg into his short story, "A Virtuoso's Collection" and in using Rugg's crime of the refusal to be human in the creation of the frustrated seeker after the unpardonable sin, "Ethan Brand" (see 199).

022. _____. "The Man With the Cloaks: A Vermont Legend." American Monthly Magazine, January, 1836.

REPRINT EDITION: The Works of William Austin, 1778-1841, Irvine, CA, American Biography Service, 1988.
RESEARCH SOURCE: Fisher, B.F., "William Austin," Supernatural Fiction Writers, pp.693-696.

CRITICAL SYNOPSIS: Another story of spiritual dislocation and psychic anguish is Austin's "The Man With the Cloaks." If Austin had written his version of the Rip Van Winkle legend in allowing Peter Rugg no homecoming, he provides an equally Gothic doom for the frigid and uncharitable John Grindall. When he denies a freezing stranger the use of his warm cloak, Grindall denies brotherly love and cuts himself off from humanity. The stranger freezes to death, but his apparition reappears to impose a penance on Grindall's conscience. He must give away a cloak each day for a year to atone for his inhumanity and to regain warmth of heart. Within the tale's allegorical structure, the spectral stranger represents Grindall's lost spirit of brotherhood come back to haunt him, but the chief Gothic feature is perhaps the deadness of Grindall's own heart. An admiring Hawthorne found in the story another study of the terrors of self-isolation, a theme which he would use in a story which resembles Austin's parable of guilt, "The Man of Adamant" (see 201).

023. Bailey, Charles. The Drop of Blood; or, The Maiden's Rescue. Springfield, MA: William B. Brockett, 1845.

CRITICAL SYNOPSIS: The teaser title of this 40 page primitive paperback promises grand Gothic gore, but the tale proves to be a love-and-identity story marketed under a horror title. The rescued maiden is Isabel Langburt, the rescuer, Frederick Marshall. The two meet often in a lover's cave in defiance of her harsh father, Sylvester Langburt, who is neither her true father nor a Langburt but the renegade nobleman, Sir Charles Tileston. The tyrannical patriarch has employed a villain, Robert Demerring, to filch money and to perform other clandestine activities. "I would make her a minister to my carnal appetites," sneers Demerring as he spies on Isabel. Elements of the sentimental Gothic romance saturate the plot. The Langburt estate on the outskirts of Boston is rendered as a lonely locale of lurking terror in which the sanctuary of the lovers' cave is contrasted with the hazards of the family house. Like Clara Wieland (see 063), Isabel hears a mysterious voice and is approached by a haglike old woman who melodramatically demands that she "swear not to yield to any entreaty of thy father as thou callest him; he would wed thee to the devil incarnate!" The murky genealogy and the timely revelation of her true parentage are also characteristic of the domestic Gothic mode which often involves a complex quest for one's true origins, identity, and family ties. By making the family itself not a circle of comfort, but a place of hazard, deception, and imposture, the writer adhered to a strategy that had proved its value for the appeal of the domestic Gothic novel in long or short form.

024. Bangs, John Kendrick. Toppleton's Client; or, Spirit in Exile. New York: Charles L. Webster, 1893.

REPRINT EDITION: The Works of John Kendrick Bangs, Irvine, CA, American Biography Service, 1985.
RESEARCH SOURCE: Bleiler, E.F., "J.K. Bangs," Supernatural Fiction Writers, pp.725-729.

CRITICAL SYNOPSIS: Bangs specialized in humorous horror, but he avoided the ghoulish and repulsive in the Gothic predicaments of his foolish characters. Thus, his use of the supernatural is sometimes contrasted with the sardonic and cruel wit of his contemporary, Ambrose Bierce. Bangs also has some obvious ties with his predecessor in the craft of sportive Gothic, Washington Irving. Dire events and grotesque twists of fate befall his characters, to be sure, and the supernatural world is always more powerful than the natural world. But the tone always borders on risible irony and sly fun which diminishes the shock power of the stories but makes them undeniably amusing. His creatures from the other side, for example, are typically more pests than menaces. The human fools who are thrust into dealings with these comic devils or ghosts are called upon to outguess them in a contest of wits, and the human beings usually lose. The novel, Toppleton's Client, is a splendid example of Bangs's comic Gothic techniques. The ghosts of two unscrupulous lawyers are locked in a dispute over the possession of a body while the body's rightful occupant is left corpseless. Young Toppleton is asked to enter the case to recover the body for the bodiless lawyer ghost, never mind the poor original owner who is ignored in these litigations! The willing but bungling Toppleton accepts the bodiless ghost as his "client" but loses his own young body when he foolishly forfeits it to the client for temporary use until a permanent body can be obtained. Apparently, possession remains nine tenths of the law even in the Gothic world and Toppleton is compelled to make the best of the decrepit and wornout body he has been allotted by the spectral lawyers. There is no element of savage satire on lawyers and the law in any of this as there might have been had the story been written by Bierce, only absurd punishment for a fool's handling of an absurd situation. Prior to the work of Bangs, the American ghost story almost always offered a rationalized ending which permitted the entrapped character a way back to the natural world. But for Toppleton, whose case is hopeless, there is no such exit.

025. _____. "The Spectre Cook of Bantletop." The Water Ghost, and Others. New York: Harper, 1894.

REPRINT EDITION: The Works of John Kendrick Bangs, Irvine, CA, American Biography Service, 1985.
RESEARCH SOURCE: Cox, Virginia L., "John Kendrick Bangs and the Transition from Nineteenth to Twentieth-Century American Humor," Dissertation Abstracts International 31 (1971): 4762A (Ohio State University).

CRITICAL SYNOPSIS: If water ghosts can be disposed of by deep freezing, annoying servants, in this case a seventeenth century cook who was dismissed from her position without being paid, can be outwitted in other ways to put a stop to their haunting habits. The spectre cook haunts the kitchen and disturbs the routine of the household while demanding several million pounds in back wages. The American who now owns the estate uses his Yankee ingenuity when he appeals to the culinary ghost's British superiority to put her to rest. The amusette features Bangs's usual clever treatment of supernatural material in its contest between English snobbery and American shrewdness.

026. _____. "The Water Ghost of Harrowby Hall." The Water Ghost, and Others. New York: Harper, 1894.

REPRINT EDITION: New York, Irvington, 1972.
RESEARCH SOURCE: Bleiler, E.F., "J.K. Bangs," Supernatural Fiction Writers, pp.725-729.

CRITICAL SYNOPSIS: Each Christmas Eve the narrator is annoyed by a phantom whose substance consists of cold water and whose chief business is to get everything and everyone within Harrowby Hall sopping wet. The narrator tries many ways of exorcising this annual dousing but the wet Christmases continue. Almost at his wit's end, he is assisted by the weather, a sort of natural solution to a supernatural problem. On one very cold Christmas Eve the dripping demon is coaxed outdoors where the water ghost is frozen solid and stored away permanently in the narrator's icehouse, now become a morgue for troublesome water spirits. Although Bangs reduced the Gothic's awesome apparition to the status of the nuisance spook, he also produced a delightful comic Gothic bauble.

027. _____. "The Amalgamated Brotherhood of Spooks." Over the Plum Pudding. New York: Harper, 1901.

REPRINT EDITION: The Works of John Kendrick Bangs, Irvine, CA, American Biography Service, 1985.
RESEARCH SOURCE: Bleiler, E.F., "J.K. Bangs," Supernatural Fiction Writers, pp.725-729.

CRITICAL SYNOPSIS: An amusing Gothification of an institution that Bangs knew well, the American labor union. Like other American workers at the end of the Nineteenth Century, the ghosts have organized and are agitating for fairer hauntings. The narrator who is also a writer makes a mistake when he ridicules the Amalgamated Brotherhood of Spooks and finds himself deprived of the right to write, or blacklisted by the union of spooks. Earlier Gothic victims had to fear being closed up in a castle or mansion; Bangs's victim must fear a closed shop.

028. Barthelme, Donald. The Dead Father. New York: Farrar, Straus, 1975.

REPRINT EDITION: Baltimore, Penguin Books, 1984.
RESEARCH SOURCES: Barth, Melissa E., "The Dead Father," Survey of Modern Fantasy Literature, pp.347-349; Gordon, Lois, Donald Barthelme, Boston, Twayne, 1981.

CRITICAL SYNOPSIS: The shattered narrative and antistructure of The Dead Father give to this Gothic fantasy a kind of surreal logic of its own. The novel resists facile synopsis but resembles in some respects Nathanael West's visceral voyage inside the intestines of the Trojan Horse, The Dream Life of Balso Snell (1931). The first Gothic novelist, Horace Walpole, had installed a giant figure within the walls of the first haunted castle in The Castle of Otranto (1764). Barthelme's book also relies upon gigantism for its central effect. The quest to convey the father's enormous

3,200 cubit corpse to its grave is the basis for the action. Absurd encounters, wild adventures, and polymorphous conversations make up a sort of mock odyssey as the son drags the father's corpse to its waiting grave. The corpse voyage is interrupted at one point by the reading of a bizarre pamphlet by one, Peter Scatterpatter (a pun on "pater"?) called "A Manual for Sons." The book can be interpreted as a mock mythology which ridicules the ancient theme of the search for the father coupled with the Homeric journey. Instead of confinement within a crazy castle, the hero must drag the huge corpse of his father through a nightmare landscape filled with Gothic surprises. Characters in older Gothic fiction wander down dim corridors looking for a way out their entrapment. Characters in the modern Gothic are enmeshed in cerebral windings and turnings in the dark castle of the mind.

029. Bates, Arlo. "The Intoxicated Ghost." The Intoxicated Ghost, and Other Stories. Boston: Houghton Mifflin, 1908.

REPRINT EDITION: Salem, NH, Ayer (Short Stories Index Series), 19-72.

CRITICAL SYNOPSIS: In the vein of Gothic comedy as practiced by J. K. Bangs (see 024-027), the story of a tipsy spook is not original with Bates but he does bring touches of cleverness to this supernatural figure of fun. The intoxicated ghost is one, Major Mc Hugh, a Revolutionary war hero who often returns to visit his ancestors but never seems to come back sober. The drunken ghost also has a purpose and mission. Having concealed the family jewels at his death, he would now carry them back with him to the other side to flash at his fellow phantoms and thus elevate his standing in high ghost society. Retaining the jewels and tricking him out of his secret becomes the basis for the plot which pits the living Mc Hughs against their alcoholic ancestor. Although the conflict is different, Edgar Allan Poe's tale, "The Angel of the Odd," also uses alcoholic fantasy to bring together the two worlds.

030. Beagle, Peter. A Fine and Private Place. New York: Viking Press, 19-60.

REPRINT EDITION: New York, Ballantine, 1988.
RESEARCH SOURCE: Van Becker, David, "Time, Space, and Consciousness in the Fantasy of Peter S. Beagle," San Jose Studies 1 (19-75): 52-61.

CRITICAL SYNOPSIS: Beagle's first novel is raucous Gothic comedy. Its title, taken from the poem, "To His Coy Mistress" by Andrew Marvell, rings with irony since the Bronx cemetery where the hero, Jonathan Rebeck, has taken up residence with a companion raven is hardly a "private place." To the contrary, the dead surrounding Rebeck's mausoleum home are constantly awake and gregarious. Thus, the central situation of the novel--conversations with the dead in their own marble domain--becomes a grotesque burlesque of the novel of talk and the so-called Shavian novel of lofty ideas. Readers of Thomas Love Peacock's vociferous novels, Headlong Hall (1816) and Nightmare Abbey (1818), will instantly recognize Beagle's literary roots and methods of comedy. The names of the characters stand for various life views, the extreme fantasist, the unyielding realist, the bookish idealist, and so forth. Rebeck himself is a failed druggist who has come to the graveyard because he could not cure the ills of those who sought his medicines. His corpse companions are Michael Morgan, a murdered professor of history, Laura Durand, a woman who was cold in life but is warm in death, and Doris Klapper an aggressive sensualist and master builder of garish mausoleums. The sole, sane voice rising above the friction of crazy talk is that of the raven, Poe's bird, but in this case, the conveyer of sarcastic wisdom. When the raven feeds Rebeck early in the novel, it is not manna that he brings in his beak, but baloney. Inspired baloney is what follows when the dead begin to talk. In composing a witty necromantic fantasy, Beagle also transforms a traditional Gothic site, the graveyard, into a place of hilarious post-mortem education.

031.   _____. Lila, the Werewolf. Santa Barbara, CA: Capra Press, 1974.

REPRINT EDITION: Dark Imaginings, A Collection of Gothic Fantasy, eds. Robert Boyer, Kenneth Zahorski, New York, Dell Publishing, 1978.
RESEARCH SOURCES: Samuelson, David N., "Peter S. Beagle," Supernatural Fiction Writers, pp.987-991; Tobin, Jean, "Werewolves and Unicorns: Fabulous Beasts in Peter Beagle's Fiction," Forms of the Fantastic, eds. Jan Hokenson, Howard Pearce, Westport, CT, Greenwood Press, 1986, pp.181-189.

CRITICAL SYNOPSIS: First published in 1969, then retitled "Farrell and Lila the Werewolf," the story is a good example of one type of Gothic fantasy in which every detail of the story is realistic, ordinary, and probable with the exception of a single unbelievable fact or event. Here, the incredible fact is the strange, father-daughter relationship that exists between Joseph Farrell and Lila Braun. Lila is a sweet, delicate, and perfect child except when the moon is full. The mutilated corpses of neighbors' dogs and cats can only mean the impossible, that Farrell's little ward is a werewolf. Farrell realizes that he is somehow being tested by being given the care of a superbeast and he meets the monthly problem with tenderness and tolerance rather than terror and revulsion. Thus, the usual conditions of the monster story are turned around when the human character finds out that he is living with and being asked to love and to accept a monstrosity. While Farrell passes the test, the real brute of the story turns out to be Lila's "normal" and prudent mother, Bernice, who exploits (or feeds off) her daughter's lycanthropy. When Farrell finally sees Bernice as the "real werewolf" the point about the monsterism of society is driven home. Beagle's manipulation of the monster question finds parallels in the earlier treatment of the theme in Crane's novella, "The Monster" (see 102).

032.   Beale, Charles Willing. The Ghost of Guir House. Cincinnati: Editor Publishing, 1897.

REPRINT EDITION: Five Victorian Ghost Novels, ed. E.F. Bleiler, New York, Dover Publications, 1971.

CRITICAL SYNOPSIS: The novel offers plenty of supernatural content, but only minimal terror. The format is that of a time journey and dream quest which convey the protagonist, Paul Henley, to a crumbling mansion in the deep woods of colonial Virginia. Here, he is received and entertained by the strange squire, Ah Ben, and his beautiful grand daughter, Dorothy, who is seemingly his prisoner. Thus, the prime ingredients of a successful Gothic are on hand but Beale misdirects the situation toward a spiritualist love

story rather than a tale of horrible persecution and paternal menace. Like previous grail castles or magic mansions, Guir House
does not exist except in the overwrought imaginings of a romance-
starved young mind. When Ah Ben informs Paul Henley that he has
entered a mirage and is living in a dream, Paul still declines to
return to reality and pledges his love to Dorothy. But she sacri-
fices her own happiness by insisting that Paul reawaken, which he
does, to find himself alone in a decaying ruin and unsure how he
came there. Politely spooky, the novel often charms by its descriptions, but never awes or overwhelms by a superior presence of
evil as a good Gothic does after assembling its cast behind the
walls of the haunted mansion.

033.   Beaumont, Charles [Charles Nutt]. "The Vanishing American." The Hun-
       ger and Other Stories. New York: Putnam, 1957.

       REPRINT EDITION: New York, Bantam Books, 1959.

       CRITICAL SYNOPSIS: The story first appeared in Modern Fantasy and
       Science Fiction, 1955, and strikes a kind of moral in the truth
       that we only discover how to live after we are dead. To get the
       idea across, the posthumous narrator, Mr. Monchell, undergoes all
       of the sensations of a conscious corpse able to hear, see, and
       feel, but not able to communicate his post-mortem consciousness.

034.   _____. "The Howling Man." Night Ride and Other Journeys. New
       York: Bantam Books, 1960.

       CRITICAL SYNOPSIS: Investigating a mysterious cry or horrid moan
       in a dark building by night is a standard Gothic excursion. A
       young American recuperating from an illness in the German monas-
       tery of Schwartzhof is disturbed by awful howls coming from the
       bowels of the building. Upon investigation, he finds that the
       caged howler is no one less than Satan himself now a prisoner in
       what was once the capital of all evil in the western world. The
       tale obviously plays with the passage in Revelation, 20:2 which
       reveals Satan bound for a thousand years, combining the Biblical
       prophecy with the amoral curiosity of young Americans travelling
       abroad. There are also overtones of the myth of Pandora's box and
       her impetuous act. Anxious to see the Prince of Evil at his full
       strength, he releases the devil from his cell to wreak havoc upon
       the world once more. The story offers a more-than-satisfactory
       Gothic atmosphere and cleverly pursues a sinister "what if" pre-
       mise in the American's self-serving gesture.

035.   Bellamy, Edward. "The Blindman's World." The Blindman's World, and
       Other Stories. Boston: Houghton-Mifflin, 1898.

       REPRINT EDITION: The Blindman's World and Other Stories, Ada, OK,
       Garrett, 1968.
       RESEARCH SOURCE: Martin, Jay, "Ghostly Rentals: Ghostly Purchases:
       Haunted Imaginations in James, Twain, and Bellamy," The Haunted
       Dusk: American Supernatural Fiction, 1820-1920, eds. Howard Kerr,
       John W. Crowley, Charles L. Crow, Athens, GA, Georgia UP, 1983,
       pp.121-131.

       CRITICAL SYNOPSIS: The futurist fantasy is eerie, but not terrify-
       ing. An astronomer falls asleep at his telescope and makes a vi-
       sionary excursion to the planet, Mars, where he has a haunting
       glimpse of the future and comes to an awareness of earthly limita-

tions. Martians lack all power of memory but more than compensate for their missing sense of the past by prodigious insight and foresight. When he awakens, the astronomer realizes that only by dreaming prophetically forward can any civilization fulfill its higher ends. Consciousness bound by memory is the Platonic cave from which we must seek exits or remain blind prisoners of the past.

036.   Bennett, Emerson. The Phantom of the Forest: A Tale of the Dark and Bloody Ground. Philadelphia: John E. Potter, 1868.

CRITICAL SYNOPSIS: Although the title suggests a haunted forest Gothic, the 503 page novel turns out to be a romantic adventure with certain resemblances to the scenes, situations, and characters of Cooper's The Last of the Mohicans (1826). The action takes place on the fringes of the frontier in the "dark and bloody ground" of the Ohio country where the principals of the story, Henry Colburne and Tom Sturgess are on a scouting expedition through the dense forests when they hear "a wild and prolonged shriek that sounded as if made by the throat of a woman." Local rumors of "a creature with eyes like coals of fire, teeth, claws, and covered with scales" seem confirmed by the awful yowl. While the mystery of the phantom voice hangs fire, Colburne meets and falls in love with Isaline Holcombe who is travelling to Kentucky to join her father, a retired Revolutionary War officer. With her is the somewhat sinister and repellent Charles Hampton, a Byronic character whose real name, purposes, and identity are hidden from Isaline. A duel between Hampton and Colburne is interrupted by the terrible scream from the depths of the forest and Colburne sees a dark, humanoid form leap from a tree and disappear. As the party proceeds down the Ohio River toward Lexington, Kentucky, the howls persist and they encounter the savage half-breed, Methoto, the redskin equivalent of the Gothic novel's lecherous cleric. After numerous captures and escapes, Henry and Isaline arrive at a destroyed settlement with Methoto and the villainous Hampton in pursuit. Rescue and revelation now follow when the phantom of the forest is at last explained and brought on as an agent of justice. The traitorous Hampton is exposed as a renegade whiteman who murders other whites in the pay of the Indians. The phantom is revealed as the lunatic girl, Helen Mervine. The murder of her father by Methoto's father drove her mad and caused her to wear a hairy mask over her face. The bestial masquerade had been her only recourse. With identities settled and both red and while villains exposed and punished, Henry and Isaline are ready for unimpeded happiness. The half-breed as neo-Gothic villain, the haunted forest as natural substitute for the haunted castle, and the delayed natural explanation of a seemingly supernatural voice all relate the novel to the American Gothic tradition.

037.   Betts, Doris. Beasts of the Southern Wild. New York: Harper & Row, 1973.

REPRINT EDITION: 3 by 3: Masterworks of Southern Gothic, ed. Lewis P. Simpson, Atlanta, Peachtree Press, 1985.
RESEARCH SOURCE: Simpson, Lewis, "Introduction," 3 by 3, pp.vii-xiv.

CRITICAL SYNOPSIS: Notable examples of recent Southern Gothic in this collection of tales are "Hitchhiker," "Burning the Bed," "The Glory of His Nostrils," and "The Spider Gardens of Madagascar."

"Beasts of the Southern Wild" is a Poesque tale reminiscent of "The Pit and the Pendulum" (see 385). In the opening scene of Poe's story, the prisoner faces the inquisitors and is consigned to the pit. In the opening scene of Betts's story, the narrator, a female white prisoner held in a black controlled jail, must face the Chooser in the Choosing Room. "The Chooser sits on an iron stool. Negro, of course, in his forties. Jim Brown used to look like him; but he has thin lips; I must insist on that: thin lips. I am beginning to be afraid. I've been beaten now, been raped, other things." The Gothic tale (printed in italics) alternates with the mundane existence of Carol Walsh, highschool English teacher, who fantasizes herself into the situation of the victim. Simpson comments that this story and others in the Southern Gothic mode "respond to the terror and pathos of the self's difficult, maybe impossible, attempt to achieve a meaningful identity."

038. Bierce, Ambrose. "Chickamauga." In the Midst of Life: Tales of Soldiers and Civilians. San Francisco: E.L.G. Steele, 1891.

REPRINT EDITION: In the Midst of Life and Other Stories, afterword Marcus Cunliffe, New York, New American Library-Signet, 1961.
RESEARCH SOURCES: Reed, Eugene E., "Ambrose Bierce's 'Chickamauga': An Identity Restored," Revue des Langues Vivantes 28 (1962): 49-53; Rubens, Philip M., "The Gothic Foundations of Ambrose Bierce's Fiction," Nyctalops 2, number 7 (1978): 29-31.

CRITICAL SYNOPSIS: One of the most successful as well as one of the most anthologized of Bierce's battlefield Gothics, "Chickamauga" is probable the most repulsive of his Civil War pieces. Bierce himself had participated in the September 1863 battle which took its name from "the river of death." His tale approaches those responses of numbing horror and hideous disgust to be seen in the nauseous vaults and sepulchral rapes of Monk Lewis in The Monk (1795). At its most shocking and repulsive, the physical Gothic seeks an emetic response, a shock so strong that it sickens. The ingenious construction of the story and the deliberate withholding of information are factors in the horror. Events are perceived or misperceived from the point of view of a six year old child but narrated by a Biercian central intelligence who manages these events with cynical hindsight and foresight. The child is seen playing soldiers' games near the battlefield just as the battle is ending and Bragg's army begins its retreat across Chickamauga Creek. The wounded make up a sort of calvalcade of agony on parade. A first moment of unbearable horror comes when the child gleefully mounts a crawling soldier to "play horse." The horror image is unforgettable: "The man sank upon his breast, recovered, flung the small boy fiercely to the ground as an unbroken colt might have done, then turned upon him a face that lacked a lower jaw--from the upper teeth to the throat was a great red gap fringed with hanging threads of flesh and splinters of bone." The horror image is repeated when the child leads the wounded men to his home only to find his house ablaze and his mother in splinters. But it is the culminating horror image of the dead mother coupled with the shocking revelation that the child is a deaf mute which makes "Chickamauga" the peerless example of battlefield Gothic at its point of maximum horror and revulsion. What the mute child sees is "The greater part of the forehead torn away, and from the jagged hole the brain protruded, overflowing the temple, a frothy mass of gray, crowned with clusters of crimson bubbles--the work of a shell." No one awakens from a Biercian nightmare of war.

039. _____. "The Damned Thing." In the Midst of Life: Tales of Soldiers and Civilians. San Francisco: E.L.G. Steele, 1891.

REPRINT EDITION: Ghost and Horror Stories of Ambrose Bierce, ed. E.F. Bleiler, New York, Dover Publications, 1964.
RESEARCH SOURCES: Cruce, Stark, "The Color of 'The Damned Thing': The Occult as Suprasensational," The Haunted Dusk: American Supernatural Fiction, 1820-1920, eds. Howard Kerr, John W. Crowley, Charles L. Crow, Athens, GA, Georgia UP, 1983, pp.211-227; Grenander, M.E., "Bierce's Turn of the Screw: Tales of Ironical Terror," Western Humanities Review 11 (1957): 257-264.

CRITICAL SYNOPSIS: A tale in four parts which mixes horror and humor, the work could be described as Bierce's version of an anatomy lesson. The presence of "the damned thing" verifies the strange scientific fact that "There are sounds that we cannot hear.... There are colors that we cannot see," a scientific finding for which the main character pays with his life. Each story part is adorned with a gruesome caption as with the coroner's inquest at the opening. "One Does Not Always Eat What is on the Table" refers to the dissected corpse of Hugh Morgan, the man torn to pieces by the damned thing. Part Two, an eye-witness account of the mutilation by William Harker is called "What May Happen in a Field of Wild Oats," the spot where the damned thing had attacked and shredded Morgan. Part Three is vintage Bierce in its graphic detailing of the mutilated torso: "The chest and sides looked as if they had been beaten with a bludgeon. There were dreadful lacerations; the skin was torn in strips and shreds." Thus, the joke book chapter title, "A Man Though Naked May Be in Rags," assumes a grisly accuracy. The final part, "An Explanation from the Tomb," is a fragmentary account of the damned thing from Morgan's diary. Morgan had seemingly been pursuing and investigating this invisible creature without a name and on the day that Harker saw him in the field of oats he had finally found his answer. Thus, the tale follows a familiar Biercian formula of relating a horrid event within a number of conflicting contexts and yielding no certain conclusions about what actually happened and why. Only the inescapable fact of the horror remains.

040. _____. "The Eyes of the Panther." In the Midst of Life: Tales of Soldiers and Civilians. San Francisco: E.L.G. Steele, 1891.

REPRINT EDITION: Ghost and Horror Stories of Ambrose Bierce, ed. E.F. Bleiler, New York, Dover Publications, 1964.
RESEARCH SOURCE: Woodruff, Stuart C., The Short Stories of Ambrose Bierce, A Study in Polarity, Pittsburgh, Pittsburgh UP, 1964.

CRITICAL SYNOPSIS: A story of the human beast or were-panther and also a story of sheer horror which substitutes bestial savagery for maternal affection. The metamorphosed woman is one, Irene Marlowe. A gruesome reunion with her husband, Charles, will convey some idea of Bierce's handling of the human-into-beast theme: "Cowering on the floor against a wall was his wife, clasping a child. As he sprang toward her, she broke into laughter, loud, long, and mechanical, devoid of gladness and devoid of sense--the laughter that is not out of keeping with the clanking of a chain. Hardly knowing what he did he extended his arms. She laid the babe in them. It was dead--pressed to death in the mother's embrace."

041. _____. "The Middle Toe of the Right Foot." In the Midst of Life: Tales of Soldiers and Civilians. San Francisco: E.L.G. Steele, 1891.

REPRINT EDITION: Ghost and Horror Stories of Ambrose Bierce, ed. E.F. Bleiler, New York, Dover Publications, 1964.
RESEARCH SOURCES: Hill, Larry L., "Style in the Tales of Ambrose Bierce," Dissertation Abstracts International 34 (1973): 3400A (University of Wisconsin).

CRITICAL SYNOPSIS: A story of supernatural revenge with Poe-like overtones written in Bierce's spare but waspish and macabre style. The wife-murderer, Grossmith, is drawn into a duel with his dead wife's lover. There is a commotion in the dark in the empty house where the murder had occurred, the old Manton House. Morning reveals an indisputable anatomical clue beside the body of the slain Grossmith, a woman's footprint showing a missing middle toe. Gertrude Manton's revenge from beyond the grave is complete. The monstrous footprint or the track of the thing from the nightside is a horror motif going back to the raid of Grendel on the Mead Hall in Beowulf, but Bierce has reused it with considerable macabre power.

042. _____. "The Moonlit Road." In the Midst of Life: Tales of Soldiers and Civilians. San Francisco: E.L.G. Steele, 1891.

REPRINT EDITIONS: Ghost and Horror Stories of Ambrose Bierce, ed. E.F. Bleiler, New York, Dover Publications, 1964.
RESEARCH SOURCES: Woodruff, Stuart Cowan, "The Short Stories of Ambrose Bierce: A Critical Study," Dissertation Abstracts 23 (1962): 1713-1714 (University of Connecticut).

CRITICAL SYNOPSIS: No supernatural event is more common in the pages of Gothic fiction than the confrontation with the apparition of a slain relative. Bierce's story is built around this fearsome event, but he gives it freshness as well as his customary cynical undercut. The story concerns the murder of the mother and is told three times, first by the son of the Hetman family, then by the father of the house, and finally by the victim herself, the late Julia Hetman, speaking posthumously in ghostly form through a medium. The story rapidly accumulates various Gothic effects. The son, Joel Hetman, Jr., is summoned home from college when his mother is strangled. Shortly thereafter, his father vanishes from the moonlit road after seeing someone or something loom up in his path, a manifestation unseen by the son. The middle narrative, "The Statement of Caspar Grattan," reenacts the murder of the wife by the husband and her subsequent reappearance on the moonlit road, an event which causes his derangement. The final narrative recreates the murder from the strangled wife's point of view and is a small set piece of Gothic suspense and fear, the approach of the thing on the stairs, the door to the chamber being thrown open, "the strangling clutch upon my throat." Unaware that her murderer is her husband, she attempts a reunion from beyond the grave but her manifestation on the moonlit road has driven Hetman mad. Nor has she been able to make contact with her skeptical son. The spectre of the murdered mother has the last gloomy word from her state of living death when she remarks: "Soon he, too, must pass to this Life Invisible and be lost to me forever."

043. _____. "An Occurrence at Owl Creek Bridge." In the Midst of Life: Tales of Soldiers and Civilians. San Francisco: E.L.G. Steele, 1891.

REPRINT EDITION: Ghost and Horror Stories of Ambrose Bierce, ed. E.F. Bleiler, New York, Dover Publications, 1964.
RESEARCH SOURCE: Rubens, Philip M., "The Literary Gothic and the Fiction of Ambrose Gwinett Bierce," Dissertation Abstracts International, 37 (1976): 1555A (Northern Illinois University).

CRITICAL SYNOPSIS: The battlefields of the American Civil War constituted a natural Gothic environment for Bierce. Examples of human helplessness, brutality, stupidity, wasted courage, and baseness were drawn from his personal memories of carnage at Missionary Ridge, Chickamauga, Lookout Mountain, and Resaca. Here in the midst of life, death came to a terrible and supreme focus in the strivings of the soldiers. The confluence of the death moment and the life moment, the one absurd event overlapping the other, is the subject of what is arguably Bierce's most famous short story, "An Occurrence at Owl Creek Bridge." The mental effect of the death moment during a fall or descent had previously been studied by Poe in "A Descent into the Maelström" (see 382) where the fatal experience results in the hero's salvation. But Bierce's universe permits no such miracles although his entrapped soldiers and civilians may want to believe in transcendence and escape. The situation is heavy with gruesome irony as the Confederate Spy, Peyton Farquhar, "a rope loosely encircling his neck," stands on the makeshift gallows of a railroad bridge awaiting the sergeant's command that will commence his hanging. It comes, but to Farquhar's astonishment he does not lose consciousness at the death moment but instead feels enraptured and freed thinking that the rope has snapped. In his euphoric plunge into the creek, he seems transported to a kind of Eden, making a visionary homecoming and feeling the embrace of his wife. Here, at the apex of extreme vitality and joy, the story pivots or twists grotesquely and abruptly. "As he is about to clasp her, he feels a stunning blow upon the back of the neck; a blinding white light blazes all about him with a sound like the shock of a cannon--then all was darkness and silence! Peyton Farquhar was dead." The reader is left with only one more bleak horror among the occurrences of a war which admitted of no miracles or resurrections.

044. _____. "One of the Missing." In the Midst of Life: Tales of Soldiers and Civilians. San Francisco: E.L.G. Steele, 1891.

REPRINT EDITION: In the Midst of Life and Other Stories, afterword Marcus Cunliffe, New York, New American Library-Signet, 1961.
RESEARCH SOURCES: Ringe, Donald A., American Gothic, pp.183-184; Berkove, Lawrence I., "Arms and the Man: Ambrose Bierce's Response to War," Michigan Academician 1 (1969): 21-30.

CRITICAL SYNOPSIS: For the immobilization of the victim and the proximity of death, this tale of the Civil War (the battle of Kennesaw Mountain) challenges Poe's famous horror story, "The Pit and the Pendulum." As in Poe's tale, there is a single character in an unbearable situation of entrapment. Poe's victim has been placed in the pit and beneath the pendulum by the Inquisition for a crime he can neither remember nor name. Bierce's victim, the sniper, Private Jerome Searing, has been placed in his fatal predicament by the brutal fortunes of war. From his hiding place in a small

shed on an abandoned plantation, the Federal sharpshooter prepares
to line up a Confederate victim in the sights of his hairtriggered
rifle when suddenly a random shell crashes into the structure collapsing it and pinning him beneath the debris. Not only do we get
a instantaneous ruin or a wrecked building required for a good
Gothic, but we also get death in the midst of life as Searing's
"head was as rigidly fixed as in a vise; he could move his eyes,
his chin--no more." What he sees is the muzzle of his own rifle
now aimed at the exact center of his forehead and poised to go off
at the slightest movement. About to bestow death on another just
moments before, he now becomes the recipient. The gruesome brilliance of the situation is heightened by its credibility, for horrible chance of just this sort is a common element of warfare. Unable to bear the strain of waiting for his death, Private Searing
manages to free one hand and press the trigger after many excruci-
ating hours of staring into the impersonal, metallic eye. Poe's
victim is granted mercy by a miraculous liberation; Bierce's victim apparently dies of unbearable relief when he depresses the
trigger and receives no shot. Unknown to Searing, his rifle had
fired when the building was wrecked. A good Gothic tale can sometimes convey the reader to the limits of fear without any reliance
on the supernatural. In this area, Bierce's after action report of
a missing man is one of the best.

045.　　　　　. "The Death of Halpin Frayser." Can Such Things Be? New
York: Cassell, 1893.

REPRINT EDITION: Ghost and Horror Stories of Ambrose Bierce, ed.
E.F. Bleiler, New York, Dover Publications, 1964.
RESEARCH SOURCES: Mc Lean, Robert C., "The Deaths in Ambrose
Bierce's 'Halpin Frayser,'" Papers on Language and Literature 10
(1974): 394-402; Stein, William Bysshe, "Bierce's 'The Death of
Halpin Frayser': The Poetics of Gothic Consciousness," ESQ: A
Journal of the American Renaissance 18 (1972): 115-122.

CRITICAL SYNOPSIS: One of the masterworks of Biercian Gothic, the
story contains some elements to seen elsewhere in Bierce's work.
These include the situation of the lost hunter, a dream excursion,
an Oedipal theme featuring an encounter with a phantasmic mother,
sinister sound effects, and "that most dreadful of all existen-
ces...a body without a soul." The Gothicism of the story is in the
ambiguous psychological mode challenging all interpretations of
what actually happened and calling into question the reality of
reality itself. The dreamer, Halpin Frayser, has a grisly reunion
with the murdered mother, Catherine Larue, a terror so gigantic
that it apparently causes his death. This is a story of mood
rather than plot and action, but as William Bysshe Stein remarks,
"If there is a criminal at large he is for Bierce the creator of
the mind of man: the trickster God (Descartes' Dieu trompeur) who
delights in betraying every aspiration for truth or certitude that
the creatures of His creation harbor in their thoughtless
thought."

046.　　　　　. "The Secret of Macarger's Gulch." Can Such Things Be? New
York: Cassell, 1893.

REPRINT EDITION: Ghost and Horror Stories of Ambrose Bierce, ed.
E.F. Bleiler, New York, Dover Publications, 1964.
RESEARCH SOURCE: Davidson, Kathy N., "Restructuring the Ineffable
and Ambrose Bierce's 'The Secret of Macarger's Gulch,'" Markham

Review 12 (1982): 14-19.

CRITICAL SYNOPSIS: A tale of suggestive terror rather than explicit horror, the plot involves a time passage in a dream to the
sources of a murder. The narrator, Elderson, while hunting quail
in Macarger's Gulch, takes shelter in a cabin, falls asleep, and
dreams of a strange city (Edinburgh) and of a couple in a strange
room. Dream intersects with reality "as if two pictures, the scene
of my dream, and my actual surroundings, had been blended, one
overlying the other." The narrator then experiences the actual
presence of the murdered woman although she never directly appears. In a postscript, Elderson is informed by Morgan that he had
previously visited the cabin in the Gulch and there found the battered skeleton of the murdered woman. This story is not much more
than an exercise in Gothic acoustics, especially the indescribable
moan in the darkness.

047. _____. "One Summer Night." The Collected Works of Ambrose Bierce.
New York and Washington, DC: Neale, 1909-1912.

REPRINT EDITION: The Stories and Fables of Ambrose Bierce, ed. Ed-
ward Wagenknecht, Owings Mills, MD, Stemmer House, 1977.
RESEARCH SOURCE: Wymer, Thomas L., "Ambrose Bierce," Supernatural
Fiction Writers, pp.731-737.

CRITICAL SYNOPSIS: Mencken wrote of Bierce that "Death to him was
not something repulsive, but a sort of low comedy--the last act of
a squalid and rib-rocking buffoonery." This little nugget of cya-
nide demonstrates the accuracy of Mencken's point. The chief character is a victim of premature burial whose coffin is dug up "one
summer night" by two medical students and their black servant,
Jess. Bierce favored the supernatural jolt or grisly shock which
he delivers here with cold enthusiasm when the coffin lid is
pulled back. It is an old moment in the pages of Gothic horror but
freshly handled by Bierce and as is his custom Bierce is able to
inject a note of gleeful burlesque into the gruesome situation.

048. Bird, Robert Montgomery. Calavar; or, The Knight of Conquest, A Romance of Mexico. Philadelphia: Carey, Lea, & Blanchard, 1834.

REPRINT EDITION: New York, AMS Press, 1978.
RESEARCH SOURCES: Cowie, Alexander, Rise of the American Novel,
pp.247-249; Kilman, Joan Collins, "Robert Montgomery Bird: Physician and Man of Letters," Dissertation Abstracts International 39
(1978): 1571A (University of Delaware).

CRITICAL SYNOPSIS: In the vein of Scott and Cooper but more realistic in its treatment of the villains of history, this romance of
Mexico during the Spanish conquest uses such real events as the
Battle of Otumba and the massacre of Spaniards on the noche triste
as sanguinary backdrop. But Calavar also qualifies as Gothified
history in its presentation of the life and fortunes of the half-
mad knight, St. John Calavar and his romantic nephew, Amador.
These soldiers of fortune whose names sound so much like characters in a Gothified saga or one of the heroic dramas of the Restoration period have come to the new world to serve with Cortez.
Against a background of looting, betrayal, bloodshed, torture, and
massacre, their intricate heroic drama or Gothic melodrama is
played out to its destructive end.

049. _____. The Hawks of Hawk Hollow, A Tradition of Pennsylvania. Philadelphia: Carey, Lea, & Blanchard, 1835.

REPRINT EDITION: New York, AMS Press, 1978.
RESEARCH SOURCES: Cowie, Alexander, Rise of the American Novel, pp.250-251; Dahl, Curtis, Robert Montgomery Bird, New York, Twayne, 1963.

CRITICAL SYNOPSIS: A romance of the American Revolution containing Gothic overtones and episodes. The setting is the wilderness reaches of the Delaware Water Gap in Pennsylvania, ideal Gothic territory. Bird's landscapes are never Edenic, but instead, zones of violence and danger where characters can lose both their way and their humanity. The plot has all of the genealogical complications and complex entanglements of action expected in an English Gothic romance. The time is the year following the surrender of the British at Yorktown, but the war continues on the frontier in the shape of a family feud between the Tory Gilberts and the patriot Falconers. Neither side has a premium on virtue and the feud that pits the Gilberts (called the Hawks because of their wild and predatory behavior) against the equally ambitious and scheming Colonel Falconer and his nephew, Henry, creates a picture of barbarous rivals in a barbaric environment. Unlike Cooper, Bird was not prone to idealizations of human nature or nature itself on the primitive American frontier. The complex plot also admits a mysterious stranger who interrupts the wedding of Henry Falconer and Catherine Loring, murdering the first and abducting the second. This is precisely the sort of episode--the nuptial which ends in violence--that many English Gothic writers had used to lubricate the gears of terror and bring a villain to genealogical justice. When the stranger, Sterling (actually, Oran Gilbert) is visited in his prison cell by the phantom of Henry Faulkner, he responds to this Gothic cue by committing suicide, thus clearing the way for another marriage, this time a successful one, between Catherine and Hyland Gilbert who is now disclosed as the natural son of Colonel Falconer and Jesse Gilbert. Through this myth of family harmony, Bird expresses the uneasy balance of forces in American frontier life without overlooking the permanent potential for violence in the American character.

050. _____. Nick of the Woods; or, The Jibbenainosay. A Tale of Kentucky. Philadelphia: Carey, Lea, & Blanchard, 1837.

REPRINT EDITION: ed. Curtis Dahl, New Haven, CT, College & University Press, 1967.
RESEARCH SOURCES: Bryant, James C., "The Fallen World in Nick of the Woods," American Literature 38 (1966): 352-364; Cowie, Alexander, Rise of the American Novel, pp.253-254; Ringe, Donald A., American Gothic, pp.110-111; Winston, Robert P., "Bird's Bloody Romance: Nick of the Woods," Southern Studies: An Interdisciplinary Journal of the South 23 (1984): 71-90.

CRITICAL SYNOPSIS: There are no noble savages in this Gothic romance of the American forest. As Oral Coad has observed of the conversionary process from English to American Gothic, "the caverns of America's hills supplant the Gothic vaults of Europe, and the redskin proves no less terrifying than the spectre of the castle." Donald A. Ringe extends Coad's statement by designating Bird's Nick of the Woods "the most Gothic of border romances [and] the culmination of a line of development--the naturalization of

Gothic techniques and devices--that Cooper had begun in The Spy (see 097)." Nick of the Woods or Jibbenainosay (the spirit-that-walks) as he is known to the Indians, is more savage than any savage, a demonic and barbaric reincarnation of Cooper's woodsman, Natty Bumppo. He roams the Kentucky forests like a bloody, avenging phantom or superhuman warrior mutilating and slaughtering every redman he can find and reserving an especially brutal ardor for the Shawnees and their chief, Wenonga. Nick's monomania to hunt down and exterminate every living Indian is on a par with Ahab's destructive obsession with the white whale in Moby Dick (see 324). The gory spirit of sanguinary atrocity which had once characterized the pages of M.G. Lewis's Gothic, The Monk (1795) has been transported intact to the Kentucky frontier in "a wantonness of malice and lust of blood which even death could not satisfy." But this bloodthirsty Pathfinder has not always haunted the wild landscape. In his other identity before he was forced to witness the murder of his wife and children by Shawnees Nick had been the gentle Quaker, Nathan Slaughter, as passive and peaceful as Nick is brutal and violent. Bird has his character vibrate between these two polar personalities, for Nick of the Woods is both a frontier Gothic and a novel of the double life. And here Bird touches upon a profound American Gothic theme concerning the darker side of the American character. Lurking beneath the innocence and optimism, there is something dark and dreadful and capable of primal evil. It is just this permanent stain of evil on the American Oversoul that the feared Indian-hater comes to embody.

051. Blish, James. Black Easter. Garden City, NY: Doubleday, 1968.

REPRINT EDITION: ed. David G. Hartwell, Boston, Gregg Press, 19-80.
RESEARCH SOURCES: Aldiss, Brian, "James Blish: The Mathematics of Behavior," Foundation 13 (1978): 43-50; Ketterer, David, "'Imprisoned in Tesseract': Black Easter and The Day After Judgement by James Blish," Missouri Review 7 (1984): 243-263; Stableford, Brian, A Clash of Symbols: The Triumph of James Blish, San Bernardino, CA, Borgo Press, 1979.

CRITICAL SYNOPSIS: A mushroom cloud rising over Vatican City, an exploding cross, the fiery destruction of William Blake's illustrations of Dante, and demonic voices whispering that God is dead are among the horror elements of this futuristic Gothic. Science runs amuck and pushes civilization under the terminal shadow of the silenium bomb while religion watches helplessly as the world of traditional values moves toward cataclysm, a black Easter. The characters are straightforward allegorizations of the forces contending in the nuclear age. The Jesuit, Father Domenico, is set against the agnostic power-monger, Theron Ware. Baines, the cynical munitions manufacturer and the superspy, Adolph Hess, contribute to the impending holocaust through an agency which seems to be a mock-UN, the Consolidated Warfare Service. In older forms of the Gothic, the menace comes from a dark and tyrannical past; in nuclear Gothic, the not-so-impossible horrors of the future generate the shock. In this regard, Blish's Black Easter has interesting connections with Mary Shelley's doomsday novel The Last Man (1826) where the closing scenes depict a peopleless earth under a "black sun."

052. Bloch, Robert. "The Feast in the Abbey." Weird Tales, January, 19-35.

REPRINT EDITIONS: The Opener of the Way, Sauk City, WI, Arkham
House, 1945; Sudbury, UK, Neville Spearman, 1974.
RESEARCH SOURCE: Guérif, Francois, "Robert Bloch: Du Noir Gothique
Au Noir Polar," Europe 664-665 (1984): 105-108.

CRITICAL SYNOPSIS: An early tale published when Bloch was only
seventeen, but exhibiting a sound grasp of the requirements of an
effective Gothic story. The content suggests Bloch's reading in a
special type of early Gothic fiction, the monastic shocker in
which the principal background was a monastery or convent and the
principal action some diabolic or ghoulish deed by depraved cler-
ics. In Bloch's modernized version, an assembly of cannibalistic
monks invite the narrator to a great feast in the abbey. All is
highly festive until the abbot reveals to him that the main course
was the flesh of his brother. By using a lofty style, skilled irony and the décor of the monastic shocker, Bloch gives new horror
to an ancient Gothic motif which goes back to the legend of Thyes-
tes and the feast of flesh.

053. _____. "Yours Truly, Jack the Ripper." Weird Tales, July, 1943.

REPRINT EDITION: The Opener of the Way, Sudbury, UK, Neville
Spearman, 1974.
RESEARCH SOURCE: Larson, Randall D., The Complete Robert Bloch: An
Illustrated, International Bibliography, Sunnyvale, CA, Fandom Un-
limited, 1986.

CRITICAL SYNOPSIS: The unsolved murders of the famous London killer and the vivid correspondence of the Ripper to the London police make up the substance of one of Bloch's best-known tales.
Bloch's hypothetical Ripper is an "immortal fiend," a deathless
demon who might reappear elsewhere in time. Yet, he has charming
gifts as a talker and connoisseur of macabre wit.

054. _____. Psycho. New York: Simon and Schuster, 1959.

REPRINT EDITION: Mattituck, NY, Aeonian Press/Amereon, 1980.
RESEARCH SOURCE: Wiater, Stanley, "Interview: Robert Bloch," Fantasy Newsletter 47 (1982): 19-20, 35.

CRITICAL SYNOPSIS: An established classic of cinema-Gothic Ameri-
cana, Bloch's horror novel furnished the material for Alfred
Hitchcock's 1960 shocker, perhaps the ultimate and certainly the
most analyzed American horror film. At the headwaters of the Gothic tradition in Walpole's Castle of Otranto (1764), psychopathic
peril had stalked the corridors of an enclosed Gothic world in the
dual personality of the villain, Manfred, "whose virtues were always ready to operate when his passion did not obscure his reason." It is fascinating to observe the survival of Otrantoesque
devices and predicaments in the equally psychopathic world of
Bloch's motel Gothic. All of the original Gothic objects and
events are on hand, Americanized but still highly recognizable.
The stock figure of the entrapped and menaced maiden, however,
gains some added horror stature in Bloch's work since she is not
permitted to exit alive from his version of the haunted castle.
Bloch's Mary Crain and Hitchcock's Janet Leigh die horribly in a
modernized shower room version of the chamber of horrors, a violation of the heroine's rescue and exit from the castle which had
become nearly mandatory for the sentimental Gothic ending. Readers

and film viewers never quite recovered from this shocking departure from the formula. In addition, a strong rational character,
in this case the detective, proves helpless against irrational
forces and becomes a victim of the psychopath. The psychopath is
Norman Bates, the young operator of a now-deserted motel who is
two personalities in one body, dutiful son of a dead mother and
schizophrenic maniac who enters the personality of the mother he
killed. Norman Bates is especially likely to become old Mrs. Bates
just after some homicidal outburst as he does after the murders of
Mary Crain and the detective. Every haunted castle or homicidal
motel needs a terrible family secret which should not be disclosed
until the climax. When a swinging lightbulb illuminates the ghastly remains of Norman's dead mother and Norman himself become his
mother again the curse of the Bateses is revealed and all easy
psychological explanations go down the drain as profusely as the
heroine's blood had gone down the drain earlier. The success of
Psycho, a Gothic thriller which refused to grant its readers a way
out of the irrational world, demonstrates a fact of high horror
art: that there is dreadful pleasure in the nagging fear that evil
is mightier than good and chaos more probable than order. The
Americanization of this traditional Gothic theme is the achievement of Psycho.

055. _____. "The Man Who Collected Poe." Bogey Men. Moonachie, NJ:
Pyramid Publishers, 1963.

REPRINT EDITION: Selected Stories of Robert Bloch, San Francisco,
CA, Underwood, Miller, 1987.
RESEARCH SOURCE: Elliot, Jeffrey, "Robert Bloch," Fangoria Octo-
ber, 1979, pp.43-47.

CRITICAL SYNOPSIS: This comic piece is a sort of oblique tribute
to the master of American horror art, who, along with H.P. Lovecraft, inspired Bloch's craft. Written in several of Poe's own
styles and drawing upon Poe's own tales for its situations, the
tale's crowning touch is the appearance of Poe's own corpse, the
premium acquisition for a man who collected Poe.

056. _____. American Gothic. London: W.H. Allen, 1975.

REPRINT EDITION: New York, St. Martin's/Warner Publishing Servi-
ces, 1987.
RESEARCH SOURCE: Collins, Tom, "Robert Bloch: Society as Insane
Asylum," Twilight Zone June 1981, pp.13-17.

CRITICAL SYNOPSIS: Shows Bloch's longstanding interest in what may
be an American cultural phenomenon, mass killings by a psychotic. In 1893 during the Chicago World Fair, a pharmacist named H.H.
Holmes carved a niche for himself in American horror annals by
murdering twenty-seven people. American Gothic recreates the
homicidal career of Holmes in the person of G. Gordon Gregg, a
midwestern Bluebeard or Gilles de Rais responsible for the deaths
of several dozen girls. The novel's title seems in part a grim
jest at the expense of Grant Wood's famous painting.

057. _____. "The Skull of the Marquis de Sade." The Skull of the Marquis de Sade, and Other Stories. London: Robert Hale, 1975.

REPRINT EDITION: Selected Stories of Robert Bloch, San Francisco,
CA, Underwood, Miller, 1987.

RESEARCH SOURCE: Daniels, Les, "Robert Bloch," Supernatural Fiction Writers, pp.901-907.

CRITICAL SYNOPSIS: Merits comparison with F. Marion Crawford's chiller, "The Screaming Skull" (see 107). The animated skeleton had often appeared in Gothic fiction as an avenging agent or even a partner in conversation for the villain during his final hours. Here, the antiquarian, Christopher Maitland, acquires the skull of the famous sadist and the wickedest man of the Eighteenth Century, but alas, poor Yorick, the skull of the Marquis de Sade does not seem to wear a grisly grin as do most skulls. This flaw is a disappointment to the collector. However, the narrator's befuddlement over this rare sobriety in a skull will soon be set straight in horrifying fashion when events make it known that Sade's skull smiles only when it is about to devour a victim. This is gruesome comedy told with flashes of macabre wit.

058. Botsford, Margaret. Adelaide. By a Lady of Philadelphia. Philadelphia: Dennis Heartt, 1816.

RESEARCH SOURCE: Petter, Henri, Early American Novel, pp.196-199.

CRITICAL SYNOPSIS: Sentimental fiction concentrating on domestic tyranny and the indifference of parents to the needs of their daughter. The influence of Richardson may be seen in Botsford's drawing of character and of Mrs. Radcliffe in her depiction of male villainy and sublime landscaping. A further influence is Charles Brockden Brown's novel of seduction, Ormond; or, The Secret Witness (see 065), although Botsford's heroine is a far more passive sufferer than Brown's Constantia Dudley. The heroine, Adelaide Delmont, is a personage of extreme sensibility whose absentee father coerces her into a loveless marriage with the Marchese di Vironaldi. Although he lacks the supernatural stature of Mrs. Radcliffe's archfiends, Montoni (The Mysteries of Udolpho) and Schedoni (The Italian), Vironaldi has other Gothic endowments. One of the main melodramatic scenes depicts violence at a wedding, a common episode in maiden-centered Gothic fiction. As she is dragged to the altar by Vironaldi, Adelaide swoons while her sinister seducer is challenged to a duel and eliminated by a champion of virtue. All parties are happy when Adelaide's vicious father dies of disappointment over the failure of his scheme of enforced marriage. What the reader got in the novel were the stock figures from the English Gothic cast transplanted to a Philadelphian locale. Botsford made some efforts, however, to Americanize the tormented maiden of this cast. Thus, the moral contrast of wicked European males set against virtuous American females that forms the basis for the conflict anticipates a pattern of later American Gothics such as James's The Portrait of a Lady (see 241).

059. Bowline, Charley. The Iron Tomb; or, The Mock Count of New York. Boston: George H. Williams at the Office of "The Uncle Sam," 18-52.

CRITICAL SYNOPSIS: The scenes "written with a free hand" take place at Astor House, the Battery, Trinity churchyard, Hoboken, and other New York City sites. The dark doings of the novel are somewhat imitative of George Lippard's metropolitan Gothic and terrifying pictures of the underworld in such books as The Quaker City; or, The Monks of Monk Hall (see 288). The mock count is the foreign renegade, Le Chandau, intriguer, poisoner, master crimi-

nal, and pursuer of the beautiful heiress, Carolina Raymond, who
seems to be the victim of one of the count's poison plots. In his
various schemes, the count is assisted by the dissipated young New
Yorker, Conrad Daring, who administers the poison to Carolina as
an agent of the count's revenge upon her for favoring the good
Doctor, Elbert Richland. The primary Gothic episodes take place in
the fetid den of Mrs. Selgins's groggery, a front for a body-
snatching operation. In a back room, stolen corpses are boiled
down and the skeletons sold to physicians and medical students.
This grisly work is performed by the deformed black servant, Bubo,
who is delighted when he learns that the beautiful body of Carolina is to be delivered for processing. The rescue of the still-
living Carolina from the iron tomb in Trinity churchyard and the
grisly justice meted out to the mock count climax the narrative.
Like Juliet, Carolina had reposed in a deathlike sleep in the
vault of her ancestors. She is revived by Doctor Richland's medical skill and her place of live burial taken by the mock count Le
Chandau who is entombed, assailed by rats and cadaverous damps,
and slowly expires. Frightened into a renunciation of his evil
city life by "the seducer's doom," Conrad Daring becomes an hon-
est, hardworking Yankee serving on a Hudson riverboat between New
York and Troy. The metropolitan Gothic mixes elements of horror
with the emergent features of the American success parable. The
evil represented by foreigners and blacks eventually loses out to
natural American virtue, persistence, and hard work.

060. Bradbury, Osgood. The Haunted Castle; or, The Abducted Niece. New
York: Robert M. De Witt, 1857.

RESEARCH SOURCE: Railo, Eino, The Haunted Castle: A Study of the
Elements of English Romanticism, New York, Humanities Press, 19-
64.

CRITICAL SYNOPSIS: Several horror titles by this author suggest
the persistence of plagiarized Gothic imitations into the mid-
century. In the same year as the 100 page double-columned chapbook, The Haunted Castle, we find a companion Gothic by the same
author, Female Depravity; or, The Hour of Death. The Haunted Castle and this short Gothic are essentially the same shocker written
twice, one as a villain-centered saga of suffering and supernatural menace and the other as the same story told in maiden-centered
form. The menaced maiden, who never seems to be able to find her
way out the haunted castle although she is able to enter with relative ease, is lifted without change from the romances of Mrs.
Radcliffe. The villainess is also transferred without much alteration from the Matilda character of Lewis's The Monk (1796) and
given all of the voluptuous malice of perhaps the most exalted
Gothic example of female depravity in the English tradition, William Henry Ireland's The Abbess (1799). Like their English counterparts, these small Gothics, once cheaply manufactured and sold
for pennies, are now considered prime rarities.

061. Bradbury, Ray. Something Wicked This Way Comes. New York: Simon and
Schuster, 1972.

REPRINT EDITION: New York, Bantam Books, 1983.
RESEARCH SOURCES: Burt, Donald C., "Poe, Bradbury, and the Science
Fiction Tale of Terror," Mankato State College Studies 3 (1968):
76-84; Johnson, Wayne L., Ray Bradbury, New York, Frederick Ungar,
1980; Mogen, David, Ray Bradbury, Boston, Twayne, 1986; Pierce,

Hazel, "Ray Bradbury and the Gothic Tradition," Ray Bradbury, eds. Joseph D. Olander, Martin H. Greenburg, New York, Taplinger, 1980, pp.165-185.

CRITICAL SYNOPSIS: The Green Town of the novel is Bradbury's Gothified version of Our Town, the opposite of Wilder's pastoral and elegiac microcosm of American life. The encroachment of something wicked is the work of a demonic carnival operated by two entrepeneurs of deception and chaos, the carnival owners, G.M. Dark and C.G. Cooger. These itinerant charlatans are played off against their Green Town counterparts, the two thirteen year old boys, William Holloway and James Nightshade. Arriving in Green Town several days before Halloween, the supernatural carnival offers a special attraction for the boys, a carousel which functions as a time change machine. A ride in one direction brings ageing. A ride in another direction on the wheel of time propels the rider backward into childhood. Both proprietors seem to have ridden their time wheel many times since both Dark and Cooger also have youthful identities as the boys, Robert and Jed. The figure most aware of the wickedness of manipulated time that has come the town's way is Charles Holloway, father of Jim whose resistance to the time temptations of the carousel and whose reliance on the power of laughter to counter evil enables him to survive a deadly threat by the carnival's Dust Witch and to prevent the boys from running off and joining the wicked road show. An entertaining fantasy, the novel can also be viewed as a piece of Gothic allegory, for it is darkly didactic in some special senses. There is no refuge from the evil within ourselves and we are constantly visited by Pandaemonium in alluring forms. Face the fear, know it by riding its wheel of fortune, then send the carnival on its way until it returns the following year.

062. Brennan, Joseph Payne. "Canavan's Back Yard." Nine Horrors and a Dream. Sauk City, WI: Arkham House, 1958.

CRITICAL SYNOPSIS: Meditative and eerie rather than directly horrifying, the story is a good index to the muted horror art of Brennan. The narrator, a bookseller, stares compulsively into the back yard adjoining his premises. Someone or something seems to beckon. The area itself is a wicked zone with a reputation for metamorphosing those who stray into it. A witch had cursed the ground three hundred years before. But these perilous circumstances only intensify the attraction for the bookseller who eventual yields to the lure of the evil place, and with awful consequences. Another tale among the nine horrors in Brennan's collection, "Levitation," also deserves mention. It is contrived, but effective, and brings off its climax with some macabre wit. A mesmerist chooses a young male subject from an audience, places him in a deep trance, levitates him, and promptly perishes of cardiac arrest in mid-performance. With no one able to abort the levitational trance, the young man simply drifts off into the air apparently never to come down again. This gruesome bit of comedy recalls one of Poe's tales where the horror of hypnotism is featured, "The Facts in the Case of M. Valdemar" (see 388).

063. Brown, Charles Brockden. Wieland; or, The Transformation. New York: H. Caritat, 1798.

REPRINT EDITIONS: ed. Fred Lewis Pattee, New York, Hafner Publishing, 1960; eds. Sidney J. Krause, S.W. Reid, Alexander Cowie,

Kent, OH, Kent State UP, 1977.
RESEARCH SOURCES: Fiedler, Leslie A., "Charles Brockden Brown and the Invention of the American Gothic," Love and Death in the American Novel, pp.106-148; Frank, Frederick S., "Wieland," Survey of Modern Fantasy Literature, pp.2126-2131; Gilmore, Michael T., "Calvinism and Gothicism: The Example of Brown's Wieland," Studies in the Novel 9 (1977): 107-118; Nye, Russel B., "The Early Novel: Charles Brockden Brown's American Gothic," American Literary History: 1607-1830, New York, Alfred A. Knopf, 1970, pp.241-244; Shelden, Pamela J., "The Shock of Ambiguity: Brockden Brown's Wieland and the Gothic Tradition," De Kalb Literary Arts Journal (Clarkston, GA) 10 number 4 (1977): 17-26.

CRITICAL SYNOPSIS: Brown adapted the Radcliffean version of the English Gothic Romance to the American environment and character, and in so doing, launched an American school of Gothicism. Wieland is a dark and violent fable of moral horror and mental terror whose Gothic content is a means of questioning the optimistic assumptions of the newly founded republic. The history of the Wieland family is recited in retrospect and with great intensity by Clara Wieland whose strength of character and pessimistic view of enlightenment ideals distinguish her from the swooning maidens of Radcliffean narrative. The family malady or moral curse hanging over the Wielands takes the odd form of a religious psychosis or theomania. Early in the novel the patriarch of the Wielands perishes spectacularly by means of spontaneous combustion while attempting to commune directly with the Almighty in a private temple on the banks of the Schuylkill River. This first Gothic death initiates a series of weird and bloody events as the House of Wieland sinks into chaos and madness. The son of the house, Clara's brother Theodore, deludedly believes that the voice of God has commanded him to take the lives of his wife and children. The strange death of her father, her brother's violent dementia, and her own heritage of insanity as a Wieland drive Clara toward a terminal horror of self, the fundamental American Gothic condition. As she peers into the dark mirror of her memory, she expresses what will become the dark center of the American Gothic experience: "Now was I stupefied in tenfold wonder in contemplating myself. Was I not likewise transformed from rational and human into a creature of fearful attributes?" Into this dark and fallen world slinks the enigmatic figure of Carwin (Cain, plus "RW" but no last name), the first and one of the most memorable of American Gothic villains. Carwin is a ventriloquist or biloquist as well as a demonic practical joker on a diabolic scale who engages in acts of power purely for amoral pleasure. "'My only crime,'" he tells Clara, "'was curiosity.'" The main Gothic crisis occurs when Clara is about to be slaughtered by her brother when Carwin intercedes from a distance with his ventriloquial power imitating God's voice and ordering the lunatic to "hold!" After Theodore's suicide, the wrecker of order moves onward into the unplumbed Pennsylvania wilderness in quest of new victims. Clara is left to sort out her anguished memories and to reckon with her own tendencies to madness and violence, a first lonely survivor of the American paradise lost. As may be seen, Brown's American Gothic prototype fixed a sophisticated model for later American Gothicists by addressing the cultural fallacy that a freedom from Europe guaranteed radical innocence. Thus, Wieland stands forth as a first effort to articulate the shallowness of a transcendental outlook which excluded evil from the content of the American Oversoul. The dark and tragic world of Wieland foreshadows all of the conditions of later

American Gothics. Neither a rationalist's Eden nor an idealist's paradise, it is fallen world replete with death, darkness, aliena- tion, guilt, mental and moral displacement, and the gloom of fami- ly decay and decline.

064. _____. Arthur Mervyn; or, The Memoirs of the Year 1793. Philadel- phia: H. Maxwell, 1799.

REPRINT EDITION: ed. Warner Berthoff, New York, Holt, Rinehart & Winston, 1962.
RESEARCH SOURCES: Frank, Frederick S., "Perverse Pilgrimage: The Role of the Gothic in the Works of Charles Brockden Brown, Edgar Allan Poe, and Nathaniel Hawthorne," Dissertation Abstracts 29 (1968): 1866A-1867A (Rutgers University); Bernard, Kenneth, "Ar- thur Mervyn: The Ordeal of Innocence," Texas Studies in Language and Literature 6 (1965): 441-459; Hume, Robert D., "Charles Brock- den Brown and the Uses of Gothicism: A Reassessment," ESQ: A Jour- nal of the American Renaissance 18 (1972): 10-18.

CRITICAL SYNOPSIS: In Brown's second novel, the urban Gothic be- gins to assume some of its later features. Instead of a haunted castle, Brown offers a more contemporary site of terror, the city of Philadelphia during an epidemic of yellow fever. The public burial teams, the stench of death, the disintegration of civic or- der and safety, and an atmosphere of dreadful night give the novel some unique Gothic dimensions. The plot is also more complicated on the surface than that of Wieland (see 063) since the titular character is something of a Yankee bumpkin and picaro who is ex- posed to a rapid and startling series of adventures as he travels through the metropolis enroute to the dark grail of adulthood. But Arthur Mervyn's encounter with the dark world is similar to that of Clara Wieland in that he is called upon to confront and to con- trol the Gothic aspects of his unknown self, i.e., substitute for vulnerable innocence a guilty self-wisdom. Young Mervyn, the some- what unreliable author of these memoirs of the plague year, is a genuine American type. An optimistic and rustic simpleton who be- lieves unquestioningly in the goodness of human nature and the greatness of America, he will undergo a stern moral education dur- ing his sojourn in the city. Driven from his father's household in the country, he comes to Philadelphia, and takes employment with a fascinating master criminal, Welbeck, a commercialized portrait of the Gothic villain who lives in society only in order to live off it. Welbeck's evil talents and his pernicious schemes for control- ling the lives of others infatuate and repel Mervyn who becomes a kind of unconscious pupil to this corrupt father figure. Arthur Mervyn's involvement with Welbeck also entangles him in a series of Gothic incidents. There is a secret chamber in Welbeck's house where the inquisitive Arthur stumbles upon "the body of a man, bleeding, ghastly, and still exhibiting the marks of convulsion and agony." Shortly thereafter, he is forced to participate in the interment of Watson in "darksome and murky recesses." He is bedev- iled by the unbearable nightmare of the pit and his own premature burial, and while he dreams, his unconscious body is placed in a coffin by one of the public burial teams collecting plague vic- tims. These Gothic experiences and others within the haunted soci- ety of the city give the novel an unmistakable fabric of local horror and foreshadow an American Gothic mode. And in Arthur Mer- vyn's contraction of the yellow fever virus, Brown is able to sym- bolize with some success the fact that no American is immune to the timeless diseases of the soul and spirit as active in the new

world as in the old. The metaphor of the haunted city and its destruction of innocent vision of self would attract the attention
of Hawthorne who was certainly thinking of Brown's Gothic novel in
the character and adventures of young Robin in the much-admired
story, "My Kinsman, Major Molineux" (see 202).

065. _____. Ormond; or, The Secret Witness. New York: H. Caritat, 17-
99.

REPRINT EDITIONS: ed. Ernest Marchand, New York, Hafner, 1962;
eds. Sidney J. Krause, S.W. Reid, Kent, OH, Kent State UP, 1981.
RESEARCH SOURCES: Christophersen, Bill, "Charles Brockden Brown's
Ormond: The Secret Witness as Ironic Motif," Modern Language Studies 10 number 2 (1980): 37-41; Ringe, Donald A., American Gothic,
pp.39-40; Warfel, Harry R., Charles Brockden Brown: American Gothic Novelist, Gainesville, FL, Florida UP, 1949, pp.125-140.

CRITICAL SYNOPSIS: Ormond is Brown's second novel in which the
city under plague is introduced as a substitute for the haunted
castle under supernatural duress. The female narrator, Sophia
Westwynd Courtland, who has come into contact with the villain,
gives the novel certain parallels with Wieland (see 063). Ringe
comments on Brown's use of the plague-ridden city as horror symbol: "A feeling of intense fear pervades these scenes in Ormond.
The characters face the horror of the plague with enervating terror and perceive the gruesome effects of sickness and death. The
stench of the disease fills the atmosphere, and the horror of
physical dissolution is constantly held before the eyes of the on-
looker." Against this background of pestilence and the universal
threat of infection moves the strange and blighted figure of Ormond, a sort of personification of the plague itself. He is clever, resourceful, verbally artful, unscrupulous, and maintains powerful connections with the Illuminati and other European secret
societies. The victim of Ormond's charades and schemes is the worthy and beautiful Constantia Dudley, whose blind and bankrupt
father, Stephen Dudley, is brutally murdered by Ormond's repulsive
accomplice, Craig. The climactic chapters of the novel are heavily
Gothic in pace, tone, and setting as Ormond decides to break Constantia's will by holding her prisoner in "a solitary and darksome
abode" and terrifying her with such spectacles as the corpse of
the murdered Craig. She is also repeatedly threatened with necrophiliac rape unless she submits to his advances while she still is
alive. Brown's rhetoric of emergency derives directly from the
English Gothic fiction of the period with the descriptions of impending sexual crisis modeled upon Mrs. Radcliffe's scenarios:
"The mansion was desolate and lonely. It was night. She was immersed in darkness. She had not the means, and was unaccustomed to
the office of repelling personal injuries. What injuries she had
reason to dread, who was the agent and what were his motives, were
subjects of vague and incoherent meditation." In English Gothic
fiction, the persecuted maiden typically remains passive victim
and helpless sufferer awaiting her deliverance from the terrible
house but never effecting it herself. The American maiden in distress, however, declares her independence, turns upon her tormentor, and in a gesture of freedom for all harassed Gothic virgins,
stabs Ormond to death (the wound, incidentally, refuses to bleed).
Thus, the perverted theories of power as embodied in the European
villain are countered by a spirited American heroine who refuses
to submit to them. The old Gothic theme of the endangered maiden
is reconstructed to express the superiority of American democratic

values over European aristocratic attitudes.

066.   . Edgar Huntly; or, The Memoirs of a Sleep-Walker. Philadelphia: H. Maxwell, 1799.

REPRINT EDITION: ed. David Stineback, New Haven, CT, College &
University Press Services, 1973.
RESEARCH SOURCES: Bernard, Kenneth, "Edgar Huntly: Charles Brockden Brown's Unsolved Murder," Library Chronicle 33 (1967): 30-53;
Berthold, Dennis, "Desacralizing the American Gothic: An Iconogra-
phic Approach to Edgar Huntly," Studies in American Fiction 14
(1986): 127-138; Kimball, Arthur G., "Savages and Savagism: Brockden Brown's Dramatic Irony," Studies in Romanticism 6 (1967): 214-
225; Krause, Sidney J., "Edgar Huntly and the American Nightmare,"
Studies in the Novel 13 (1981): 294-302; Schulz, Dieter, "Edgar
Huntly as Quest Romance," American Literature 43 (1971): 323-335;
Toles, George, "Charting the Hidden Landscape: Edgar Huntly," Early American Literature 16 (1981): 133-153.

CRITICAL SYNOPSIS: Haunted castle is transformed into haunted forest complete with a hideous pit and spectral Indians in this outstanding early example of naturalized American Gothic fiction. The
tortured and winding narrative is cast in the form of letters from
Edgar Huntly to Mary Waldegrave, with the sanity and reliability
of both the narrator and the strange and violent characters of his
dream life held in constant abeyance. If the ideal structure of
the novel of terror is vortical, then Brown certainly attained
such a structure in the convolutions of this nocturnal novel. Much
of the novel's midnight action probes the irrational world of
sleep. Throughout the story, Brown is able to convey an image of
American life as uncontrollable and unintelligible nightmare in
his dark reply to the claims of American optimism. The opening of
the novel, one of the most effective night scenes in Gothic literature, finds Huntly spying upon the somnambulist, Clithero Edny,
observing him as he digs a pit at the base of a great tree in the
depths of the forest and sobbing as he works. Whose grave is being
prepared in this gruesome night ritual? Gradually and to his
mounting self-horror, Huntly loses rational grip on his own life
and becomes a sleep-walker, and therefore, in a sense assumes the
place of the man in the pit. In Brown's hands, the sinister phenomenon of somnambulism becomes a psychological metaphor for the
dark and unknown recesses of the unconscious mind, the new Gothic
castle within us all. The climax of Huntly's Gothic journey
through himself occurs in the famous episode of the man in the
pit, a horror episode to be found in several English Gothic novels
prior to Brown, and raised to new heights of horror in Poe's "The
Pit and the Pendulum" (see 385). Without warning, Huntly awakens
in a cold, dark abyss, a vast and irregular underground compartment whose exact shape and depth he cannot determine. He is assailed by pain, delirium, hunger, the growls of a beast, and the
silhouettes of marauding savages. He has no recollection of how he
came to be stranded in the cave although the suggestion that he
too has become a guilty sleep-walker is one explanation. With this
realization that there is a nightside to every human intelligence,
Brockden Brown fixes the novel's theme of the fragility and vulnerability of the rational self. In Huntly's pit experience we may
note the origin of the the deeper strains of American Gothicism
summed up by Donald A. Ringe: "The dark world of Gothic terror
would seem therefore to be more real than the bright and ordered
world of the rationalists....The external world of Gothic terror

in Edgar Huntly is no chimera that can be easily dismissed by the influx of light, either physical or mental. It is, rather, an accurate indication of the reality that lies within the tortured minds of the protagonists, a reality that is not to be changed by any simple means."

067.   Bryant, William Cullen. "The Legend of the Devil's Pulpit." The Talisman for MDCCCXXVIII, New York, 1827.

REPRINT EDITION: William Cullen Bryant, Representative Selections, ed. Tremaine Mc Dowell, Cincinnati, American Book, 1935.

CRITICAL SYNOPSIS: In the comic Gothic vein of Washington Irving, the tale has none of the morbid grandeur of Bryant's famous graveyard poem, "Thanatopsis." The voice here is that of the wry folklorist who teases the reader with playful terrors while allowing him to feel superior to the credulous characters. The Satanic congregation at worship is what the main character, the Knickerbocker tailor, William Vince, is convinced he has seen during a nocturnal visit to New Jersey. Blacks who are mistaken for ghosts, a foolish rational skeptic, Dr. Magraw, and a satiric sermon by the devil suggest the risible tone. But Bryant was also capable of working in the serious Gothic vein as indicated by his straight tales of terror in The Talisman.

068.   _____. "The Indian Spring," The Talisman. New York, 1830.

REPRINT EDITION: William Cullen Bryant: Representative Selections, ed. Tremaine Mc Dowell, Cincinnati, American Book, 1935.

CRITICAL SYNOPSIS: What are the consequences when a rationalist runs squarely up against an irrational experience which he can neither explain nor expel from memory? Perhaps he undergoes a conversion to the Gothic view of life as something irreducibly mysterious and beyond all natural cause. The narrator of this piece "finds it the easier belief to ascribe it to a cause above nature." The narrator is a young hunter who falls asleep near a spring by a glade in the deep woods while hunting along the west bank of the Susquehanna River. It is the time after the Revolution and the whites have come to rule the wilderness after the removal of the Indians. The narrator meditates "upon the ancient inhabitants of these woods" and awakens to find himself staring into the glaring eyes of a spectral brave, "an Indian, a real Indian, the very incarnation of the images that had been floating in my fancy." Ghostly encounter turns into a kind of historical parable when the redskin spectre pursues the young white man through the forest causing him to abandon first his shoes, then his hat, and finally his musket. Thus, the savage drives the civilizer from his virgin territory. Just as the Gothic villain sometimes overtakes the maiden in the depths of the haunted castle, so the ghostly Indian overtakes the young hunter, driving him to ask himself the guilty question about the whiteman's rape of the wilderness and the displacement of its natural people: "I turned my head, and there again stood the Indian with that eternal, intolerable glare of the eyes....Was this figure some restless shadow, that could haunt only its ancient wilderness, and was excluded from every spot reclaimed and cultivated by the whiteman?" It is never made clear whether the young hunter has hallucinated the figure in a dream of guilt or whether indeed he had actually encountered the wronged spirit of the first Americans when had paused to rest at the Indian spring. This tale is a good example of how the American imagination frequently remade the Gothic to focus on cultural guilts and anxieties.

069. _____. "The Skeleton's Cave" in Tales of the Glauber Spa. New York: Harper, 1832.

REPRINT EDITION: New York, Irvington Publishers, 1972.
RESEARCH SOURCE: Griffith, Clark, "Caves and Cave Dwellers: The Study of a Romantic Image," Journal of English and Germanic Philology 62 (1963): 551-568.

CRITICAL SYNOPSIS: There are touches of the cave predicament of Brown's Edgar Huntly (see 066) in Bryant's ingeniously conceived "The Skeleton's Cave." A vigorous subspecies of the tale of terror, grotto or cavern Gothic, wherein a subterranean excursion climaxes in an encounter with an animated skeleton is a second possible source. On the western frontier in the early 1800's, a party of explorers consisting of Father Ambrose, the rugged French man, Le Maire, and the delicate Miss Emily find themselves entombed when a fierce storm causes a landslide that seals the cavern's mouth where they have taken shelter. But just as an unfortunate stroke of nature brings about their entrapment, so an equally accidental act of nature will liberate them from the skeleton's cave where, according to local legend, Indians had once sought shelter in similar circumstances and perished horribly. To work properly in evoking terror, every Gothic tale needs some version of the isolated enclosure. In the American mode of the Gothic, such enclosures were often natural rather than architectural and to be found in the depths of the wilderness rather than the depths of the castle or abbey. And the incarceration of characters within these caves and forests often led to a dark enlightenment.

070. Bunkley, Josephine M. The Escaped Nun; or, Disclosures of Convent Life. New York: De Witt & Davenport, 1855.

RESEARCH SOURCES: Rogers, Katherine M., "Fantasy and Reality in the Fictional Convents of the Eighteenth Century," Comparative Literature Studies 22 (1985): 297-316; Werner, Stephen, "Diderot, Sade, and the Gothic Novel," Studies on Voltaire and the Eighteenth Century 114 (1973): 273-290.

CRITICAL SYNOPSIS: In the anti-Catholic vein of the early English Gothic, the novel is a lurid and sensational exposé of the secrecy, severity, and condoned sadism of the convent. The narrative of the abused nun had longstanding ties with the early Gothic novel by way of Denis Diderot's La Réligieuse (1796) and enjoyed a widespread vogue in the American Gothic. The narrative's full title gives some idea of Bunkley's purposes and readership: The Escaped Nun; or, Disclosures of Convent Life, and The Confessions of a Sister of Charity, Giving a More Minute Detail of their Inner Life, and a Bolder Revelation of the Mysteries and Secrets of Nunneries Than Have Ever Before Been Submitted to the American Public. Respectfully Dedicated to the Protestants of America. Bunkley's fugitive nun is not reticent about her duty to "warn parents and guardians against the wiles and cunning ways of Jesuits." The chapter titles of her narrative read like a roster of Gothic occurrences. "The Art of Hypocrisy," "Forced Ceremony," "Misere," "Maceration" [coercive wasting away], "Hair Cloths and Scourges," "Inveigling Girls into Convents," "My Life Threatened," "The Cave of the Sea Wolf," "The Mad Nun," "Refined Cruelty," "The Scourge Applied," "The Wanderer in the Corridors," "A Vision of the Devil and the Virgin Mary," "The Subterranean Passage," and "Midnight Adventures in the Convent" are terrifying topics worthy of Monk Lewis. Like Agnes in The Monk and a thousand other monastic victims, the escaped nun's most harrowing experiences take place in the subterranean depths. In "The Subterranean Cell" she vividly recalls her incarceration and punishment. "When I had reached the bottom of the stairs my feet were bloody, my limbs were bruised, my situation would have softened hearts of flint. With large keys, the Superior opened the door of a gloomy subterranean cell, where they threw me upon a mat half rotted by the damp of previous bodies." Thus did the American Gothic accommodate and exploit the tradition of Catholic monstrosity and atrocity inherited in part from English Gothic fiction. Credibility is a vital consideration for the escaped nun, who habitually reminds the reader that she has not simply imagined these horrors. "I have seen Americans who might deny all this," she constantly demurs. "I sometimes wish they could be but half an hour in one of those awful places which I have known!"

071. Burgess, Gelett. The White Cat. Indianapolis, MN: Bobbs-Merrill, 19-07.

CRITICAL SYNOPSIS: The inventor of "Goops" and "Purple Cows" made at least one foray into Gothic territory in the amusing novel of dual personality and hypnotic possession, The White Cat. But Burgess's irrepressible sense of nonsense continually undermines the somber mood required of thrilling or dark fiction. The situation of a young girl possessed and manipulated by a sinister hypnotist seems borrowed from George Du Maurier's Trilby (1894) except that Burgess's heroine survives the leechings of her Svengali to be rescued by that most American of palladins, a handsome young architect who specializes in middle class homes.

072. Burks, Arthur J. "Vale of the Corbies." Black Medicine. Sauk City, WI: Arkham House, 1966.

CRITICAL SYNOPSIS: Probably should be called ornithological Gothic and first published in Weird Tales, 1925. This grim little shocker seems based on the old English ballad, "The Twa Corbies" or three ravens who pick clean the bones of a fallen knight and discuss their cadaverous feast in the ballad's dialogue. In Burks's story the narrator repeatedly visits an eerie valley where the ravens who seem to possess it become increasingly more aggressive. Finally, the body of the narrator, or what is left of it, is found after the ravens have finished their grisly feast. The horror climax echoes the gruesome imagery of the old ballad: "Ye'll sit on his white hause-bane,/And I'll pike out his bonny blue een./Wi' ae lock o' his gowden hair/We'll theek our nest when it grows bare."

073. Burnett, Mrs. Frances Hodgson. In the Closed Room. New York: Mc Clure, 1904.

RESEARCH SOURCE: Shelden, Pamela J., "American Gothicism: The Evolution of a Mode," Dissertation Abstracts International 35 (1974): 1634A-1635A (Kent State University).

CRITICAL SYNOPSIS: The inhabitant of the closed room is a ghost-

ly child. Spectral children such as the little girl found here or
Miles and Flora in James's The Turn of the Screw (see 245) are not
special to American Gothic works, but their appearance does confirm Pamela Shelden's argument that there is "no clean split between English and American Gothicism, only continuum and refine-
ment of that which the early Gothicists had sensed and explored
intuitively."

074. Butler, Ellis Parker. "Dey Ain't No Ghosts." The Best Ghost Stories.
New York: Boni and Liverright, 1919.

REPRINT EDITION: Humorous Ghosts, ed. Dorothy Scarborough, New
York, Putnam, 1921.

CRITICAL SYNOPSIS: Told in black dialect, the story is about Little Mose whose nocturnal visit to the pumpkin patch ends in a rendezvous with some spectres. But not wishing to terrify the boy (or
the reader), the ghosts inform him very solicitously that "Dey
ain't no ghosts."

075. Cable, George Washington. "La Belle Dame Plantations." Scribner's
Monthly Magazine, April, 1874.

REPRINT EDITION: Literature of the United States, eds. Walter
Blair, Theodore Hornberger, James E. Miller Jr., Chicago, Scott,
Foresman, 1966.
RESEARCH SOURCE: Hill, Cason Louis, "A Bibliographical Study of
George Washington Cable and a Check List of Criticism, 1870-1970,"
Dissertation Abstracts International 38 (1978): 4816A (University
of Georgia).

CRITICAL SYNOPSIS: Reprinted in the collection, Old Creole Days
(1879), the story has some elements that are analogous with the
destruction of Poe's House of Usher (see 379) as well as some
foreshadowing of twentieth century Mississippi Gothic. The patriarch of the venerable plantation of the beautiful damsels, old
Colonel Jean Albert Henri Joseph De Charleu-Marot, engages in a
struggle for ownership of territory with his Choctaw relative, In-
jin Charlie. His grand mansion on the banks of the river stands,
like Roderick Usher's sinking house, for family decay, decline,
and imminent madness. Although the tale lacks the overt and sustained moods of terror to be found in Poe's tale, Cable's story
has its Gothic moments, especially when the Colonel collapses in
front of old Charlie, a fall which is simultaneously reflected in
the crumbling of the plantation house into the Mississippi: "Old
Charlie stood tranfixed with horror. Belles Demoiselles, the realm
of maiden beauty, the home of merriment, the house of dancing, all
in the tremor and glow of pleasure, suddenly sunk, with one short,
wild wail of terror--sunk, sunk, down, down, down, into the merciless, unfathomable flood of the Mississippi." Other great houses
that have been built on a lie in Southern Gothic will follow the
fate of the Colonel's plantation.

076. _____. "Jean Ah-Poquelin." Old Creole Days. New York: Scribner's, 1879.

REPRINT EDITION: Old Creole Days, foreword Shirley Ann Grau, New
York, New American Library-Signet, 1961.
RESEARCH SOURCES: Christophersen, Bill, "'Jean Ah-Poquelin': Ca-
ble's Place in Southern Gothic," South Dakota Review 20 (1982):

55-66; Stone, Edward, "Usher, Poquelin, and Miss Emily: The Progress of Southern Gothic," <u>Georgia Review</u> 14 (1960): 433-443.

CRITICAL SYNOPSIS: Cable's tale is a superb example of "Delta Gothic," a story which forms a Gothic trio in American literature consisting of Poe's "The Fall of the House of Usher" (see 379) and Faulkner's "A Rose for Emily" (see 131). Cable seems aware of Poe's Gothicism, just as Faulkner seems aware of Cable's Gothicism. Central to all three tales is a haunted mansion containing hidden relatives and presided over by a strange, hermit-like being who has severed all ties with the outside world. In Cable and Faulkner, the Gothic environment speaks directly to the clash of cultures and collision of past and present. The decaying, interior world of the old Creole, Jean Poquelin, is threatened from without by the progressive aims of the community. Jean's house is a Gothic fortress precariously stationed in the midst of a swamp where it blocks the path of the roadbuilders and modern improvers. The description of the decaying dwelling indicates that Cable was thinking directly of Poe's sinister mansion: "The house was of heavy cypress, lifted up on pillars, grim, solid, and spiritless, its massive build a strong reminder of days still earlier. Its dark, weatherbeaten roof and sides were hoisted up above the jungly plain in a distracted way, like a gigantic ammunition wagon stuck in the mud and abandoned by some retreating army." Fearful rumors circulate about the haunted house and its proprietor and his long-missing brother, Jacques Poquelin, who will make a cadaverous entry at the climax of the tale. Insular, mysterious, defiant, and ultimately doomed along with his house, Jean Poquelin is a Creole version of the Gothic's half-evil man ruling over a dying world. "His eye, large and black, was bold and open like that of a war horse, and his jaws shut together with the firmness of iron." When the governor's secretary, Little White, visits the house with a proposal for putting through the new road, he is met by a foul odor of decay and a transient glimpse of a white, ghostly figure, possibly the missing brother. The modern world decides that it must have both its road and an answer to the mysteries of the house and a noisy raid called a "charivari" is planned to flush old Jean out of his lair. But Little White greets the crowd with the bleak words "He's dead." Then, by lantern light, the mob is shown an impromptu funeral and given an answer to the mystery of the missing brother. At the climax, a superb Gothic scene, a little cart bearing a coffin and attended by Poquelin's African mute passes through the gates, and "there behind the bier, with eyes cast down and labored step, walked the living remains--all that was left--of little Jacques Poquelin, the long-hidden brother--a leper, as white as snow. Dumb with horror the cringing crowd gazed upon the walking death." This explained Gothic climax vies in power with the cadaverous resurrection of Madeline Usher or the loathsome necrophilia of Miss Emily's secret love in Faulkner's "A Rose for Emily" (see 131). Cable's place as a Gothic writer seems assured by the superbly crafted horror of this tale.

077. Cannon, Charles. <u>Father Felix, A Tale</u>. New York: Edward Dunigan, 18-45.

RESEARCH SOURCE: Tarr, Sister Mary Muriel, <u>Catholicism in Gothic Fiction: A Study of the Nature and Function of Gothic Materials in Gothic Fiction in England (1762-1820)</u>, Washington, DC, Catholic UP, 1946; Ann Arbor, MI, UMI Press, 1980.

CRITICAL SYNOPSIS: From its beginnings, Gothic fiction had been virulently anti-Catholic. The monastery was a place of sexual crime and supernatural danger; the monk or abbot was portrayed as a lecherous fiend exploiting the elaborate rituals of Catholicism to terrify and mystify his victims. The sentimental and philosophical Gothic, Father Felix, inverts these anti-Catholic sentiments to present a good priest in conflict with Protestant bigots and fanatics. The moral lesson that "bigotry is not confined to any sect or creed" is reiterated by this benign cleric whose efforts to save Julia Baldwin from the frenzied delusions of Millerism, a radical sect of the 1840's which advocated Christ's second coming, and the bigoted attitudes of the Dutch Reformers toward the Catholic faith, finally fail. Much of the novel is a pro-Catholic polemic with the various characters representing various religious positions. From her Hudson Valley homestead, Julia is beset by the Reverend Mr. Cleaver who warns her against the "poison of Popery." She is also tempted by the atheism of the intellectual widow, Mrs. Dowd, who inveighs against "the idolatrous worship paid by Catholics to this symbol of man's redemption." Despite Father Felix's efforts, Julia Baldwin eventually dies apparently as a result of a Millerite frenzy. Other features of the Gothic tradition which survive in this novel are an inset tale, "The Soldier of Mary," modeled after Eugène Sue's Wandering Jew, and spooky Hudson River landscapes done seemingly in imitation of Mrs. Radcliffe's sublimely gloomy scenery.

078. Capote, Truman. Other Voices, Other Rooms. New York: Random House, 1948.

REPRINT EDITION: New York, Random House, 1968.
RESEARCH SOURCES: Blake, Nancy, "Other Voices, Other Rooms: Southern Gothic or Medieval Quest?" Delta: Revue Centre d'Etudes et les Recherches sur les Ecrivains du Sud Etats-Unis 11 (1980): 31-47; Malin, Irving, New American Gothic, pp.50-52; Reed, Kenneth T., Truman Capote, Boston, Twayne, 1981.

CRITICAL SYNOPSIS: In both spirit and letter, this novel is pervasively Gothic. "Other Voices, Other Rooms," says Kenneth T. Reed, "is less a novel than it is a Gothic romance: brooding, sinister, mysterious, inward-reaching, lyrical and shadowy. The only sense of reality in it is psychological realism." The search for the father which terminates in horror and confrontation with the self which ends in terror are conjoined in the homecoming journey of the thirteen year old protagonist, Joel Harrison Knox, whose return to Skully's Landing is a visit to a type of underworld and hell. Joel has been summoned home for a reunion with the father he has never known (Ed Sansom) after his mother's death. He is driven to Skully's Landing by the sinister negro, Jesus Fever, where he undergoes a series of Gothic experiences much like other sons in search of kinsmen in the Gothic underworld. Hawthorne's "My Kinsman, Major Molineux" (see 202) is an early example of the pattern. Made to sleep in the bed where his mother died and where his bizarre cousin, Randolph, had shown symptoms of madness, he awakens to see Miss Amy (his father's new wife) in the act of killing a bluejay. Two central horrific events dominate the narrative. From an upper window in the house, Joel beholds a queer old lady gazing down upon him with a peculiarly sexual expression. And when the encounter with the missing father finally comes, he is horrified to find an invalid so badly paralyzed and comatose that his attention can only be gained by bouncing a tennisball at his bedside. A pair of girl twins, Idabel and Florabel, Jesus Fever's wild niece, Missouri (Zoo), the proprietor of a wicked carnival, Miss Wisteria, and a black hermit living in a ruined hotel, Little Sunshine, all act as grotesque guides in Joel's journey to selfhood and adulthood. One traditional Gothic technique involves the sequence of shock or shudder, long delay, mounting mystery, and belated natural explanation for seemingly inexplicable events. Capote's variation on the young man's Gothic quest adheres to such a formula which originates with Mrs. Radcliffe. The sexy hag peering out of the upper window was actually Cousin Randolph in one of his transvestite masquerades. The paralyzed father came to be so when Randolph shot him in the back, possibly out of homosexual jealousy. The other mysteries of Skully's Landing such as the hanged mule found dangling over the hotel bannister and the seduction of Joel by Miss Wisteria while they ride the Ferris wheel are eventually clarified as "natural" happenings in the psychologically aberrant world of the boy's lost kinsman. But the Radcliffean resolution in no way detracts from the perverted energies of this paradigm of American Gothicism.

079. _____. "The Headless Hawk." The Tree of Night and Other Stories. New York: Random House, 1949.

REPRINT EDITION: Selected Writings of Truman Capote, New York, Random House, 1963.
RESEARCH SOURCES: Johnson, Thomas Slayton, "The Horror in the Mansion: Gothic Fiction in the Works of Truman Capote and Carson Mc Cullers," Dissertation Abstracts International 34 (1973): 2630A (University of Texas at Austin); Malin, Irving, New American Gothic, pp.82-83.

CRITICAL SYNOPSIS: One of the most popular pieces of horror machinery for the Gothic writers as far back as Horace Walpole and C.R. Maturin had been the animated portrait or prophetic picture. A modification of the haunted portrait which hides the soul of a character is Wilde's famous Picture of Dorian Gray (1891). Capote's story recalls both the classic Gothic and the decadent novel of Wilde. There are only two characters and each is a mirror image of the other. Both are isolated, rootless, lacking solid identity, and take the form of the headless hawk of the quotation from the Book of Job which furnishes the tale's title. The girl, D.J., has run away from an insane asylum carrying with her a painting which she sells to Vincent Walters, the manager of a picture gallery in Manhattan. The macabre painting is like a chilling illustration taken from one of the Gothic chapbooks or a nightmare scene from one of the surrealist masters. The scene depicts "a headless figure in a monklike robe reclining complacently on top of a tacky vaudeville trunk; in one hand she held a flaming blue candle, in another a miniature gold cage, and her severed head lay bleeding at her feet." One glance at the painting is enough to possess and accuse the "quite headless" Vincent Walters, an almost Jamesian or Prufrockian character who has failed to live. "He was a poet who had never written poetry, a painter who had never painted, a lover who had never loved." No wonder then that the mocking contempt of self shown in the painting should drive him to a form of suicide when he seizes a pair of scissors and attacks the headless figure. Capote's Gothic renders a horribly unforgettable portrait of one of society's selfless creatures who "knows not the light" and never will.

080. _____. "Shut a Final Door." The Tree of Night and Other Stories. New York: Random House, 1949.

REPRINT EDITION: Selected Writings of Truman Capote, New York, Random House, 1963.
RESEARCH SOURCE: Freese, Peter, "Das Motiv des Doppelgängers in Truman Capotes 'Shut a Final Door' and E.A. Poe's 'William Wilson," Litteratur in Wissenschaft und Unterricht (Kiel) 1 (1968): 40-48.

CRITICAL SYNOPSIS: The main character, the failed businessman, Walter Ranney, is one of life's little losers. He is the sort of unselfconscious failure to which Robert Browning might have applied his term, "losel," "a lost soul past hope." For Walter Ranney, "failure was definite, a certainty, and there is always peace in certainties." But the midnight ring of the telephone shatters this comfortable illusion. The Gothic element in the tale is an ingenious modernization of the supernatural voice, a device as old as the Gothic genre itself. Here, the spectral voice takes the form of an unidentified long distance telephone caller who seems to have Ranney's number whether he is hiding out in a sleasy New York City apartment or sharing a room with a club footed woman in Saratoga. When the anonymous caller rings Ranney, the message is always the same: "You know me, Walter. You've known me a long time." Thus, the spectral voice of conscience calling him over the long distance of memory summons Walter to account. In childhood, he had plagiarized a poem and passed it off as his own. In manhood, he had coaxed a homosexual into a taxi, then slammed the door on the startled lover. In courtship, he had belittled and denied his only friend, Rosa Cooper. These crimes of conscience and denials of self are all known to the caller who will not let Walter forget. The tale ends with a tableau of misery and failure as Walter, alone and in the darkened room, pushes his face down into the pillow to drown out the ring of destiny.

081. _____. "A Tree of Night." The Tree of Night and Other Stories. New York: Random House, 1949.

REPRINT EDITION: The Grass Harp, The Tree of Night, and Other Short Stories, New York, New American Library, 1968.

CRITICAL SYNOPSIS: A superb Gothic piece, the story commences on a deserted railroad platform where a young female college student waits alone to board a night train after attending the funeral of an uncle. The icicles hang from the roof of the platform "like vicious teeth." This is the premonitory Gothic image suggesting that the maiden is about to enter the house of death. In this case, the chamber of horrors is the dismal railroad car. It is filled with sleeping passengers in the postures of cadavers, it is dismal, smoky, and reeking of rotten, half-devoured fruit scattered in the aisle. The coffin-car reminds the young woman, Kay, "of terrors that once, long ago, had hovered above her like haunted limbs on a tree of night." Without insisting upon the point, it should be clear that she has entered a rolling stock version of the haunted castle or a house of horrors on wheels. Her encounter with a pair of swindlers, the only riders awake in the car, fixes the Gothic nature of her trip. She is accosted by a man and woman whose travelling act is a deadly fraud since they go from town to town performing mock funerals and living entombments. The man is a mute but his partner glibly talks Kay into a kind of trance in the "malicious moonshine," then filches her purse. This is a spiritual rape of sorts, since the evil couple deprive the maiden of her will power and emotional defenses. In atmosphere and action, this story conforms to all of the expected requirements of that kind of Gothic which allows no return to the entrapped maiden from her awful fate in the depths of the castle. In its portrayal of the defeat of innocence, "The Tree of Night" is among the most chilling tales of terror in the American Gothic canon.

082.   . In Cold Blood. A True Account of a Multiple Murder and its Consequences. New York: Random House, 1966.

REPRINT EDITION: New York, New American Library, 1971.
RESEARCH SOURCE: Perry, J. Douglas Jr., "Gothic as Vortex: The Form of Horror in Capote, Faulkner, and Styron," Modern Fiction Studies 19 (1973): 153-167.

CRITICAL SYNOPSIS: Capote's experimental non-fiction novel conforms to a pattern of Gothic structure described by J. Douglas Perry as "parallel[ing] the most pervasive Gothic image and form: the fear of being drawn down and the image of the whirlpool find[ing] their expression in a structural vortex composed of a series of rings or levels." Capote's heavily documentary style and cold-blooded factual account of the execution of a Kansas family by two young men draws the reader downward and inward into the murder's maelström, factual level by factual level. By using objective and impersonal techniques of reportage, Capote creates a chronicle with its own moods of horror. Central to the horror effect is the motiveless nature of the quadruple murder or thrill killing of Herbert Clutter and his family on November 15, 1959, by Richard Hickock and Perry Smith. The youthful killers were captured in Las Vegas, tried, and hanged on April 14, 1965. Capote's chronicle details these events without moralizing or imposing judgements. The effect of horror is cumulative rather than immediately shocking and follows the Gothic pattern of an inexorable descent into a dark vortex.

083. Carr, John Dickson. It Walks by Night. New York and London: Harper, 1930.

REPRINT EDITION: New York, Zebra, 1986.
RESEARCH SOURCE: Herzel, Roger, "John Dickson Carr," Minor American Novelists, ed. Charles A. Hoyt, Carbondale, IL, Southern Illinois UP, 1971.

CRITICAL SYNOPSIS: When the decapitated body of the handsome French athlete, the Duc de Saligny, is discovered by Inspector Bencolin on the eve of the Duke's marriage to Madame Louise Laurent, the policeman is baffled. Anticipating just such a hideous crime, Bencolin had taken every precaution to guard the gaming room in the Paris club where the Duke was to spend the evening before his wedding. Yet, someone or something, either by natural means or supernatural dexterity had walked by night and breached the chamber to behead the Duke. Implausible enough, this is still the stuff of good mystery and perhaps no less far-fetched than the simian homicides of Poe's "The Murders in the Rue Morgue." Like Poe's detective, Monsieur Dupin, Carr's Gallic sleuth operates by intuition and super-logic. Another horrid homicide follows the decapitation of the Duke, but by examining the subtle clues rather than the obvious trail of gore, the detective prevails at last. As

in Poe's famous Parisian story, we have crime and punishment conducted in a heavy Gothic atmosphere of dark streets, dim chambers,
and mutilated victims.

084.   _____. The Burning Court. London: Hamish Hamilton, 1937.

REPRINT EDITION: New York, International Polygonics, 1985.
RESEARCH SOURCES: Sheridan, Daniel, "Later Victorian Ghost Stories," Gothic: The Review of Supernatural Horror Fiction 2 (1980):
33-39.

CRITICAL SYNOPSIS: A detective novel which turns into a novel of
horror in its final chapter, The Burning Court departs from the
usual formula of the mystery solved, the criminal outwitted and
apprehended, and domestic tranquillity restored. Carr had usually
adhered to this formula which dates back to the castle investigators of Mrs. Radcliffe. In Radcliffean Gothic, all seemingly supernatural enigmas were finally exposed as natural phenomena when
brought under the cold light of reason. Of the four main characters in Carr's novel, two are supernatural personages, demons masquerading as human beings, whose supernaturality is not revealed
until the final chapter (called "Verdict"). The characters are Edward and Marie Stevens, Mark Despard, and Gaudan Cross. Edward is
a boringly normal individual, but like Walter Mitty, he harbors a
capacity for fantasy. He thinks he knows his wife, and he thinks he
controls his world, two assumptions which will be badly shaken by
events. Perusing the writings of the criminologist, Gauden Cross,
he comes upon an 1861 picture of a poisoner about to go the guillotine. Disturbingly, every feature of the murderess resembles Marie Stevens, his wife, and it is this jolt of some past life hidden that reorients Stevens to the supposed normality of his surroundings. Everything and everyone are now suspiciously and terrifyingly altered in his mind's eye as he has been pushed into the
Gothic world. Just as the maiden had looked to the hero for release from the haunted castle, so Stevens now looks to the detective for delivery from an evil universe. And things seem to be
going in this direction until the unexpected death of the detective by poison and a stunning final chapter which reverses the
Radcliffean formula. All that had been presumed natural turns out
to be supernatural after all, and a malign supernatural as well.
His dear wife, Marie, really was the murderess in the old picture.
She is no woman at all but a timeless demon in league with Gaudan
Cross, another demon, in a scheme to punish all those who would
deny the existence of the supernatural world. The woman he loved
and the detective he looked to for rational protection turn out to
be partners in conspiracy. This interesting reversal of rationalized Gothic has parodic overtones, but this does not prevent at
least a third of the book from being read as a novel of horror.
One modern reader (Joseph Sanders) has summed up Carr's application of Gothic methods: "Carr utilized outrageously Gothic trappings in scrupulously constructed puzzle plots." Another highly
satisfactory Gothic by Carr is Castle Skull, Harper, 1931.

085. The Castle of Altenheim; or, The Mysterious Monk. Philadelphia: A.
     I. Dickinson, 1836.

CRITICAL SYNOPSIS: In its earliest phase, the Gothic novel and the
historical romance of an imaginary middle ages were one in the
same genre. Thomas Leland's Longsword, The Earl of Salisbury (17-
62) and Sophia Lee's The Recess: A Tale of Other Times (1783)

startled and excited their audiences by blending frantic female victims, dark medieval settings, hidden rooms and secret passageways, fiendish pursuers, ghastly death, supernatural incident, and timely rescue with the real events and personages of a violent and remote epoch. This anonymous American specimen of Gothified history uses the early days of the Holy Roman Empire as a backdrop for its garish action. The Castle of Altenheim holds many secrets, not the least of which is the imperial identity of the castle's mysterious monk. The American readership remained susceptible to this early type of Gothic romance throughout the nineteenth century, and, looking at the abundance of twentieth century Gothic titles which incorporate history or pseudo-history, it might be argued that this kind of Gothic has never lost its popularity.

086. Cather, Willa. <u>Sapphira and the Slave Girl</u>. New York: Alfred A. Knopf, 1940.

REPRINT EDITION: New York, Vintage-Random House, 1975.
RESEARCH SOURCE: Rosowski, Susan J., "Willa Cather's American Gothic: <u>Sapphira and the Slave Girl</u>," <u>Great Plains Quarterly</u> 4 (1984): 220-230.

CRITICAL SYNOPSIS: Willa Cather's writings would seem to be located at the opposite pole from Gothic horror. Her Nebraska novels such as <u>O Pioneers!</u> are American pastorales celebrating the western landscape and its people. Examined more closely, however, there are Gothic personalities and events in nearly all of her books. The sinister Wick Cutter, for example, in <u>My Antonia</u> is cut from the same pattern as the monastic rapist villain of early Gothic fiction. The terrifying presence of Ivy Peters in <u>A Lost Lady</u> is summed up in one horror image as he slits the eyes of a young woodpecker before moving on to a sadistic possession of the lost lady's home and soul. Then, there is "The Stone Lips" chapter in <u>Death Comes for the Archbishop</u>, a kind of muted live burial episode in which the Bishop "found himself in a lofty cavern, shaped somewhat like a Gothic chapel, of vague outline,--the only light within was that which came through the narrow aperture between the stone lips." Given these Gothic overtones elsewhere in her work, it is not surprising that Willa Cather should have attempted a bona fide Gothic novel in her dark saga of the antebellum south, <u>Sapphira and the Slave Girl</u>. Susan Rosowski has written of this book's Gothicism that Cather "drew upon the Gothic tradition, placing within her study of manners the familiar plot of an innocent young woman trapped within a castle and sexually threatened by its villainous owner. She transplants the castle to America and she makes its owner female. But Gothic elements remain, and they are the fiber from which the novel is made." The Gothic heroine-villainess of the tale is Sapphira Dodderidge Colbert, owner of a large manor house in Back Creek Valley in the Virginia backwoods where she and her miller husband rule over a world of slaves with their power unchallenged and their position feared by the locals. Capricious, cold, and sometimes malevolent, Sapphira schemes against the mulatto slave girl, Nancy Till, placing her in sexually threatening situations and seeing to her persecution in other ways. The mill house where the mulatto maiden is incarcerated is a cryptlike setting of perpetual Gothic danger where the sensation of premature burial lies as heavily as the decayed air of the dark, drafty hallways and rotten staircases. But whether she is white or black, the American Gothic heroine has an independence and resourcefulness which extends back to Brockden

Brown's Constantia Dudley in Ormond (see 065). With the aid of the
young abolitionist, Rachel Blake, Nancy Till escapes from Sapphira's castle and moves along the underground railroad to freedom
and Canada. Her evil plans thwarted, Sapphira withdraws into herself and isolates herself from the outside world only to find herself locked in a struggle with death. Although it is a minor and
uncharacteristic novel in the Cather canon, Sapphira and the Slave
Girl must be considered a major contribution to the growth of the
American Gothic, an anti-pastoral view of the American experience
in which depravity is as strong as innocence and "in which the irrational assumes distinctively new world forms."

087. Cave, Emma. Little Angie. New York: Coward, Mc Cann & Geoghegan, 19-
77.

RESEARCH SOURCE: Sullivan, Jack, "Two Ways to Write a Gothic: Little Angie and The Shining," New York Times Book Review, February
20, 1977, p.8.

CRITICAL SYNOPSIS: If the novel is not a parody of the entire "female" Gothic genre, then Cave's Little Angie must be the purest of
pure Gothics, "a concise and elegant" modern Mysteries of Udolpho.
Little Angie is the naive American heiress, Angela Mac Clintock.
Her English countryside holiday turns into the grimmest of Gothic
ordeals when she is made the prisoner of Fox Hall and compelled to
occupy the upper bedroom where her villain host, Sir Peregrine
Palfrey Devonwood Donisthorpe, harasses, terrifies, interrogates,
menaces, and violates her repeatedly and in an interesting variety
of ways. The schedule includes regular sexual assault, closet incarceration, and more sadistic games than the Marquis de Sade ever
thought of playing. Outwardly horrified and hysterical, Angela
doesn't mind too much because deep down she is as responsive as
any other Gothic heroine to the secret delights of brutal sex and
solitary fear. Assisted capably by his dwarfish Butler, Sir Peregrine does his best to comply with the desired Gothic stimuli.
Again, if the novel is not the shrewdest of parodies, then it must
be taken as the Gothic's Gothic of the 1970's. Reviewing it and
comparing the book to Stephen King's The Shining, (see 261) Jack
Sullivan found Little Angie to be both high Gothic and brilliant
satire all at once. "The author treats her most menacing apparition scenes as a joke, not only explaining them away in the penul-
timate scene (as Mrs. Radcliffe and her contemporaries were fond
of doing), but making the 'surprise' explanation absurdly predict-
able to everyone but the heroine/victim. But gullibility is also a
red herring. 'Little Angie' is so named because of the heroine's
consistent fantasy of childlike helplessness, her masochistic devotion to her own victimization." Occasionally, a Gothic parody
can be so close to the model that it becomes the real thing.

088. Chambers, Robert W. "In the Court of the Dragon." The King in Yellow. New York and Chicago: F. Tennyson Neely, 1895.

REPRINT EDITION: The King in Yellow, and Other Horror Stories, ed.
E.F. Bleiler, New York, Dover Publications, 1970.
RESEARCH SOURCE: Clark, Kenneth, "Robert W. Chambers Reclassi-
fied," Journal of the Long Island Book Collectors 3 (1975): 18-
20.

CRITICAL SYNOPSIS: Unexplained supernatural or preternatural
events give the story its memorable Gothic power. Action is once

more motivated by a character's reading of the noxious play, "The King in Yellow" which infects him with almost unbearable physical anguish and mental agony. He enters the Church of St. Barnabé hoping to gain solace but the organ and organist thunder out a hideously dissonant and "wicked music" which only increases his discomfort. Suddenly, the protagonist is the object of the demon organist's baleful stare, "a look of hate, intense and deadly: I have never seen any other like it." The damning glance fills the narrator with blasphemous impulses and he rushes from the church into the Parisian streets where he has three chance encounters with the fearful organist, the creature who would claim his soul. The final encounter is in the Court of the Dragon, the narrator's street, in a narrow passage that leads from the Rue de Rennes. Here, he is cornered defiantly against the massive iron doors and claimed by the emissary of the King in Yellow. The postscript is one of the best instances of ambiguous horror in Chambers's work. Perhaps his body had never left the church since he had fallen asleep during the sermon. But it is also equally possible that his soul had been tempted to pursue the demon organist and has temporarily left his body to do so. Does the body join the soul in death, or does he relapse into nightmare, or does the King in Yellow return to claim the body now that he possesses the soul of the sufferer, or has the protagonist gained at last the relief that he had originally sought? The ending makes it impossible to know: "And now I heard his voice, rising, swelling, thundering through the flaring light, and as I fell, the radiance increasing, increasing poured over me in waves of flame." Salvation and destruction are ambiguously united into a single grand and eerie moment.

089.   _____. "The Mask." The King in Yellow. New York and Chicago: F. Tennyson Neely, 1895.

REPRINT EDITION: The King in Yellow, and Other Horror Stories, ed. E.F. Bleiler, New York, Dover Publications, 1970.
RESEARCH SOURCE: Weinstein, Lee, "Robert W. Chambers," Supernatural Fiction Writers, pp.739-745.

CRITICAL SYNOPSIS: Gothic fantasy involving the lethal atmosphere of art and the artist's studio with some strong hints of studio scenes in Wilde's The Picture of Dorian Gray (1891). The horror themes are similar to Alcott's "Marble Woman" (see 008) but instead of a figurative petrifaction of the young woman by the sculptor, the artist's power to turn flesh into stone is literal. The triangle of characters, the female victim, the male victimizer, and the helpless hero, all three enclosed within the dangerous and deadly world of art, comprise a typical Gothic cast. The cold and sinister sculptor, Boris Yvain, has found a chemical solution which renders organic matter into stone, a sort of ultimate preservative or embalming agent. Beginning his experiments with animals and flowers, he moves on to human beings and specifically to the woman who loves him, Genevieve, whom he petrifies. These events are reported by the narrator, Alec, who watches in helpless horror as the woman he loves becomes the sculptor's stone curio. The tale climaxes after Boris's suicide when Alec comes to reside in his studio in which a sealed and forbidden chamber holds all of the living things changed to stone figures by Boris's terrible fluid, including the marble-ized Genevieve. In a Gothicized version of sleeping beauty, Alec enters the chamber and emerges from behind the mask of self-deception by reviving her with a kiss. The warmth of love triumphs over the coldness of art as Alec "sprang through the hallway of the marble room. The doors flew open, the sunlight streamed into [his] face and through it in a heavenly glory, the Madonna smiled, as Genevieve lifted her flushed face from her marble couch, and opened her sleepy eyes."

090.   _____. "The Yellow Sign." The King in Yellow. New York and Chicago: F. Tennyson Neely, 1895.

REPRINT EDITION: The King in Yellow, and Other Horror Stories, ed. E.F. Bleiler, New York, Dover Publications, 1970.
RESEARCH SOURCE: Weinstein, Lee, "Chambers and The King in Yellow," Romantist 3 (1979): 51-57.

CRITICAL SYNOPSIS: A well-crafted story of insistent horror even in the midst of the pleasures of the artist's life. Several characters in these Chambers stories are ushered into the presence of evil and death when they read passages from a drama called "The King in Yellow." The play is bound as a yellow book, a forbidden and poisonous volume of devil lore whose words are fatal and whose depraved leaves can corrupt by the merest touch. This literary source of evil is coupled with the cadaverous figure of death's coachman to yield a subtle and satisfying tale of terror. The two principals of the story are a Washington Square artist and his nude model, Mr. Scott and Tessie Reardon. Their relationship is strictly professional until Tessie relates a terrifying dream to Scott and he in turn relates nearly the same nightmare to her. The church next to the artist's studio is presided over by a hideous watchman whose face is like a "coffin worm" and holds a repulsive attraction for the artist. The fatal watchman also appears in Tessie's dream as the driver of a hearse containing Scott's body and coffin. "You--you were in the coffin, but you were not dead." His nightmare is precisely the same and out of their mutual nightmare grows a love which prevents her from posing any longer in the nude. When the figure with the white puffy face mutters "Have you found the yellow sign?" the artist remembers the evil book with poisonous yellow binding and seeks it in his library to discover the answer to the face's awful question. Playfully, Tessie seizes the volume and the touch is fatal. Scott hears the dull, crunching wheels of the hearse's approach, hears death at the door of the studio as "the bolts rotted at his touch," hears Tessie's sigh of death "for I knew that the King in Yellow had opened his tattered mantle." No one is able to explain "the horrible decomposed heap" on the studio floor, the foul remains of the church watchman who must have been dead for several months. The chilling craftsmanship of the tale and the entrance of the cadaverous coachman make it one of Chambers's best fairytales of fear.

091.   _____. "The Harbor-Master." In Search of the Unknown. New York: Harper, 1904.

REPRINT EDITION: The King in Yellow, and Other Horror Stories, ed. E.F. Bleiler, New York, Dover Publications, 1970.

CRITICAL SYNOPSIS: A suspenseful story of abnormal zoology and the creature from the depths. The researcher, Halyard, whose scientific training makes him skeptical of such marine monsters as the Kraken and the fabled harbor-master, is swiftly converted to belief in oceanic monsters when the thing from the deep rises to the surface. "But the horror of the thing were the two gills that swelled and relaxed spasmodically, emitting a rasping, purring sound. The harbor-master had gathered himself into a wet lump, squatting motionless in the bows under the mast; his lidless eyes were phosphorescent, like the eyes of of a living codfish...and the next I knew the harbor-master ran at me like a colossal rat, just as the boat rolled over and over through the surf, spilling freight and passengers among the sea-weed-covered rocks."

092. Chesnutt, Charles Waddell. The Conjure Woman. Boston and New York: Houghton, Mifflin, 1899.

REPRINT EDITIONS: Ann Arbor, MI, Michigan UP, 1969; Saint Clair Shores, MI, Scholarly Press, 1977.
RESEARCH SOURCES: Andrews, William L., The Literary Career of Charles W. Chesnutt, Baton Rouge, LA, Louisiana State UP, 1980; Hemenway, Robert, "Gothic Sociology: Charles Chesnutt and the Gothic Mode," Studies in the Literary Imagination 7 (1974): 101-119.

CRITICAL SYNOPSIS: This collection of negro folk tales by the black author, Charles W. Chesnutt, is narrated and framed by Uncle Julius Mc Adoo, a former slave. African magic or "Conjure" underlies and unifies the various stories in which the conjure woman, Aun' Peggy, or the conjure man, Uncle Julius, employ thaumaturgic powers to depict the darker side of slavery and the Gothic situation of blacks entrapped within a culture which denies their selfhood and dignity. In "Mars Jeems's Nightmare," the violence that was condoned and encouraged by white supremacy is shown with a brutal force, but in most of the stories, the Gothicism of racism is more subtly condemned. Tales containing the Gothic motifs of flight, terror of authority, pursuit, separation from family, cultural enclosure, and metaphoric live burial are "Hot-Foot Hannibal," "The Conjurer's Revenge," and "The Marked Tree." For the black imagination, American society before and after the Civil War was a haunted and foreboding society. Hence, the devices of Gothicism could be made to express the nightmare realities of racism.

093. Clemens, Samuel Langhorne [Mark Twain]. "A Ghost Story." Sketches, New and Old. Hartford, CT: American Publishing, 1875.

REPRINT EDITION: The Complete Short Stories of Mark Twain, ed. Charles Neider, Bantam Books, 1957.
RESEARCH SOURCE: Gribben, Alan, "'When Other Amusements Fail': Mark Twain and the Occult," The Haunted Dusk: American Supernatural Fiction, 1820-1920, eds. Howard Kerr, John W. Crowley, Charles L. Crow, Athens, GA, Georgia UP, 1983, pp.171-189.

CRITICAL SYNOPSIS: The story commences as a hair-raiser and a near parody of the pulsating style of one of Poe's homicidal monologues. The narrator has taken a room in the top floor of an old deserted building in New York. He awakes in "shuddering expectancy...when the bedclothes began to slip away slowly toward the foot of the bed as if someone were pulling them!" Literally every single Gothic sound effect in the whole orchestra of terror is now brought into play as the narrator's horror mounts at the presence of some unseen night visitor. He hears "a heavy footstep, the step of an elephant it seemed to me." He hears "the clanking of chains faintly...muttered sentences, half-uttered screams that seemed smothered violently; and the swish of invisible garments, the rush of invisible wings." Every known Gothic screw is turned very hard until by a bluish light the gigantic ghostly guest materializes from a vaporous cloud. At this point Twain wrenches the narrative from the Gothic to the comic because the narrator finds himself staring into the friendly face of "the naked, muscular, and comely, the majestic Cardiff Giant," Barnum's famous archeological fraud. The giant has not had a chance to sit down for a century and when he does so as he begins to explain his visit to the narrator he ruins all of the furniture in the room. It seems that the giant is condemned to wander and haunt until his colossus now exhibited in the museum across the street is given proper burial again. In absolute disgust, the narrator points out that "you have been haunting a plaster cast of yourself--the real Cardiff Giant is in Albany. Confound it! Don't you know your own remains?" Thoroughly humiliated, the marble-footed phantom trudges off in embarrassment imploring the narrator not "to let this get out." The ghost story is remarkable for its welding of the two moods of high Gothicism and ludicrous revelation. The reader is completely unaware that he is being spoofed until the very moment when the petrified spook emerges from the lethal nimbus. Poe too had played with the idea of the goofy Gothic night guest in the tale, "The Angel of the Odd."

094.   _____. "The Golden Arm." Oral Performance for the Women of Bryn Mawr College, March 23, 1891.

REPRINT EDITION: The Literature of the United States, eds. Walter Blair, Theodore Hornberger, James E. Miller, Jr., Chicago, Scott, Foresman, 1966.
RESEARCH SOURCES: Kaplan, Justin, Mr. Clemens and Mr. Twain: A Biography, New York, Simon and Schuster, 1966, pp.309-310; Kemper, Steven E., "Poe, Twain, and Limburger Cheese," Mark Twain Journal 21 (1981-82): 13-14.

CRITICAL SYNOPSIS: "On the platform I used to tell a negro ghost story that had a pause in front of the snapper on the end, and that pause was the most important thing in the whole story." So Twain described this little piece of Gothic stagecraft in "How to Tell a Story." The perfectly timed delay at the climax is indeed vital to the success of the jolt that scares the "farthest-gone auditor" but the Gothic detailing which builds to the pause is equally important to the effect. The three hundred words of the tale contain almost every element of the tale of terror. We have the night time, a burial and disinterment of a dead wife by "a monsus mean" man to get her precious golden arm, a storm, a cadaverous voice howling above the wind its little chorus of terror which runs throughout the piece, "Who got my golden arm?" Then there follows isolation, pursuit by the armless corpse, numbing fear, a dreadful footstep, a bedroom visitation by the dead and possibly murdered wife who has come to retrieve her golden arm. Finally, the armless corpse stands at the mean man's bedside and from beneath the sheets "he seem to feel someth'n cold, right down 'most agin his head! (pause)" Then, Twain's pause and lunge at the nearest frightened young lady in the audience and the snapper, "You've got it!" Twain might have called this little bit of ghoulish stagecraft "How to write a Gothic novel in three hundred words."

095. Cline, Leonard. The Dark Chamber. New York: Viking Press, 1926.

CRITICAL SYNOPSIS: An utterly formulaic Gothic, yet the book still

has much to recommend it in its marvelous management of the haunted castle and its stereotyped machinery. Stylistically as well,
Cline makes the passions of his characters real and fascinating in
their otherworldliness. Even hostile reviewers, such as the historian, Allan Nevins, writing in the Saturday Review admired
Cline's reworking of shopworn Gothic patterns. Within the context
of the fantasy, the characters are rendered with a "gruesome credibility. Yet, even in its failure the book has qualities which
inspire unusual respect," said Nevins. The book might be designated "Hudson River Gothic," since its architectural setting is a
frowning mansion on the New Jersey Palisades, Mordance Hall. Master of the mansion is the nearly insane recluse, Richard Pride. He
performs strange experiments within the dark chamber and drives
his erotically starved wife into a fatal affair with the family
secretary. The victimized and imprisoned daughter, Janet, and a
rescuing stranger, who also collects notes and writes the strange
story of Pride's evil house, complete the Gothic cast. Suicide,
pathos, mysterious disappearances, voluptuous fits of passion, and
a crumbling family seat with a personality and biology of its own
yield a Gothic's Gothic. This is not the great American novel, but
it is a readable and pleasurable shocker by a writer whose expertise in timing a horrific climax is almost unmatched.

096.   Coates, Robert M. The Eater of Darkness. New York: Contact Edi-
        tions, 1926.

RESEARCH SOURCE: Pierce, Constance, "'Divinest Sense': Narrative
Techniques in Robert Coates," Critique: Studies in Modern Fiction
19 number 2 (1977): 44-52.

CRITICAL SYNOPSIS: A Dadaist novel and an absurdist Gothic which
exhibits the structural distortions of Sterne, the nightmare collage of Kafka, and the stream of consciousness of Joyce. Coates
was a member of the Hemingway, Gertrude Stein circle in Paris and
an admirer of the surrealism of André Breton. In The Eater of
Darkness he experimented with literally all of the radical post-
war ideas about art and literature popularized by surrealism, and
in so doing, he produced a surreal Gothic fantasy. Reading the
novel requires the same skill and patience as reading Sterne's
Tristram Shandy (1762) or Joyce's Ulysses (1922) because its design is centripetal rather than linear; hence, we seem to get sequence without consequence as well as a structural parody of the
well-made detective novel of crime, complication, concentration,
and solution. There are several styles, numerous narrative culs-
de-sac, useless and phony footnotes, and many other violations of
the logical plot. Finally, there is no solution to the murder mystery possibly because no murder occurred. The demented hero,
Charles Dograr, goes through a series of shadowy adventures with
two mysterious figures, a man with a walking stick, and a still
stranger stranger, the eater of darkness who owns a machine capable of consuming the pall of night. But since Dograr's adventures
are narrated through the mind of his mistress, we cannot be sure
of the truth of any of them or even of their actual occurrence. No
prior Gothic character ever wandered through such a mental labyrinth as Dograr. Joyce's modern Ulysses at least achieved a homecoming or sorts; but there is no such solace for for Coates's
crazed voyager. The surrealist notion that experience is beyond
human apprehension and resistant to all control by logic is an
idea best expressed through patterns of Gothic chaos which bear
the helpless hero to the end of night.

097. Cooper, James Fenimore. The Spy, A Tale of Neutral Ground. New York: Wiley & Halsted, 1821.

REPRINT EDITION: ed. James H. Pickering, New Haven, CT, College & University Press, 1971.
RESEARCH SOURCES: Ringe, Donald A., American Gothic, pp.106-108; St. Armand, Barton Levi, "Harvey Birch as the Wandering Jew: Literary Calvinism in James Fenimore Cooper's The Spy," American Literature 50 (1978): 348-368.

CRITICAL SYNOPSIS: Like many other novels by Cooper, The Spy is an historical romance with Gothic touches and scenery woven into its fabric of intrigue, adventure, danger, and disguise. The spy is the peddler, Harvey Birch, a protean figure of mystery and multifarious disguises who serves as an intelligence agent in the American revolutionary cause. Birch is a refabricated Gothic character who comes and goes by darkness in the neutral territory of Westchester County, aiding both his Loyalist and rebel neighbors in the persons of the Wharton family and the Lawtons, their rebel adversaries. Incredibly, George Washington is deeply involved in Birch's clandestine activities since he is living incognito under the alias, Mr. Harper, in the divided household of the Loyalist, Henry Wharton. Although Birch's motives are nobly patriotic, there is an aura of demonic mystery about him. His lineage seems to be accursed by some unnamed crime, and, as Barton Levi St. Armand has suggested, he carries the traits of that guilty outcast, the Wandering Jew. The cast also includes Cooper's version of a Gothic heroine, Frances Wharton, whose rebel sympathies place her in a constant peril which Cooper presents in several scenes as Gothic entrapment and distress. To rescue her brother, Henry, from the hangman, she visits Harvey Birch's remote cabin by night and later experiences by moonlight the ghastly silhouette of noose and gallows where her brother must die in the morning. Other night scenes in the novel are similarly conceived to create Gothic shock and horror. Although The Spy is not a Gothic novel, it is nevertheless heavily dependent on Gothic situations and effects. And, as Donald Ringe points out, the book "marks an important step in the domestication of literary Gothicism in America. Cooper found in the mode a useful means for evoking one aspect of the American landscape and for transforming so native a character as Birch into a creature of mystery."

098. _____. Lionel Lincoln; or, The Leaguer of Boston. New York: Charles Wiley, 1825.

REPRINT EDITION: eds. Donald A Ringe, Lucy B. Ringe, Albany, NY, State University of New York Press, 1984.
RESEARCH SOURCES: Gross, Louis, Redefining the American Gothic: From Wieland to the Day of the Dead, Ann Arbor, MI, UMI Press, 19-89, pp.25-28; Ringe, Donald A., American Gothic, pp.121-123; Ringe, Donald A., "Cooper's Lionel Lincoln: The Problem of Genre," Long Fiction of the American Renaissance: A Symposium on Genre, ed. Paul Mc Carthy, Hartford, CT, Transcendental Books, 1977, pp. 24-30.

CRITICAL SYNOPSIS: Cooper's Gothicism is, of course, subordinate to his larger historical purposes, but Gothic scenery, devices, and characters are present in almost every one of his more than thirty published novels. The main character in this work, for example, a major in the British army of occupation during the siege of Boston during the American Revolution, shares many traits of mind with the misperceiving heroines of Mrs. Radcliffe whose imaginations constantly transform natural dangers into supernatural terrors. A strain of insanity in Major Lionel Lincoln's family further impairs his ability to govern his morbid imagination. Reginald Lincoln, Lionel's great grandfather had been driven nearly mad by his militant Protestant beliefs, and maniac tendencies had reappeared in Lionel's father whom he thinks now to be confined to a madhouse. In one respect, Lionel Lincoln's military service in the new world is his effort to escape the family curse of madness. In Gothic terms, he attempts to deny the haunted castle of self by heroic deeds in the Americas. But the spectres of Lionel's past accompany him and demand recognition. His mad father has come on the ship with the regiment under the disguise of "Old Ralph" and his step-brother, Job Pray, is already prowling about Boston when Lionel arrives. Genealogical entanglements, the normal stuff of the subplot of numerous Gothics, also lead to Lionel's eventual discovery of his true father. In several episodes, Lionel's perceptions of the natural world cause him to imagine supernatural occurrences as when he flees in panic one night when he thinks he hears the colonial dead scratching their way out of their coffins to avenge themselves upon the occupying English army. But as does his predecessor, the Radcliffean heroine, Lionel Lincoln eventually learns to regulate a sensibility that is prone to dark imaginings and in so doing he averts the madness which has afflicted his family for several generations.

099.   . The Heidenmauer; or, The Benedictines, A Legend of the Rhine. Philadelphia: Carey & Lea, 1832.

RESEARCH SOURCES: Cowie, Alexander, Rise of the American Novel, pp.136-137; Wagenknecht, Edward, Cavalcade of the American Novel, pp.20-21; Wyss, Hal H., "Involuntary Evil in the Fiction of Brown, Cooper, Poe, Hawthorne, and Melville," Dissertation Abstracts International 32 (1971): 1489A (Ohio State University).

CRITICAL SYNOPSIS: With its title taken from a ruined fortress near the Bavarian town of Dürkheim and its sixteenth-century backdrop of religious conflict between the Benedictine monks of Linburg Abbey and the Protestant Count Emich of Leiningen-Hartenburg, Cooper's novel has many of the components of the romance of the ruin, a special category of Gothic novel. As in other Gothified histories and monastic shockers, a love plot is complexly interwoven with the historical violence and mystery of Gothic times. One of Cooper's immediate sources is Scott's Gothic novel of the Vehmgericht or secret Fehmic Court, Anne of Geierstein (1829). With the exception of supernatural trappings, Cooper's Germanic romance relies on Gothic characterization, action, and atmosphere to embellish the historical theme. That theme deals with the internecine collision of two societies, an authoritarian Catholic past ruling through fear and superstition versus a Protestant future which is equally perilous. The Gothic is placed in the service of the political dialectic to produce a picture of two sets of values consuming their adherents. In his American romances, Cooper would again turn to the Gothic for exploring the conflict between the wilderness and the incursions of civilization. Cooper's imitation of the historical Gothic can claim several fine Gothic characters such as Baron Odo von Ritterstein, the hermit who patrols the ruined fortress of Heidenmauer.

100. Counselman, Mary Elizabeth. "The Shot-Tower Ghost." Half in Shadow. Sauk City, WI: Arkham House, 1978.

CRITICAL SYNOPSIS: An Alabama regionalist whose stories appeared originally in Weird Tales. This story is a whimsical Gothic tall tale about a crippled Confederate veteran who leaps into a river in an act of patriotic defiance. Now his ghost repeats the suicidal deed of defiance each year on the anniversary of his death. In tone, the story hearkens back to Irving's sportive Gothic.

101. Cram, Ralph Adams. "The Dead Valley." Black Spirits and White: A Book of Ghost Stories. Chicago: Stone & Kimball, 1895.

REPRINT EDITIONS: The Frankenstein Reader, ed. Calvin Beck, New York, Ballantine Books, 1962; Black Spirits and White: A Book of Ghost Stories, Salem, NH, Ayer Publishers, 1970.

CRITICAL SYNOPSIS: Cram was a well known architect and architectural historian whose writings on architecture prepared him well for the making of a single anthology of terror, Black Spirits and White. In 1907, he published The Gothic Quest, in 1916, The Substance of the Gothic, and in 1927, a book that could be used as a guide to the English Gothic novel, Ruined Abbeys of Great Britain. But his knowledge of high Gothic architecture does not figure directly in his most famous story of the supernatural, "The Dead Valley." The locale is northern Sweden, where the narrator and his friend come upon a noxious valley filled with poisonous vapors. They barely escape, but the narrator feels an overwhelming compulsion to return to the "dead valley." The theme of fatal allurement which had also been used by Poe in tales involving the lethal voyage is handled with subtle power by Cram. Several other tales in the volume are more traditionally Gothic in their use of horrible interiors. "Sister Madellena," for example, has all of the components of the monastic shocker. The setting is the Sicilian convent of Santa Catarina. Horrific events center on the immured nun of the title who was walled up in a window niche centuries before. Driven to see her for himself, the narrator risks a Gothic confrontation when he goes in quest of her remains.

102. Crane, Stephen. "The Monster." The Monster, and Other Stories. New York: Harper, 1899.

REPRINT EDITIONS: Maggie and Other Stories, ed. Austin Mc C. Fox, New York, Washington Square Press, 1960; The Evil Image: Two Centuries of Gothic Short Fiction and Poetry, eds. Patricia L. Skarda, Nora Crow Jaffe, New York, New American Library, 1981.
RESEARCH SOURCE: Morris, James Kelly, "Stephen Crane and the Gothic Tradition," Dissertation Abstracts International 44 (1983): 18-02A (University of Mississippi).

CRITICAL SYNOPSIS: Moments of sheer Gothic horror are not foreign to the art of Stephen Crane as illustrated when Private Henry Fleming comes upon the ant-covered corpse in the pine grove in The Red Badge of Courage (1895). The Gothicism of "The Monster," however, is a far more sustained mood. The novelette also has interesting parallels with Mary Shelley's Frankenstein (1818) in its ambiguous presentation of the theme of monsterism. Both novels raise tormenting questions about who the real monsters are supposed to be,--the hideously deformed creatures, their so-called civilized masters, or "normal" society which reacts with horror and revulsion at the sight of these subhuman things? Crane's handling of the theme of society's lack of sympathy is much more bitterly ironic that Mary Shelley's portrayal of inhumanity and indifference. But Crane's monster is fundamentally different from Victor Frankenstein's nameless creation in two respects: Henry Johnson, the monster, is unaware of his hideousness and hence is bewildered and driven mad by his effect on others: Johnson was not born a monster but became one when he was horribly burned during the perforance of a courageous act when he rescued the son of his employer, Dr. Trescott, from a fire. Dr. Trescott, a pillar of the community, befriends his negro servant to the horror of all the polite citizens of Whilomville who ostracize the Doctor and his family for harboring a monster in their home. The fire that deprives the black man of his face and the malicious rejection of both Johnson and his employer by the townspeople lend an added dimension to the story regarding the position of negroes in American life and the whole uneasy matter of race relations even after freedom had technically been granted. The reader is compelled to trace the true source of horror in this trenchant example of the American Gothic and finally to judge for himself who the real monsters are by a nervous glance in the mirror.

103.   Crawford, Francis Marion. The Witch of Prague. New York: Macmillan, 1891.

RESEARCH SOURCES: Brumbaugh, Thomas B., "The Facile Francis Marion Crawford," Markham Review 4 (1974): 70-71; Moran, John C., "Recent Interest in F. Marion Crawford: A Bibliographical Account," Romantist 1 (1977): 53-56; Moran, John C., "The Witch of Prague," Survey of Modern Fantasy Literature, pp.2136-2138.

CRITICAL SYNOPSIS: Crawford's exotic novel of hypnotism, quest, and intermittent horror is a blend of several romance genres. According to John C. Moran, The Witch of Prague is "a fantasy, a Gothic novel, a horror tale, an occult novel, and in many respects a scientific romance." To this amalgam may be added the book's Dantesque dimension in the Wanderer's search for his lost Beatrice and a Spenserian suggestion in the parallel situations of the Wanderer's relations with the witch, Unorna, which recalls the deception of the Red Cross Knight in the first book of the Faerie Queene. Although the plot appears complex it is actually a simple quest romance elaborately adorned with cabalistic detail and adventure and decorated by intertwining subplots. Like other examples of decadent art, Crawford allows the parts to predominate over any unity. Hence, such episodes as the profaning of the host by Beatrice while under hypnosis, the mockery of Unorna (whose name may be a perversion of the Spenserian Una) by one hundred animated skulls, and the atrocious description of the crucifixion of the Jewish lad, Simon Abeles, by the Prague Jews in the performance of the blood libel are subsidiary events which take precedence over the larger plot. The main story relates the attempts of the witch, Unorna, to obtain the secrets of immortality with the aid of her dwarf confederate, Keyork Arabian. She also becomes involved with two men, the wanderer who seeks Beatrice in Prague and rejects her blandishments, and Israel Kafka, who loves the Witch of Prague and is despised by her in return. Crawford's novel makes no pretenses to didactic seriousness as would a Hawthorne tale of witchcraft and the black arts. From the opening chapter where we hear the mass in the Gothic cathedral of Teyn Kirche through the blacker masses to follow, the narrative seeks only to divert the reader by suspending him between wonder and horror.

104.   _____. "The Upper Berth." <u>The Upper Berth and Other Tales</u>. London: T. Fisher Unwin, 1894; New York: Putnam, 1894.

REPRINT EDITION: <u>Classic Ghost Stories by Charles Dickens and Others</u>, New York, Dover Publications, 1975.
RESEARCH SOURCE: Moran, John C., Edward Wagenknecht, Russell Kirk, and Donald Sydney-Fryer, <u>An F. Marion Crawford Companion</u>, Westport, CT, Greenwood Press, 1981.

CRITICAL SYNOPSIS: Probably the most frequently anthologized of all of Crawford's ghostly and Gothic tales, the story makes use of a terror device introduced by Wilkie Collins in "The Traveler's Story of a Terribly Strange Bed" (1852). Whoever sleeps in the trans-Atlantic liner's upper berth in a certain cabin is doomed to kill himself because the berth had been the last resting place of a madman who committed suicide. The berth remains his by right of possession from beyond the watery grave. The story is told through the point of view of the passenger who occupies the berth just below, a powerful man who has felt the physical presence of the suicide's ghost when he has his arm broken when he attempts to seize the phantasmic intruder. There is nothing shy, gentle, or suggestive about Crawford's spectre which reeks of the gore of one of Monk Lewis's fiends from the grave. "It was something ghostly, horrible beyond words, and it moved in my grip," the narrator remembers. "It was like the body of a man long drowned, and yet it moved, and had the strength of ten men living; the putrid odour of rank sea water was about it, and its shiny hair hung in foul wet curls over its dead face." Death is stronger than life and the supernatural more powerful than natural strength in Crawford's smoothly crafted bedtime Gothic. H.P. Lovecraft judged "The Upper Berth" to be "Crawford's weird masterpiece, one of the most tremendous horror stories in all literature."

105.   _____. "The Dead Smile." <u>Uncanny Tales</u>. London: T. Fisher Unwin, 1911.

REPRINT EDITION: <u>A Century of Horror Stories</u>, ed. Dennis Wheatley, London, Hutchinson, 1935.

CRITICAL SYNOPSIS: There are overtones of "The Fall of the House of Usher" (see 379) and of the gory Gothic melodrama of the Irish Poe, Joseph Sheridan Le Fanu, in this piece. The setting is the ancient feudal seat of the dead Irish baronet, Sir Hugh Ockram, who expired with an evil smile on his face and carried the secret of the dead smile to his grave. The secret of the grinning corpse compels his son and heir, Gabriel Ockram, to make the traditional Gothic descent to the family burial vaults where the body of his father has been enshrouded but not entombed because he he was too wicked to deserve full burial. The subterranean visit is carried out with skillful attention to suspense and charnel detail in this little Gothic gem as is Gabriel's discovery of the moldy parchment in the decayed clutch of the father. It is incest which caused and still causes the corpse to wear its horrible smile. These are all old Gothic gears and gadgets, but reassembled with masterful dexterity by Crawford.

106.   _____. "For the Blood is the Life." <u>Uncanny Tales</u> [U.S. Title, <u>Wandering Ghosts</u>]. London: T. Fisher Unwin, 1911; New York: Mac-

millan, 1911.

REPRINT EDITIONS: Tales of the Undead, Vampires and Visitants, ed. Elinor Blaisdell, New York, Thomas Y. Crowell, 1947; Voices from the Vaults: Authentic Tales of Vampires and Ghosts, ed. Devendra P. Varma, Toronto, Key Porter Books, 1987.
RESEARCH SOURCE: Holman, Harriet R., "F. Marion Crawford and the Evil Eye," American Notes & Queries 9 (1971): 103-104.

CRITICAL SYNOPSIS: This is a vampire tale and narrated so skillfully that the mood of supernatural credibility is never broken. The vampire is Christina who has been murdered by the thief, Angelo. She invades his sleep, lures him to her graveside and takes his blood for her life. The thinly disguised eroticism of the vampire story is also evident in the tone which is similar in some ways to the art of Joseph Sheridan Le Fanu in his famous vampire piece, Carmilla (1871).

107. _____. "The Screaming Skull." Uncanny Tales [U.S. Title, Wandering Ghosts]. London: T. Fisher Unwin, 1911; New York: Macmillan, 1911.

REPRINT EDITION: Great Tales of Terror and the Supernatural, eds. Herbert A. Wise, Phyllis Fraser, New York, Modern Library, 1944.
RESEARCH SOURCE: Sidney-Fryer, Donald, "Francis Marion Crawford: A Neglected But Not a Forgotten Master," Romantist 3 (1979): 43-50.

CRITICAL SYNOPSIS: The narration is somewhat experimental as it is told in conversational fragments and flashbacks through the faulty memory of a retired sea captain. He has taken a cottage on the shore from a doctor (Luke Pratt) whose wife had died under mysterious circumstances. Among other curious medical relics, the cottage contains a skull which rattles with a leaden sound when shaken and is later found on the beach near the doctor's strangled body. There are strange stories about how the doctor had poisoned his wife by employing a grisly method similar to the murder of Hamlet's father. Some say that he poured molten lead into the porches of his wife's ear while she slept; thus the skull's restlessness, its screams, and its promptings to eventual revenge. These details must all be pieced together via the banter of the sea captain who sometimes fails to understand or connect the events he relates. When Captain Braddock decides to retain the skull, he seals his own horrible fate. But instead of a direct assault by the screaming skull, Crawford chose to put the climax into the form of a newspaper obituary on the "Mysterious Death of a Retired Sea Captain" who had been "bitten in the throat by a human assailant with such amazing force as to crush the windpipe."

108. Cruger, Julie Grinnell Storrow [Julien Gordon]. Vampires. Mademoiselle Réséda. Philadelphia: J.R. Lippincott, 1891.

CRITICAL SYNOPSIS: An American example of the Victorian vampire story. The short novel is conceived along the lines of psychological horror with the vampire invading the souls and wills of those humans foolish enough to venture near him. The narrator, Mr. Milburn, is helplessly fascinated by a strange clergyman, Father Nast, who lives in the same boarding house with him. There is something irresistibly evil about this man of God, a vampiric magnetism which attracts even as it repels. Milburn remembers that "to me there was a charm in his dim medieval figure, something quaint, almost Gothic, cast upon the garish background, that supplanted the crude modernity of our environment." Milburn's friend, Paton, Miss Olivia Spooner, and his cousin, Nelly, are equally infatuated by Father Nast, who is followed by them all as he travels from spa to spa and boarding house to boarding house. When Paton is found dead under strange circumstances, Milburn suddenly recalls a story from the sacred book, the Talmud, "of a man into whose ear a tiny gnat crept, and it grew, and it grew, and it grew until the man died, and when his head was opened, the gnat had grown to the size of a dove, only it was not a dove that they found there, but a creature with a beak of brass and claws of iron." But despite this awakening to the presence of evil, Milburn cannot dissociate himself from the vampire. The figure of the malign, yet alluring, priest goes back to the roots of the early Gothic hero-villain while the sophisticated treatment of mental helplessness invites parallels with the ghostly fiction of Henry James.

109. Dana, Richard Henry, Sr. "Paul Felton." The Idle Man, II, number 1. New York: Wiley & Halsted, 1821.

REPRINT EDITION: New York, Gordon Press, 1981.
RESEARCH SOURCES: Davis, David Brion, Homicide in American Fiction, 1798-1860: A Study in Social Values, Ithaca, NY, Cornell UP, 1957, pp. 191-200; Hunter, Doreen, "America's First Romantics: Richard Henry Dana, Sr. and Washington Allston," New England Quarterly 45 (1972): 3-30; Ringe, Donald A., "Early American Gothic: Brown, Dana, and Allston," American Transcendental Quarterly 19 (1973): 3-8.

CRITICAL SYNOPSIS: Gothic themes and moods in this dark and gloomy tale foreshadow the morbid universe of Hawthorne several decades later. The name of Dana's morose hero, Felton, also turns up in Hawthorne's work in the romance of the elixir of life, Septimius Felton (see 205). Dana's story reveals his interest in several of the motifs of dark or Gothic romanticism, "negative" Romanticism as some critics have termed it. The power of the imagination to destroy or to warp the capacity to love is dramatized in the strange and lonely career of Paul Felton. He has grown to manhood without ever knowing love in any form. He is ignored by his father and surrounded by crude types; thus, his artistic temperament craves relief from these frustrations in an inbred pessimism and his urge to self-isolation. Felton's marriage to the vibrant Esther Waring allows him a temporary release from the gloomy castle of self, but his dark imaginings about the untrustworthiness of all human relationships will eventually draw him backward into melancholy and misanthropic seclusion. Just as Hawthorne's isolatoe, Young Goodman Brown (see 196), comes to distrust the reality of any goodness, so Paul Felton is driven by his imagination to believe that all happiness must be illusory. Joy in general is a mere mirage, and any marital bliss is particularly deceiving. It is inevitable that he should suspect Esther of infidelity and to see her jeu d'esprit as promiscuity. Esther's exuberant nature arouses his morbid jealousy and he wanders like Byron's Childe Harold (1809-1812) into remote and desolate regions taking "a perverse satisfaction in self-torture." When he encounters the mad boy, Abel, he encounters his future self. A terrible visionary experience inside a wilderness hovel called "the Devil's Haunt"

causes a final transformation in his character from morbid misanthropy to homicidal madness. Clutching a rusty dagger, he pursues Esther, accuses her of infidelity, and fatally stabs her.
Throughout the scene, Paul Felton, like the insane Theodore Wieland (see 063), is prompted by a supernatural voice commanding him
to kill. Dana's interest in the vulnerability of the human mind
and the proximity of sanity to insanity link him with the earlier
mental explorations of Charles Brockden Brown and the probings of
Poe in his homicidal fantasies. The collective theme running from
Brockden Brown to Dana to Poe in their tales of insanity can be
thus stated: is any man ever safe from himself? Is the imagination
a faculty to be admired and trusted or is it one of the most
dreadful forces at work within the buried self?

110. Daniels, Dorothy. The Unearthly. New York: Lancer Publishing, 1977.

RESEARCH SOURCES: Ewing, Emma Mai, "Gothic Mania," New York Times
Book Review May 11, 1975, pp.10, 12-13; "Heathcliffs, Cliffhang-
ers," Newsweek April 4, 1966, pp.101-102; Radcliffe, Elsa J.,
Gothic Novels of the Twentieth Century, pp.55-58; Russ, Joanna,
"Somebody's Trying to Kill Me and I Think it's My Husband: The Mo-
dern Gothic," Journal of Popular Culture 6 (1973): 666-691.

CRITICAL SYNOPSIS: Daniels is a typical Garden Club Gothic entre-
peneur who has made a killing in paperback Gothics. Elsa Radcliffe's bibliography lists no less than seventy-two titles by
her, all so similar in plot that a summary of The Unearthly can
stand as a summary of any Daniels Gothic. The heroine, Hope Owen,
returns alone to the family plantation mansion following her mother's death. Obscure victimizations, ghostly meetings, and a vaguely menacing relationship with a strange man follow. Elsa Radcliffe's judgement upon Daniels's Gothic is severe but probably
fair. "Daniels consistently provides," says Radcliffe, "a depend-
able standard of mediocrity." The anonymous critic in Newsweek
echoes this judgement in his scornful observation about the Daniels school of Gothicism: "Neo-Gothics are cranked out by pseudonymous English and American writers, most of whom are women, some
of whom publish under several different names. The old Gothic heroine, when imprisoned in a decaying mansion, wanted only to get
away. The new one wants to redecorate." Yet, the laws of supply
and demand apply as inexorably to Gothic novel writing and reading
as they do to other human demands, and Daniels's junkfood Gothics
meet a demand. Other titles by Daniels which rank above the routine sameness of Garden Club Gothic are: The Attic Rope (Lancer,
1970), Castle Morvant (Warner, 1972), The Curse of Mallory Hall
(Fawcett-Crest, 1970), Ghost Song (Pocket Book, 1974), Mystic Man-
or (Warner, 1972), The Tormented (Paperback Library, 1969), and
Witches' Castle (Paperback Library, 1971).

111. Daniels, Les. The Black Castle. New York: Scribner's, 1978.

REPRINT EDITION: New York, Ace Books.

CRITICAL SYNOPSIS: The novel is a successful revival of a very
popular type of early Gothic fiction, the Inquisition Gothic. The
Inquisition contributes horrid character and atmosphere in Mrs.
Ann Radcliffe's The Italian; or, The Confessional of the Black
Penitents (1797), Christiane Naubert's Hermann Von Unna; Eine
Geschichte aus dem Zeiten der Vehmgerichte (1794), Lewis's Ambro-
sio; or, The Monk (1796), and "The Spaniard's Tale" in Maturin's

Melmoth the Wanderer (1820). Poe condensed the horrific elements of the lengthy Inquisition Gothics in the opening paragraph of "The Pit and the Pendulum" (see 385). Drawing upon these earlier Gothic works, Daniels sets the novel in late fifteenth-century Spain when the newly created institution of the Inquisition under the ruthless Torquemada was approaching a zenith of power. Opposing the methods of the Inquisition and seeking to curb its power is the heroic main figure, Sebastian of Villanueva. He is assisted by Margarita, a woman who knows the Inquisition and its work at firsthand, having been accused of witchcraft and seen the strappado and the rack at work. Although there may be some political message or allegory lurking in this historical Gothic, The Black Castle is primarily a tale of stunning and horrid scenery and effects.

112. Dawson, Emma. "Singed Moths." An Itinerant House and Other Stories, illus. Ernest C. Peixotto. San Francisco: William Doxey, 1896.

CRITICAL SYNOPSIS: "Singed Moths" involves satanic encounter and a disturbingly ambiguous ending. The tale is narrated from four divergent points of view, the diaries of the three sisters, Charlotte, Elizabeth, and Catherine, and their gossipy servant, Biddy. There is no way of determining the actuality of the devil's visit since each sister's evidence contradicts the others'. All of the sisters become "singed moths" who fly too near the alluring satanic flame when the devil figure, Mr. Orne, "his face swarthy with evil in the fiery glow of the sunset," invades their lives on Midsummer Eve and All Hallows. One sister reports receiving Lucifer's kiss, the seal of Satan, another hears the eerie strains of the Mephisto Waltz, and the third, Charlotte, is given a necklace whose beads are imps, a version of the diabolic gift. The effect of Orne's infiltration of the sisters' quiet lives is to transform them into the weird sisters themselves. "And over a sputtering candle, burning blue, we all nodded at each other like so many doomed witches." The ending may or may not show the strangulation of Charlotte with the devil's necklace; neither the reader nor the other two sisters can be absolutely sure because of the psychological ambiguities of the event. One other story in the collection, "Are the Dead Dead?" deserves praise for its ambiguous Gothicism. The narrator dabbles in the supernatural by associating herself with a "ghost club," only to discover that the supernatural does not allow dabbling; any involvement with it is a full involvement from which there can be no turning back. Hence, the answer to the rhetorical question, "Are the Dead Dead?" is brought home to the narrator. Death is a higher reality than life, which may be all illusion. "Sitting there so long, so still, it seemed to my strained nerves that we were like ghosts, and only the pictures on the wall had life and motion. A cold draught rushed in as at the opening and closing of some doors. A nameless fear seized me."

113. De Camp, L. Sprague and Fletcher Pratt. Castle of Iron. New York: Gnome Press, 1950.

RESEARCH SOURCE: Le Guin, Ursula, "New England Gothic," Times Literary Supplement, March 29, 1976, p.335.

CRITICAL SYNOPSIS: The title sounds promisingly Gothic but the novel is only intermittently so. Two characters who appear elsewhere in De Camp's fantastic fiction, Reed Chalmers and his research assistant, Harold Shea, enter the complex cosmos of Spenser's <u>Faerie Queene</u>, particularly the pathless forests and dark castles of Book III of Spenser's poem. The equally complicated adventure world of Ariosto's <u>Orlando Furioso</u> is also part of the elaborate plot, and some knowledge of the two great Renaissance poems is needed and assumed to appreciate the adventures of these two modern heroes at large in the exotic world of allegory. Quests, transformations, battles againsts beasts and super-beasts, and suddenly shifting sequences of elation and nightmare give the novel its Spenserian flavor and pace. Metamorphosis is a common predicament in <u>The Faerie Queene</u> as human characters find themselves changed into non-human substances or shapes. The rehumanization of these victims is often the task of the Spenserian quester as it is for De Camp's two modern knights errant. They endure the terrors of the Iron Castle of the black magician Atlantes who has changed the young woman, Florimel (in Book III, the beloved of Marinell and the pursued heroine), into a figure of snow. The Iron Castle itself is a Gothic place and recalls many dangerous castles in <u>The Faerie Queene</u> but is especially reminiscent of Book III's Castle of Busirane and its awful iron doors. With the aid of Merlin, Chalmers and Shea are able to rehumanize this snow image into a loving woman of flesh and blood. As was the case with the polymorphous Spenserian plot in which many stories are in progress simultaneously, there are many other adventures and ordeals circulating around this core quest. In certain respects, De Camp and Pratt have duplicated the complicated and multi-leveled plotting of the first Gothic novels of the Eighteenth Century where the reader loses his way almost as many times as the characters do.

114. De Ponte, Mrs. S. "A Night of Terror." <u>Thirteen Good Stories from Old and New</u>. Boston: Old and New Office, 1873.

CRITICAL SYNOPSIS: An early anthology or tea table sampler of weird, sinister, and occasionally supernatural pieces. Such literature adorned the parlors of Victorian ladies from Boston to San Francisco. "A Night of Terror" is a typical tale of ghostly return and revenge with a moral concerning fidelity to lend the tale didactic respectability.

115. Derleth, August, H.P. Lovecraft. <u>The Lurker at the Threshold</u>. Sauk City, WI: Arkham House, 1945.

REPRINT EDITION: <u>The Watchers Out of Time</u>, Sauk City, WI, Arkham House, 1974.
RESEARCH SOURCE: Tweet, Roald D., "August Derleth," <u>Supernatural Fiction Writers</u>, pp.883-890

CRITICAL SYNOPSIS: Given the label, "posthumous collaboration," by Lovecraft critics, the tale is mainly from Derleth's hand with some interpolated paragraphs by H.P. Lovecraft. Derleth consciously attempted to duplicate Lovecraft's style in this novel of supernatural horror and satanism. The lurker at the threshold of the human cosmos is Lovecraft's awful divinity from the other side, Yog Sothoth. The characters as well have a Lovecraftian weirdness about them right down to their very names. The inheritor of the haunted estate in Arkham, Ambrose Dewart, his diabolically involved ancestor, Abijah Billington, and the Indian wizard, Quamis, have the true Lovecraftian ring. But the strongest and most appealing Gothic aspect of the narrative is the old manor house of Billington itself which is ordered according to orthodox horrific plan. The desolate estate which Dewart inherits is ruinous and

overrun with decayed growth. Strange monuments almost like mega-
liths brood over the grounds and a sealed tower menacingly over-
sees all. This is certainly the Gothic skyline. The house contains
an oddly shaped window which when peered through reveals a
strange, otherworldly landscape. Both the tower and the window are
forbidden to Dewart, but precisely in the manner of earlier Gothic
explorers (usually locked-in maidens) he defies these warnings.
The Satanic ritual--a favorite Lovecraft event--explains his ancestor's dark reputation and his own tendency toward wishing to
penetrate evil mysteries. Although the climax is conventional (the
forbidden tower collapses) Derleth's Lovecraftian extravaganza can
claim some moments of pure cosmic dread especially in its display
of Gothic scenery and stagecraft.

116. _____. "No Light for Uncle Henry." Something Near. Sauk City, WI:
Arkham House, 1945.

RESEARCH SOURCE: Wilson, Alison M., August Derleth: A Bibliography, Metuchen, NJ, Scarecrow Press, 1983.

CRITICAL SYNOPSIS: The haunted room ordeal dates back to the beginnings of the Gothic tradition itself. There are several variations to the theme and Derleth's variant is to use the chamber as
the site for supernatural revenge. The spirit of the murdered
uncle possesses his nephew, Edward, who engineers the revenge by
contriving to entrap the murderer, Herbert, within the chamber by
playing on his pride.

117. _____. "The Lonesome Place." Lonesome Places. Sauk City, WI: Arkham House, 1962.

REPRINT EDITION: Horror Times Ten, ed. Alden Norton, New York,
Berkley Medallion Books, 1967.

CRITICAL SYNOPSIS: A clever piece of diablerie based on what must
be a universal childhood fear, terror of a familiar yet eerie location which must be passed on the way home from school or er-
rands. The special lonesome place here is an abandoned grain ele-
vator which overshadows the street two boys must use to make their
way from home to downtown. The brothers' secret fear grows as they
imagine the old building to be the home of some monster, and indeed, a child was mysteriously murdered some years ago in the
area. All of these fearsome facts are recalled by the grown-up
narrator who has never been able to outgrow his terror of the
lonesome place.

118. Drake, Joseph Rodman. "The Culprit Fay." The Culprit Fay, and Other
Poems. New York: G. Dearborn, 1835.

REPRINT EDITION: New York, Grolier Club, 1923.

CRITICAL SYNOPSIS: The poem is a Keatsian fantasy published posthumously in 1835 and takes as its locale the banks of the Hudson
below West Point, certainly an unlikely territory for lost maidens
and culprit feys or fairies. Although severely derided by Poe who
called this poem and others "utterly destitute of any evidence of
imagination whatsoever....We are bidden, in the first place, and
in a tone of sentiment and language adapted to the loftiest
breathings of the Muse, to imagine a race of fairies in the vicin-
ity of West Point," Poe did point out several passages which at-

tain an ideal Gothic mood of beautiful terror. Poe was also equally severe with the Gothic poem, "Alnwick Castle," by Drake's
friend and collaborator, Fitz Greene Halleck. But he also cited
several passages which reflected "the highest order of poetry" and
which might bear comparison with Keats's Gothic romance in verse,
"The Eve of St. Agnes," or Coleridge's "Christabel." The approach
to Alnwick Castle, for example, is in the high Gothic mood: "Gaze
on the Abbey's ruined pile:/Does not the succoring ivy keeping,/
Her watch around it seemed to smile/As o'er a lov'd one sleeping."

119. Dreiser, Theodore. An American Tragedy. New York: Boni and Liveright, 1925.

REPRINT EDITION: afterword Irving Howe, New York, New American Li-
brary, 1975
RESEARCH SOURCE: Riggio, Thomas P., "American Gothic: Poe and An
American Tragedy," American Literature 49 (1978): 515-532.

CRITICAL SYNOPSIS: If the traditional image of the haunted castle
becomes in later versions of the tale of terror the haunted society, then certain structural aspects of Dreiser's famous case
study may be taken as expressions of the American Gothic mode. The
novel contains a seduction, a murder, a cultural environment which
entraps or dispossesses the young hero and arouses his vanity,
some landscapes that suggest that Dreiser "turned to Poe" at one
juncture in the writing of the novel, and a grim concluding sequence of trial, punishment, and death. In M.G. Lewis's great
Gothic shocker, The Monk (1796), the criminal Ambrosio is not portrayed as entirely responsible for his brutal sexual passions and
murderous misdeeds. To some extent, the novel's horrors carry an
indictment of the social and spiritual conditions which produced
the criminal monk. Dreiser's indictment of a closed and warping
society is similar. Clyde Griffiths, the ambitious son of Kansas
City street evangelists, dreams of escaping his drab future and
rising to wealth and social prominence according to the promise
held forth by the glittering mirage of the American dream. Fate,
the environment, and his own weakness of character combine to
place him in a hopeless and tragic position within the haunted society which undermines his dreams, drives him to murder (he pre-
meditates the act and allows her to drown), and claims his life.
Perhaps the most direct influence of Gothic themes and moods in
the novel is to be found in Book Two, chapter 47, the famous
murder chapter, in which Clyde takes the pregnant Roberta Alden
out on the lonely lake with thoughts of killing her. Alone in the
rowboat on Big Bittern Lake with loons crying ominously in the
distance and the dark water inviting the dark deed, the boat
lurches, the girl screams as she strikes her head on the camera,
and Clyde capsizes the boat as he pulls back from her imploring
touch. On the surface of it, the homicide may be unintentional,
but on the deeper level, the sinister forces working against Clyde
converge in a focal moment of pure Gothic horror. "And in the
meantime his eyes--the pupils of the same growing momentarily
larger and more lurid...And then he, stirred by her sharp scream
(as much due to the lurch of the boat as the cut on her nose and
lip), rising for the unintended blow....As she sank and then rose
for the first time, her frantic, contorted face turned to Clyde,
who by now had righted himself. For she was stunned, horror-
struck, unintelligible with pain and fear--her lifelong fear of
water and drowning and the blow he had so accidentally and all but

unconsciously administered." Dreiser's American Tragedy was not conceived as a Gothic novel, but in scenes such as this, a distinct strain of American Gothicism is to be intensely felt.

120.   . "The Hand." Chains, Lesser Novels and Stories. New York: Boni and Liveright, 1927.

REPRINT EDITION: American Ghost Stories, ed. C. Armitage Harper, Boston, Houghton-Mifflin, 1928.

CRITICAL SYNOPSIS: This chilling little piece makes good use of the hand that haunts, a grisly effect which is as old as the Gothic novel itself. The story's control and craftsmanship further show that Dreiser might have written a full-length novel of horror had he been so predisposed. The plot makes use of a stock situation for the horror story, revenge from beyond the grave and by a supernatural agency in the form of a detached limb. The main character, Davidson, has murdered the sinister and lugubrious Mersereau. Mersereau dies with hand raised in a menacing gesture of doom. Hand haunting commences almost immediately as Davidson, who begins as a psychic researcher and ends as a madman, firsts sees and then feels the omnipresent hand of his victim. When Davidson's body is found in the insane asylum, the doctors give the cause of death as tuberculosis, but had they examined the corpse more closely, they would have seen the hand prints on Davidson's throat. In this story at least, Dreiser's naturalism is subordinate to his Gothicism for environmental forces are not nearly as powerful as internal psychic forces springing from the dungeons of the mind.

121. Dunlap, William. Ribbemont; or, The Feudal Baron. New York: David Longworth at the Dramatic Repository, Shakespeare-Gallery, 1803.

REPRINT EDITION: Four Plays, Delmar, NY, Scholars' Facsimiles, 19-76.
RESEARCH SOURCE: Zipes, Jack, "Dunlap, Kotzebue, and the Shaping of American Theatre: A Re-valuation from a Marxist Perspective," Early American Literature 8 (1973): 272-284.

CRITICAL SYNOPSIS: A dramatic adaptation of Mrs. Ann Radcliffe's fourth and best known Gothic romance, The Mysteries of Udolpho (1794). The noble bandit character would also have been available to Dunlap by way of numerous other sources in the period. To bring Mrs. Radcliffe to the American stage, Dunlap collaborated with John Hodgkinson.

122.   . Fountainville Abbey. New York: David Longworth at the Dramatic Repository, Shakespeare-Gallery, 1807.

REPRINT EDITION: Four Plays, Delmar, NY, Scholars' Facsimiles, 19-76.
RESEARCH SOURCES: Coad, Oral, "The Gothic Element in American Literature Before 1835," Journal of English and Germanic Philology 24 (1925): 72-93; Evans, Bertrand, "Ann Radcliffe and Gothic Drama," Gothic Drama from Walpole to Shelley, Los Angeles, CA, California UP, 1947, pp.90-115.

CRITICAL SYNOPSIS: Referred to by Coad as "the first native Gothic play," the drama is a spectacularized stage version of Mrs. Ann Radcliffe's third novel, The Romance of the Forest (1791). The secondary but more immediate source is James Boaden's Gothic drama, Fountainville Forest. Names and locales are preserved intact from the Radcliffean model as is the natural solution to the preceding supernatural events. The villainous Marquis de Montalt, the weeping Adeline, the ruined abbey, and a relentless pattern of flight, menace, and persecution proved as successful with American seekers of terror as with the English Gothic readership. When we hear Adeline exclaim, "I must be cautious, lest the sudden blast extinguish my faint guide. What's that I tread on? A dagger all corrupted by the rust," we can be certain that we are in the Gothic world.

123. Eastburn, J.W. and R.C. Sands. Yamoyden; A Tale of the Wars of King Philip. New York: Clayton & Kingsland, 1820.

CRITICAL SYNOPSIS: Plenty of Gothic imagery and morbid grandeur fills the lines of this epic of King Philip's War (1675-76). The poem is in six cantos, each a tribute to Indian valor and Puritan depravity in the extermination of the Wampannoags and the Nipmucks under Yamoyden in their tribal struggles against the white settlers. To drive home his sympathetic portrayal of the Indian cause, Sands often writes in a Gothic key to depict as luridly as possible "uncertain horror's spectral train." Gothic gloom pervades the forests "when at midnight's ghostly noon, a crimson scar deformed the moon." Other passages, such as the description of King Philip's flight to Mount Hope, teem with the dark energy of Gothic verse: "There, where the spirits of the dead, Seemed flitting through each moonlight glade,--Where pageant hosts of glory fled in mockery rose with vain parade,--In gloomy grandeur o'er his head, Where forests cast congenial shade,--Brooding mid scenes of perished state, He mused to madness on his fate." The spectral wilderness of the American Gothic, our most typical site of terror, looms over and over in the dark scenography of Yamoyden.

124. Echard, Margaret. The Dark Fantastic. Garden City, NY: Doubleday, 1947.

CRITICAL SYNOPSIS: The title refers to the danse macabre which characterizes the dark and closed world of the boarding school operated by the main character, Richard Tomlinson, somewhere in the mid-West in the 1870's. School life is filled with grotesque occurrences and people. The wife of the sexually repressed master of the school is the invalid, Abigail. Until she is terrified to death by a strange doll, her sinister control over the closed Gothic world and its dark fantastic atmosphere is almost complete. Two young women, Thorne and Judith, enter the school and compete for the erotic attention of Tomlinson. He marries Judith, the girl who frightened his crippled wife to death with her strange doll, but he continues to desire Thorne. A climax is reached when Judith is attacked by Abigail's ghost and the other characters are ejected from this scholastic version of the haunted castle. In the plot's full box will be found every single piece of the old Gothic puzzle, all regionalized and given a mid-Western tinge.

125. Elliott, Francis Perry. The Haunted Pajamas. Indianapolis, MN: Bobbs Merrill, 1911.

CRITICAL SYNOPSIS: Gothic comedy in the sportive mode of Washington Irving or John Kendrick Bangs. Supernatural humor is best carried out with a light touch or the joke will pall. Here, the comic premise, which is a good one, is overdone as the joke is repeated ad nauseam until the premise is no longer amusing. The novel starts briskly with a Harvard man determining to spend three years in English society in order to acquire a cultured accent and rid himself of other vulgar Americanisms. To assist his cultural transformation, a university friend furnishes the Harvard man with a pair of Chinese pajamas reputed to be 4,500 years old. The magical properties of the pajamas are soon evidenced when the Harvard man is changed back into one of the previous wearers every time he puts on the haunted pajamas. Such transformations are not limited to one sex as the ancient Chinese sleeping suit can just as easily turn the present wearer into a woman. How many prior persons can the Harvard man become? As the transformation joke is told over and over, the joke goes as flat as a repeated punchline.

126. Ellison, Harlan. "Grail." Stalking the Nightmare. Huntington Woods, MI: Phantasia Press, 1982.

REPRINT EDITION: New York, Berkley Publishers, 1984.
RESEARCH SOURCE: Smith, Curtis C., Supernatural Fiction Writers, pp.1015-1021.

CRITICAL SYNOPSIS: A demonic messenger offers the main character, Christopher Caperton, a visionary opportunity to know his own moment of supreme and peerless love. But this "grail" gift proves also to be a gruesomely ironic experience because with the recovery of this grail comes the dark wisdom that his moment has passed and will never come again. It is typical of Ellison's horror art to elevate standard Gothic scenes and events into parable statements about the moral life. Concerning Ellison's frequent use of visionary shock in his tales, Curtis Smith observes: "Shock is purposeful, for he is a modernist prophet who believes in the power of art to stave off the apocalypse. In 'Paulie Charmed the Sleeping Woman' (1962), a horn player performs in the cemetery at the crypt of his dead love, Ginnie, and raises her, Lazarus-like: 'We heard the noise outa that crypt. We heard her coming.'"

127. _____. "Night of Black Glass." Stalking the Nightmare. Huntington Woods, MI: Phantasia Press, 1982.

RESEARCH SOURCE: Smith, Curtis C., "Harlan Ellison," Supernatural Fiction Writers, pp.1015-1021

CRITICAL SYNOPSIS: Loss of the power to feel or a special deadness of the heart inform this Gothic tale of inner death. The main character is a sort of last survivor figure who has come through the Viet Nam War but all his friends have been killed. He comes home to find that his wife has also died. Guilt over his survival and loneliness impel him to make a kind of nocturnal quest to recover these lost loved ones. He takes a bus which brings him to a Maine beach in the dead of night. As he ponders on the solemn shore there rises from the ocean a collective cavalcade of the dead consisting of his fallen companions and his lost wife. On this "edge of the world," they come to him from the depths of a night of black glass. But the dark mirror of memory refuses to reflect any feeling in the deadest character in the tale, the survivor himself. Sometimes a grand vision of the dead can effect the redemption of the sinner, but in Ellison's story, the theme is treated with climactic pessimism. The final horror stresses that for some dead souls there can be no rebirth of feeling.

128. Endore, Guy. The Werewolf of Paris. New York: Farrar & Rinehart, 19-
      33.

      REPRINT EDITION: London, Sphere Books, 1974.
      RESEARCH SOURCES: Smith, Kirby Flower, "An Historical Study of the
      Werewolf in Literature," Publications of the Modern Language Asso-
      ciation 9 (1894): 1-42; Summers, Montague, "The Werewolf in Liter-
      ature," The Werewolf, London, Routledge & Kegan Paul, 1933.

      CRITICAL SYNOPSIS: Endore's unique novel of lycanthropy has ample
      horrors but may also be read as a novel of ideas in which were-
      wolfery functions as a symbol of social and political movements
      run wild and as a commentary on savage behavior on a mass scale,
      especially when a society is possessed by an idea. The werewolf's
      destructive rampage corresponds with the rise and fall of the 1871
      Paris Commune from September, 1970, to the massacre of "bloody
      week" in May, 1871. The lust of the werewolf for blood and flesh
      is hardly less appalling than the same lust which brought the
      slaughter of more than 30,000 Communards and ordinary Parisians by
      the Versaillesist troops. The narrative structure of the novel is
      somewhat unique and reverts to the Gothic novel's mechanism of the
      lost manuscript rediscovered. An American writer seeking material
      in Paris comes upon the history of Bertrand Caillet's trial for
      mass murder when he purchases a worthless manuscript from trash
      dealers. The facts of Bertrand's hideous career as a lycanthrope
      are given by his Uncle, Aymar Galliez, an unsympathetic relative
      who assists in the stalking and trial of his werewolf nephew. The
      chronicle of these uncontrollable crimes of bestial appetite com-
      poses the Gothic core of the novel, but again, a deliberate con-
      trast is evoked between the deeds of one Parisian werewolf and the
      deeds of the government against the Communards. Bertrand violates
      graves, assaults friends, phlebotomizes his sweetheart, Sophie de
      Blumenberg, and leaves a trail of half-devoured corpses in his
      wake, before he is apprehended with the assistance of a government
      spy, Captain Barral de Montfort. Committed to an asylum for the
      cure of his delusion, he dies there of neglect and maltreatment.
      The American writer decides to sort out these facts and write a
      book that will get at the truth of Bertrand's werewolfery. But the
      larger and more troubling question to be asked in the light of the
      events of the year of the Commune is: who are the real werewolves,
      the literal beasts, or the political beasts so possessed by an
      idea that it must be nourished by blood? Reading the novel from
      this angle makes the work less a study of the "liberated id" than
      a study of society's innate bestiality.

129. Engolls, William. The Countess; or, The Inquisitor's Punishments, A
      Tale of Spain. Boston: Gleason's Publishing Hall, 1847.

      RESEARCH SOURCE: Redden, Sister Mary Mauritia. The Gothic Fiction
      in the American Magazines (1765-1800). Washington, DC, Catholic
      UP, 1939.

      CRITICAL SYNOPSIS: A 100 page Gothic chapbook printed in double
      columns. What we have is a plagiarized reduction of the infamous
      shocker, M.G. Lewis's The Monk (1795), with an admixture of mater-
      ial lifted from shilling shockers and Inquisition Gothics such as
      William Henry Ireland's Gondez the Monk (1805). In Madrid, the
      Grand Inquisitor, Bartolme Torquemada, a "proud ecclesiatic of
      fierce and sensual expression and a disciple of pleasure," deter-

mines to have the Countess Maria of Norma, a sexual prize whose "full heaving bosom was but half-concealed by the loose dress of her boudoir." Other characters and events are crude refabrications of the most famous Gothic novel of the Eighteenth Century. The dwarf, Reinaldo, the sinister Sister Agatha, and the displaced hero, Pasamonte, step straight from the pages of Monk Lewis in this American specimen of Inquisition Gothic. An Inquisition Gothic would not be complete without a long description of the Inquisitor's "iron virgin." The machine of torture appears right on cue when the Inquisitor interrogates the maiden, Blanchette: "When this image had been disclosed by opening the doors, Bartolme contemplated it for a moment with a gleam of fiendish satisfaction. and then commanded Blanchette to advance and kiss its lips. She touched a secret spring, and in a moment the arms enclosed her form, while the fair image was changed into an instrument of torture, armed with a thousand sharp knives, which pierced her flesh in all directions, cutting her body into innumerable pieces." As Sister Mary Mauritia Redden's survey shows, a large literature of cheap and tawdry horror of this type found its way into the American magazines between 1765 and 1800. The 1847 date of this monastic shocker indicates that such Gothic fiction continued to be marketable well into the Nineteenth Century.

130. Farris, John. The Fury. New York: Warner Publishing and St. Martin's Press, 1976.

CRITICAL SYNOPSIS: Futuristic Gothic fantasy concerning a CIA-type governmental office called MORG. MORG's agents pursue the "psychic twins," Robin Sanza and Gillian Bellaver because the pair possesses extrasensory powers that the government covets for its own sinister purposes. Robin's father, Peter Sanza, devotes his life to protecting his daughter and her companion from the machinations of MORG. The original Gothic pursuit was by a monastic or baronial villain through the underground of a dark castle or abbey; the modern Gothic equivalent of the pursuit motif has two teenagers hounded by a governmental agency with a gruesomely appropriate acronym for place of death. Although the myths of mysterious victimization and female distress have been modernized, the underlying Gothic origin of these myths is still highly discernible. Parallels with Stephen King's The Firestarter (see 268) and similar Orwellian fantasies of the government as tyrannical intruder are extensively evident.

131. Faulkner, William. "A Rose for Emily." Forum. 83 April, 1930, 233-238; These 13. New York: Cape and Smith, 1931.

REPRINT EDITION: Literature, eds. James H. Pickering, Jeffrey D. Hoeper, New York, Macmillan, 1986.
RESEARCH SOURCES: Allen, Dennis W., "Horror and Perverse Delight: Faulkner's 'A Rose for Emily,'" Modern Fiction Studies 30 (1984): 685-696; Perry, J. Douglas, Jr., "Gothic as Vortex: The Form of Horror in Capote, Faulkner, and Styron," Modern Fiction Studies 19 (1973): 153-167.

CRITICAL SYNOPSIS: Certainly Faulkner's most conventional Gothic tale, the heroine's preservation of her lover's cadaver in the decaying atmosphere of her solitary mansion should be compared with earlier appearances of the necrophiliac motif in the American Gothic such as in Hawthorne's "The White Old Maid" (see 186). Miss Emily Grierson's self-enforced isolation, her strange black servant, her mysterious courtship, her purchase of arsenic, and above all, her sequestration within the "big, squarish frame house that had once been white, decorated with cupolas and spires and scrolled balconies" provide the Gothic ambience. After her funeral, the townspeople flock to investigate the interior of the Grierson mansion which reeks of foul odors and holds some hideous secret somewhere above the stairs. In a scene that is reminiscent of the visit to the vault or the breaching of the forbidden chamber in old Gothic fiction, they break down the door of the room above the stairs which no one had entered in forty years. Even though Faulkner's climax could be anticipated by any experienced reader of the tale of terror, it is still a well-timed stroke of putridity and horror, for her bed contains "what was left of him, rotted beneath what was left of the nightshirt." The title of the story does not seem to make much sense unless we take it metaphorically. The "Rose" or fond tribute is the memorial narrative itself which is remembered and spoken by an anonymous townsperson who sees and understands the love beyond the horror.

132. _____. As I Lay Dying. New York: Cape and Smith, 1930.

REPRINT EDITION: New York, Vintage-Ballantine, 1979.
RESEARCH SOURCE: Kerr, Elizabeth L. "From Otranto to Yoknapatawpha: Faulkner's Gothic Heritage," William Faulkner's Gothic Domain, Port Washington, NY, Kennikat Press, 1979, pp.3-28.

CRITICAL SYNOPSIS: The novel is written in stream-of-consciousness form with approximately sixty narrative panels or small sections assigned to the various characters of the Bundren family. The relationship of the dead mother to her children is gradually revealed through the interplay of the various narrative fragments. The main action is the funeral journey of the mother, Addie Bundren, and the subsequent adventures of her putrifying corpse and coffin as her family transports her remains back to her childhood home in Jefferson, Mississippi for burial. In the retinue are Addie's inane husband, Anse, and her four sons, Cash, Darl, Jewel, and Vardaman. During the gruesome journey, Anse bores a hole in the coffin to have a final glimpse of his departed wife and the coffin itself is almost lost when the cortege tries to ford a flooding stream. Enroute, Darl burns down a barn and Jewel is severely burned while trying to save the animals. Only one of the brothers, Cash, is anything like a balanced and normal character, while the others along with the Bundren daughter, Dewey Dell, make up a Gothic family of frenzied or psychopathic types. The novel's complex psychological structure with the dead mother's own last thoughts (as she lay dying) at the dark center suggests a labyrinthine design or a Gothic patterning which captures the dark crisscrossings of domestic tensions and disintegrating family ties.

133. _____. "Dry September." Scribner's, 89 January, 1931, 49-56; These 13. New York: Cape and Smith, 1931.

REPRINT EDITION: The Modern Tradition, Short Stories, ed. Daniel F. Howard, Boston, Little, Brown, 1972.
RESEARCH SOURCES: Brady, Ruth A.H.H., "The Reality of Gothic Terror in Faulkner," Dissertation Abstracts International 32 (1972): 5774A-5775A (University of Texas at Austin); Ferguson, Robert C., "The Grotesque in the Fiction of William Faulkner," Dissertation Abstracts International 32 (1971): 1508A (Case Western Reserve University).

CRITICAL SYNOPSIS: The alleged rape of the white spinster, Miss Minnie Cooper, by the black man, Will Mayes, forms the basis for the racial terror and unassuaged blood lust of this tense tale. Jefferson, Mississippi has seen sixty-two rainless days in the driest September within memory. Nothing apparently can relieve the ire of the weather god short of a blood sacrifice while the air itself, presided over by "the wan hemorrhage of the moon," lights the way to dusty death. A lynch party led by the war veteran, John Mc Lendon, seizes Mayes and gives him a last ride down a back road "to an abandoned brick kiln--a series of reddish mounds and weed-and-vine choked vats without bottom." Faulkner's omission of the specific details of the awful deed actually intensifies the horror of an entire community entrapped within the blood thirst. While Will is being lynched, Miss Minnie herself sits in the local pic-ture show and emits a low laugh which slowly builds to an hysteri-cal cacchination of guilt, a standard Gothic sound effect which rises to a hideous pinnacle. Had she started the rumor of a sexual assault on her which quickly led to the death of the innocent black man? The dry heat which encloses and entraps the whole town continues to exert its terrible effect on the lynchers in the story's final scene. Arriving home, Mc Clendon is unable to make love to his waiting wife and stands panting against the screen door in impotent frustration. This is one of Faulkner's bleakest Gothic tales of small town life filled with an atmosphere of vio-lence, gloom, and self-betrayal. The tale's final sentence empha-sizes the terrible closure of this world, "the dark world [which] seemed to lie stricken beneath the cold moon and lidless stars."

134. _____. Sanctuary. New York: Cape and Smith, 1931.

REPRINT EDITION: New York, Vintage-Ballantine, 1978.
RESEARCH SOURCES: Bleikasten, André.,"Terror and Nausea: Bodies in Sanctuary," Faulkner Journal 1 (1985): 17-29; Frazer, David, "Gothicism in Sanctuary: The Black Pall and the Crap Table," Mod-ern Fiction Studies 2 (1956): 114-124; Heller, Terry, "Terror and Empathy in Faulkner's Sanctuary," Arizona Quarterly 40 (1984): 344-354; Miller, James E., Jr., "William Faulkner: Descent into the Vortex," Quests Surd and Absurd: Essays in American Litera-ture, Chicago, Chicago UP, 1967, pp.31-40; Rossky, William, "The Pattern of Nightmare in Sanctuary: or, Miss Reba's Dogs," Modern Fiction Studies 15 (1969-1970): 503-515.

CRITICAL SYNOPSIS: Faulkner himself made no attempt to disguise his Gothic ends in the publication of this cruel and shocking tale. According to him, Sanctuary was to be "the most horrific tale I could imagine...deliberately conceived to make money." Settings, characters, and episodes read like an inventory of Goth-ic necessities. There is a raped maiden (Temple Drake) driven half mad by her brutal deflowering, a perverted, unnaturally monstrous villain (Popeye) who is nearly chinless and whose eyes "are two knobs of soft, black rubber," a house of horrors (the Old French-man's Place) "set in a ruined lawn, surrounded by abandoned grounds and fallen outbuildings," murder, sexual violence, and the total ineffectiveness of goodness and justice in an atmosphere of cloying evil and moral decay. Faulkner follows the Gothic formula with uncanny precision in the novel's style and imagery as well as in theme and situation. The helpless and sleeping Temple Drake just before being raped by Popeye lies with "her hands crossed on her breast and her legs straight and close and decorous, like an effigy on an ancient tomb." Her savagely beaten lover, Gowan Stevens, appears as "a wild, battered, and bloody apparition." When Temple Drake is held prisoner in the Memphis brothel, she shudders at images "in the wavy mirror of a cheap varnished dresser, as in a stagnant pool, [where] there seemed to linger spent ghosts of voluptuous gestures and dead lusts." The plot pattern too is undeviatingly Gothic. The virgin college girl, Temple Drake, and her drunken escort, Gowan Stevens, take a lover's drive but are forced off a backroad by a fallen log cut and placed for just such a purpose. They stumble through the swamps to a dilapidated house, the Old Frenchman's Place, where a gang of bootleggers led by the unspeakably vicious Popeye is in conclave. Gavin abandons her while Temple is seized, menaced, and raped in a corncrib by Popeye who uses a corncob as a copulative dagger since he is impotent. Other horrifying adventures follow in swift succession. Temple is consigned to a Memphis whorehouse by the degenerate Popeye. One of Popeye's confederates, Goodwin, is arrested, tried, convicted, and lynched by a mob despite the noble but innocuous exertions in his behalf by the lawyer, Horace Benbow. The tale's conclusion is a sort of merciless Gothic grotesque, a reversion to primal darkness. The fugitive Popeye is apprehended and hanged for a murder he did not commit. His last words from the gallows are "Fix my hair, Jack." The half mad Temple makes a futile attempt at recovering her wits in Paris, but the concluding image in the novel suggests that she is now and forever will be a spiritual corpse as she stares sightlessly at "the dead tranquil queens in stained marble...and on into the sky lying prone and vanquished in the embrace of the season of rain and death." The gruesome irony of Sanctuary's title is sounded with a vengeance in these final scenes as it is throughout this undiluted example of American Gothic horror.

135. _____. Absalom, Absalom! New York: Random House, 1936.

REPRINT EDITION: New York, Vintage-Ballantine, 1981.
RESEARCH SOURCES: Pitavy, François L., "The Gothicism of Absalom, Absalom! Rosa Coldfield Revisited," "A Cosmos of My Own": Faulkner and Yopnapatawpha, Jackson, MS, Mississippi UP, 1981, pp.199-226; Putzel, Max, "What is Gothic About Absalom, Absalom!?" Southern Literary Journal 4 (1971): 3-14; Torsney, Cheryl B., "The Vampire Motif in Absalom, Absalom!," Southern Review 20 (1984): 562-569; Whan, Edgar W., "Absalom, Absalom! as Gothic Myth," Perspective 3 (1950): 192-201.

CRITICAL SYNOPSIS: An intertwined and murky tale of family decay and decline told in various Gothic styles by three narrators. The story of Colonel Sutpen and his Mississippi mansion, Sutpen's Hundred, is recited first by his half-mad sister-in-law, Rosa Coldfield. Her recital is given to the young man, Quentin Compson, with details added by Quentin's father, the second narrator. Quentin in turn attempts to reconstruct his version of the story for his Harvard roommate, Shrevlin Mc Cannon. The legend of Colonel Sutpen is the dark saga of the great house built on crime, blood, concealment, and lies. It was Colonel Sutpen's "grand design" to found a great aristocratic line in Jefferson, Mississippi, with himself as powerful patriarch and his sons as perpetuators of the great name of Sutpen. To do so, he ruthlessly carries out his plan at the expense of the honor and lives of many others. But after his return from the Civil War, the House of Sutpen goes into gradual but steady decline until by the year 1910 the "fall" is utter and complete. Sutpen himself is murdered and the great house burns. The final image depicts the idiot black, Jim Bond, the last incestuous descendant of Sutpen's dream of power, howling and prowling about the ashes of Sutpen's Hundred. Each of the three narrators uses a style that is heavy with Gothic metaphor and the rhetoric of horror. It also seems definite that Faulkner had Poe's "The Fall of the House of Usher" (see 379) in mind when he described the House on the verge of annihilation: "It loomed, bulked, square and enormous, with jagged half-toppled chimneys, its roofline sagging a little; for an instant as they moved, hurried, toward it Quentin saw completely through it a ragged segment of sky with three hot stars in it as if the house were of one dimension, painted on a canvas curtain in which there was a tear. Now, almost beneath it, the dead furnace-breath of air in which they moved and seemed to reek in slow and protracted violence with a smell of desolation and decay as if the wood of which it was built were flesh....The house collapsed and roared away, and there was only the sound of the idiot negro left."

136. Fitzgerald, F. Scott. "The Curious Case of Benjamin Button." Tales of the Jazz Age. New York: Charles Scribner's Sons, 1922.

REPRINT EDITION: Avon Ghost Reader, intro. Herbert Williams, New York, Avon Books, 1976.
RESEARCH SOURCE: Wilt, Judith, "The Spinning Story: Gothic Motifs in Tender Is The Night," Fitzgerald/Hemingway Annual 1976, 79-95.

CRITICAL SYNOPSIS: A sophisticated and lighthearted spook caprice by the seer of the Jazz Age. Born at the age of seventy during the American Civil War, Benjamin Button is a curious case because he grows younger instead of older each year. Fitzgerald was sometimes given to Gothic pranks and horseplay. The critic, Edmund Wilson, in a piece entitled "A Weekend at Ellerslie," recalled after a houseparty weekend: "I later heard that Scott had waked up in the night and decided that he had not done justice to the possibilities of the Ellerslie ghost. He put a sheet over his head and invaded the Seldeses' room. Standing beside their bed, he began to groan in a way that he hoped was an improvement on the butler. But Gilbert started up from his sleep and gave a swipe with his arm at the sheet, which caught fire from a cigarette that the ghost was smoking inside his shroud."

137. The Five Fiends; or The Bender Hotel Horror in Kansas. Philadelphia: Old Franklin Publishing House, 1874.

CRITICAL SYNOPSIS: A 60 page dime novel Gothic western, the American equivalent of the English chapbook. The advertisement on the title page hawks the gory contents as a piece of authentic local history. "This family of fiends have for a long number of years been systematically murdering travellers who stopped at their hotel or store by a most singular method which has never been discovered until the killing of Dr. York of Kansas. This book contains full and startling details of their awful crimes. It is certain that they have murdered over one hundred people."

138. Fleming, May Agnes [Cousin May Carleton]. Victoria; or, The Heiress of Castle Cliffe. New York: Frederic A. Brady, 1862.

CRITICAL SYNOPSIS: A domestic Gothic using the familiar trappings of the orphan-become-heiress romance, but with a twist, since the heiress reverts to her humble status at the end. Victoria is the illegitimate daughter of Sir Roland Cliffe and the London actress, Vivea. Throughout childhood, a cloud shrouds both her identity and her parentage as she is raised in the household of the Weldemans whose own daughter, Barbara, bears a strange resemblance to Victoria. At sixteen, Victoria is transported to Castle Cliffe where she goes through the usual set of terrifying experiences reserved for maidens in Gothic fiction. In one of the better Gothic scenes, she is confronted by a spectral nun who tells her to beware, that she will be "thrust into the slime from which she has arisen," a prophecy which she finds pleasingly perplexing during her castle residence. Further explorations of the castle bring her into contact with mad Marguerite Shirley, a relative who predicts doom for Victoria as her wedding day and marriage to Sir Leicester Cliff approach. On the wedding day, the bridegroom fails to appear. Resuming her quest for the truth about her parentage, she is assisted by Mr. John Sweet who tells her that as a result of an exchange of infants she is Barbara Weldeman and Barbara Weldeman is the true Victoria. Now understanding the spectral nun's curse, she realizes that she has loved above her station and has no entitlement to the legacy of Castle Cliffe. The only honorable course is to join the mission of Florence Nightingale in the Crimea which Victoria-become-Barbara does with all the moral alacrity expected of the Victorian Gothic heroine. Although it lacks the scenes of domestic violence and connubial cruelty often associated with this type of "female" Gothic, the novel is a representative example of typical "female" Gothic reading fare in the mid-Nineteenth Century.

139. Francis, Mary O. [Margaret Blount]. Hallow-Ash Hall; A Story of a Haunted House. New York: Frederick A. Brady, 1864.

CRITICAL SYNOPSIS: An 80 page chapbook style horror story using the familiar Gothic trappings and settings. The Carolinian locale is well-suited to the horrid events of the tale which include the demands of a paternal ghost and a haunted chamber which is forbidden to the heroine. The long-lingering influence of Mrs. Radcliffe's maiden-centered Gothic is once again in evidence. An identical version of this Gothic was reissued by T.B. Peterson, Philadelphia, 1880, under the new title Clifford and the Actress; or, The Reigning Favorite. A Tale of Love, Passion, Hatred, and Revenge.

140. Freeman, Mary Elinor Wilkins. "A New England Nun." A New England Nun, and Other Stories. New York: Harper, 1891.

REPRINT EDITION: Irvine, CA, American Biography Service, 1988.
RESEARCH SOURCE: Hirsch, David H., "Subdued Meaning in 'A New England Nun,'" Studies in Short Fiction 2 (1965): 124-136.

CRITICAL SYNOPSIS: The horror here is of the subtle Jamesian variety since there are no terrible abbey confinements or external ghosts. The theme again bears a tinge of Hawthornesque melancholy and deals with self-imposed loneliness, self-inflicted spiritual death, and self-denial of what a Jamesian character might call "the lost stuff of consciousness." The "nun" is the reclusive Louisa Ellis who once pledged her love and life to Joe Dagget. But fifteen lonely years have passed while he made his fortune in Australia so that they might marry and she has grown ever fonder of spinsterdom and solitude while she awaited his return. In a sense, she falls in love with her seclusiveness in his long absence. She withdraws to her own private convent of the spirit, closes off all commerce with the heart, and devotes herself to herself even though she continues to honor her engagement to Joe in outward form after his return. He too has changed and now loves Lily Dyer. Neither character is willing to release the other from an empty obligation and loveless relationship. In the traditional monastic shocker, a maiden is held in the dungeons of the monastery by an evil-eyed monk bent on rape. The condition of horrid entrapment is much subtler here but Louisa's doom is no less horrifying. When Joe finally releases her from the marriage pledge, her heart undergoes a kind of transformation from human warmth to icy indifference to her own rejected humanity. The final sentences catch and modify one of Hawthorne's major moral horrors found in those characters who renounce their humaness or refuse to be human even at the price of their souls. "Louisa, all alone by herself that night, wept a little, she hardly knew why; but the next morning, on waking, she felt like a queen who, after fearing lest her domain be wrested away from her, sees it finally insured in her possession. Serenity and placid narrowness had become to her as the birthright itself."

141. _____. "The Hall Bedroom." The Wind in the Rose Bush, and Other Stories of the Supernatural. New York: Doubleday, Page, 1903.

REPRINT EDITION: The Supernatural Omnibus, ed. Montague Summers, London, Victor Gollancz, 1931.

CRITICAL SYNOPSIS: The dual structuring of the tale provides for two conflicting readings. Events concerning the disappearances from the hall bedroom of the boarding house are recollected from two quite opposite points of view. One point of view, that of the landlady who owns the house and eventual sells it to free herself of the hall bedroom and its unexplained terrors, suggests a variety of Gothic responses to these events including the orthodox reactions of unrelieved horror and shocked wonder. The other point of view, that of George Wheatcroft who has lived in the room and vanished from it leaving his journal behind, allows a non-Gothic reading of the events which runs sharply counter to fear, dismay, and horrified premonition. Because of the ambivalent presentation of these two sets of evidence, the reader can never be sure of the real nature and meaning of the supernatural experiences occurring in the hall bedroom. Wheatcroft's journal, for instance, recounts only pleasant if fantastic experiences while he lived in the room. He fell under the spell of a lovely landscape painting and was literally absorbed by it, passing into another dimension which turned out to be a pastoral and Edenic existence. The abortive last entry in his journal hints that the other side was so much more pleasant than this world that he decided to re-enter it voluntarily by way of the hall bedroom and never return. Who possesses the truth about the strange room and furthermore what is the true nature of the supernatural,--is it something malign under a benign disguise, or something benign under a malign disguise? The lasting power of the tale lies in such ambivalences.

142. _____. "Luella Miller." The Wind in the Rose Bush, and Other Stories of the Supernatural. New York: Doubleday, Page, 1903.

REPRINT EDITION: The Best Stories of Mary Wilkins Freeman, ed. Henry W. Lanier, Saint Clair Shores, MI, Scholarly Publications, 1971.

CRITICAL SYNOPSIS: A Jamesian sense of evil pervades this remarkable variation on the traditional vampire tale. Although there are no dripping fangs, gore-clotted corpses, or stakes driven through the heart at sunrise, the victims of the vampire in this story are just as numerous and just as dead. Luella Miller is a classic parasitic personality, a vampire of the spirit whose ordinary and mild-mannered temperament belies her sinister ability for attaching herself to other people and getting them to devote all of their energies to her while she reaps the rewards and does no work. Her husband, Erastus Miller, is an early victim of her psychic vampirism and leech-like character, as is her sister, Lily, who begins caring for Luella after her husband's death and expires within a year drained dry of all life force and emotional virility. This is the subtle pattern of vampire attack throughout the story as Luella is able to use her fraudulent helplessness and weakness to suck the life force from the souls of others. This odd case of spiritual vampirism is narrated by Lydia Anderson who is forced to allow at the end of the tale that there is neither any poetic justice nor any reduction in Luella's special brand of evil even after her death. At the conclusion the narrator is alarmed when she is shown a vision of Luella from beyond the grave. In the awful vision, the vampire appears at the head of a retinue of her victims--all those she had drained of spirit in life--who continue to serve her and submit to her after death. Luella Miller's vampirism is eternal. Although the conception of the psychic vampire is not new or unique to Freeman (see for example Dr. John Polidori's The Vampyre and Joseph Sheridan Le Fanu's Carmilla), Freeman's normalization of the foul creature imparts a new degree of horror to her rendering of the vampire myth.

143. _____. "The Shadows on the Wall." The Wind in the Rose Bush, and Other Stories of the Supernatural. New York: Doubleday, Page, 1903.

REPRINT EDITION: Who Knocks? Twenty Masterpieces of the Spectral for the Connoisseur, ed. August Derleth, New York, Rinehart, 1946.
RESEARCH SOURCE: Oaks, Susan, "The Haunting Will: The Ghost Stories of Mary Wilkins Freeman," Colby Library Quarterly 21 (1985): 208-220.

CRITICAL SYNOPSIS: A mood piece. The shadows are the restless spectres of a quarreling family who have hastened one another's deaths. Their outlines haunt the parlor walls of the family home. Wilkins often depicted destructive domestic hatred in spectral terms in her single collection of supernatural stories.

144. _____. "The Southwest Chamber." The Wind in the Rose Bush, and Other Stories of the Supernatural. New York: Doubleday, Page, 1903.

REPRINT EDITION: The Fireside Book of Ghost Stories, ed. Edward Wagenknecht, Indianapolis, IN, Bobbs-Merrill, 1947.

CRITICAL SYNOPSIS: A well-made domestic Gothic tale that makes excellent use of a standard figure of the haunted castle or abbey, the spectre-in-residence. The spectre in this case refuses to vacate the chamber where she died before her house passed to her nieces, Amanda and Sophia Gill, by inheritance. The old lady had developed a desperate hatred for her sister and the house with the haunted chamber becomes something of a burden and punishment upon her sister's children. They rent out the room and try to play down the terror associated with the Southwest Chamber but the stubborn ghost keeps making its presence felt. A roomer is the victim of an odd nocturnal attack and the local minister, who is called in to assuage the spirit, is also thwarted by the spectre. In a well-timed climax, the spectre-in-residence asserts its permanent right to remain in the chamber by manifesting itself in a mirror to Sophia Gill, who is then compelled to acknowledge the ghost's rights to occupancy. Both the action and title of Freeman's story demonstrate her debt to one type of Gothic novel, the sealed or perilous apartment and its attendant spectre, a category of Gothic fiction dating back to the work of Mrs. Radcliffe and originating in the forbidden chamber device of Mrs. Radcliffe's predecessor, Clara Reeve, in The Old English Baron (1777).

145. _____. "The Vacant Lot." The Wind in the Rose Bush, and Other Stories of the Supernatural. New York: Doubleday, Page, 1903.

REPRINT EDITION: The Best Stories of Mary Wilkins Freeman, ed. Henry W. Lanier, Saint Clair Shores, MI, Scholarly Publications, 1971.
RESEARCH SOURCE: Diomedi, Claudette A., "Mary Wilkins Freeman and the Romance-Novel Tradition," Dissertation Abstracts International 31 (1972): 4155A-4156A (University of Maryland).

CRITICAL SYNOPSIS: Gothic acoustics and unexplained supernatural events mark this tale of inescapable family guilt. Like Hawthorne's Pynchons (see The House of the Seven Gables, 200), the Townsends have settled near Boston in a fine mansion, but it is a house overshadowed by ancestral crime and cruelty. The vacant lot next to the house is inhabited by nebulous figures, strange sounds, and eerie lights. These ghosts of the Townsend past have apparently stalked the family to its new home and are living in the Gothic remains of a destroyed house which once stood on the vacant lot. At least, the murky outlines of a ghostly house can be seen on the vacant lot by night. Wilkins's horror art is not designed to startle or terrify. Instead, she uses Gothic situations and sinister moods to evoke an atmosphere of what H.P. Lovecraft called "uncanny tragedy."

146. _____. "The Wind in the Rose Bush." The Wind in the Rose Bush, and Other Stories of the Supernatural. New York: Doubleday, Page, 1903.

REPRINT EDITION: The Best Stories of Mary Wilkins Freeman, ed. Henry W. Lanier, Saint Clair Shores, MI, Scholarly Publications, 1971.
RESEARCH SOURCES: Bendixen, Alfred, The Wind in the Rose Bush and Other Stories, Chicago, Academy Chicago, 1986; Westbrook, Perry D., Mary Wilkins Freeman, New York, Twayne, 1967.

CRITICAL SYNOPSIS: Another gentle chilling mood piece. Her style can occasionally remind the reader of the somberness of Hawthorne in such pieces as "Fancy's Show Box," "Snowflakes," and "The Sister Years." The main character, Rebecca, is anxious to see the little girl, Agnes, again. But the parents of the child find ways of delaying the reunion. Meanwhile, Alice catches a glimpse of Agnes outside the window and there are other unexplained sightings

as well. On a windless day, a rosebush nevertheless shakes violently and other supernatural stirrings of nature are felt and
heard. The revelation that little Agnes had perished of neglect
ends the story and also terminates Rebecca's naive assumptions
about the natural kindness of parents. Like Hawthorne's tales,
Freeman's ghostly sketches of New England life usually contain a
somber moral.

147. Freneau, Philip. "The House of Night." The Poems of Philip Freneau.
Written Chiefly During the Late War. Philadelphia: Francis Bailey,
1786.

REPRINT EDITION: Poems of Freneau, ed. Harry Hayden Clark, New
York, Hafner Publishing, 1960.
RESEARCH SOURCES: Bowden, Mary Weatherspoon, Philip Freneau, Boston, Twayne, 1976; Leary, Lewis, "The Dream Visions of Philip Freneau," Early American Literature 11 (1976): 156-173.

CRITICAL SYNOPSIS: Freneau's Gothic verse was first published in
The United States Magazine for August, 1779. The poem is a nightmare excursion in 136 quatrains containing a splendid confluence
of Gothic imagery and scenery. Like a charnel wanderer in a graveyard poem by Gray, Thomas Warton, or Edward Young in one of the
Night Thoughts, Freneau's Gothic wanderer (an undertaker) enters
the House of Night and beholds all of the resplendent horrors of
death's abode. He converses with Death himself who lies dying in
his own dark palace as he ponders a suitable epitaph for himself.
The wanderer undertakes to assist Death in this task, an act which
seems to hasten Death's death. The poem concludes with the funeral
of Death and a gloomy meditation on the certainties of the grave
and the vanity of human pomp. In theme, this is a standard and un-
distinguished graveyard poem by an American poet, but in imagery,
it holds some superior flights of the Gothic imagination. The memorable picture of Death upon his deathbed, for example, suggests
that Freneau had studied various Gothic death scenes for inspiration and had decided to give the poem his own version of the
ghastliest of deaths. The scene is conceived as a Gothic encounter
when Death faces the guest in the House of Night: "Turning to view
the object from whence it came,/My frighted eyes a horrid form
survey'd;/Fancy, I own thy power--Death on the couch,/With flesh-
less limbs, at rueful length was laid./Around his bed, by dull
flambeaux' glare,/I saw pale phantoms--Rage to madness vext,/Wan,
wasting grief, and ever musing care,/Distressful pain, and poverty
perplext./Sad was his countenance, where only bones were seen,/And
eyes sunk in their sockets, dark and low,/And teeth, that only
show'd themselves to grin."

148. Frost, Robert. "The Witch of Coös." New Hampshire: A Poem with Notes
and Grace Notes. New York: Henry Holt, 1923.

REPRINT EDITION: A Pocket Book of Robert Frost's Poems, intro.
Louis Untermeyer, New York, Washington Square Press, 1969.
RESEARCH SOURCES: Dedinger, Lloyd N., "The Ghoul-Haunted Woodland
of Robert Frost," South Atlantic Bulletin 38 (1973): 87-94; Le-
gris, Maurice, "The Joyful Killer of 'The Witch of Coös,'" Studies
in the Humanities (Indiana, PA) 9 number 1 (1981): 30-32; Marcus,
Mordecai, "The Whole Pattern of Robert Frost's 'Two Witches': Con-
trasting Psycho-Sexual Modes," Literature & Psychology 26 (1976):
69-78.

CRITICAL SYNOPSIS: Some critics have called Robert Frost a "poet of terror" and this judgement seems undeniably true of the voice heard in such poems as "Desert Places" and "Design" in which pastoral beauty gives way to Gothic horror. But Frost's most direct connection with an American Gothic tradition is to be seen in "The Witch of Coös," a New Hampshire shocker. The spine chiller consists of a dialogue within a monologue. The narrator pauses to spend an evening with a mother and son at their lonely farmstead. The mother turns out to be a witch and her son, her lifelong companion if not her willing familiar. But this witch, it would seem, is more haunted than haunting, beset as she is by a household problem, an animated skeleton barricaded in the attic where it has been a prisoner for more than forty years. Forty years before, it broke loose from its grave in the cellar and tried to escape from the house, but it was tricked into the attic where the door was nailed shut by the witch's husband, Toffile Lajway. "Where it wants to get is back into the cellar, where it came from. It left the cellar forty years ago and carried itself like a pile of dishes up one flight from the cellar to the kitchen, another from the kitchen to the bedroom, another from the bedroom to the attic." Although the bones do not walk nightly as they certainly would in an English shilling shocker, their presence in the attic has certainly unhinged the old witch and perhaps driven her to hallucinate the supernatural incidents she relates to the guest. One homely but hair-raising Gothic scene is the witch's recollection of how she had flung open the door to find the skeleton poised at the cellar threshold. The description here is unadulterated Gothic in the old style of the English Schauerroman or shudder novel: "A tongue of fire flashed out and licked along the upper teeth. Smoke rolled inside the sockets of his eyes." In utter panic, she "struck the hand off brittle on the floor, and fell back from him on the floor myself." At the conclusion of the narrative, when the son remarks "We never could find out whose bones they were," his witch mother informs him in a confessional outburst that "They were a man's his father killed for me. I mean a man he killed instead of me." Mother and son have borne the homicidal secret--the skeleton in their closet--for many years, but only the mother heard and touched those mobile bones on the night of its ghastly ascent from the cellar. Hence, the ghostly recital ends on a cryptic note of horrible truth blurted out to a stranger at long last; the guest departs in a dual mood of sympathy and awe. Frost's shrewd assemblage and manipulation of the Gothic parts yields a superb poem of terror which goes deeply to the center of a persistent theme in Frost's work, an acquaintance with the night.

149. Gaddis, William. Carpenter's Gothic. Baltimore, MD: Viking, 1985.

REPRINT EDITION: Baltimore, Penguin, 1986.
RESEARCH SOURCE: Comnes, Gregory A. Jr., "William Gaddis and the Cosmological Novel," Dissertation Abstracts International, 48 (19-87): 126A (Claremont Graduate School).

CRITICAL SYNOPSIS: The novel is quite a gripping modernization of a standard Gothic situation wherein the husband plots to obtain the wife's inheritance and uses Gothic means to reach his nefarious goals. The scheming husband is the Viet Nam War veteran, Paul Booth, who is obsessed with founding a financial empire in Africa and the near east. To these ends, he schemes to frighten his wife out of her inheritance and pursues his scheme by renting a Victorian mansion on the banks of the Hudson. The great house has the

usual sinister history and is now the property of an alcoholic ge-
ologist. Carpenter's Gothic, that style of ornamentation whereby
wood is designed to imitate the stone tracery of medieval buildings, comes into full play in alarming the wife. The reviewer for
The New York Times Book Review (July, 1985) praised this novel as
yet another successful foray into Gothicism by a writer who has
dealt in Gothics on previous occasions. "It is an unholy landmark
of a novel, an extra turret added on to the ample, ingenious, au-
dacious Gothic mansion William Gaddis has been slowly building in
American letters."

150. Garland, Hamlin. The Tyranny of the Dark. London: Harper, 1905.

REPRINT EDITION: The Collected Works of Hamlin Garland, Irvine,
CA, American Biography Service, 1988.
RESEARCH SOURCE: Kaye, Francis W., "Hamlin Garland: A Closer Look
at the Later Fiction," North Dakota Quarterly 43 number 3 (1975):
45-56.

CRITICAL SYNOPSIS: A novel of perverse spiritualism bordering on
Gothic moods and themes. The central situation concerns the special psychic powers of Viola Lambert who is highly sensitive to
the spirit world and can communicate with the other side. Her tal-
ented extrasensory consciousness is exploited by her egotistical
parents who use or abuse Viola in their desire to communicate with
the dead. Because of her unusual psychic powers, Viola is denied
childhood, companionship, and love by her father and mother and
frequently confined to the darkness of her chamber for many hours.
Garland's foray into the conditions of Gothic romance is not to be
understood as a critique of spiritualism about which he remained
ambiguous. Rather, the novel repeats in spiritualistic terms a
prime crisis of earlier Gothic fiction, the confinement to the
dark and harassment of an innocent young woman with evil emanating
from her close relatives. Garland's other writings have attracted
generous criticism, but this unusual novel of danger and distress
has been almost totally ignored. Studying it gives Garland a niche
in the American Gothic tradition.

151. Gerould, Katharine Fullerton. "Louquier's Third Act." Valiant Dust.
New York: Scribner's, 1922.

CRITICAL SYNOPSIS: Along with another story, "Belshazzar's Letter," the above tale concerns the losing struggle of human beings
with superior psychic forces. The retired actor, Louquier, living
in solitude and hoping to end his days tranquilly, is attacked by
some aggressive, malign, and invisible force he can neither name
nor stave off. In the losing struggle, the actor succumbs to violence and plays his last and least coveted role.

152. Gilman, Charlotte Perkins. "The Giant Wistaria." New England Magazine. June, 1891.

CRITICAL SYNOPSIS: Appears to derive its heroine, a Puritan adul-
tress, from the character of Hester Prynne in Hawthorne's The
Scarlet Letter (see 197). Despotic parents, a favorite character
type for Gilman, force her into a loveless marriage and residence
in a lonely mansion represented by the gloomy overhang of the giant wisteria. After her death, the ghost of the young mother escapes from this house of confinement and horror.

153. _____. "The Yellow Wallpaper". Boston: Small, Maynard, 1899.

REPRINT EDITION: Eight Strange Tales, ed. Victor Ghidalia, Greenwich, CT, Fawcett Publications, 1972.
RESEARCH SOURCE: Fleenor, Juliann E., "The Gothic Prism: Charlotte Perkins Gilman's Gothic Stories and Her Autobiography," The Female Gothic, Montreal, Eden Press, 1983, pp.227-241.

CRITICAL SYNOPSIS: This much-anthologized tale was first published in The New England Magazine for 1892. Central to the story is the traditional horror motif of live burial, but presented in figurative and symbolic rather than literal terms. The tale is narrated in the form of extracts from a secret journal kept by an unnamed mother who has been brought by her physician husband to a country house to recuperate from a severe nervous disorder following the birth of her child. So severe are her depression and anxiety that the symptoms of a peculiar condition known as post partum depression can be inferred. Conveyed to the nursery in the upper floors of the mansion, she becomes the "victim" of an over-solicitous and over-loving family and particularly of her practical and paternalistic husband, John. She is permitted to do nothing but rest and to stare at the four walls which are papered with hideous labyrinthine patterns in decayed yellow. Since she is not allowed to write, she must conceal her journal upon the approach of John and other relatives who have removed her child and now constantly watch over her. With consummate skill, Gilman has converted and psychologized the classic Gothic ordeal of the menaced maiden sealed up within a chamber of horrors and also given us a modern version of a woman killed with kindness. In effect, she is denied a self. As she steadily withdraws into a fantasy life, the awful paper becomes increasingly animated and seemingly contains some shadowy female form, a figure behind the wallpaper which is struggling to get out. Reading the paper more deeply even as she becomes progressively insane, she comes to understand that the woman buried beneath the disgusting patterns of the wallpaper is herself, a creative being trying to escape from the stale patterns imposed upon her life. At the tale's climax, the female prisoner involves herself directly and defiantly with the entrapped woman by attacking the wallpaper and tearing it away. She also bites the bed, that symbol of marital servitude and torment, and as her unperceiving husband watches in horror, she slips into the serenity of madness. She locks the room from within, throws the key into the garden, and begins to crawl along the walls on all fours even creeping over the body of her fainted husband in her endless circuit. This is domestic Gothic, but rendered in a horrifying new key. Poe's Madeline Usher had clawed her way out of a copper sheathed sarcophagus, but Gilman's madwoman in the attic asserts her identity against the world of male authority by going mad. When she says calmly to the horrified John, "I've got out at last in spite of you and Jane," she means that she is truly disinterred --but at an awful price.

154. _____. Unpunished. unpublished novel.

CRITICAL SYNOPSIS: A detective novel with numerous horror elements and some bold departures from the standard formula. The victimizer and victim is the sadistic and callous Wade Vaughn, a character who might have been at home in many Gothic novels since he is "the most tyrannical male and unqualified villain in the Gilman canon." His bad deeds include driving his wife to suicide and the sexual

abuse of his sister-in-law, Jacqueline Warner. Thus, his murder
astounds no one, including the two detectives who begin to piece
together the evidence, Jim and Bessie Hunt. The manner of the
killing is curious, almost a parody of the bizarre crime motif.
Vaughn's corpse shows signs of poisoning and bludgeoning. Additionally, he has been shot in the head and there are cord marks on
his throat from strangulation. Either the murder was committed in
group style, or the killer made sure of his crime in four posi-
tively certain stages. All of these clues, however, are false
leads. At the coroner's inquest, testimony is offered to show that
no murder had occurred after all since the direct and only cause
of death was cardiac arrest. The final and highly satisfactory
twist is offered when the Hunts learn that the abused sister-in-
law, the "unpunished" Jacqueline Warner, had performed a spectral
masquerade by appearing to Vaughn in the dead of night in the
death mask of her sister. Fright, not guilt, had induced the heart
attack. Plenty of strong Gothic detail fills the narrative and the
portrait of Wade dates back to the sexual evil of the early Gothic
villains of Mrs. Radcliffe and Monk Lewis.

155.　Glasgow, Ellen. "The Shadowy Third." The Shadowy Third and Other
Stories. Garden City, NY: Doubleday, Page, 1923.

REPRINT EDITION: Beware After Dark! The World's Most Stupendous
Tales of Mystery, Horror, Thrills, and Terror, ed. T. Everett Har-
ré, London, Macaulay, 1929,

CRITICAL SYNOPSIS: This tidy tale of spectral revenge should be
compared with the situation of the wife in Charlotte Perkins Gilman's "The Yellow Wallpaper." (see 153) A wealthy young physician
employs a nurse to assist him in a scheme to drive her insane in
order that they may enjoy her inheritance. Although severely persecuted, the wife maintains her grip on her mind but has periodic
visitations from her dead child. Eventually, the phantom child intervenes to expose the husband's conspiracy. The tale is narrated
in a sophisticated manner so as to be both persuasive and chilling. Although not usually considered a supernaturalist, this story
and several others in the collection, notably the tale "Whispering
Leaves" in which young Pelham is safeguarded from theatening relatives by an apparitional black mammy, show Glasgow's excellent
knowledge of the Gothic tradition and her ability to reset the
Gothic in local colors.

156.　Gorman, Herbert S. The Place Called Dagon. New York: Doran, 1927.

CRITICAL SYNOPSIS: A novel of witchcraft and the sabbat set in the
Berkshires. Dr. Dreeme, an idealistic man with little or no experience of evil, comes to the village of Marlborough where he comes
into contact with the strange and solitary Westcott family. Their
ancestry extends back to the witches of Salem whose evil remains
are contained in a collective burial site which also serves for
celebrations of the sabbat. The witch cemetery is a place called
Dagon where the elder Westcott presides over black rites and is
even rumored to have performed human sacrifice. Investigating
these rumors, Dr. Dreeme learns that a young woman is to be sacri-
ficed to Satan by the warlock and his crew. Like Hawthorne's Young
Goodman Brown before him (see 196), he attends the Sabbat and sees
evil at its height, but with quite different results. While the
novel has some fine sequences of terror and some very accurate
devil lore, the ending is notably weak. Westcott is killed and the

devil cult which had infected almost the entire community immediately dies out.

157. Goyen, William. The House of Breath. New York: Random House, 1949.

REPRINT EDITIONS: New York, Persea Books, 1986.

CRITICAL SYNOPSIS: In its lyric style and in its evocation of the
American Gothic theme of loneliness, the novel is highly reminiscent of Sherwood Anderson's Winesburg Ohio (see 014). This is a
book of interwoven moods and a plotless reverie delivered by several nostalgic narrators. The prime voice is that of Christie
Ganchion who is entrapped within memories of the town of Charity,
Texas, and imprisoned still more completely within the specific
memory of the "house founded on a fragile web of breath." Other
remembering characters too are haunted by the spectres of memory
and morbid regret which overwhelm them in Proustian waves of sadness, loss, and spiritual death. Without any reliance on an external story, the novel achieves its ends and occasionally attains
dark poetic beauty through its elegiac flights and falls. Staring
at a spider, Ganchion remembers and returns to the house of breath
by way of his epitaphic imagination. "Some appetite waits and
lurks in the world, you remark; it is some great hunger, insect
and rodent and decay hunger. This seems suddenly to be a law of
the universe. Insect, mold, rat, rust, death--all wait for and get
the human plunder in the end to carry the carrion away....The dead
of this house lie fastened in what web stretched over what blue
kingdom?--bits of wings and antennae, all debris." Like Anderson's
Winesburg or Edgar Lee Masters's Spoon River Anthology (1915), the
Gothicism of Goyen's book strikes a deeper chord of terror that
resounds in the loneliness of the soul.

158. Grau, Shirley Ann. The Black Prince, and Other Stories. New York:
Alfred A. Knopf, 1954.

REPRINT EDITION: 3 by 3: Masterworks of the Southern Gothic, ed.
Lewis P. Simpson, Atlanta, Peachtree Press, 1985.
RESEARCH SOURCES: Rose, Alan H., Demonic Vision: Racial Fantasy
and Southern Fiction, Hamden, CT, Archon, 1976; Schlueter, Paul,
Shirley Ann Grau, Boston, Twayne, 1981.

CRITICAL SYNOPSIS: "The Black Prince" is the second Gothic fable
in a collection of Gothic fables of identity. Two other pieces,
"Miss Yellow Eyes" and "The Way of a Man," contain Gothic moments
and characters. The epigraph for "The Black Prince," "How art thou
fallen from heaven, O Lucifer, son of the morning!" (Isaiah 14:12)
hints that the tale will involve a Satan figure and a demonic
encounter. Alberta Lucy and Maggie Mary Evans have just such an
encounter when Stanley Albert Thompson, the prince of darkness,
enters their lives. Thompson can apparently materialize and dema-
terialize, can turn candle wax into silver coins, and has many
other cabalistic qualities. Although she recognizes him to be
evil, Alberta Lucy is tempted by the fiend from whom she receives
endless supplies of silver. Resenting the devil's interference in
his love affair, Willie, a bar owner, casts a silver bullet from
Thompson's coins, then shoots the fiend in the chest. But the devil is not destroyed as his eyes take on a silver glint and he
calmly walks away taking Alberta Lucy with him. The pair now pass
into local legend and are sometimes seen when barns, beginning
with Willie's barn, burn suspiciously or when crops go bad. Speak-

ing of a fellow southern Gothicist, Flannery O'Connor, Grau has said, "You can get so turned around in your Gothic trappings that you lose sight of where you are." Grau's own Gothic, therefore, strives to define itself as a mood rather than a mode, a touch rather than a heavy application.

159. Gregory, Franklin. The White Wolf. New York: Random House, 1941.

CRITICAL SYNOPSIS: A novel of lycanthropy set in the Pennsylvania Dutch region. The family of Pierre de Camp-d'Avesnes have settled here hoping to begin life anew and rid themselves of the strain of werewolfery which extends back to their European ancestor, Hugues d'Avesnes. But savage symptoms begin to show up in one of the daughters of the household, Sara, whose whereabouts are often unaccounted for and whose lupine tendencies are a source of worry to her lover, David Trent. There are rumors of midnight peregrinations and child molestation and murder and there are also several spottings of a great white wolf in the nearby countryside. When a lucky photograph of this strange beast is taken and developed, the print reveals the features of Sara. While there are some good lonely landscapes and while the lupine lore follows the traditions of lycanthropy with reasonable accuracy, the novel begins too turgidly and moves too slowly to be regarded as a shocking success.

160. Grubb, Davis. "One Foot in the Grave." Twelve Tales of Suspense and the Supernatural. New York: Charles Scribner's Sons, 1964.

CRITICAL SYNOPSIS: The story was featured in Weird Tales in 1948. The risible quality of the title carries over into the sinister comedy of the piece when the cliché literally turns out to be true. Henry's severed foot is indeed in the grave, having been buried before the rest of him after an industrial accident which dismembered him. The amputated limb which insists upon a life of its own and behaves independently of its former body is hardly a new premise upon which to build a Gothic burlesque. Dickens had introduced a variation on the theme in the willful gyrations of Silas Wegg's wooden leg in Our Mutual Friend (1865). One could almost say that there is Gothic mischief afoot throughout the story since the restless member refuses to stay buried even though it had been interred with full and solemn ritual. Although the tone and situation are far too farcical to sustain a mood of fear, this is a clever little Gothic fillip.

161. Hall, Leland Boylston. Sinister House. Boston: Houghton Mifflin, 19-19.

CRITICAL SYNOPSIS: The reviewer in The Dial compared the Gothicism of the novel to the brooding atmosphere of James's The Turn of the Screw (see 245) and there are striking similarities. The modern, model town of Fosby has one old and sinister house, a sort of defiant architectural symbol of a past that resists modernization and mechanization. The sinister house is loathed by the narrator, Pierre Smith, but is almost religiously revered by its tenants, the Griers. Secretly, the Griers have taken up residence in the house to lay claim to the inheritance of its dead owners. Soon Julia Grier is beset by the spectre in residence who drives her into an admission of their guilty motives. When the Griers confess their selfish designs, the spectre goes away. Although this tidy Gothic would seem to support some heavy moral themes concerning the purification of the generations, its main business was to

amuse or divert the reader, not to erect a stern moral parable in
the manner of Hawthorne. Hall's novel enjoyed some success as a
typical book club Gothic.

162. Halyard, Harry. The Chieftain of Churubusco; or, The Spectre of the
Cathedral, A Romance of the Mexican War. Boston: F. Gleason, 18-
48.

CRITICAL SYNOPSIS: A 100 page dime novel Gothic printed in double
columns and illustrated by several gruesome woodcuts. The historical background of "our romantic and eventful story" is General
Winfield Scott's campaigns against Puebla and Churubusco in August
1847. As is common with many Gothic chapbooks, there are two
plots, a love story and a terror story, ingeniously spliced on the
final page of the romance. The love story graphs the misfortunes
and separations of the young American officer, Captain Charles
Warren of Scott's command, and the Mexican beauty, Lauretta Vare-
re. The mysterious Chieftain of Churubusco operates under the
name, Mazarra, for most of the tale with his real identity with-
held until the final page of resolutions, dispensations, and nup-
tials. The Gothic segments of the narrative concentrate on the
sufferings and alarms of Lauretta and her servant, the blind girl,
Vanilla Canalzo. The spectre of Churubusco Cathedral, "a glimpse
of white mantle seen through the deep gloom of the charnel house,"
makes frequent appearances but is less terrifying than pathetic
and moves mechanically toward the disclosure of the secrets of
story in an inset chapter entitled "The Spectre's History." A single sample of dialogue will suggest the level of the entire dime
shocker. Upon first encountering the spectre, we hear Lauretta exclaim "'Good heavens, Vanilla,' as she gave over her frantic attempts to force a passage to the church above. 'What can be the
meaning of all this? I will scream for help' burst Lauretta who
then uttered a loud, terrific shriek which was then answered by
its own echoes." To counter the Gothic maiden who is required to
scream on cue, the chapbooker brought a Yankee skeptic into the
Cathedral catacombs, Mr. Solomon Snubbins of Waldurburrur, Maine.
It is the gropings and investigations of Snubbins which eventually
unmasks the identity of the spectre who is no spectre at all but
the young woman, Annette Clayton, who had been abducted in Texas
and thrust into a Mexican nunnery. All that seemed supernatural
had been the result of her masquerade. An American soldier lover
is quickly found for Annette and the romance ends with a triple
nuptial made even more triumphant by General Scott's capture of
Mexico City. This type of throwaway Gothic was a close relative of
the Victorian penny dreadful and massively marketed by the house
of Beadle and Adams or cheap publishers such as Gleason for quick
consumption and tawdry thrill. Halyard is a typical supplier of
such cheap horrors and is writing to fill the publisher's a speci-
fied page quota.

163. _____. The Haunted Bride; or, The Witch of Gallows Hill, A Romance of Olden Time. Boston: F. Gleason, 1848.

CRITICAL SYNOPSIS: A 100 page chapbook style historical Gothic
dealing with the Salem witchcraft panic. In the usual manner of
Gothified history, the short novel mingles actuality with violent
fantasy. The sanguinary and sensational presentation of the events
of 1691-1692 should be compared against Hawthorne's less direct
Gothicism in his handling of witchcraft themes in such tales as
"The Hollow of the Three Hills." (see 182) Halyard's witch may be

based on Martha Carrier, alluded to by Cotton Mather as "that rampant hag and queen of hell" and executed by hanging on Gallows Hill on August 19, 1692.

164. Harper, Vincent. The Mortgage on the Brain. New York: Doubleday, 1905.

RESEARCH SOURCE: Kerr, Howard, Mediums and Spirit-Rappers and Roaring Radicals: Spiritualism in American Literature, 1850-1900, Urbana, IL, Illinois UP, 1972.

CRITICAL SYNOPSIS: A novel of villainous mesmerism, dual personality, and the perils of spiritualism. Psychic possession and mind control for perverted purposes are American Gothic themes extending back to the early terror of Charles Brockden Brown. The mystical sciences such as animal magnetism and hypnotism became something like substitute religions or faiths for certain groups in the late nineteenth century. The mesmeric glance and the all powerful will that could paralyze the moral sense of a victim were apt subjects for the American Gothicist. Harper's novel should be compared with another contemporaneous treatment of psychological perversion, Garland's The Tyranny of the Dark (see 150).

165. Harris, George Washington. "Dad's Dog-School." Sut Lovingood. Yarns Spun by a "Nat'ral Born Durn'd Fool." Warped and Wove for Public Wear. New York: Dick & Fitzgerald, 1867.

REPRINT EDITIONS: Sut Lovingood, ed. Brom Weber, New York, Grove Press, 1954; ed. M. Thomas Inge, New Haven, CT, New College and University Press, 1966.
RESEARCH SOURCES: Fisher, Benjamin Franklin IV, "George Washington Harris and Supernaturalism," Publications of the Mississippi Philological Association 1 (1982): 18-23; Rickels, Milton, "The Imagery of George Washington Harris," American Literature 31 (1959): 173-187; Wilson, Edmund, "Poisoned!" New Yorker 36 (1955): 150-154.

CRITICAL SYNOPSIS: Many of the comic sketches of Mark Twain's contemporary folklorist and southwestern humorist, G.W. Harris, exhibit features of the American Gothic nightmare. Beneath their homespun wit and Tennessee mountain dialect, the demonic, grotesque, sadistic, and morally demented tone and tendencies of southern American Gothic are all-too-audible. The themes of hatred, family disorder, and fundamental human ugliness were pointed out by Edmund Wilson. Others have noted strong links with the Gothic of Faulkner and Flannery O'Connor in Harris's gruesome humor and emphasis on natural and unnatural human brutality. In the Sut Lovingood sketch, "Dad's Dog-School," the father has himself sewn up in the bloody hide of a freshly slaughtered bull to demonstrate to his son how a dog may be taught how to bite and hang on viciously when properly instructed, a lesson in conditioned cruelty which backfires on the teacher. Strange and malign supernatural events are the basis for several other folklore and local color pieces. "'Hark from the Tomb' Story" uses Gothic acoustics. A story published in The Chattanooga Daily American Union for October 31, 1867, "Saul Spradlin's Ghost," solves the problem for Halloween readers of how to exorcise a pesky family spook. As in the Gothic work of Ambrose Bierce, humor and horror are so intertwined in Harris's vision of life as to be inseparable.

166. Harris, Joel Chandler. "A Ghost Story." <u>Nights with Uncle Remus</u>. Boston and New York: Houghton, Mifflin, 1881.

REPRINT EDITION: <u>American Ghost Stories</u>, ed. C. Armitage Harper, Boston, Houghton, Mifflin, 1928; Philadelphia, Century Bookbindery, 1982.

CRITICAL SYNOPSIS: The ghost story is recited by 'Tildy who craftily plays upon the old folk practice of placing coins on the eyelids of the dead "fer to hol' um down." A man takes a terrible risk when he steals this eye money ("roun' shiny silver dollars") from a dead woman's eyelids. When the wronged ghost returns to retrieve the coins, the thief's own eyes grow large with terror. The idea of a supernatural payback is carried out with great skill and appropriate gestures. "'I want my money! Oh, gim me my money!' ...As she reached this climax, 'Tildy sprang at Daddy Jack and seized him, and for a few moments there was considerable confusion in the corner." One other "Night" successfully mixes folk and Gothic elements, the tale "Spirits Seen and Unseen."

167. Harte, Francis Brett. <u>Gabriel Conroy</u>. Hartford, CT: American Publishing, 1876; Boston: Houghton, Mifflin, 1876.

REPRINT EDITIONS: New York, Irvington Publishers, 1970.

CRITICAL SYNOPSIS: Unexpectedly, the large canon of stories by the western regionalist, Bret Harte, contains a number of examples of the pure tale of terror as well as ghostly pieces with a satiric twist. Parts of his novel of high adventure, Gabriel Conroy, might be called "Gold Rush Gothic" in tone and movement. There are episodes of cannibalism, murders, savage lynchings, hair breadth escapes by night, and a sensational trial scene. The plot is a tangle of love, loyalty, villainy, and betrayal all brought to a dénouement in the earthquake scene at the end. The novel's violent theatrics, however, are weakened by the stereotyped characters who are somewhat like a cast of Dickens's London eccentrics given western drawls and moved to San Francisco. The desperado, Jack Hamlin, is the same character as every other gambler, freebooter, and sluice robber in Harte's work. The soldier-of-fortune, Colonel Starbottle, is amusing and exotic only within the limits of his stereotype, and the thick witted Gabriel Conroy disappoints even as an anti-hero. Harte would exhibit better control of Gothic moods and circumstances in his short fiction, some of which employs a traditional English Gothic setting as in the slick little comedy of horror, "The Ghosts of Stuckeley Castle" (see 169).

168. _____. "A Ghost of the Sierras." <u>Drift from Two Shores</u>. Boston: Houghton, Osgood, 1878.

REPRINT EDITION: <u>Drift from Two Shores</u>, Salem, NH, Ayer Publishers, 1973.

CRITICAL SYNOPSIS: A mining camp ghost story capped by a twist. The teller of the story and his audience are lying on their backs in a grove of pines. The Doctor, who has "some skill as a raconteur," regales the other miners with the tale of the Cave City ghost, the murdered inhabitant of a haunted cabin. Following the murder, an old prospector down on his luck had taken up residence in the cabin with his only companion, a great old yellow dog, but the dog had seen something on the threshold and had taken to the hills "and neither the threats nor cajoleries of his master could ever make him enter the cabin again." The Doctor himself had come upon the haunted cabin and heard for himself the strange noises and weird groans. He had also seen the widening red pool of human blood on the door sill which had driven the dog mad. Throughout the telling of the story the mining party's Mexican vaquero, Juan Ramirez, has been growing more and more nervous. At the Doctor's mention of blood, he suddenly makes a guilty dash for safety thus revealing himself to be the murderer. The Doctor, pistol blazing, interrupts his story to pursue the man responsible for the ghost of the sierras. "Was it the murdered man's ghost, Doctor?" we all panted in one quick breath. "Ghost be damned! No. But in that Mexican vaquero--that cursed Juan Ramirez, I saw and shot at his murderer." The terminal twist with its strained frontier morality defaces an otherwise promising ghost story which lacks an ending of its own.

169. _____. "The Ghosts of Stuckeley Castle." Colonel Starbottle's Client, and Some Other People. New York: Houghton, Mifflin, 1892.

REPRINT EDITION: Colonel Starbottle's Client, Salem, NH, Ayer Publishers, 1970.

CRITICAL SYNOPSIS: A clever spoof of that most horrific of Gothic ordeals, the night spent alone within a haunted castle. The first author in the Gothic tradition to make good use of the situation was Clara Reeve in The Old English Baron (1777), an early Gothic in which young Edmund Twyford subjects himself to the ordeal of the fatal chamber within Lovel Castle. Stuckeley Castle is well stocked with all of the mandatory equipment for such an experience. It has forbidden chambers, shadowy turrets, mysterious sounds, and a history of horrible events extending back to Roman times. As the narrator is quick to point out, "It was rich in a real and spiritual estate of tapestries, paintings, armor, legends and ghosts," adding satirically that "Everything the poet could wish for, and indeed some things that decent prose might have wished out of it, were there." Seeking a Gothic thrill, the "Western Barbarian" (presumably one of those crude Americans) receives permission of the present owner to spend Christmas eve alone within Stuckeley Castle. While wandering through the portrait gallery, the Barbarian is seized by a zany idea. Why not "try on a certain breastplate and steel cap that hung over an oaken settle?" Immediately upon doing so, the doors of the gallery fly open and a troop of ghosts "in the habiliments of a bygone age" come filing in. So far, events have adhered to the schedule of terror set forth in Gothic novels of this sort. But something is quite wrong with these ghosts of Stuckeley Castle, for they are all spectral tourists who are being given an excursion through the Castle by a "ghostly Cicerone" who points out all of the building's modern improvements down to the most recently installed electrical fixture. One of the ghostly tourists finds and puts on the Barbarian's discarded hat and the deed snaps the dream and ends his absurd vision. Dining the next day at Audley Friars, the Barbarian is informed by his host that two girls had gone into the Castle the night before "to give you a start of some kind...but by Jove, they got the biggest kind of fright themselves, for they declare that something dreadful in armor was sitting in the gallery." The Barbarian's discreet denial of the existence of the Stuckeley Castle ghosts ends Harte's skillful and knowledgeable spoof of the self-imposed evening of horrible confinement.

170. _____. "The Mystery of the Hacienda." The Bell-Ringer of Angels, and Other Stories. Boston: Houghton, Mifflin, 1894.

REPRINT EDITION: A Hollow of the Hills, New York, Irvington Publishers, 1979.

CRITICAL SYNOPSIS: The main character, Dick Bracy, inherits the huge Hacienda de las Osos and moves in with his relative, Aunt Viney. His pretty cousin, Cecily, accompanies them. Mysterious events soon begin to occur and Dick is especially astonished by the shadowy appearances and disappearances of a beautiful young woman who approaches him in the rose garden. The mysterious visitant bears some resemblance to Cecily, but she also bears the marks of some great sorrow. His involvement with the spectral stranger deepens into a kind of forbidden love to the dismay of his aunt and to the mounting dread of Cecily who feels alone and abandoned within the great casa. A neighbor, Dona Felipa, tells a melancholy story of the seduction and destruction of the beautiful Rosita, an anecdote which awakens Dick to the fact that he has become enamoured of her ghost. Meanwhile, Cecily too has had a mysterious visitor, one of Rosita's cruel seducers in apparitional form. "'And kissed you?'" said Dick. 'Oh, Dick, Dick! do you think he really did it? The horror of it, Dick! to be kissed by a--a--man who has been dead a hundred years!'" Realizing that they are both menaced by demon lovers who haunt the great hacienda, Dick and Cecily kiss and embrace for the first time and find miraculously that their love conquers terror. Harte's Gothic novella transports all of the moods of Radcliffean Gothic to the Californian frontier and does so with considerable knowledge of the more delicate requirements of the novel of terror.

171. Harvey, Alexander. "The Forbidden Floor." The Toe and Other Tales. New York: Mitchell Kennerley, 1913.

REPRINT EDITION: The Toe and Other Tales, Salem, NH, Ayer, 1973.

CRITICAL SYNOPSIS: In one of the first Gothics, The Old English Baron (1777) by Clara Reeve, is to be found the form's original forbidden apartment or haunted chamber. The remainder of the house, mansion, or castle might be safe enough and open to visitors, but one chamber or one closed wing of the building had been permanently reserved for Gothic horror by Clara Reeve. The persistence and usefulness of the sealed suite is evident in many Gothic survivals. In "The Forbidden Floor," for example, the curious narrator is allowed to satisfy his curiosity about the ancient Bowers Mansion with the exception of the chambers of the top floor which hide some delectable Gothic secret. A wicked son of the House of Bowers is said still to inhabit the forbidden floor while a beautiful, ghostly woman in eighteenth-century dress has been seen above the staircase over the years. The major moment of Gothic experience comes when the beautiful ghost guides the narrator to the forbidden floor and in the chamber at the top gives herself to her earthly lover. The act of spectral lovemaking which occurs only once a century seems to be done in expiation for the terrible crimes of the bad Bowers males who are condemned to pace the forbidden floor forever.

172. Hassall, Miss. [Leonora Sansay]. Secret History; or, The Horrors of St. Domingo, in a Series of Letters, Written by a Lady at Cape

François to Colonel Burr. Philadelphia: Bradford & Inskeep, 1808.

CRITICAL SYNOPSIS: A Defoe-like eyewitness report, the letters are full of humanitarian sentiments and sensational descriptions of the brutality of the French and the Creoles toward the natives and blacks during the period of General Rochambeau's occupation of the islands. The Europeans have made them "an abode of pleasure and luxurious ease where vices reign at which humanity must shudder." Among the horrors that are graphically depicted, the correspondent singles out the fate of the white girl Adelaide to illustrate how white cruelty is matched by black cruelty. Seized by the black chief, Dessalines, "the monster gave her to his guard, who hung her by the throat on an iron hook in the marketplace, where the lovely, innocent, unfortunate victim slowly expired." Similar atrocious accounts mingled with sentimental aphorisms adorn the narrative. The head of the slave girl, Coomba, on a stake and the public execution by slow fire of three blacks accused of burning their master's plantation are typical anecdotes of horror. Fiction presented as fact in order to sensationalize the horrors of empire appealed to an audience which would later struggle with the moral question of slavery in the United States.

173.   Hawkes, John. The Beetle Leg. New York: New Directions, 1961.

REPRINT EDITION: New York, New Directions, 1967.
RESEARCH SOURCES: Frohock, W.M., "The Drowning of American Adam: Hawkes' The Beetle Leg," Critique 14 (1973): 63-74; Greiner, Donald J., Comic Terror: The Novels of John Hawkes, Memphis, TN, Memphis State UP, 1973; Rovit, Earl, "The Fiction of John Hawkes: An Introductory View," Modern Fiction Studies 11 (1964): 150-162.

CRITICAL SYNOPSIS: A nightmarish parody of the American western, this strange and violent novel of cultural sterility and despair was well-described by the reviewer in Commonweal (January 25, 19-52) as "the concrete irrationally observed and rationally recorded." The central event is the death by premature burial of a construction worker, Mulge Lampson, during the building of an irrigation dam. The haunting effect of this terrible death on his friends and neighbors is the substance of the novel which adheres to the Hawkes formula of a maximum flow of violent and bizarre action accompanied by a minimal or non-existent story line. The cast of the American western—particularly such films as Shane and High Noon—is all present in gruesome caricature or distorted stereotype. A true grit sheriff hunts down sexual deviants instead of rustlers and gunslingers. Mulge's brother, Luke Lampson, hooks a drowned baby while trolling for the body of his brother in the artificial lake which still hides Mulge's remains. The dude strangers in town, the Campers, undergo strange and violent experiences while a mysterious gang called the Red Devils wreaks more sadistic havoc than any well-trained corps of Gothic gremlins or banditti infesting a castle or abbey. The most sinister and strangest character among these grotesques is the medicine man, Cap Leech, "a midnight vivisectionist in a cat hospital" who holds the power of life and death in his hands. While these characters interact in a kind of collage of violence, the dam itself disintegrates a "beetle leg" at a time as it moves steadily toward the ruin of the great slide. The novel ends with a twisted version of the traditional street shootout between good and bad men, but the good guys are no longer distinguishable from the bad and the traditional gunfight concludes in chaos rather than in the restoration of order and justice. The Gothic novel often replaces mundane or complacent value systems with nightmares of cultural and personal disorder. In this respect, The Beetle Leg is a most effective Gothification of the reassuring patterns of the American western.

174. _____. "The Goose on the Grave." Lunar Landscapes. New York: New Directions, 1969.

RESEARCH SOURCE: Berryman, Charles, "Hawkes and Poe," Modern Fiction Studies 29 (1983): 643-654; Scholes, Robert, "Lunar Landscapes," New York Times Book Review, July 13, 1969, p.4.

CRITICAL SYNOPSIS: If the inexplicably violent event is a perennial trademark of the high Gothic, then Hawkes's short novel deserves to be regarded as very high modern Gothic. The best and perhaps the only way of describing Hawkes's violation of traditional structures is to suggest that "The Goose on the Grave" is something like what Fielding's Tom Jones would have been like had it been written by Franz Kafka. A grotesque picaresque combines with the surreal anti-structure of the novel to yield a queer and disturbing blend of humor and horror, or "comic terror" as one critic has labeled it. The locale is Italy, but it is fantasized Italy of some indeterminate time. The principal character is the orphaned wanderer, Adeppi, whose mother has been abducted by three priests on white donkeys. In the novel's final episode, Adeppi witnesses her burning alive and all of his strange adventures in between the abduction and the burning are additional versions of odd and unexplained violence, betrayal, brutality, or perversion of body and spirit. Like the traditional picaresque hero, he is repeatedly misled or deceived by false preceptors and placed in situations of sexual endangerment. The mad soldier, Nino, puts a pistol to Adeppi's head. The sexual criminal, Jacopo, an accordianist, takes further advantage of Adeppi. The religious fanatic, Arsella, and her blind husband, Pipistrello, force him to vend cheap religious souvenirs. All of these encounters are accompanied by images of horror or religious void such as the madonna with empty, childless arms that Adeppi sees at one point or the horrid painting of the bleeding heart in Arsella's bechamber before which she prostrates herself. But perhaps the most grotesque of his encounters is with the warped priest, Dolce, who worships the agony of Christ's passion and goes about wearing "this exact expression...showing to strangers only his insignificant suspicion, a trembling chin meanly concealing the images of wind-beating locks and thorns." It is Dolce who deliberately stages the burning of Adeppi's mother, but the grisly event has no apparent effect on Adeppi whatsoever. Absurdity, disconnectedness, ludicrous sadism, indifference to religious and sacred values, mockery of history, and motiveless cruelty project all of the conditions of modern or nuclear doom--a collective fate well-suited to a Gothic presentation--the utter meaninglessness of religion, art, human relationships, and finally of life itself.

175. Hawthorne, Hildegarde. "Perdita." Shapes That Haunt the Dusk, eds. W.D. Howells and H.M. Alden. New York: Harper, 1907.

CRITICAL SYNOPSIS: Delicate Gothic fantasy involving the reappearances of the spectral child, Perdita.

176. Hawthorne, Julian. Archibald Malmaison. London: R. Bentley, 1879; New York: Funk & Wagnalls, 1884.

RESEARCH SOURCE: Park, Martha M., "Archibald Malmaison: Julian Hawthorne's Contribution to Gothic Fiction," Extrapolation 15 (1973): 103-116.

CRITICAL SYNOPSIS: This Gothic novelette of the dual consciousness centers on the unstable personality of the main character and is said to be Julian Hawthorne's best contribution to the genre of horror. There is little philosophizing and moralizing in the story and almost complete attention to pure horror of both the internal and external varieties. Archibald Malmaison (the surname means "bad house") is afflicted with a strange malady which manifests itself in abrupt alterations of personality, memory chasms, and vacillations between normal intelligence and near idiocy. He even forgets for a time the woman he loves, Kate Battledown, causing her to marry one, Richard Pennroyal, sworn foe of the Malmaison family. When Archibald's brother, Edward, is killed in a duel with Pennroyal, he becomes the heir to the family estate but the inheritance is soon challenged by Pennroyal who brings the claim that Archibald is illegitimate. Within the Malmaison mansion there is a secret chamber or ancient vault to which Archibald conducts Kate as his bride-to-be after killing Pennroyal and sinking his body in a nearby lake. It is at this juncture that he suffers another of his strange attacks, and, having decorated the secret chamber as a wedding suite and left Kate in her wedding dress, he forgets her and leaves her locked within the chamber for several years. When he returns to the bridal suite, thinking that only a few hours have passed, he finds only her corpse in a rotted dress and dies of guilt and despair several months later. This creepy tale is heavily embellished with numerous Gothic devices including secret passageways, pictures with accusing eyes, and the strange mental condition of the unstable hero. The fact that no moral is drawn and no final explanations are ever offered for the secrets contained in the horrible room indicate the son's desire to separate his sense of horror and gloom from the moralized Gothicism of his father, Nathaniel Hawthorne.

177. _____. "Ken's Mystery." David Poindexter's Disappearance and Other Tales. New York: D. Appleton, 1888.

REPRINT EDITIONS: Salem, NH, Ayer, 1976.

CRITICAL SYNOPSIS: The influence of Victorian sensation fiction and the penny dreadfuls such as the notorious Varney the Vampyre; or, The Feast of Blood (1847) is clearly evident in this vampire story. The main character is an artist and antiquarian whose passion for the past and morbid curiosity eventually bring him to a lethal rendezvous with the vampire. While traveling in Ireland, Keningale comes upon the sixteenth-century legend of a beautiful woman, Ethelind Fionguala, who was seized and ravaged by a clutch of vampires. Obsessed with the location of her grave, Keningale investigates many cemeteries and headstones until he finally discovers her resting place. Guarding the grave is a strange and lovely woman who demands Keningale's ring as a gift for her vigilance. Bestowing the ring upon her, he suddenly finds himself caught up in a vertiginous time shift which conveys him to the Sixteenth Century. Confronting him at the threshold of the open grave is the undead Ethelind Fionguala, her aggressive features now showing all the tell-tale marks of the vampire. The Gothic content of this work and others by the son of the famous American author show how dedicated Julian Hawthorne was to the shock and thrill qualities of Gothicism in contrast to Nathaniel Hawthorne's reticence and coolness toward direct displays of gore and horror.

178. Hawthorne, Nathaniel. Fanshawe. Boston: Marsh & Capen, 1828.

REPRINT EDITION: The Complete Novels and Selected Tales of Na-thaniel Hawthorne, ed. Norman Holmes Pearson, New York, Modern Li-brary, 1937.
RESEARCH SOURCES: Baym, Nina, "Hawthorne's Gothic Discards: Fan-shawe and 'Alice Doane,'" Nathaniel Hawthorne Journal 1974, pp. 105-115; Goldstein, Jesse Sidney, "The Literary Source of Haw-thorne's Fanshawe," Modern Language Notes 60 (1945): 1-8.

CRITICAL SYNOPSIS: Hawthorne began his literary career as he ended it, with an experiment in Gothic decor and incident wherein the Gothic material itself occupies the thematic foreground rather than the atmospheric background. Fanshawe self-consciously draws upon the novels of Scott and the Gothic novelists, especially the work of Charles Robert Maturin, for its scenes, character rela-tionships, and overwrought style. The influence of Maturin's Mel-moth the Wanderer (1820) is to be seen in the self-isolated and scholarly hero, Fanshawe, and in the name which Hawthorne chose for the president of Harley College in this "college" novel, Dr. Melmoth. Affixed to Chapter VIII is an epigraph taken from Matu-rin's Gothic drama, Bertram; or, The Castle of St. Aldobrand (18-16). The plot is a conventional love story embellished with ele-ments of violence and morbidity and occasionally reminds the reader of the fated love of Ravenswood for Lucy Ashton in Scott's The Bride of Lammermoor (1816). The lovely ward of Dr. Melmoth, Ellen Langton, is sought after by Edward Walcott and by the asce-tic and studious Fanshawe who is momentarily forced out of his scholarly role when he rescues Ellen from a would-be kidnapper and seducer, accomplishing the rescue simply by means of an accusing downward glance from atop a cliff. In return for his noble ges-ture, Ellen offers to marry Fanshawe, but the idealistic intellec-tual refuses a life of domestic bliss to devote himself to his studies and proceeds to retire from the world. This slight and trite romance plot allowed the young Hawthorne to practice and perfect his craft of building Gothic moods and exploring the char-acter of the high minded isolatoe, a figure which Hawthorne would continue to develop and investigate. The tragic misanthropy of Young Goodman Brown (see 196) and the intellectual pride of Ethan Brand (see 199) have their imaginative genesis in Fanshawe's gloomy self-absorption. Fanshawe proved to be an important and necessary failure for Hawthorne in the proper adaptation of Gothic materials. Even the most Gothic scene in the book, the menacing of Ellen in the midst of the forest beneath a great cliff, is awk-wardly managed by Hawthorne. When the seducer ascends the cliff to get at Fanshawe, he loses his footing and falls over the precipice to his death. Hawthorne moralizes over the death of the villainous Butler: "The goodness and the nobleness of which his heart was not destitute, turned, from that time, wholly to evil, and he became irrecoverably ruined and irreclaimably depraved." Hawthorne's great subject, the mystery of evil and its growth, is certainly present in Fanshawe. Finding a way of placing the potent devices and effects of the Gothic at the service of his moral art became for Hawthorne an early problem of form, a problem which he had begun to solve even with the failings of his first novel.

179. _____. "Alice Doane's Appeal." The Token, 1835; Hawthorne's

<u>Works</u>, XIII, ed. George Parsons Lathrop. Boston: Houghton, Mifflin, 1883.

REPRINT EDITION: <u>Nathaniel Hawthorne's Short Stories</u>, ed. Newton Arvin, New York, <u>Vintage-Ballantine</u>, 1974.
RESEARCH SOURCES: Baym, Nina, "Hawthorne's Gothic Discards: <u>Fanshawe</u> and 'Alice Doane,'" <u>Nathaniel Hawthorne Journal</u> 1974, pp. 105-115; Markus, Manfred, "Hawthorne's 'Alice Doane's Appeal': An Anti-Gothic Tale," <u>Germanisch-Romanische Monatsschrift</u> 25 (1975): 338-349.

CRITICAL SYNOPSIS: A heavily overwrought Gothic tale, the story exhibits workbook qualities as it examines the author's problem of how to write (or how not to write) an American Gothic. There are actually two tales or a story-within-a-story. Carrying a manuscript in his pocket, a young author guides two lady companions to the summit of Gallows Hill to the site of the execution and burial of witches, then recites aloud to them some fragments of a work which he has in progress. The strange and gloomy narrative contains all that lady readers of Gothic fiction might desire,--and more. It has incest, murder, wizardry, graveyards, a congregation of spectres, midnight gloom, lonesome settings, and even the stern spirit of Cotton Mather "that my hearers...mistook for the visible presence of the fiend himself." The plot is the very stuff of Gothic melodrama, involving a three-way illicit sexual rivalry which the young author calls "that impure passion which alone engrosses all the heart." Competing for the love of Alice Doane are Walter Brome and Alice's brother, Leonard Doane, a fatal rivalry which leads to Brome's murder following Leonard's visit to a wizard. The narrative is cast in the shape of Leonard Doane's belated confession which also contains his sister's guiltridden appeal to the phantom of Walter Brome to be absolved of her double sexual sin of incest and adultery. There are powerful echoes of some of Hawthorne's most successful Gothic endeavors in this "Gothic discard." The cavalcade of the dead come alive in a grand vision of evil looks ahead to the dark and loathsome brotherhood which welcomes Young Goodman Brown to his destiny while the concealment of carnal passion anticipates the sexual themes of <u>The Scarlet Letter</u>.

180. _____. "Graves and Goblins." <u>New England Magazine</u>, June, 1835.

REPRINT EDITION: <u>The Centenial Edition of the Works of Nathaniel Hawthorne</u>, ed. William Charvat, Columbus, OH, Ohio State UP, 1978.
RESEARCH SOURCE: Bezanson, Walter E., "The Hawthorne Game: 'Graves and Goblins,'" <u>Emerson Society Quarterly</u> 54 (1969): 73-77.

CRITICAL SYNOPSIS: A posthumous monologue delivered by the spectre of a young man who died before he could fullfill himself as a lover. If he haunts at all, he haunts with delicacy and solicitude. "In death, I bring no loathsome smell of the grave, nor ghostly terrors,--but gentle, and soothing, and sweetly pensive influences." He has known many other ghosts, the spirits of patriots, politicians, and even writers, who are condemned to search for fame, or power, or some other earthly goal because their ambitions did not die with their bodies. Because he seeks only a higher love, the spectre narrator hopes to become pure spirit someday and rise above his graveyard home. In a Poe-like scene, he recalls visiting the "ancestral vault" of a young maiden and finding that her tomb was empty. "She had taken her trackless flight, and had found a home in the purest radiance of the upper stars, leaving me to knock at the stone portal of the darksome sepulchre. But I know --I know, that angels hurried her away, or surely she would have whispered ere she fled!" This morbid sketch is Hawthorne's "Annabel Lee," a true prose poem contribution to the American graveyard school.

181. _____. "The Gray Champion." Twice-Told Tales. Boston: American Stationers, John B. Russell, 1837.

REPRINT EDITION: Twice-Told Tales and Other Stories, ed. Quentin Anderson, New York, Washington Square Press, 1960.

CRITICAL SYNOPSIS: The tale is a fine example of a political ghost story which blends New England history with fable and fantasy. The "hoary apparition" of the Gray Champion is no less than the legendary and venerable spirit of liberty itself, "the type of New England's hereditary spirit." He appears whenever and wherever oppression casts its shadow over the people's freedom or whenever and wherever domestic tyranny threatens to crush the people's rights. The specific occasion of the story is the final days of the harsh administration of King James II's royal governor, the despotic Sir Edmund Andros. The specific locale of the story is Boston's King Street on an April evening in the year 1689 where Andros has assembled his troops "to strike terror by a parade of military force, and to confound the opposite faction by possessing himself of their chief." Suddenly from the midst of the crowd there emerges the imposing figure of an old man clad in the Puritan fashion of the old Massachusetts Bay Colony. By means of a gesture and a command, the grim-visaged champion of the people confronts Andros and drives him back with a warning glance and a curse. "Back, thou that wast a governor, back! With this night thy power is ended--tomorrow the prison!--back, lest I foretell the scaffold!" Andros retreats, the people surge forward, liberty is restored and the Gray Champion "fades from their eyes, melting slowly into the hues of twilight, till where he stood there was an empty space." Thus, does Hawthorne transform the avenging spectre of the castle into the righteous phantom of liberty and alter the supernatural eye of various Gothic ghosts into the potent glance of the spirit of American freedom.

182. _____. "The Hollow of the Three Hills." Twice-Told Tales, Boston: American Stationers, John B. Russell, 1837.

REPRINT EDITION: Twice-Told Tales and Other Short Stories, ed. Quentin Anderson, New York, Washington Square Press, 1960.
RESEARCH SOURCE: Doubleday, Neal Frank, "Hawthorne's Use of Three Gothic Patterns," College English 7 (1946): 250-262.

CRITICAL SYNOPSIS: A story of witchcraft set "In those strange old times when fantastic dreams and madman's reveries were realized among the actual circumstances of life." A lady has a rendezvous with a witch at an appointed hour near the mantling pool within the hollow of the three hills, a dismal site reserved for some "impious baptismal rite." Placing her head on the witch's knees, she is given several visions of the parents she had shamed, the husband she had betrayed, and the child she had abandoned. The Gothic sketch ends with the morbid vision of someone's funeral, perhaps a foreshadowing of the sinner's death. When the witch attempts to revive the kneeling lady, "she lifted not her head" from the hag's lap. Had she perished of guilt? Hawthorne never answers the question but concludes the story with the witch's chuckle over her "sweet hour's sport." This is an early Hawthorne story, but told with a chilling mastery of Gothic atmosphere and event. The pre-Gothic source for the story derives from Hawthorne's absolute recall of Bunyan's The Pilgrim's Progress. In Part II, Greatheart describes the witch, Madame Bubble, as follows: "This woman is a witch and it is by virtue of her sorceries that this ground is enchanted. Whoever doth lay his head down in her lap had as good lay it down on that block over which the axe doth hang."

183. _____. "The Minister's Black Veil." Twice-Told Tales. Boston: American Stationers, John B. Russell, 1837.

REPRINT EDITION: Selected Tales and Sketches of Nathaniel Hawthorne, ed. Michael J. Colacurcio, Baltimore, Penguin, 1984.
RESEARCH SOURCES: Allen, M.L., "The Black Veil: Three Versions of a Symbol," English Studies 47 (1966): 286-289; Barry, Elain, "Beyond the Veil: A Reading of Hawthorne's 'The Minister's Black Veil,'" Studies in Short Fiction 17 (1980): 15-20.

CRITICAL SYNOPSIS: First published in The Token for 1836, the tale demonstrates Hawthorne's manner of transposing a terror motif to the requirements of his moral symbolism. In this case, the motif is the famous black veil behind which lurks the horror of all horrors in Mrs. Ann Radcliffe's The Mysteries of Udolpho (1794). In Mrs. Radcliffe's Gothic romance, the black veil's sole purpose is to stimulate unbearable dread for several hundreds of pages by leaving unanswered the terrible question, "What lies behind the veil which was so horrible that it caused the heroine, Emily St. Aubert, to swoon away in abject terror when she looked behind it?" But Hawthorne imbues the black veil with a profounder mystery when he transfers the terror object to the features of the Reverend Mr. Hooper, the "minister" of the tale's title. For unexplained reasons and for more than twenty years, the Reverend Mr. Hooper has taken the veil thus keeping his face hidden from his congregation, his fiancée, and even from himself. Was his sudden decision to wear the black veil for the remainder of his mortal life an act of conscience and compassion or an act of cold isolation and egotism? Whatever his motive, the effect is an appalling separation of Hooper from all humanity. "That piece of crepe seemed to hang down before his heart, the symbol of a fearful secret between him and them," and even after his death Hooper's black emblem of universal mourning and withdrawal is worn in the grave. "Still veiled, they lay him in his coffin, and a veiled corpse they bore him to the grave." The superficial horror of the Radcliffean question is darkened by Hawthorne's genius into a question about the primal mystery of evil itself, for the question now becomes "Why is the veil worn?" And why at the moment of his death should the minister see "on every visage a Black Veil?" For sheer visionary gloom alone, "The Minister's Black Veil" is one of Hawthorne's most successful transformations of a Gothic object into a symbol of the impenetrable moral darkness at the core of the human heart.

184. _____. "The Prophetic Pictures." Twice-Told Tales. Boston: American Stationers, John B. Russell, 1837.

REPRINT EDITION: Twice-Told Tales and Other Short Stories of Nathaniel Hawthorne, ed. Quentin Anderson, New York, Washington

Square Press, 1960.
RESEARCH SOURCE: Doubleday, Neal F., "The Gothic Naturalized: 'The Prophetic Pictures,'" Hawthorne's Early Tales: A Critical Study, Durham, NC, Duke UP, 1972, pp.109-117.

CRITICAL SYNOPSIS: The animated or the peripatetic portrait may well be the most common of all the Gothic devices. Certainly, its reappearances after Walpole had introduced it in The Castle of Otranto (1764) confirm its durability as a prop of terror. When the motif is combined with the power of the painter to capture the subject's secret soul when the portrait is made, it gains a terrifying intensity. The newly married couple, Walter and Elinor Ludlow, are first sketched, then done in oil by an artist with these "preternatural" powers. The finished portraits are terrifyingly prophetic, as they foreshadow the fates and darker passions of the couple. Walter Ludlow begins to take on the malicious qualities of his portrait as the work of art begins to possess the mortal subject. He is about to stab Elinor when the painter intervenes to "interpose himself between the wretched beings with the same sense of power to regulate their destiny as to alter a scene upon the canvas. He stood like a magician controlling the phantoms which he had evoked." The artist's intervention is not a moral act, but an egotistical assurance to himself that he retains the power of life and death through his art. From these Gothic events, Hawthorne draws a stern moral: "Could the result of one or all our deeds be shadowed forth and set before us--some would call it Fate and hurry onward, others be swept along by their passionate desires, and none be turned aside by the PROPHETIC PICTURES."

185.   _____. "The Wedding Knell." Twice-Told Tales. Boston: American Stationers, John B. Russell, 1837.

REPRINT EDITION: Twice-Told Tales, and Other Short Stories of Nathaniel Hawthorne, ed. Quentin Anderson, New York, Washington Square Press, 1960.
RESEARCH SOURCE: Lundblad, Jane, Nathaniel Hawthorne and the Tradition of the Gothic Romance, New York, Haskell House, 1964.

CRITICAL SYNOPSIS: The tale concerns the "late union of two early lovers," the widow Mrs. Dabney and Mr. Ellenwood, "quite a secluded man, selfish, like all men who brood over their own hearts." As the bride enters the church, the bell sends forth a deep and funereal knell and rings seemingly of its own accord. As the bride awaits the arrival of the groom, the bell keeps up its dismal pealing when suddenly "a dark procession paced into the church." In the midst of the spectral procession stands the horror of horrors, "the bridgroom in his shroud." He extends a grisly invitation to the shocked widow: "'Come, my bride!' said those pale lips. 'The hearse is ready. The sexton stands waiting for us at the door of the tomb; let us be married; and then to our coffins!'" Was her intended indeed an animated corpse come to lead her down the aisle to the grave? Or is the spectre bridegroom simply a made-up figure in a morbid charade? The central Gothic ambiguity is never resolved, but the cadaverous union is solemnized with "the death knell tolling through the whole till its deep voice overpowered the marriage words." The tale's weird power derives from Hawthorne's skillful adaptation of a pair of Gothic devices: the bell in the tower which rings by itself or by supernatural touch; and the deceased beloved who conveys the maiden to the tomb. Francis Lathom's Gothic novel, Midnight Bell (1798) and

Mary Meeke's thriller, Midnight Weddings (1802) were available to Hawthorne, although the ropeless bell and the cadaverous husband were to be found throughout the tradition.

186. _____. "The White Old Maid." Twice-Told Tales. Boston: American Stationers, John B. Russell, 1837.

REPRINT EDITION: Seven Masterpieces of Gothic Horror, ed. Robert D. Spector, New York, Bantam Books, 1963.
RESEARCH SOURCE: Rupprecht, Eric S., "Nathaniel Hawthorne," Supernatural Fiction Writers, pp.707-715.

CRITICAL SYNOPSIS: One of the purest, yet one of the least known, of Hawthorne's Gothic tales, the story has affinities with Faulkner's "A Rose for Emily" (see 131) and might well be Faulkner's prime source. An atmosphere of decay and the introduction of putrid detail at the climax also set the tale apart from Hawthorne's customarily subtle Gothicism. The tale begins with a corpse kiss by moonlight as the young maiden, Edith, "presses her living lips to the dead ones" of a young man. Her passionate kiss is interrupted by another young woman who flings herself on the deathbed, "her head pillowed beside that of the corpse, and her hair mingling with his dark locks." The two women pledge to meet years later to settle the matter of possession and they seal their bargain with a lock of the dead man's hair. As the years pass, the village becomes the abode of a lonely old woman who hides her person in a shroud of white, roams the streets by night, habitually hangs around houses of mourning and death, and always joins any funeral cortege on its way to the graveyard. Like the Reverend Hooper's black veil, her winding sheet is the white old maid's appalling curtain placed between herself and the world. The climax occurs in a dark old mansion deserted since the death of Colonel Fenwicke. Strange noises, foul odors, and the obligatory blood curdling shriek bring a party of investigators led by the local clergyman. Upstairs in the great bedroom they collide with the horror of horrors, for there, "clutching a lock of hair, once sable, now discolored with a greenish mold," sits the white old maid with her rival lover kneeling with her forehead in the white old maid's lap. Both are dead and have been so for some time. Hawthorne points no moral at all over this gruesome reunion, but simply terminates the story at the pinnacle of horror, certainly a radical departure from his usual procedure in his dark parables of the moral life.

187. _____. "The Haunted Mind." Moral Tales II. The Flower Basket; or a Selection of Interesting Stories, ed. Samuel Griswold Goodrich. New York: Nafis and Cornish, 1840.

REPRINT EDITION: Twice-Told Tales, and Other Stories, ed. Quentin Anderson, New York, Washington Square Press, 1960.
RESEARCH SOURCE: St. Armand, Barton Levi, "Hawthorne's 'Haunted Mind': A Subterranean Drama of the Self," Criticism 13 (1971): 1-25.

CRITICAL SYNOPSIS: Not a tale but a nocturne or night sketch describing that moment of suspended terror bewteen sleep and waking when "the things of the mind become dim spectres to the eye" and when "the imagination is a mirror, imparting vividness to all ideas, without the power of selecting or controlling them." Hawthorne's haunted mind expresses the quintessential themes of the

American Gothic: a castle of the solitary and guilty self from which there can be no easy exit to light and innocence; a dungeon or tomb of the heart which holds its secret guilts and dark necessities, a prison which "holds its hell within itself." The night sketch contains one of the best statements of the content and theme of the American Gothic to be found in the literature. Like many American Gothic questers, the narrator finally beholds a "nightmare of the soul; this heavy, heavy sinking of the spirits; this wintry gloom about the heart; this indistinct horror of the mind, blending itself with the darkness of the chamber." This same unknown or darker self would later be identified by Emily Dickinson as the prime phantom of American Gothicism, the "superior spectre more near" that should "startle most."

188.   . "Edward Randolph's Portrait." Twice-Told Tales. Boston: American Stationers, John B. Russell, 1842.

REPRINT EDITION: Twice-Told Tales and Other Short Stories of Nathaniel Hawthorne, ed. Quentin Anderson, New York, Washington Square Press, 1960.
RESEARCH SOURCES: Ringe, Donald A., American Gothic, p.153; Stein, William B., Hawthorne's Faust: A Study of the Devil Archetype, Gainesville, FL, Florida UP, 1953; Turner, Arlin, "Hawthorne's Literary Borrowings," Publications of the Modern Language Association 51 (1936): 543-562.

CRITICAL SYNOPSIS: One of four "Legends of the Province House," the tale appears to draw directly upon one of Mrs. Radcliffe's main instruments of terror to achieve its effect, that prop being the veiled portrait which so terrified Emily St. Aubert in The Mysteries of Udolpho (1794). The period of the story is 1770, the year of the Boston Massacre. Revolutionary ferment grips the citizens of Boston as Governor Hutchinson prepares to sign the order allowing British troops to land in force. With his niece, Alice Vane, and his kinsman, Francis Lincoln, he discusses a gloomy portrait heavily veiled in silk which hangs in his chamber in the Province House. Its blackened figure can barely be discerned but it does reveal a posture of great anguish like a figure in the terminal throes of death. Hutchinson tells his relatives that the painting depicts his ancestor, Edward Randolph, a traitor to freedom since he had helped to annul the provincial charter. As an expression of revulsion and warning, Alice removes the silk drapery to expose Hutchinson to the face of guilt in all its horrible detail. The expression is one of inexpressible agony but Hutchinson still signs the wicked order. Directly after the Boston Massacre, he is discovered dead, his face contorted exactly into the same look of agony worn by Edward Randolph. Hawthorne had once more taken a familiar Gothic symbol, the sentient portrait, and filled it with political and moral symbolism transforming the painting into the icon of the guilty conscience itself.

189.   . "Old Esther Dudley." Twice-Told Tales. Boston: James Munroe, 1842.

REPRINT EDITION: Twice-Told Tales and Other Short Stories of Nathaniel Hawthorne, ed. Quentin Anderson, New York, Washington Square Press, 1960.
RESEARCH SOURCE: Ringe, Donald A., American Gothic, p.157.

CRITICAL SYNOPSIS: One of four "Legends of the Province House," the tale is an historical fantasy which uses the person of the hag as a symbol of the decadent royal past. She laments the passing of all the royal governors who lived in the Province House, especially Sir William Howe, and consorts with their memories. She has retained the key to the Province House bestowed upon her by Howe at his departure and she insists that the British are winning the war by inverting each of Washington's victories into a Tory success. When Governor Hancock arrives to take possession of the Province House in the name of the United States of America, Old Esther collapses and dies with "God save King George" on her lips. She is Hawthorne's witch of the dead political past, bedeviled by delusions of British authority.

190. _____. "The Birthmark." Mosses from an Old Manse. New York and London: Wiley and Putnam, 1846.

REPRINT EDITION: The Celestial Railroad and Other Stories, afterword R.P. Blackmur, New York, New American Library, 1974.
RESEARCH SOURCE: Doubleday, Neal F., "Hawthorne's Use of Three Gothic Patterns," College English 7 (1946): 250-262.

CRITICAL SYNOPSIS: Although not exactly an overreaching scientist of Victor Frankenstein's type in Mary Shelley's Frankenstein (1818), the main character in "The Birthmark" persuades himself that he can use his superior scientific knowledge to improve upon or amend nature's flawed work. The man of science is Aylmer. His wife, Georgiana, becomes the subject of his experiment in perfection since she bears a tiny birthmark in the shape of a hand which Aylmer would remove. Since the mark symbolizes for Aylmer "his wife's liability to sin, sorrow, decay, and death," he would save her from these evils and purify her through his science. Assisting Aylmer is a Caliban-like creature named Aminadab whose brutish nature obviously represents the darker side of Aylmer's self. The powerful potion which Aylmer's research has developed is finally administered to the consenting Georgiana with the result that the birthmark is eradicated but the patient dies. His attempt to perfect only destroys the thing he loves most. The story demonstrates Hawthorne's distrust of theoretical science and his abhorrence of the Faustian cravings of the human intellect.

191. _____. "Egotism; or, The Bosom Serpent." Mosses from an Old Manse. New York and London: Wiley and Putnam, 1846.

REPRINT EDITION: The Complete Novels and Selected Tales of Nathaniel Hawthorne, ed. Norman Holmes Pearson, New York, Modern Library, 1937.
RESEARCH SOURCES: Ringe, Donald A., American Gothic, p.175.

CRITICAL SYNOPSIS: The Gothic motif of a snake residing within the human body was an apt subject for the tale of terror as shown by Holmes's use of the idea in Elsie Venner (see 216). Hawthorne's literal knowledge of Spenser's Faerie Queene also made the idea of a bodily serpent available to him, for in Faerie Queene, I.iv.31, we read of the figure of Envy: "And in his bosome secretly there lay/An hateful Snake, the which his taile uptyes/In many folds, and mortall sting implyies." Convinced that his stomach contains a living, growing snake, Roderick Elliston spurns the company of his lovely wife, Rosina, and imagines that everyone else harbors such a viper in his or her bosom. His own bosom serpent, however, is the most anguishing of all, for it gnaws him constantly. And indeed, when other people place their hands on the madman's breast, "they were inexpressibly horror-stricken to feel the monster wriggling, twining, and darting to and fro within his narrow limits." Hawthorne even lingers over a moment of high horror when he describes Elliston "before a looking glass, with his mouth wide open, watching in hope and horror, to catch a glimpse of the snake's head far down within his throat." His sculptor friend, Herkimer, and Rosina eventually bring Elliston to a mansion and a garden hoping to effect his recovery or perhaps even to expel the bosom serpent. At the fountain in the garden a sort of miracle occurs when Roderick remembers a family prophecy that the Ellistons shall harbor serpents in their bosoms until they learn to think of others and love outside themselves. As Roderick asks Rosina to forgive him for his coldness toward her, "the sculptor beheld a waving motion through the grass, and heard a tinkling sound, as if something had plunged into the fountain." The fiend of envy has departed from Roderick's body at last. But the moralized ending does not detract from the horrid possibility that his body had for a time nourished a real snake.

192.   _____. "Fire Worship." Mosses from an Old Manse. New York and London: Wiley and Putnam, 1846.

REPRINT EDITION: Mosses from an Old Manse, Short Story Index Reprint Series, Salem, NH, Ayer Publishers, 1979.

CRITICAL SYNOPSIS: Not exactly a story but more of a pyrotechnic meditation. The unnamed narrator deplores the imprisonment of the primal element of fire within modern cast iron stoves. The holy fire of God and the hell fire of Satan have been replaced by the "cheerless and ungenial stove." The writer's inspiration by open fireplace and hearth is now denied to him by this abominable modern invention. The comic meditation concludes with the sarcastic reflection that our ancestors fought willingly to preserve their flaming altars and the hearths. He will not answer the call to "Fight for your stoves." This is Hawthorne in a lighter or Irvingesque mood.

193.   _____. "Monsieur du Miroir." Mosses from an Old Manse. New York and London: Wiley and Putnam, 1846.

REPRINT EDITION: Complete Short Stories of Nathaniel Hawthorne, Garden City, NY, Doubleday, 1959.
RESEARCH SOURCE: Stein, William B., Hawthorne's Faust: A Study of the Devil Archetype, Gainesville, FL, Florida UP, 1953.

CRITICAL SYNOPSIS: "Mr. Mirror" is Hawthorne's wry contribution to the literature of the doppelgänger or double, a character who frequently found his way into Gothic novels such as James Hogg's Memoirs and Confessions of a Justified Sinner (1824). The narrator indulges himself in a rambling series of reflections on his reflection, some comic and others more solemnly philosophic. The narrator wonders if Monsieur du Miroir will accompany him to his tomb and also muses on the strangeness of a companion at once so constant and familiar. Thus, Hawthorne is able to work in the theme of solipsistic terror or terror of the unknown self: "There is something fearful in bearing such a relation to a creature so unperfectly known, and in the idea that, to a certain extent, all which concerns myself will be reflected in its consequences upon him." At the end of the sketch, the narrator tries to make contact with the mysterious shape and is no longer sure which is the reality and which the image. Is it he or is it Monsieur du Miroir who has the objective existence? "So inimitably does he counterfeit that I could almost doubt which of us is the visionary form.... Thus do mortals deify, as it were, a mere shadow of themselves, a spectre of human reason." In its ultimate Gothic form, the reflection could be expected to descend from the mirror and overwhelm or displace the human being, but Hawthorne seldom extends any Gothic motif to such a violent climax.

194.   . "Rappaccini's Daughter." <u>Mosses from an Old Manse</u>. New York and London: Wiley and Putnam, 1846.

REPRINT EDITION: <u>The American Tradition in Literature</u>, eds. Sculley Bradley, R.C. Beatty, E. Hudson Long, New York, W.W. Norton, 1967,
RESEARCH SOURCE: La Regina, Gabriella. "'Rappaccini's Daughter': The Gothic as Catalyst for Hawthorne's Imagination," <u>Studi Americani</u> 17 (1971): 29-74.

CRITICAL SYNOPSIS: If characterization in "Ethan Brand" (see 199) shows the result of Hawthorne's Gothic reading in Maturin's <u>Melmoth the Wanderer</u> (1820), "Rappaccini's Daughter" reveals his response to the arcane and lethal Italian villains of Mrs. Ann Radcliffe. The gaunt and sinister Dr. Rappaccini who dresses like Prospero or Faustus and speaks in the idiom of Milton's Satan is also a point-by-point reincarnation of Mrs. Radcliffe's Montoni in <u>The Mysteries of Udolpho</u> (1794), and more particularly, her horrible monk, Father Schedoni, in <u>The Italian; or, The Confessional of the Black Penitents</u> (1797). He maintains a toxic garden, a sort of perverted Eden filled with luxuriant but deadly flowers and plants. The poisoned garden also serves as his laboratory for some obscene mithridatic experiment performed upon his own daughter, Beatrice. This persecuted maiden is beautiful but highly poisonous, having been slowly contaminated by the insane science of her Gothic father. Dr. Rappaccini is the coldest villain in all of Hawthorne's collection of marble-hearted fiends, for he "care[d] infinitely more for science than for mankind. His patients are interesting to him only as subjects for some new experiment." A young man, Giovanni Guasconti, gazes upon the poisonous Eve in her forbidden paradise and falls in love with her despite warnings to avoid her touch at all costs. Determined to free Beatrice from the hideous experiments of her "awful father," he offers her a purifying antidote, but when she drinks the elixir, it causes her instant death. From a dark portal, Dr. Rappaccini gazes upon the youth's attempt to cure the maiden "with a triumphant expression" as the antidote runs its deadly course. His evil experiment has apparently been a crowning success. The gruesome and merciless ending achieves an almost Poe-like horror in the narrator's grotesque epitaph for the miserable Beatrice: "As poison had been life, so the powerful antidote was death." The triumph of evil is the single most powerful form of climax for the Gothic tale. In "Rappaccini's Daughter," Hawthorne attains his most remorseless Gothic climax.

195.   . "Roger Malvin's Burial." <u>Mosses from an Old Manse</u>. New York and London: Wiley and Putnam, 1846.

REPRINT EDITION: <u>Selected Tales and Sketches of Nathaniel Hawthorne</u>, ed. Michael J. Colacurcio, Baltimore, Penguin, 1984.

CRITICAL SYNOPSIS: First published in The Token for 1832, the story deals with strange guilt and even stranger retribution for that guilt. Events are based the last battle of the Indian fighter and scalp hunter, John Lovewell (1725). The tale's terror lies in Hawthorne's reuse of the Gothic motif of the unburied corpse which seeks interment or revenge upon those who left the body to rot and denied it final rest. Two of Lovewell's men, old Roger Malvin and Reuben Bourne, have barely escaped from the battle with their lives and Roger Malvin has been mortally wounded. They reach an oak glade where the dying Malvin urges Reuben Bourne to leave him in order to reach safety. Bourne is exhorted to send help if he can and to marry old Malvin's daughter, Dorcas. Intending to carry out these promises, young Bourne fixes a bloody cloth to an oak and makes his way back to the settlement where he conceals from Dorcas the unburied condition of her father. For some eighteen years while the corpse of Roger Malvin vainly awaits decent burial Bourne's concealment becomes his private crime and the crime becomes an agony of conscience which eventually drives him back into the wilderness with Dorcas and with his handsome woodsman son, Cyrus. One evening, father and son set out in opposite directions to kill a deer. Either an appalling coincidence or the hand of God now takes over to bring Bourne to a terrible but just accounting for his abandonment of the dying Malvin. Hearing a rustling in an oak grove, Bourne fires at the noise and rushes forward to claim his game. In the very spot where Roger Malvin lay dying so many years before, the dead Cyrus now reclines, felled by the bullet from Bourne's musket. As usual, Hawthorne imbues the moment of horror with deeper moral meaning when Reuben confesses his deed to Dorcas and prays for the first time in eighteen years. "Then Reuben's heart was stricken and the tears gushed out like water from a rock. The vow that the wounded youth had made the blighted man had come to redeem."

196. _____. "Young Goodman Brown." Mosses from an Old Manse. New York and London: Wiley and Putnam, 1846.

REPRINT EDITION: Nathaniel Hawthorne's Short Stories, ed. Newton Arvin, New York, Vintage-Ballantine, 1974.
RESEARCH SOURCES: Cook, Reginald, "The Forest of Goodman Brown's Night: A Reading of Hawthorne's 'Young Goodman Brown,'" New England Quarterly 43 (1970): 473-481; Hurley, Paul J., "Young Goodman Brown's 'Heart of Darkness,'" American Literature 37 (1966): 410-419.

CRITICAL SYNOPSIS: First published in the New England Magazine for 1835, the tale reverses the journey made by Young Goodman's Brown's fellow pilgrim into the darkness, Robin Molineux (see 202). Brown undertakes a night journey into a haunted wilderness which commences as an amoral adventure and terminates in the loss of Brown's soul. Unlike Robin Molineux who comes to accept his membership in the loathsome brotherhood of mankind, Young Goodman Brown fails to recover from the moral shock of his voyage into the interior of his own heart of darkness. The allegory begins with Brown's departure from his new wife, Faith, when he undertakes a mission into the forest which can be seen as nothing less than Brown's going to the devil. His attendance is expected at a diabolic communion presided over by a sable clad figure of "once angelic nature" who welcomes Brown to the communion of his race and prepares to touch his forehead with blood. Enroute to the devil's

meeting, Brown has encountered all of the citizens of Salem village he had revered and trusted for their purity and virtue. He
now finds all of the authority figures of his childhood already
members of Satan's congregation and waiting to receive him if he
will only accept the polluting stain of blood at the highpoint of
the infernal rite of baptism. Dismayed by the universal vision of
evil, Brown's faith in human goodness is severely shaken and at
the critical moment he resists the devil's touch, thus rejecting
both his own nature as well as the Satanic invitation to manhood
and membership in the tainted community of humankind. On the very
threshold of dark wisdom, Brown's quest aborts in what seems to be
the abrupt collapse of a nightmare or destructive dream. Hawthorne
omits any description of Young Goodman Brown's return from the
witch meeting in the depths of the wilderness, perhaps because his
quest for self was incomplete and his moral education therefore a
failure. Back in the village, the sullen and misanthropic Brown
can only see the human condition as hopelessly evil and he coldly
withdraws. His refusal to be human or to acknowledge evil within
himself show that his experience has turned him into a type of
moral monster whose soul has preceded his body in a premature
spiritual death. This powerful story relies for many of its effects upon Hawthorne's redesigning of Gothic apparatus and action.
Hideous shrieks and similar horrid acoustics, lurid lightning effects, the sordid paraphernalia of the coven or witches' conclave,
and the presence of the Devil himself give the tale an atmosphere
of moral evil that marks the American Gothic tale at its profound-
est level.

197.   _____. The Scarlet Letter. Boston: Ticknor, Reed, and Fields, 18-
50.

REPRINT EDITION: ed. Sculley Bradley, New York, W.W. Norton, 19-
61.
RESEARCH SOURCES: Chisholm, Richard M., "The Use of Gothic Materials in Hawthorne's Mature Romances," Dissertation Abstracts International 31 (1970): 382A (Columbia University); Kaftan, Robert A.,
"A Study of the Gothic Techniques in the Novels of Nathaniel Hawthorne," Dissertation Abstracts 29 (1968): 1899A (Michigan State
University); Lewis, Paul, "Mournful Mysteries: Gothic Speculation
in The Scarlet Letter," American Transcendental Quarterly 44 (19-
79): 279-293.

CRITICAL SYNOPSIS: Fascination with elements of the eighteenth-
century Gothic novel infuse Hawthorne's most famous romance of
concealed sin, guilt, retribution, and the evil imperfections of
humans and their social institutions. Hawthorne had found that
Gothicism could provide a point of view for exploring the ambiguity of human experience along with a profound sense of the uncertainty and confusion of life. In The Scarlet Letter, deep moral
mysteries arise out of the sexual transgression of the hero and
heroine to yield some tragic examples of what Hawthorne calls "the
dark problem of this life." Like the closed and tyrannical Roman
Catholic world of such English Gothic novels as Lewis's The Monk
(1796), the merciless world of seventeenth-century Calvinist New
England where civil and Old Testament law are one in the same
imparts a vision of "life-long sorrow...dark necessity...and stern
and sad truth" for the secret "sinners," Hester Prynne and the
Reverend Arthur Dimmesdale. Convicted of adultery, Hester Prynne
is compelled to wear the scarlet badge of shame in the form of the
red A. With her illegitimate child, Pearl, she endures the oppro-

brium of the community. Her co-habitor, the minister Dimmesdale, hides his fatherhood of the child, but suffers mounting agonies of conscience over his adulterous and hypocritical life. Like Lewis's Father Ambrosio, Dimmesdale's sermons are "fraught with all the terrors of the tempest, while he inveighed against the vices of humanity." (Monk, chapter 1) Hester's husband, the old physician or "leech," Roger Chillingworth, proceeds to rack the soul of Dimmesdale in his vengeful quest to expose Hester's seducer. Hawthorne suggests at one point that a red letter A has actually formed upon the minister's flesh over his guilty heart even as his conscience and Chillingworth's cold probings torment him with all the pains of hell. The novel also presents several memorable night scenes on the scaffold or pillory and it is on this site of suffering and humiliation that Dimmesdale finally perishes in Hester's arms as he confesses his guilt. But the vilest of the three sinners remains Roger Chillingworth, the novel's most derivative Gothic character and a character motivated by a cold curiosity which becomes an even colder hatred. Like Dr. Rappaccini or Ethan Brand, Chillingworth is a paradigm of Gothic diabolism who comes to enjoy the invasion of the darker places of another human soul for its own evil sake. Dimmesdale's judgement upon Chillingworth is both accurate and just: "That old man's revenge has been blacker than my sin. He has violated, in cold blood, the sanctity of a human heart." Unlike the traditional female prisoner of the Gothic castle who survives her sufferings to return to a traditional world, Hester Prynne insists upon a new world for herself and her rejection of the society which had rejected her must be seen as a challenge by a free woman to the wicked orthodoxies that have bound her.

198.   . "The Devil in Manuscript." The Snow Image, and Other Tales. London: Henry G. Bohn, 1851.

REPRINT EDITION: The Complete Novels and Selected Tales of Nathaniel Hawthorne, ed. Norman Holmes Pearson, New York, Modern Library, 1837.
RESEARCH SOURCE: Stein, William B., Hawthorne's Faust: A Study of the Devil Archetype, Gainesville, FL, Florida UP, 1953.

CRITICAL SYNOPSIS: The narrator pays a visit to the failed author, Oberon, on a cold December evening. In a mad dialogue with the narrator, Oberon reviles his own writings and denounces the publishers who have rejected his work. Much of his work has been devoted to devil lore and he has come to believe that the fiend himself lives in his manuscripts which he now flings into the flaming fireplace. He thinks he catches a glimpse of the devil smirking at him from the midst of the flames. As the embers shoot up the chimney "like a demon with sable wings" someone in the street below shouts the alarm of "fire!" It seems that the author was successful after all since his writings have "set the town on fire." Oberon, the king of fairyland, and Nathaniel Hawthorne, the king of dark fantasy, converge in this comic tale of the perils of the imaginative life.

199.   . "Ethan Brand: A Chapter from an Abortive Romance." The Snow Image, and Other Tales. London: Henry G. Bohn, 1851.

REPRINT EDITION: Twice-Told Tales, and Other Short Stories, ed. Quentin Anderson, New York, Washington Square Press, 1960.
RESEARCH SOURCE: Stein, William B., "Faustian Symbolism in the

Gothic Romance," Hawthorne's Faust: A Study of the Devil Achetype, Gainesville, FL, Florida UP, 1953, pp.35-50.

CRITICAL SYNOPSIS: The immediate Gothic source for the tale is C. R. Maturin's widely read Gothic novel, Melmoth the Wanderer (18-20). With fiery eyes and stony heart, Maturin's accursed outcast wanders through time visiting various sufferers at the extremes of anguish and trying to trade his doom of the never-ending life for theirs. Hawthorne's Ethan Brand has spent many years on a similar futile and perverted quest, having gone in search of the unpardonable sin and sought it everywhere over the earth except within the black cavern of his own heart. As with Melmoth's perverse pilgrimage, the quest has hardened and dehumanized Ethan Brand turning him from man into fiend full of Satan's own "pale ire, envy, and despair." The action of the story concerns Ethan Brand's final days on earth, or more precisely, his final nights since the tale takes place almost entirely in the night time in Brand's old haunts atop Mount Graylock near North Adams, Massachusetts. Here, the lime burner, Bartram, and his little son, follow their trade and tend their lime furnace. One evening, they are startled by a fearful "roar of laughter, not mirthful, but slow and even solemn." Ethan Brand has returned. He offers to tend the kiln throughout the night but his real purpose is to stare deeply into the infernal fire and to meditate upon hellfire as the primal element of his existence. Standing on the edge of the blazing lime kiln and uttering a prayer of Satanic defiance, Ethan Brand casts himself into the fiery pit with a contemptuous shout of universal hatred which rings through the mountains. The suicide scene is a high Gothic death whose rhetoric of pyrotechnic horror is comparable to the death of Lewis's Father Ambrosio, hero-villain of The Monk (1796), or in cruder Gothic terms, the sensational death of Varney the Vampyre (1847) who hurls himself into the erupting crater of Mount Vesuvius. "Ethan Brand stood erect and raised his arms on high. The blue flames played upon his face, and imparted the wild and ghastly light which alone would have suited its expression; it was that of a fiend on the verge of plunging into his gulf of intensest torment....'Come, deadly element of fire, henceforth my familiar friend. Embrace me as I do thee!'" The next morning, Bartram and his son discover Brand's skeleton amidst the ashes. The skeleton holds a heart of pure marble. Other Gothic elements in this most Gothic of Hawthorne's tales of the night include an encounter with the Wandering Jew and reverberations of demoniac laughter, both Melmothian borrowings.

200.   _____. The House of the Seven Gables. Boston: Ticknor, Reed, and Fields, 1851.

REPRINT EDITION: ed. Seymour L. Gross, New York, W.W. Norton, 19-67.
RESEARCH SOURCES: Curran, Ronald T., "'Yankee Gothic': Hawthorne's 'Castle of Pyncheon,'" Studies in the Novel 8 (1976): 69-80; Hamada, Masjiro, "The House of the Seven Gables: Ni Okeru Gothic Romance Teki Yoso," Studies in English Literature (Tokyo) 45 (1968): 49-61; Lundblad, Jane, Nathaniel Hawthorne and the Tradition of the Gothic Romance [first title: Nathaniel Hawthorne and the European Literary Tradition], New York, Haskell House, 1964.

CRITICAL SYNOPSIS: The novel is an important example of the American Gothic romance at its highest point of development. R.T. Curran has shown that Hawthorne's "Castle of Pyncheon" is a democratized version of the European Gothic romance or a new type of horror novel, a "Yankee Gothic." "In remodeling The House of the Seven Gables after a standard Gothic protoypical plot, Hawthorne was recasting the story line to suit his own ambivalent faith in American democracy." The technology of terror worked out so precisely by Hawthorne conforms almost completely to the format of the first Gothic novel minus its supernatural absurdities, Horace Walpole's Castle of Otranto (1764). An ancestral crime and curse hover over the house and its occupants until the usurper is exposed and ownership of the building is properly restored. The interior of the castle now become a haunted house is filled with supernatural or mysterious objects and events as Hawthorne follows Walpole's Gothic idea of endowing the architecture and furnishings with a life of their own. Living portraits, animate and sentient mirrors, ghostly music from an ancient harpsichord, hidden manuscripts, and the gruesome death of the villain are only a few of many Gothic parts installed by Hawthorne to turn the screws of destiny. In the Seventeenth Century, the estate had once been the property of one Matthew Maule, accused of wizardry by the politically powerful Colonel Pyncheon who coveted the property. Maule went to his death with a curse on his lips against the Colonel and all his descendants. The action of the novel takes place in the Nineteenth Century. The house is in the hands of the absentee owner, Judge Jaffrey Pyncheon, seemingly a pillar of the community of Salem but actually a cruel and grasping hypocrite who persecutes his relatives, Hepzibah and Clifford Pyncheon, the house's caretakers. Other prisoners of the castle correspond to figures in Walpole's cast. Young Phoebe is the democratic equivalent of the aristocratic Isabella, the menaced maiden of Otranto. The mysterious daguerrotypist or photographer, Holgrave, is the Yankee Gothic counterpart of the rightful and rescuing heir to the castle, Walpole's young Theodore. The death of Judge Pyncheon in Chapter XVIII as he slumps in agony in the great chair before the picture of his evil ancestor and the marital union of the wronged house of Maule with the tainted house of Pyncheon in the union of Holgrave and Phoebe adhere to Gothic patterns found in the English parent form. But Hawthorne's close use of Walpole's Gothicism does not detract from his Americanization of the Gothic form in The House of the Seven Gables. Hawthorne's terrors and spectres are moral reminders of the pervasive presentness of the past whose historical and psychological reality will not be denied.

201. _____. "The Man of Adamant: An Apologue." The Snow Image, and Other Tales. London: Henry G. Bohn, 1851.

REPRINT EDITION: Selected Tales and Sketches of Nathaniel Hawthorne, ed. Hyatt Waggoner, New York, Holt, Rinehart, 1974.
RESEARCH SOURCE: Ringe, Donald A., American Gothic, p.157.

CRITICAL SYNOPSIS: A gruesome parable of misanthropy, frigidity of heart, and determined self-doom, the story shows the influence of the Gothic villain, the superman who risks everything for evil. There are only two main characters, Richard Digby, a man petrified by his own proud delusion that he is the only righteous man on earth, and Mary Goffe, whose appearance in the story as a redeeming spectre fails to soften Digby's adamantine heart. The setting is a cavern in the depths of the forest to which Digby has withdrawn with his Bible and his gun to pursue his plan of self-salvation and to sever himself absolutely from his fellow creatures. "Here I can offer up acceptable prayers, because my voice

will not be mingled with the sinful supplications of the multitude. Of a truth, the only way to heaven leadeth through the narrow entrance of this cave, and I alone have found it!" From this
dismal Gothic enclosure--a barren symbol of Digby's stony heart--
he will never reemerge. When visited in his solitude by Mary Goffe
who appeals to him to renew his fellowship to save his soul, he
drives her away with contemptuous words. But these are no sooner
spoken than Digby is transformed into a man of stone or adamant
while the reader is told that "Mary Goffe had been buried in an
English churchyard, months before; and either it was her ghost
that haunted the wild forest, or else a dream-like spirit typify-
ing pure Religion." The "simultaneous shriek" when a group of
children uncover the petrified corpse of Digby in its gloomy recess also recalls a common event in the early novel of horror when
a wall is pulled down or a slab pushed aside to reveal the horror
of horrors. A vaulted chamber of horrors, a religious egomaniac,
an apparitional visitation and a stupendous transformation wherein
flesh becomes stone illustrate Hawthorne's familiarity with standard Gothic properties and effects and also his desire to change
the literal objects of the tale of terror into terrifying symbols
of the warped and wasted moral life.

202. _____. "My Kinsman, Major Molineux." The Snow Image and Other
Tales. London: Henry G. Bohn, 1851.

REPRINT EDITION: Selected Tales and Sketches of Nathaniel Hawthorne, ed. Michael J. Colacurcio, Baltimore, Penguin, 1984.
RESEARCH SOURCE: Doubleday, Neal Frank, "'That Tinge of the Marvelous': Hawthorne's Gothic Habit," Hawthorne's Early Tales: A
Critical Study, Durham, NC, Duke UP, 1972, pp.52-62.

CRITICAL SYNOPSIS: The story was originally published in The Token
for 1832 and might have been one of "The Seven Tales of My Native
Land" which Hawthorne had discarded. The pattern of the story is
the night journey taken by the young initiate into the evil of the
world and the deeper evil of the self. On the psycho-cultural level, the journey takes the young man from the forest to the city
and from a colonial past into the violence of a revolutionary present. Thus, the allegory connotes the movement of the young nation
from rural to urban and from foreign domination to revolutionary
freedom. The central character is young Robin Molineux, a bird out
of nest for the first time and a bumpkin figure embodying both the
timeless delusions of youth and the naivete of young America on
the threshold of war. Crossing a river and entering the dark city
streets, Robin makes several inquiries about the whereabouts of
his kinsman, Major Molineux, whom he supposes a celebrity of power, prestige, wealth, and influence. Each of these inquiries as
Robin makes his way through the forbidding urban labyrinth receives an ominous or cryptic response which Robin misinterprets.
Furthermore, his question is often met by sarcastic laughter in
the tavern, barber shop, and streets which are thronged with muffled citizens seemingly hurrying to some festive nocturnal event.
Three of Robin's encounters are with a strikingly grotesque man
with an unforgettably demonic face, "one side blaz[ing] an intense
red, while the other was black as midnight. The effect was as if
two individual devils, a fiend of fire and a fiend of darkness,
had united themselves to form this infernal visage." Hawthorne's
refabrication of the stock Gothic scene in which maiden confronts
villain in the subterranean maze of the haunted castle is brilliantly done. Later, Hawthorne's new version of the Gothic villain

is identified within the allegory as nothing less than "war personified" and it remains for Robin to complete his education by recognizing and accepting his true kinsman in this Satanic father figure. At the climax, Robin is made to watch a cavalcade of violence as a parade swings in view with the bifaced demon at its head as grand marshal. When a cart pauses before Robin, he has his reunion with Major Molineux at last and it is a terrible moment of dark enlightenment for him, for "there in tar-and-feathery dignity," sits the once-mighty Molineux. The horror of the moment also becomes Robin's moment of understanding and he joins in the mob's peals of laughter. By doing so, he rejects his false kinsman and acknowledges his true kinship with the self-evil written into the features of the bifaced fiend and night rider. Offering multiple opportunities for Gothic interpretation, the tale depicts the entanglement of the victim in a new version of the castle maze, the darkest corridors of the American experience. The positive consequences of the night journey for Robin Molineux should be compared against the negative results of the same night journey into the hidden recesses of the self made by Young Goodman Brown (see 196).

203. _____. "The Wives of the Dead." The Snow Image and Other Tales. London: Henry G. Bohn, 1851.

REPRINT EDITION: The Celestial Railroad and Other Stories, afterword R.P. Blackmur, New York, New American Library, 1979.
RESEARCH SOURCES: Newlin, Paul A., "'Vague Shapes in the Borderland': The Place of the Uncanny in Hawthorne's Gothic Vision," ESQ: A Journal of the American Renaissance 18 (1972): 83-96; Stephenson, Edward R., "Hawthorne's 'The Wives of the Dead,'" Explicator 25 (April, 1967): item 63.

CRITICAL SYNOPSIS: A superbly crafted story which employs the terror of suggestion rather than the horror of direct revelation. The ambiguity which Hawthorne maintains between dream occurrences and actual events is perhaps unmatched elsewhere in Hawthorne's oneiric tales and sketches. The two wives are the sisters-in-law, Mary and Margaret, whose husbands have recently been reported dead on "two successive days." Thus, they sit together in "a parlor on the second floor of a small house...nursing their mutual and peculiar sorrows." Margaret had married Mary's brother, a soldier slain in the Indian wars in Canada. Mary had married Margaret's brother, who had died in a shipwreck at sea. Thus, the tale has a sort of morbid geometry in its structure of mutual grief. Each wife receives a visit while the other sleeps from a harbinger of good news. Margaret is told by the night messenger that her husband did not fall in battle and is returning home. Mary is told by another night visitor that her husband's brig was not lost after all and that her husband lives. Out of compassion for the other, each wife keeps her good news of the miraculous "resurrection" to herself: "Shall I waken her to feel her sorrow sharpened by my happiness? No; I will keep it within my own bosom till the morrow." But did any of these events occur or had each wife dreamt of her husband's return? The reader never knows because morning never comes. Instead, Hawthorne sustains the ambivalence between elation and bereavement to the very end in this tale before sunrise.

204. _____. The Marble Faun; or, The Romance of Monte Beni. Boston: Ticknor and Fields, 1862.

REPRINT EDITION: ed. Maxwell Geismar, New York, Pocket Books, 19-58.
RESEARCH SOURCE: Elder, Marjorie, "Hawthorne's Marble Faun: A Gothic Structure," Costerus: Essays in English and American Language and Literature 1 (1972): 81-88.

CRITICAL SYNOPSIS: Many successful Gothic novels revolve around a central brutal event sometimes supernatural in character, and in this respect, Hawthorne's Marble Faun adheres to Gothic convention. The Italian hero, young Donatello, saves a beautiful woman, Miriam, from a relentless and demonic stranger who has been stalking her by hurling the dark intruder from the Tarpeian Rock. Two other characters who witness Donatello's act are morally implicated in his virtuous crime, the American sculptor, Kenyon, the New England maiden, Hilda, both art students in Rome. Hawthorne shifts all emphasis from the violent deed itself to its psychological aftermath and corrosion of soul which threatens the four young people. The sensuous and Dionysian relationship between Donatello and Miriam changes into a mutual moral guilt after the destruction of the menacing stranger, but their suffering also has the positive effect of reaffirming their humanity. The Apollonian and intellectual relationship between Kenyon and Hilda is also transformed by the crime as Hilda finally rejects her frigid Puritanism by divulging her secret knowledge of the crime and criminal in a moment of passionate confession. Revising Gothic devices, situations, and characters, Hawthorne created an allegory of the heart in The Marble Faun, using the various Gothic properties to reenact the fall of man. The ancient catacombs and other subterranean enclosures, Hilda's Tower, the Owl Tower, and a tower among the Apennines, the edges of precipices, and a chapter called "The Spectre of the Catacomb" all strongly suggest the Gothic setting of the novel. But perhaps the most pronounced Gothic feature is Hawthorne's innovative reuse of the device of the living statue. Young Donatello bears such a close resemblance to the famous marble faun of Praxiteles that the statue itself appears to have come to life in the body of the young man. Transformed by his crime and subsequent suffering, the Faun loses his innocence but gains a soul through his sin. Of the Gothic world Hawthorne reveals in The Marble Faun, Donald Ringe observes that "it provides the appropriate vehicle for expressing those somber truths which Hawthorne believed Americans of his generation needed most to know."

205.   . Septimius Felton; or, The Elixir of Life. Boston: Osgood, 1872; London: Henry S. King, 1872.

REPRINT EDITION: The Elixir of Life Manuscripts, The Centennial Edition of the Works of Nathaniel Hawthorne, ed. William Charvat, Columbus, OH, Ohio State UP, 1977.
RESEARCH SOURCE: Hull, Ramona E., "Hawthorne and the Magic Elixir of Life: The Failure of a Gothic Theme," ESQ: A Journal of the American Renaissance 18 (1972): 97-107.

CRITICAL SYNOPSIS: In his last romances, Hawthorne allowed the recessant Gothic element to come into the foreground of his plots and characters. Most critics agree that this reversal of emphasis was an artistic error. Yet, the unfinished or abortive romances dealing with the secret of immortality are among American literatures most interesting "failures." Septimius Felton is at once a historical romance of the American revolution, a Gothic romance of entangled genealogies and dark motives, and a tale of how love can

sometimes flow from hatred or goodness become the byproduct of
evil. Except for the Faustian hero, Septimius Felton, the characters are stereotypical reproductions of characters to be found in
the works of Godwin, Scott or Cooper, romance writers admired by
the young Hawthorne. The innocent young woman, Rose Garfield, the
witchlike Sybil Dacy, the American soldier, Robert Hagburn, and
the comic physician, Dr. Portsoaken, and the old halfbreed, Aunt
Keziah, strut and fret their hour on Hawthorne's stage without
much consequence. What really interests--even obsesses--Hawthorne
in this late fragment is Felton's search for the power of life and
death that the secret elixir grants its possessor. The search, of
course, brings disaster to himself and others as the possession of
the elixir becomes a terrible curse. An ancient manuscript containing the dark formula, the murder of a British officer, an interrupted wedding, deception, revenge, scenes at graveside, and
the death of a beautiful woman indicate how heavily embroidered
Hawthorne's plot is with the standard Gothic fabric. So heavy and
frontal is the Gothicism of the last fragments, however, that the
great moral issues that Hawthorne had brought to tragic focus in
his best writings are almost entirely eclipsed for the sake of the
Gothic itself. Effect displaces idea as Ramona Hull has explained
in her critique of the late Hawthorne. "In the unfinished works,
where [the elixir and the alchemist] are meant to be the central
subjects of the plot and where the reader must accept them literally, the Gothic devices become mere trappings without real substance. After Hawthorne's return to America, Gothicism failed
him."

206. _____. The Ancestral Footstep; Outlines of an English Romance.
Boston: Copyright by Rose Hawthorne Lathrop, 1882.

REPRINT EDITION: The Centenary Edition of the Works of Nathaniel
Hawthorne, ed. William Charvat, Columbus, OH, Ohio State UP, 19-
78.
RESEARCH SOURCES: Calhoun, Thomas O., "Hawthorne's Gothic: An Approach to the Last Four Fragments," Genre 3 (1970): 229-241; Davidson, Edward Hutchins, "The Romance of England and 'The Ancestral Footstep,'" Hawthorne's Last Phase. New Haven, CT, Yale UP;
Yale Studies in English Number 111, 1949, pp.13-29.

CRITICAL SYNOPSIS: These are the scattered bones of an unfinished
Gothic romance done in the English Gothic manner. The work is possibly the most fragmented and broken of the four closing fragments
of Hawthorne's literary career for it breaks down into three disparate segments. The plot abounds in Gothic contraptions and situations including that well-worn genealogical motif of the lost
heir but the fact that there is no artistic unity or integration
is confirmed by Hawthorne's meditative postscript wherein he
broods about the problem of making this disjointed outline into a
good romance. Also evident is his interest in Gothic shock for its
own sake as shown when Hawthorne observes that "if well done, this
would produce a certain sort of horror, that I do not remember to
have seen effected in literature." The superficiality of Hawthorne's failed vision is quickly apparent in the detached plotting of the three parts. In part one, Middleton, an American lawyer who has returned to England for the purpose of finding his ancestral roots, visits a pensioners' hospital and makes the acquaintance of old Hammond who recounts to Middleton the gory legend of the bloody footprint of Smithell's Hall. Suspecting some
link with his family name, Middleton goes to the ancient manor

house to investigate but before he can start probing the chambers he is met by Squire Eldredge. The enraged Squire strikes Middleton with the butt of his musket causing the loaded weapon to discharge and the Squire to fall mortally wounded by an accidental shot through the heart. Here, the first narrative aborts. Hawthorne now retells Middleton's story but his encounter with Squire Eldredge is now cordial. With Hammond, he is given a tour of the old house and is conducted to the ghostly chamber where indeed a bloody footprint stains the threshold. There is some sinister connection between the generational crime represented by the bloody footstep and Middleton's English heritage. Part two ends with Middleton's generous renunciation of his English claims and his union with Hammond's grand-daughter, Alice. Part three resumes back at the pensioners' hospital where Middleton is invited to undergo that most Gothic of testing experiences by spending a night in the forbidden chamber of Smithell's Hall. Following the procedures established by Mrs. Radcliffe's inquisitive maidens, he searches the recesses of a great cabinet and comes across a secret compartment containing the documents which hold the secret to his heritage. Reverting to his previous character, the Squire plots to murder Middleton but his suicide interrupts the contemplated homicide. Middleton emerges from the morass of events having determined his heritage and become an ambassador. The third version of the thrice-told tale is not fully narrated but sketched or outlined. Apparently because of his preoccupation with Gothic effects and the gadgetry of shock, Hawthorne was unable to give any artistic order or moral meaning to Middleton's quest. Having used Gothic parts and characters to good advantage in his earlier fiction, Hawthorne suffers an almost complete artistic collapse when he allows these same Gothic parts to grow larger than the moral whole.

207. _____. The Dolliver Romance. The Complete Writings of Nathaniel Hawthorne, ed. Julian Hawthorne. Boston: Houghton, Mifflin, 1882.

REPRINT EDITION: The Elixir of Life Manuscripts, The Centennial Edition of the Works of Nathaniel Hawthorne, ed. William Charvat, Columbus, OH, Ohio State UP, 1977.
RESEARCH SOURCE: Curran, Ronald T., "The Reluctant Yankee in Hawthorne's Abortive Gothic Romances," Nathaniel Hawthorne Journal 1974, pp.179-194.

CRITICAL SYNOPSIS: This Gothic fragment left incomplete at Hawthorne's death appeared posthumously in the Atlantic Monthly, then in book form in 1876. The treatment of the theme of the immortalizing elixir is somewhat unusual since the old scientist, Dr. Dolliver, who inherits the drug of youth would use the powerful fluid only for selfless ends. Hence, Hawthorne strikes a moral contrast with his earlier handling of the theme of the elixir in "Dr. Heidegger's Experiment." The characters are also reminiscent of earlier figures in Hawthorne such as Dr. Rappaccini, Colonel Pyncheon, and The Scarlet Letter's child, Pearl. The plot hinges upon a struggle for power and possession, a typical conflict in Gothic fiction. The possessor of the elixir, old Dr. Dolliver, lives with and cares for his great grand-daughter, Pansie. He restores himself to youth solely to be able to continue his care and protection of the child, not for egotistic ends. His secret is threatened by Colonel Dabney, a repulsive and tyrannical landowner, who wishes to possess the immortalizing agent solely in order to regain the vigorous evil which has made him a powerful young man in the region. Hawthorne concentrates the ultimate in Gothic melodra-

ma in the moment of the Colonel's death when he quaffs the entire
vial of the elixir. The overdose brings first an instantaneous
restoration of youth, then an instantaneous mouldering of the features and a writhing death. "Then he laughed, a wild, exulting ha!
ha! with a strange triumphant roar that filled the house and re-
echoed through it; a sound full of fierce, animal rapture--enjoy-
ment of sensual life mixed up with a sort of horror." The direct
exposure of gory violence and a gruesome expiration indicate again
just how completely Hawthorne had turned to a reliance on direct
Gothic horror to achieve a moral effect in his final period.

208.   . Dr. Grimshawe's Secret. The Complete Writings of Nathaniel
      Hawthorne, ed. Julian Hawthorne. Boston: Houghton, Mifflin, 1882.

      REPRINT EDITION: The Centenary Edition of the Works of Nathaniel
      Hawthorne, ed. William Charvat, Columbus, OH, Ohio State UP, 19-
      78.
      RESEARCH SOURCE: Curran, Ronald T., "Hawthorne as Gothicist," Dis-
      sertation Abstracts 30 (1970): 4404A-4405A (University of Pennsyl-
      vania).

      CRITICAL SYNOPSIS: The fragmentary romance was edited by Haw-
      thorne's son, Julian, who first published it in 1882. Hawthorne
      reverted to a common plot pattern of the English Gothic romance
      best summed up under the variable title, the orphans of the cas-
      tle. The disinherited children who eventually unravel the secret
      of their heritage are the brother and sister, Ned and Elsie, wards
      of Dr. Grimshawe. They reside in a New England village, but some
      secret relating to their English inheritance takes them back to
      England and to their ancestral home after the death of their
      guardian. The family secret involves a bloody footprint left be-
      hind by the vanished heir who disappeared during the reign of
      Charles I. Chicanery and politics during the time of Cromwell have
      deprived the estate of its rightful lineage. The solution of the
      mystery of the vanished heir and the bloody footprint falls to Ned
      (now Edward Redclyffe), who undertakes to establish his family
      name and claim. With the help of his old tutor, Colcord, they ex-
      plore the estate, Redclyffe Hall, for clues. Their investigations
      turn up a very old man hidden in the Hall, so old in fact that he
      seems to be a fugitive from Cromwell's time. The lost and appar-
      ently immortal ancestor has been found in the person of the long-
      missing master, Sir Edward Redclyffe. The line is reestablished,
      all secrets cleared up, and young Edward named to rightful owner-
      ship of the estate. All of this detail is highly Gothic in the
      manner of the first Gothic romances, but not very original. And
      the moral theme, so imperative to a successful Hawthorne romance,
      is almost negligible. Of the four posthumous fragments, Doctor
      Grimshawe's Secret is the least interesting and the most slavishly
      mechanical with regard to its revival of conventionalized Gothic
      material.

209. Hazelton, Frank. The Mysteries of Troy. Founded Upon Incidents Which
      Have Taken Place in the City. Troy, NY: Troy Publishing, 1847.

      CRITICAL SYNOPSIS: A 38 page romance of domestic distress and the
      tribulations of the fallen woman inside the urban maze. The title
      page confers a different, if quaint, title on the work: The Belle
      of the Hudson; or, Mysteries at the Head of Navigation. The hero-
      ine and fallen woman, Laura Lerow, resides in a district of Troy,
      New York known as "Mount Olympus," an apparent euphemism for a

district of the city where women of loose or lost virtue and other
social outcasts congregate. Having had a child out of wedlock, she
still hopes for redemption and respectability by marrying Clarence
Merton, a city man of pleasure and an unscrupulous seducer who
would "make her his victim." The seduction scheme forms the core
of the Trojan mystery, a saga which sees the rise of the fallen
woman and the fall and reformation of the seducer. Much of the action occurs in the gloomy and dangerous maze of city streets and
back alleys where criminals prowl and where life itself is base
and short. The city as new Gothic environment had first appeared
in Charles Brockden Brown's Arthur Mervyn (see 064) and would continue to develop in the many urban Gothics of the Nineteenth Century.

210. Hearn, Lafcadio. "The Soul of the Great Bell." Some Chinese Ghosts.
Boston: Roberts, 1887.

REPRINT EDITION: New York, Irvington Publishers, 1972.

CRITICAL SYNOPSIS: A peculiarly chilling blend of the sentimental
and the gruesome by the American master of the bizarre Oriental
tale. In ancient China lives the master bell-maker and campan-
ologist, Kouan-Yu. But the masterpiece he is working on remains
flawed and resists all proper casting. It seems that a virgin must
be found and her living body and blood mixed with the molten metal
in order that the great bell may be properly casted. Kouan-Yu de-
spairs of achieving his masterwork until his young daughter volunteers herself as the needed ingredient. Before the horrified father can stop her, she plunges into the vat of molten metal leaving behind a silver slipper. Despite her horrible death, her soul
is always heard in the mournful tolling of the great bell. While
there is much horror here, the tale is told as a beautiful legend
of limitless sacrifice.

211. Hershey, Robert B. Death's Echo. Dallas, TX: Cottonwood Press, 19-
70.

CRITICAL SYNOPSIS: A formulaic but still effective modern Gothic.
Its publication by a relatively unknown press certainly kept
Death's Echo from the wider readership that it deserved, since the
novel has more than the average artistic merit to offer along with
its Gothic thrills. The cover description is a fair summation of
the book's Gothicism. "This novel offers a fast moving story in
the American Gothic tradition. Once you have entered the weed
grown, unkempt grounds of the Drummond estate with its massive old
home sitting on its knoll, boarded up, deserted, ugly, and deteri-
orating, you won't look back. Instead, you will move anxiously
through the book with Russ York, the Executor, Wilmer Benson, the
Attorney, and Ed Wilson, the Trustee, until you discover the true
and frightening meaning of Paragraph the Twelfth of the Will. As
Betsy Drummond arrives home from college for the last time, married to Bryce Gleason, a love-hate struggle commences and ends
only after Betsy discovers a truth she sought but doubted she
would ever find. This is a tale of love, mystery, and violence.
But to give even a bare outline of the basic plot would be unfair
at this point because it would expose too much of the book's unusual story and its bizarre dénouement." Typically, it is the brutal
husband who imprisons the wife. Death's Echo uses this situation,
but in reverse fashion.

212. Heyse, Paul. At the Ghost Hour. trans. Frances A. Van Santford. New
York: Dodd, Mead, 1894.

CRITICAL SYNOPSIS: Four books were published under the collective
title, At the Ghost Hour. These were: The Fair Abigail, The Forest
Laugh, The House of the Unbelieving Thomas, Mid-day Magic. Their
popularity with American readers makes them outstanding examples
of Gothic imports and translations. The Fair Abigail is a vampire
tale using the aftermath of the Franco-Prussian War for its historical setting. The Forest Laugh deals with the hauntings of the
ghost of a crippled boy. Perhaps the superior Gothic book is Mid-
day Magic, the sensitive story of the ghostly child, Little Lis-
beth, who is killed trying to save a pet rabbit from a dog, then
returns as a ghostly protector of helpless animals.

213. Hoffman, Charles Fenno. "Ben Blower's Story; or, How to Relish a
Julip." Graham's Magazine, September, 1842.

REPRINT EDITION: Gothic Tales of Terror: Classic Horror Stories
from Great Britain, Europe, and the United States, 1765-1840, ed.
Peter Haining, New York, Taplinger, 1972.

CRITICAL SYNOPSIS: This tall tale by the Knickerbocker author and
friend of Irving might be called "Steamboat Gothic." The narrator
is encased in the riverboat's hot water boiler and proceeds to report his horrifying claustrophobic situation in minute detail. "I
threw my arms about and looked eagerly for the opening by which I
had entered the horrid place--yes, looked for it, and felt for it,
though it was the terrible conviction that it was closed--a second
time brought home to me--which prompted my frenzied cry." He can
hear the fireman preparing to stoke the flames and feel the water
becoming increasingly hotter. Miraculous delivery comes when the
prisoner within the boiler discovers a mallet and marline spike
and drives a hole to freedom. Noticed and rescued at last, he
cools off with a much relished julip. It is interesting to compare
Ben Blower's predicament with the heating and contracting chamber
of Poe's famous Gothic tale, "The Pit and the Pendulum," (see 385)
which was first published the following year in The Gift for 1843
or with William Mudford's horrid thriller appearing in Blackwood's
Magazine in 1830, "The Iron Shroud."

214. Holland, Isabelle. Trewlawny. New York: Weybright & Talley, 1974.

RESEARCH SOURCE: Abartis, Caesarea, "Ugly-Pretty, Dull-Bright,
Weak-Strong Girl in the Gothic Mansion," Journal of Popular Culture 13 (1979): 257-263.

CRITICAL SYNOPSIS: Holland specializes in cliffhanging romances of
the maidenly plight such as Trewlawny and another Gothic of the
same year, Kilgaren: A Novel. Trewlawny's heroine, Kit, is a sort
of Nancy Drew for senior citizens and a direct descendant of
10,000 incarcerated maidens. Her haunted castle is Trewlawny Fell,
a gloomy manor house on the Maine coast. She travels to the evil
house with the noblest of purposes hoping to establish an artists'
colony but this philanthropic project is delayed by the usual
Gothic happenings and spectral difficulties. One should not be too
condescending either about the popularity or the literary quality
of these "garden club" Gothics. This one displays both a technical
acquaintance with the requirements of the genre and good grasp of
the patterns of Gothic plotting.

215. Holman, Jesse Lynch. The Prisoners of Niagara; or, Errors of Educa-
     tion. Frankfort, KY: William Gerard, 1810.

     RESEARCH SOURCE: Petter, Henri, Early American Novel, pp.383-386.

     CRITICAL SYNOPSIS: A sentimental historical romance of the Ameri-
     can Revolution with intermittent Gothic scenes and effects. The
     hero's name is Evermont, a Rousseauistic and emotionally undisci-
     plined young man who is imprisoned at Fort Niagara by the British.
     The heroine is Zerelda who promises to marry Barville, a British
     officer, after hearing of Evermont's death in a duel. After many
     adventures and complex misunderstandings against the background of
     America's struggle for independence, Evermont and Zerelda are fi-
     nally married and thereafter emancipate their slaves and devise an
     enlightened system of education for their newborn son. The novel
     shows strong traces of the Gothic romance in its early chapters
     which reflect the influence of Charles Brockden Brown's wilderness
     Gothic, Edgar Huntly (see 066). Evermont's encounters with the
     ghost of a fellow prisoner, Anderville, show touches of Radclif-
     fean Gothic technique as well.

216. Holmes, Oliver Wendell. Elsie Venner; A Romance of Destiny. Boston:
     Houghton, 1861.

     REPRINT EDITION: Psychiatric Novels of Oliver Wendell Holmes,
     Westport, CT, Greenwood Press, 1971.
     RESEARCH SOURCES: Gross, Louis, Redefining the American Gothic:
     From Wieland to the Day of the Dead, Ann Arbor, MI, UMI Press, pp.
     3, 42, 51; Pridgeon, Charles T. Jr., "Insanity in American Fiction
     from Charles Brockden Brown to Oliver Wendell Holmes," Disserta-
     tion Abstracts 31 (1970): 1766A-1767A (Duke University).

     CRITICAL SYNOPSIS: The Lamia myth of the beautiful maiden whose
     other self is a poisonous snake informs Holmes's schizophrenic
     case study of the strange woman, Elsie Venner, a serpentine hero-
     ine said to have been based in part on the New England mystic,
     Margaret Fuller (1810-1850). The toxic or mithridatic maiden had
     also interested Hawthorne in his portrait of the deadly Beatrice
     in "Rappaccini's Daughter" (see 194). Elsie Venner's case is
     Holmes's investigation of the validity of the bosom serpent of
     original sin, the central Calvinist tenet, as the source of moral
     evil in human character. Or is morality at the bottom really a
     question of physiological and biological factors as symbolized by
     Elsie Venner's pre-natal toxification, since her mother had been
     bitten by a rattlesnake during her pregnancy? The warfare between
     science (which would treat Elsie Venner for a psychiatric ailment)
     and religion (which would attribute her condition to Eve's taint-
     ing by the serpent in the Garden of Eden) forms the intellectual
     core of the novel, although there is enough violence and weird
     spiritualism to maintain a high level of Gothic horror. Elsie ap-
     pears to have hypnotic and curative powers to go with her strange,
     serpentine nature, and proves these when the man she adores, Ber-
     nard Langdon, is bitten by a rattlesnake. Her cousin, Richard Ven-
     ner, schemes to have her money and assaults Langdon when Elsie
     displays too much affection for his rival. Bernard will not return
     her love, however, and in fact rejects her reptilian advances even
     after she has saved his life. The refusal seems to precipitate the
     illness which takes the life of the snake lady. Holmes, himself a
     medical man and a foe of the rigid Calvinist explanation of human

conduct, attempts to show how Elsie Venner was a victim of heredi-
ty and how she might have been saved by science instead of condemned by religion. To illustrate his point, he chose a most sinister and repulsive psychosis, the serpent complex. In Lewis's The
Monk (1796), the fatal woman, Matilda, sucks the venom of the poisonous cientepedoro from the Monk's veins, thus saving him for future crimes.

217.   Howard, Robert Erwin. Skull-Face and Others. Sauk City, WI: Arkham
House, 1946.

RESEARCH SOURCE: E.F. Bleiler, "Robert E. Howard," Supernatural
Fiction Writers, pp.861-868.

CRITICAL SYNOPSIS: This short and shoddy pulp Gothic originally
appeared in Weird Tales for 1929. Using all of the elements of the
Lovecraftian thriller, Howard pursued a favorite theme, the modern
world menaced by a supernatural foe from another age. But the villainous force here is an unlikely Lovecraftian reincarnation in
the form of the mummified Kathulos, a skull faced survivor from
Atlantis who emerges from the Sea of Senegal to threaten the earth
with domination. The forces of civilization in the person of the
scientific investigator, John Gordon, and the heroic narrator,
Costigan, eventually subdue Howard's Fu Manchu style figure. The
modern monster tale frequently allows for the return of the thing
in a sequel story. To this end, Kathulos is checked but not permanently removed and may still rise again since he is not destroyed.
"The return of..." was becoming a mandatory formula for the monster saga. Howard was also capable of working in the orthodox
Gothic vein as shown in such suggestive titles as "The Rattle of
Bones," "The Hills of the Dead," "The Horror from the Mound," and
"The Valley of the Worm."

218.   Howells, William Dean. "His Apparition." Questionable Shapes. New
York: Harper, 1903.

REPRINT EDITION: Short Story Index Reprint Series, Salem, NH, Ayer
Publishers, 1974.

CRITICAL SYNOPSIS: The story has a muted supernatural incident,
but Howells's principal subject is the generous moral gesture of
the main character, Hewson. His stay at a resort hotel is interrupted by a spectral visit which he considers both significant and
a secret worth guarding. Eventually, however, he does tell of his
ghostly visitor and the ghost story is widely repeated by his
wife. Her dissemination of the supernatural experience scares away
all potential clientele and ruins the business of the hotel. Out
of generosity and fine conscience, Hewson buys the hotel, later
remembering that the ghostly visit had come on the same day of the
year that he had met his wife, the spreader of the ruinous tale.
Howells also tried his hand at spookiness and mystery in a collection of tales entitled Between the Dark and the Daylight (Harper,
1907) but his literary temperament was generally inimical to the
Gothic spirit. The tale, "A Case of Metaphantasmia" or thought-
transference does have its chilling moments.

219.   _____. "Though One Rose from the Dead." Questionable Shapes. New
York: Harper, 1903.

REPRINT EDITION: Short Story Index Reprint Series, Salem, NH, Ayer

Publishing, 1974.

CRITICAL SYNOPSIS: Uses the figure of the "posthumous heroine" or dead beloved whose affection transcends the grave. The Alderlings are a devoted couple and vow to remain together even after death. Thus, Mrs. Alderling's voice can be heard calling to him after death. Howells was too much the anti-romantic realist, however, to allow the tale to become a Poe-like resurrection. Given Howells's general literary career, it is slightly astonishing that he attempted any forays into Gothicism whatsoever. But even the master realist could not resist a few experiments in psychic Gothicism.

220. Ingraham, Joseph Holt. Howard; or, The Mysterious Disappearance. A Romance of the Tripolitan War. Boston: Edward P. Williams, 1843.

CRITICAL SYNOPSIS: An historical romance and love triangle with intermittent Gothic motions and emotions by the extravantly virtuous or extragantly wicked characters. The background is the retaliation in 1801 by the United States Navy against the pirates of Algiers, Tunis, and Tripoli. Duncan Dudley returns to Virginia from the Tripolitan War to press his suit for the hand of Isabel Sumpter, daughter of Judge Sumpter; she in turn is in love with Duncan's brother, the reckless and restless Howard Dudley. The Dudley brothers are intellectual opposites, but moral twins in their patriotism, selfless sacrifice, and regard for one another. When Howard suddenly and mysteriously vanishes, secretly joining the fleet bound for Tripoli, he creates the impression that he has died, thus leaving Isabel free to love Duncan. But distress follows distress when the schemer, Hamilton Woodhall, has Duncan falsely accused and tried for the murder of his brother even though no corpse has been offered in evidence. Woodhall's mind and methods, his motiveless malignity, link him to earlier American Gothic villains, particularly the mysterious criminals of Charles Brockden Brown whose evil is sometimes motivated purely by the desire to do evil under the guise of good. The melodramatic death of Woodhall during his trial for murder, the reunion of the two brothers in Tripoli, and the double marriage back in Virginia, complete the moral cycle of disaster and triumph. Having dramatized his moral, Ingraham capsulated it in the final sentences of the romance: "Let the reader long pause before he condemns another from the evidence of circumstance, however strong they may appear in his own eyes and those of the world."

221. _____. The Spectre Steamer and Other Tales. Boston: United States Publishing Company, 1846.

CRITICAL SYNOPSIS: "A true story for the most part," the eighteen page tale, "The Spectre Steamer," might be called "Riverboat Gothic." Travelling up the Mississippi from New Orleans on the steamer, St. Louis, in the spring of 1839, the narrator has a harrowing experience. Near Horseshoe Bend, the steamer pilot, Paul Fink, tells the narrator of a strange ship "which has been runnin' alone this past twelve-month and has never yet got to her port." The pilot explains that there had been a rivalry between his captain and Captain Hugh Northrup of the steamer, Lucifer. Northrup had vowed brashly to reach New Orleans in three days "or drive her to the devil," an arrogant boast which came true when the Lucifer became the Flying Dutchman of the river. Now, anyone who encounters the spectre steamer and her skeletal captain is fated to die within seven days of the sighting. As the pilot finishes his story, the

Lucifer looms up ahead with the ghastly figure of the captain be-
seeching food for himself and his cadaverous crew. The destructive
climax sees the St. Louis pulled after the Lucifer into a river of
molten fire. The narrator, who somehow survives, insists upon the
authenticity of these events. In its use of realistic detail and
common speech to recount impossible happenings, the story can be
considered a Gothified version of a Mississippi tall tale; and
since one of the characters is the cousin of the famous riverboat
roughneck, Mike Fink, its extravagant supernaturalism conforms to
the superhuman deeds of that frontiersman.

222. Ingram, Eleanor Marie. The Thing From the Lake. Philadelphia: Lippincott, 1921.

REPRINT EDITION: Supernatural and Occult Fiction Series, eds. R.
Reginald, Douglas Menville, Salem, NH, Ayer Publishing, 1976,

CRITICAL SYNOPSIS: Referred to by the supernaturalist, E.F. Bleiler, as "shopgirl Gothic," the novel follows a Radcliffean pattern
of building terror, but undermines its own Gothic effects by re-
sorting to an unsatisfying natural explanation for the supernatu-
phenomena filling the story. The main character is a songwriter,
Roger Locke. Following the route laid down by earlier Gothic wanderers, he buys an old and desolate Connecticut farmstead, goes
there to reside by himself, and immediately collides with the supernatural world and its denizens. Thus, his skeptical, unsenti-
mental, hard-headed nature is put to the test. The main evidence
of an insistent supernatural world is the old house's female phantom, a mysterious lady who appears to Locke and is somehow linked
with the stagnant and gloomy pond which verges on the house. The
tarn beneath the House of Usher was never more dank. To match his
ghostly visitations, Locke is also the victim of cloying nightmares and finds his mental stability slipping from beneath him as
result of the dark lady, the darker lake, and a recurrent monster
which stalks through his dreams. Having built an atmosphere of supernatural dread, the novel falls back upon the weakest of Gothic
endings, the plausible explication by means of natural cause and
effect. From a scientist friend who comes to visit Locke, he
learns that all of his horrific experiences had been hallucinations caused by his inhalation of the methane gas fumes emitted by
the lake.

223. Irving, Washington. "The Legend of Sleepy Hollow." The Sketch Book
of Geoffrey Crayon, Gent. New York: C.S. Van Winkle, 1819-1820.

REPRINT EDITION: The Sketch Book, afterword Perry Miller, New
York, New American Library, 1961.
RESEARCH SOURCE: Thompson, G.R., "Washington Irving and the Ameri-
can Ghost Story," The Haunted Dusk: American Supernatural Fiction,
1820-1920, eds. Howard Kerr, John W. Crowley, Charles L. Crow,
Athens, GA, Georgia UP, 1983, pp.13-36.

CRITICAL SYNOPSIS: There is no finer blend of comedy and terror,
of hilarity and horror, than in this classic American short story
and able spoof of the spectral encounter. Riding alone at night
after listening to a round of ghost stories at a quilting party,
the school master, Ichabod Crane, is accosted by the figure of the
headless Hessian horseman who aims a round object at Ichabod's
head. The description of the night meeting at the old bridge indicates that Irving knew the Gothic well and might have written ser-

ious tales of terror had he so chosen: "In the dark shadow of the grove, on the margin of the brook, he beheld something huge, mis-shapen, black, and towering. It stirred not, but seemed gathered up in the gloom, like some gigantic monster ready to spring upon the traveler." In the morning, the remains of a shattered pumpkin are found, but not Ichabod Crane, who has been scared out of his wits, out of Sleepy Hollow, and out of his suit for the hand of Katrina Van Tassel. Irving found the excesses of the typical Goth-ic tale both laughable and a rich source of material for express-ing his disbelief in the supernatural. In this respect, Irving's use of the Gothic resembles Mrs. Radcliffe. Where she finally de-nied or explained away any actual supernatural terrors, he often turned the serious into the ludicrous.

224. _____. "The Spectre Bridegroom." The Sketch Book of Geoffrey Cra-yon, Gent. New York: C.S. Van Winkle, 1819-1820.

REPRINT EDITIONS: The Evil Image: Two Centuries of Gothic Short Fiction and Poetry, eds. Patricia L. Skarda, Nora Crow Jaffe, New York, New American Library, 1981; Romantic Gothic Tales, 1790-1840, ed. G.R. Thompson, New York, Harper & Row, 1979.
RESEARCH SOURCES: Bell, Michael Davitt, "Strange Stories: Irving's Gothic," The Development of American Romance, Chicago, Chicago UP, 1980, pp.77-85; Clendenning, John, "Irving and the Gothic Tradi-tion," Bucknell Review 12, number 2 (1964): 90-98.

CRITICAL SYNOPSIS: The genre of terror is well-mocked almost point-by-point in this Germanic hairraiser. At the outset, the be-mused narrator reminds the reader: "It is well known that the for-ests of Germany have always been as much infested with robbers as its castles by spectres." But the names of the story's principal characters, the Baron of Katzenellenbogen (or cat's elbow) and his rival, Herman Von Starkenfaust (or strong fist) announce Irving's satiric purposes even before the presentation of the ghoulish horseman who abducts the Baron's daughter. The ghastly rider is no deceased hero after all but young Herman engaging in the same sort of midnight charade by which Brom Bones had wooed and won Katrina Van Tassel in "The Legend of Sleepy Hollow." (see 223) Irving's wit was attuned to the ludicrous excesses of the Germanic shocker which yet remained a popular type of short Gothic in the magazines when The Sketchbook appeared in 1820.

225. _____. "Dolph Heyliger." Bracebridge Hall; or, The Humourists, A Medley by Geoffrey Crayon, Gent. New York: C.S. Van Winkle, 1822.

REPRINT EDITION: Bracebridge Hall; or, The Humourists, A Medley by Geoffrey Crayon, Gent., The Complete Works of Washington Irving, ed. Henry A. Pochmann, New York, Twayne, 1977.
RESEARCH SOURCE: Getz, John R., "Irving's 'Dolph Heyliger': Ghost Story or Tall Tale?" Studies in Short Fiction 16 (1979): 67-68.

CRITICAL SYNOPSIS: A long short story which leaves the question of the existence of an actual supernatural unresolved and the ghostly episodes unexplained. Dolph Heyliger, a "longbow drawer" or teller of tall tales, recites the story of how he got rich implying that a spook had been his financial assistant and guided him to the place of a buried treasure. But other details of the biography do not square with this supernatural explanation. As a lad, he disap-peared briefly from his home in New York City only to turn up mar-ried to the pretty and wealthy Marie Vander Heyden of Albany. Nei-

ther his whereabouts, his wooing, nor his sudden wealth can be accounted for by Dolph's narrative. In the majority of his tales
which use the supernatural, the Gothic is mocked as a false view
of reality and reason is ranked above imagination. But the ambiguous Gothic of "Dolph Heyliger" and the story's numerous loose ends
make it an exception to Irving's customary skeptical comedies of
terror.

226. _____. "The Adventure of My Aunt." Tales of a Traveller. Philadelphia: Carey & Lea, 1824.

REPRINT EDITION: Washington Irving's Tales of the Supernatural,
ed. Edward Wagenknecht, Owings Mills, MD, Stemmer House, 1982.
RESEARCH SOURCES: Masiello, Lea, "Speaking of Ghosts: Style in
Washington Irving's Tales of the Supernatural," Dissertation Abstracts International 44 (1983): 1792A (University of Cincinnati).

CRITICAL SYNOPSIS: An instance of Irving's comic deflation of the
high Gothic tale. The story uses the durable object of terror, the
picture with moving eyes, as the basis for comedy and undercut-
ting. The common sense moral seems to deny the existence of any
and all supernatural phenomena. There is always a trick or explainable illusion behind every phantom if the menaced character
will only investigate as does the aunt who is threatened by the
moving eyes of the portrait in the story. Instead of simply fainting as would a regulation Gothic maiden, the aunt arms herself and
probes behind the portrait to find and to apprehend a lurking robber. Other travellers narrate spooky tales to explore or to debunk
the reality of the supernatural. The aunt's story is followed by
the "Adventure of the German Student" (see 227) in which the real
existence of the supernatural is treated ambiguously.

227. _____. "Adventure of the German Student." Tales of a Traveller.
Philadelphia: Carey & Lea, 1824.

REPRINT EDITION: The American Tradition in Literature, eds.
Sculley Bradley, Raymond C. Beatty, E. Hudson Long, New York, W.W.
Norton, 1967.
RESEARCH SOURCES: Devlin, James E., "Irving's Adventure of the
German Student,'" Studies in American Fiction 7 (1980): 92-95; Lu-
pack, Barbara Tepa, "Irving's German Student," Studies in Short
Fiction 21 (1984): 398-400; Ringe, Donald A., "Irving's Use of the
Gothic Mode," Studies in the Literary Imagination 7 (1974): 51-
65.

CRITICAL SYNOPSIS: A serious and sustained atmosphere of high
Gothic terror is not Irving's customary Gothic mode since he pre-
fers the comic twists afforded by the "sportive Gothic," but such
an unbroken mood of horror is present throughout the "Adventure of
the German Student." The German student is the lonely and sullen
Gottfried Wolfgang, a Frankensteinian recluse who takes chambers
in Paris just as the Reign of Terror is reaching its full fury.
Brooding heavily over esoteric subjects, his meditations are
filled with the image of a beautiful dark haired woman. Seeking
relief, he wanders the streets and draws near the scaffold of the
guillotine on the Place de Grève where he is shocked to see the
haunting creature of his dreams seated on the steps of the "horrible engine." They retire to Wolfgang's chamber where she gives
herself to him. In the morning, he leaves her lying in bed "to

seek more spacious apartments suitable to the change in his situation," but upon returning he discovers her corpse. A policeman enters, unfastens a black collar around her neck, and the decapitated head promptly rolls on the floor. She was part of the guillotine's bloody quota on the previous day. The realization that his evening of love was in reality a necrophiliac embrace proves so unbearable to the German student that he has to be dragged screaming to the madhouse. Although the tale contains no winking wordplay or ironic undercuts, some critics have still insisted that the entire tale with its overwrought Gothic characterization and effects must be read as Irving's burlesque of the heavyhanded and outrageously supernatural German tale of terror, or the Schauerroman.

228. Jackson, Daniel Jr. Ilonzo and Melissa; or, The Unfeeling Father. Plattsburgh, NY: Printed for the Proprietor, 1811.

RESEARCH SOURCES: Davidson, Kathy N., "Isaac Mitchell's The Asylum; or, Gothic Castles in the New Republic," Prospects: An Annual Journal of American Cultural Studies 7 (1982): 281-299; Petter, Henri, Early American Novel, pp.316-319; Reed, Edward B., "Letter," Nation, December 8, 1904, p.458.

CRITICAL SYNOPSIS: A plagiarized reduction of Isaac Mitchell's noteworthy American Gothic romance, The Asylum (see 338). "Groping to find the stairs, as she came near their foot, a black object, apparently in human shape, stood before her, with eyes which resembled glowing coals, and red flames issuing from its mouth. As she stood fixed in inexpressible trepidation, a large ball of fire rolled slowly along the extended hall and burst with an explosion which seemed to rock the building in its deepest foundations. Melissa closed her eyes and fell senseless to the floor." This highly Gothic event occurs not in remote Apennines of Mrs. Radcliffe's Italy but within a haunted castle in colonial Connecticut where Melissa Bloomfield has been conveyed by her father to compel her to marry the repulsive Mr. Bowman. Rescue from the terrible castle in Connecticut by her ardent lover, Alonzo, is delayed by his involvement in the cause of the American Revolution. Shipwrecked and aided by Benjamin Franklin in Paris, Ilonzo eventually makes his way back to Charleston, South Carolina, where he throws himself upon the grave of the Melissa he supposes dead. This sets the stage for a major stock spectacle of the sentimental Gothic, the heroine's miraculous reunion with her lost admirer and the reformation of the cruel father who belatedly explains that he had staffed the castle in Connecticut with artificial horrors to terrify his daughter. The phantoms who tormented Melissa are revealed to be Tory smugglers. In its several forms, Mitchell's colonial Gothic won a wide following and can be judged the transitional link between the high-minded Gothicism of Charles Brockden Brown and the Gothic excitement found in Cooper's romances of the forest.

229. Jackson, Shirley. Hangsaman. New York: Farrar, Straus, and Giroux, 1951.

REPRINT EDITION: New York, Popular Library, 1976; New York, Arbor House, 1986.
RESEARCH SOURCE: Nardacci, Michael L., "Theme, Character, and Technique in the Novels of Shirley Jackson," Dissertation Abstracts International 41 (1979): 674A (New York University).

CRITICAL SYNOPSIS: Jackson's fascination with the multiple personality and with schizophrenic breakdown are reflected in the disturbing chronicle of Natalie Waite, whose personality undergoes a
bifurcation into an introverted self and an extroverted self.
Natalie is a college freshman who becomes psychologically involved
with the mysterious Tony and nearly surrenders herself to absorp-
tion or suicide. The climactic episode takes places in the depths
of the forest when Tony leads Natalie to a decisive encounter with
her evil self, but Natalie finally repels the perverse embrace of
her dark lady thus expelling the wicked double from her psyche.
Jackson would again return to this theme, which can be traced back
in the Gothic tradition to James Hogg's Private Memoirs and Confessions of a Justified Sinner (1824), in her 1954 novel, The
Bird's Nest (see 230).

230. _____. The Bird's Nest. New York: Farrar, Straus, and Giroux, 19-
54.

REPRINT EDITION: New York, Ace Books, 1958.
RESEARCH SOURCE: Friedman, Lenemaja, Shirley Jackson, Boston,
Twayne, 1975.

CRITICAL SYNOPSIS: To write this novel of threatened self-
disintegration, Jackson had carefully studied a psychiatric text
by Morton Prince, The Disintegration of a Personality (1905). She
also responded to certain character relationships in Hawthorne's
Gothic fiction, namely the physician's perverted quest to violate
the soul of another human being under the guise of benign motives.
The character of the malign doctor appears in Chillingworth in The
Scarlet Letter (see 197), Doctor Rappaccini, (see 194), and to
some degree, in the scientist, Aylmer, of "The Birthmark" (see
190), all possible models for Jackson's prying psychiatrist, Dr.
Victor Wright. He treats the heroine, Elizabeth Richmond, for an
acute case of mutiple schizophrenia since Elizabeth's self is dis-
persed among four discrete and contesting personalities. Elizabeth
is a fragile woman who resides in a Gothic house with her slightly
crazy aunt, Morgen Jones, and suffers great guilt through several
of her selves for the death of her mother. Obsessed with guiding
her back to a wholeness of self, Dr. Wright quite "wrongly" tries
to eliminate only her wicked or demonic personalities leaving only
the good self. It falls to the aunt to protect Elizabeth from this
attempt to perfect her by ruling out an aspect of the self which
must be faced and acknowledged, the demon within us all. Elizabeth
Richmond is one of the few heroines in Shirley Jackson's work to
emerge from her ordeal without going mad or dying in some violent
way like Tessie Hutchinson who is stoned to death by her neighbors
in the famous prairie Gothic tale, "The Lottery" (1949). In fact,
she acquires both a whole self and a new name, Victoria Morgen. Of
Shirley Jackson's expert modern Gothic, John G. Parks observes:
"Gothic fiction is an effective mode for her exploration of the
violations of the human self,--the aching loneliness, the unendurable guilt, the disillusion and disintegrations, the sinking into
madness, the violence and lovelessness."

231. _____. The Sundial. New York: Farrar, Straus, and Giroux, 1958.

REPRINT EDITION: Baltimore, Penguin, 1986.
RESEARCH SOURCE: Oppenheimer, Judy, Private Demons: The Life of
Shirley Jackson, New York, Putnam, 1988.

CRITICAL SYNOPSIS: Jackson's most successful technical imitation of the eighteenth-century Gothic novel, particularly the prototype of the genre, Walpole's Castle of Otranto (1764). Only Italianate naming and medieval costuming and scenery would be required to transform the novel's mad household of Halloran into a classic tale of terror. Maddest of the Halloran lot is the matriarch of the house, Aunt Fanny, an apocalypticalist extraordinaire who believes in nothing but the imminent end of the world on a specific day in August, who regularly receives ghostly visitations from her father, and who fortifies herself within the old house to await the coming of doomsday. The interior of the house rivals Walpole's original Gothic castle in its abundance of Gothic contraptions. A sentient portrait, crepuscular statues, bosom serpents, Macbethian weather, and a terminal storm which seems to confirm Aunt Fanny's belief that the end of the world is at hand are just of few examples of Jackson's borrowings from Walpole's first Gothic warehouse of devices and effects. The central device and symbol is the sundial itself, a possessive reminder of the false human control over cosmic time and a pointer which fixes the impending ruin of the world. Having assembled the Halloran family for a stupendous Gothic climax resembling Walpole's collapsing castle at the end of Otranto, Jackson terminated the novel on the brink of doom without actually fulfilling Aunt's Fanny's prophecy. This anticlimax or non-ending may seem to weaken the novel's Gothicism; actually, it enhances her tenebrous vision of social and psychological chaos.

232. _____. The Haunting of Hill House. New York: Viking, 1959.

REPRINT EDITION: Baltimore, Penguin Books, 1984.
RESEARCH SOURCES: Kittredge, Mary, "The Other Side of Magic: A Few Remarks About Shirley Jackson," Discovering Modern Horror Fiction, Mercer Island, WA, Starmont House, 1985, pp.3-12; Parks, John G., "Chambers of Yearning: Shirley Jackson's Use of the Gothic," Twentieth Century Literature 30 (1984): 15-29.

CRITICAL SYNOPSIS: The infernal skyline of Gothic romance is in full view in Jackson's Haunting of Hill House, a novel of gripping Gothic power and audible presences. This book is most definitely her Gothic's Gothic with all of the internal requirements of the genre on hand. The organically evil character of the house itself dominates the story and supplies the sound effects which include terrible chambers of horror and midnight hammerings. The fated family of older Gothic fiction includes the lonely and suicidal Eleanor Vance, her clairvoyant and lesbian friend, Theodora, the psychic investigator and Gothic skeptic, Dr. Montague, and the pathological liar, Luke. Although they occupy the dark house together, they are each actually alone and held in solitary confinement by their egos and dreams. They have all come to Hill House ostensibly to investigate its psychic secrets and sinister manifestations but the real spectres and dark desires turn out to be themselves, and especially Eleanor, whose suicidal derangement is reflected in various ways in the crazy angularity of the House. The House itself is a twentieth-century reproduction of Poe's Usher. Its facial features and powers of observation mark the coming of the guests. It is "a place of despair, more frightening because the face of Hill House seemed awake, with a watchfulness from the blank windows and a touch of glee in the eyebrow of a cornice." This Gothic ends in violence and death when Eleanor, rejected by the others, crashes her car into a tree in a futile gesture of rebellion against the dark knowledge which her residence at Hill House has brought her.

233. _____. We Have Always Lived in the Castle. New York: Viking, 19-62.

REPRINT EDITION: Baltimore, Penguin Books, 1984.
RESEARCH SOURCES: Sullivan, Jack, "Shirley Jackson," Supernatural Fiction Writers, pp.1031-1036; Woodruff, Stuart, "The Real Horror Elsewhere: Shirley Jackson's Last Novel," Southwest Review 52 (19-67): 152-162.

CRITICAL SYNOPSIS: A psychotic world comes vividly to life before the eyes of the reader in this stunning Gothic performance, probably Shirley Jackson's ne plus ultra tale of terror. Because the narrator, Mary Katherine (called "Merricat") Blackwood is a mad woman, the reader can never be sure of the validity of the events she reports. But hallucinatory or not, we can be sure about the horrible lucidity of her narrative. "I have often thought," Merricat begins her story, "that with any luck at all I could have been born a werewolf, because the two middle fingers on both my hands are the same length. I dislike washing myself, and dogs, and noise. I like my sister Constance, and Richard Plantagenet, and Amanita Phalloides, the death cup mushroom. Everyone else in my family is dead." Her narrative is a veritable Gothic argosy of fatal events and strange people. Sister Constance, Uncle Julian, and Merricat are the last of the Blackwood line, all of the others having perished from poisoned sugar. Constance was suspected of the mass murder of her relatives and is now guarded by Merricat from the vengeful suspicions of the villagers. The ancient family estate is their fortress and Merricat is the self-appointed family protector. Suddenly, a mysterious relative, Charles Blackwood, appears to upset their isolated security and events gather quickly toward a Gothic climax. A fire watched gleefully by the sadistic villagers rages through the house but the novel cannot end with this conflagration. Merricat and Constance will always live in their castle, even a destroyed one. The final exchange underscores the cold horror of their psychotic bliss. "I wonder if I could eat a child if I had the chance?" (said Merricat). "I doubt if I could cook one," said Constance. "Poor strangers," I said. "They have so much to be afraid of." The "castle" can only be the castle of lunacy, the mind's last resort for happiness. The book is Jackson's final, and in many ways, her finest Gothic statement.

234. _____. "The Possibility of Evil." Saturday Evening Post, September 18, 1965.

RESEARCH SOURCE: Parks, John G., "'A Possibility of Evil': The Key to Shirley Jackson's Fiction," Studies in Short Fiction 15 (1978): 320-323.

CRITICAL SYNOPSIS: Of the seventy-one year old spinster heroine, Miss Adela Strangeworth, we read: "As long as evil existed unchecked in the world it was Miss Strangeworth's duty to keep her town alert to it....There were so many wicked people in the world and only one Strangeworth left in the town." Thus, she lives alone in her old house on Pleasant Street, minding her roses and minding everyone else's business, the moral watchdog of the neighborhood who is ever alert to "possible evil lurking nearby." Nearly everyone in town has received one of her unsigned letters of accusation or recrimination, for hate mail is Miss Strangeworth's special method of ferreting out evil--and her poisonous pen is ever busy. One day, however, enroute to the mailbox with the day's quota of dark warnings she chances to drop several letters which are retrieved by some passing teenagers. The next morning, her mail brings an unsigned letter to her with the message "Look out at what used to be your roses." Her letters to the vile world have been answered. The possibility of her own moral evil was something she had never considered until that morning's post. Evil everywhere and in everyone except the self had also been the moral perversion of Hawthorne's Young Goodman Brown (see 196). One of Jackson's great themes--cruelty hiding behind morality--is set forth in this story of self-depraved isolation.

235.   . "The Rock." <u>Come Along With Me</u>. New York: Viking, 1968.

RESEARCH SOURCE: Sullivan, Jack, "The Haunted Mind of Shirley Jackson," <u>Twilight Zone Magazine</u> July-August 1984, pp.71-74.

CRITICAL SYNOPSIS: Sophisticated and subtle Gothic story about a young woman's courtship by death in the form of the self-effacing Mr. Johnson. His gradual attachment to the heroine is accompanied by a gradually building of a malign and fatal atmosphere that reminds of the growth from terror to horror in the famous story, "The Lottery".

236.   . "The Visit." <u>Come Along With Me</u>. ed. Stanley Edgar Hyman. New York: Viking Press, 1968.

CRITICAL SYNOPSIS: The supernatural tale is pure household Gothic. The spectral experiences of the heroine, Margaret, remain unexplained at the end of the narrative. They may be hallucinations or she may just as equally have been visited by real ghosts during her stay in the haunted house. While in the house, she is visited by a most unusual pair of lovers, a Byronic young man and an old lady who has "died for love." While the masculine ghost retains his youth, the feminine ghost is subject to the ravages of age. Since the old lady's name is also Margaret, the dark psychic connection between the young guest and the ageing spectre is established. Taking the mysterious house a step further, the possibility that young Margaret is being absorbed into the structure of the house itself is suggested by the atmosphere of the tale. Jackson's Gothic frequently inquires into the elusive nature of reality or what we want to perceive as reality. This usage of the Gothic is summed up by Jack Sullivan who writes of "The Visit," that the tale "is the most intricate and lyrical of Jackson's supernatural tales; it presents her world at its most lonely and brilliantly artificial, a succession of mirrors, doublings, and possibilities within possibilities, where lost connections between people continually multiply." The dark labyrinth of the mind, then, is Shirley Jackson's corridor to horror.

237. Jacobi, Carl Richard. "Revelations in Black." <u>Revelations in Black</u>. Sauk City, WI: Arkham House, 1947.

REPRINT EDITION: Sudbury, UK, Neville Spearman, 1974.

CRITICAL SYNOPSIS: A fantasy of the dark lady somewhat reminiscent of Poe's "Ligeia" (see 377). The narrator wanders into a strange garden and encounters a woman in black. She offers him a book containing the biography of a maniac wherein he discovers the horrid details of his own dreamlife. Other Gothic pieces in the set include "The Satanic Piano," an instrument with a mind of its own, and the chilling tale, "Last Drive," in which a reckless driver's body which is being taken to the morgue cannot resist rising and taking the wheel of the hearse.

238. James, Henry. "The Last of the Valerii." A Passionate Pilgrim, and Other Tales. Boston: James R. Osgood, 1875.

REPRINT EDITION: The Madonna of the Future and Other Early Stories, foreword Willard Thorp, New York, New American Library, 19-62.
RESEARCH SOURCE: Banta, Martha, Henry James and the Occult: The Great Extension, Bloomington, IN, Indiana UP, 1972.

CRITICAL SYNOPSIS: Clear echoes of Hawthorne's Marble Faun (see 204) imbue this tale. The Gothic motif of the statue-come-alive is also used with considerable mysterious effect. The young American girl, Martha, marries the handsome Conte Valerio, the last of the Valerii. The couple take up residence at the ancient Roman Villa Valerio, an archeological pleasure palace "filled with disinterred fragments of sculpture—nameless statues and noseless heads and rough-hewn sarcophagi which made it deliciously solemn." At Martha's insistence, exploratory excavations are made on the estate and a magnificent statue of Juno is unearthed. Soon the Juno exerts its strange power over the Conte, becoming for him a stony beloved and "monstrous heritage of antiquity." Now locked in a mortal struggle against the Juno, Martha can only eliminate her rival by reentombing the living statue in the "dreadful earth," a live burial of sorts. "By the time we reached the edge of the grave, the evening had fallen and the beauty of our marble victim was shrouded in a dusky veil." In many Gothic novels or tales, it is not unusual for a colossus to come to life and descend from its pedestal. It is unusual within the Gothic tradition, however, for mortal characters to repel the supernatural power of the statue, but the Jamesian heroine does just this in order to save her husband from a sinister and pagan past.

239. _____. "The Romance of Certain Old Clothes." A Passionate Pilgrim, and Other Tales. Boston: James R. Osgood, 1875.

REPRINT EDITION: The Complete Tales of Henry James, ed. Leon Edel, Philadelphia, J.B. Lippincott, 1961.
RESEARCH SOURCE: Edel, Leon, "Introduction," The Ghostly Tales of Henry James, New Brunswick, NJ, Rutgers UP, 1948, pp.v-xxxii.

CRITICAL SYNOPSIS: This tale of the supernatural first appeared in The Atlantic Monthly for February, 1868. In this early story, James shows a good command of the eerie as well as a debt to Hawthorne's subtle ghostliness although he opts for a ghastly climax that is closer to Poe's endings than Hawthorne's. The names and the plot carry other reminders of Hawthorne's suggestive supernaturalism, particularly the melodramatic build up to the death moment. The sisters Viola and Perdita Willoughby (named for Shakespearean heroines) vie for the love of Arthur Lloyd. He chooses Perdita although he is also attracted to Rosalind, but Perdita soon dies in childbirth making Arthur promise on her deathbed that her fine clothes will be kept from all hands by being locked up in a great trunk until their daughter comes of age. When Arthur remarries he chooses the sister, Viola, who is obsessed with possessing her dead sister's old clothes. The great and forbidden iron chest where the trusso is kept is itself a refurbished Gothic relic. "There was a sullen defiance in its three great padlocks and its iron bands, which only quickened her desires." She gains the key to the chest and ascends to the attic to rifle the trunk and it is here that Arthur Lloyd later discovers his dead wife in a posture of abject terror. Unlike Hawthorne, who would certainly favor an ambiguous explanation for the death, James leaves no doubt that the hands of the dead sister had risen from the trunk to destroy the violator. "On her limbs was the stiffness of death, and on her face, in the fading light of the sun, the terror of something more than death. Her lips were parted in entreaty, in dismay, in agony; and on her bloodless brow and cheeks there glowed the marks of ten hideous wounds from two vengeful ghostly hands."

240. _____. "The Ghostly Rental." Scribner's Monthly, September, 1876.

REPRINT EDITION: The Complete Tales of Henry James, ed. Leon Edel, Philadelphia, J.B. Lippincott, 1961.
RESEARCH SOURCES: Elkins, Charles L., Supernatural Fiction Writers, pp.337-344; Martin, Jay, "Ghostly Rentals, Ghostly Purchases: Haunted Imaginations in James, Twain, and Bellamy," The Haunted Dusk: American Supernatural Fiction, 1820-1920, eds. Howard Kerr, John W. Crowley, Charles L. Crow, Athens, GA, Georgia UP, 1983, pp.123-131.

CRITICAL SYNOPSIS: A tale of ghosts and guilt with an abundance of supernatural detail and locale. As in The Turn of the Screw (see 245), however, James does not give quite enough definite information to confirm the genuineness of the spectres. There are also two stories in progress simultaneously, the tale of the ghostly rental paid by a guilty father to the phantom of his daughter, and the narrator's own involvement with the possible ghosts of the father and daughter. The narrator (unnamed) is a young divinity student who develops a friendship with a fascinating old man, Captain Diamond. Diamond confesses his burden of terrible guilt by telling the narrator that long ago he had disinherited his daughter and banned her from his house because she had given her love to an unacceptable young man. The "ghost" of the daughter now roams the corridors of the old house which the impoverished old captain visits four times a year to collect a ghostly rental of $133 which is all he has to live on. Interested but skeptical, the narrator offers to collect the old man's payment in order to view the ghost for himself, but when he goes to the haunted house, he finds the daughter alive. Guiltily, she explains her spectral charade to the narrator who meanwhile receives news of the sudden death of Captain Diamond. At the same instant, the father's ghost appears to the daughter, but not to the narrator. Was it real or a product of her guilty conscience? In more than one of his Gothic tales, James would leave the reality of the characters' supernatural experience unresolved thus adding to the probability of the actual existence of a spirit world.

241. _____. The Portrait of a Lady. New York: Houghton, Mifflin, 18-82.

REPRINT EDITION: ed. Robert D. Bamberg, New York, W.W. Norton, 19-75.

RESEARCH SOURCES: Nettels, Elsa, "The Portrait of a Lady and the Gothic Romance," South Atlantic Bulletin 39 (1974): 73-82; Unrue, Darlene H., "The Occult Metaphor as Technique in The Portrait of a Lady," Henry James Review 2 (1981): 199-203.

CRITICAL SYNOPSIS: Various episodes and character relationships inform the Gothicism of James's lengthy novel of the moral trials of the young American heroine, Isabel Archer, amidst the corruptions of the old world. The central Gothic situation involves Isabel's literal and psychological imprisonment within the Palazzo Roccanera by the schemers, Madame Merle, and Gilbert Osmond. The Jamesian Gothic concept of victimization teems with echoes of Hawthorne's psychological peril and Mrs. Radcliffe's imagery of danger. Isabel's place of confinement, Palazzo Roccanera, has as much to offer the suffering heroine as any previous haunted castle or awful abbey. From Isabel's point of view, "it was the house of darkness, the house of dumbness, the house of suffocation....When she saw this rigid system close about her, draped though it was in pictured tapestries, that sense of darkness and suffocation of which I have spoken took possession of her; she seemed shut up with an odour of mould and decay." Equally compelling are James's references to the great Gothic villains in his portrayal of Osmond who desires Isabel only for her inheritance while continuing his relationship with his mistress, Madame Merle. "Under all his culture, his cleverness, his amenity, under his good nature, his facility, his knowledge of life, his egotism lay hidden like a serpent in a bank of flowers." But unlike her predecessor, the earlier Gothic heroine, the American lady, Isabel Archer, chooses to remain with the shallow Osmond for the sake of his illegitimate daughter, Pansy, by Madame Merle. Radcliffean heroines are always granted a blissful release from the castle; the Jamesian version of the heroine chooses to remain within the castle of a painful marriage so that another might enjoy the freedom of choice in later life that her sacrifice makes possible.

242. _____. "Sir Edmund Orme." The Lesson of the Master. New York: Macmillan, 1892.

REPRINT EDITION: Great Tales of Terror and the Supernatural, eds. Herbert A. Wise, Phyllis Fraser, New York, Modern Library, 1944, RESEARCH SOURCES: Lind, Sidney P., "The Supernatural Tales of Henry James: Conflict and Fantasy," Unpublished Doctoral Dissertation, New York University, 1948; Ringe, Donald A., American Gothic, pp. 186-187.

CRITICAL SYNOPSIS: At all points, a Gothic ghost story and one of James's finest achievements in dealing with the common theme of spectral retribution. The tale's frame device is also a familiar piece of Gothic business, the mysterious manuscript which contains the account of a young suitor, a mother and her daughter, and the wronged phantom of Sir Edmund Orme who haunts Mrs. Marden and her daughter, Charlotte, because the mother had spurned his love many years before and jilted him to marry another. The ghost of Sir Edmund Orme is presented as an agent of justice come to bring the cruel mother to a reckoning and to save the daughter from repeating her mother's sins of the heart. There are several excellent confrontation scenes and moments of high Radcliffean suspense including the climactic manifestation when Charlotte accepts the narrator's proposal of marriage with the ghost looking on and Mrs. Marden collapsing into a lethal state of terror. James's manipulation of the Gothic in this tale and elsewhere deserves further attention because in "keeping the objects of terror significantly vague and merely suggesting the sinister quality they possess, he creates a kind of impression which stimulates the reader to conjure up in his own imagination a greater sense of horror than could ever be attained through a detailed description of the objects that suggest it. For this reason, James's ghostly tales are much superior to those of Howells, who describes too little, and those of Bierce, who describes too much." (Ringe, American Gothic)

243. _____. "Owen Wingrave." The Private Life. London: J.R. Osgood, Mc Ilvaine, 1893; New York: Harper, 1893.

REPRINT EDITION: The Complete Tales of Henry James, ed. Leon Edel, Philadelphia, Lippincott, 1962.
RESEARCH SOURCE: Probert, K.G., "Christopher Newman and the Artistic American View of Life," Studies in American Fiction 11 (1983): 203-215.

CRITICAL SYNOPSIS: Ilustrates James's reuse of a stock Gothic ordeal, the night of terror spent within the haunted chamber of the ancestral mansion. The hero, Owen Wingrave, is the scion of a military family whose moral values are unyieldingly militaristic. All male Wingraves are supposed to follow the soldier's life and die bravely on the field of honor. But James's pacifist character heroically defies his family's crude code of honor, first by refusing to enter the military academy at Sandhurst, then by proving his better courage by accepting the challenge of his wife-to-be by spending a night inside the Wingrave family's haunted room. Family legend has it that centuries ago another Wingrave father had killed his son in the chamber for a similar refusal to follow the military traditions of the house. By the ordeal of the horrible room, father and fiancée hope to shame Wingrave into an acceptance of manly duty. He keeps the awful appointment and displays a better courage than the courage of the warrior, but is found dead when the room is entered the next morning. James's severe moral climax inverts the usual heroic outcome for the young man who undergoes the ordeal of the haunted chamber as found in one of the earliest Gothic novels, Clara Reeve's Old English Baron (1777).

244. _____. "The Altar of the Dead." Terminations. London: William Heinemann, 1895.

REPRINT EDITION: Henry James, In the Cage and Other Tales, ed. Morton Dauwen Zabel, Garden City, NY, Doubleday, 1958.
RESEARCH SOURCE: Shelden, Pamela J., "Jamesian Gothicism: The Haunted Castle of the Mind," Studies in the Literary Imagination 7 (1974): 121-134.

CRITICAL SYNOPSIS: A mood piece in which the Gothic is internal rather than external. The theme is psychological captivity and spiritual attrition. The main characters are Stransom and his dead beloved, Mary Antrim. He remembers the anniversary of her death each year by placing candles on the altar of the dead in a church in "a great grey suburb of London." Remembrance of the dead by candles becomes a morbid obsession with Stransom whose adoration and memorialization of the dead at his own altar is the sole passion of his life. "He had given himself to his Dead, and it was good: this time his Dead would keep him." Entrapment within morbid memory and fatality of soul instead of physical entrapment and physical death show James's imaginative alterations in the traditional Gothic patterns.

245. _____. The Turn of the Screw. The Two Magics. London: Heinemann, 1898.

REPRINT EDITIONS: ed. Robert Kimbrough, W.W. Norton, 1966, ed. Robert Kimbrough.
RESEARCH SOURCES: Heilman, Robert B., "The Freudian Reading of 'The Turn of the Screw,'" Modern Language Notes 63 (1947): 433-445; Mackenzie, Manfred, "The Turn of the Screw: Jamesian Gothic," Essays in Criticism 12 (1962): 34-38; Schleifer, Ronald, "Trap of the Imagination: The Gothic Tradition, Fiction, and The Turn of the Screw," Criticism 22 (1980): 297-319.

CRITICAL SYNOPSIS: Certainly the most debated and possibly the most misread or overread of James's ghostly tales, this famous horror story turns its screws of meaning upon the sanity, neurosis, or downright insanity of the main narrator, an unnamed governess who has come to the lonely English country house of Bly to care for two children, Miles and Flora, after the strange death of the previous governess, Miss Jessel, and her alleged lover, Peter Quint. That James had the English Gothic novel in mind, and more particularly, the Radcliffean variety of Gothic fiction in which the heroine is often deceived by supernatural appearances, is made clear by the narrator's direct allusion to The Mysteries of Udolpho (1794) at the outset of chapter four: "Was there a 'secret' at Bly--a mystery of Udolpho or an insane, an unmentionable relative kept in unsuspected confinement?" The governess narrator's memories are also struck through with Gothic figures and metaphors so characteristic of the English Gothic heroine as when she refers to "the inner chamber of my dread." Even if her apparitional experiences are panicky projections of her repressed wants and fears, they are real enough from her point of view. Hence, whether we read The Turn of the Screw as James's refined study in hysteria or as his revival of the Gothic novella in its purest form, the tale has all of the artistic requirements of the superior ghost story: unrelieved suspense, mounting fear, an inexplicable and unbearably horrible dénouement. Like most Gothic heroines, the governess has a moral mission to perform during her sojourn within the castle. She conceives of herself as the savior of little Flora whose soul and body are now possessed by the debauched spirit of her forerunner, Miss Jessel. Miles too must be saved, or at least forced to confess that his mind and soul have been taken over by the vicious valet, Peter Quint ("Quint was so clever--he was so deep"). After numerous optical encounters with the spectres of the depraved couple on the great lawn, on the staircase, and atop the house's towers (to the approval of all Freudian theorists), the governess confronts little Miles with her "evidence" that he is under the evil influence of Quint and the child dies in her arms in a scene that some readers have called a sublimated sexual assault. Whatever really happens in The Turn of the Screw, the mechanics of the story are undeniably Gothic to the highest degree and its power to frighten remains unrivalled. This is true whether we choose to read it as a Freudian casebook or as a genuine Radcliffean romance taken one step further by James than Mrs. Radcliffe herself would ever allow in the death of little Miles.

246. _____. The Sacred Fount. New York: Charles Scribner's Sons, 19-

01.

REPRINT EDITION: intro. Leon Edel, New York, Grove Press, 1953.
RESEARCH SOURCE: Sklepowich, E.A., "Gossip and Gothicism in The
Sacred Fount," Henry James Review 2 (1981): 112-115.

CRITICAL SYNOPSIS: A convoluted and labyrinthine novel whose insular style creates a dark and hazardous narrative route for the
reader. The novel concerns a refined form of psychic vampirism as
the unnamed narrator, a guest at a weekend house party at a grand
English country house, secretly fixes himself upon the lives of
Guy and Grace Brissenden, two other guests, for the purpose of
testing his arcane theory that in any marriage of two people of
uneven ages the older partner will always drain off the vitality
and intelligence of the younger partner thus exploiting the younger as a fountain of youth. If the theory is valid, Grace Brissenden must be vampirizing her husband's energies of personality, or
to put the case in the metaphor of the narrator, she must be
drinking from his "sacred fount" refreshing herself but leaving
him in a condition of spiritual and physical dryness. The narrator
then applies his vampiristic theory to another guest, the intelligent and virile Gilbert Long, and apparently decides to further
his investigation by seeking to identify Long's "sacred fount,"
his energy source, from among the guests. Another woman, Lady
John, further complicates the narrator's search for evidence of
his theory. Eventually, he singles out the attractive but debili-
tated May Server, then contrives or imagines a rematching that
will bring the two depleted personalities, Guy Brissenden and May
Server, to a psychic recovery by pairing them according to their
mutual weakness. The law of stronger-weaker personalities which
the narrator thinks that he has extrapolated through his weekend
of research is instantaneously refuted, however, when Mrs. Brissenden suggests that he is deranged and dismisses the theory of
the sacred fount of personality as a mere "house of cards." As
well as being a psychological parable of the perils of the imagination, the novel can be read as a strange case of psychological
leeching or vampirizing. In his unwarranted prying into the inner
lives of others, the narrator is driven by dark motives similar in
their perversity to certain characters in the work of Hawthorne
whose curiosity about power impels them to violate the sacred centers of the soul.

247.   _____. "The Beast in the Jungle." The Better Sort. London: Methu-
en, 1903.

REPRINT EDITION: Henry James, Selected Short Stories, intro. Quen-
tin Anderson, New York, Rinehart, 1957.
RESEARCH SOURCES: Salzburg, Joel, "The Gothic Hero in Transcenden-
tal Quest: Poe's 'Ligeia' and James' 'The Beast in the Jungle,'"
ESQ: A Journal of the American Renaissance 18 (1972): 108-114;
Smyth, Paul Rockwood, "Gothic Influences in Henry James's Major
Fiction," Dissertation Abstracts International 41 (1981): 4063A
(Michigan State University).

CRITICAL SYNOPSIS: Refined psychological terror is the focus of
the story which stages its climax in a cemetery. The main character, John Marcher, is plagued by the inner fear of involvement in
life, an anxiety toward any passionate immersion in the drama of
life. He therefore stands back from life rejecting each passionate
experience out of a dread of failure or a deep fear that he will

be unworthy of the moment when it comes to him. "As each item of experience comes," wrote James in the Preface for the New York Edition, "with its possibilities, into view, he can but dismiss it under this sterilising habit of the failure to find it good enough and thence to appropriate it. He is afraid to recognize what he incidentally misses." Marcher's terror of living is his particular beast in the dreadful jungle of experience. Thus when the moment of potential passion and aliveness comes to Marcher in the form of an attachment to May Bartram he cringes in abject terror at the beast of experience and finally refuses to live. May, who might have saved Marcher from his own special deadness, is killed by the rejection. The gloom of Marcher's self-isolation parallels the withdrawal of certain Hawthorne isolatoes, namely Richard Digby, the man of stone, in "The Man of Adamant" (see 201). In the novella's final scene, Marcher visits the grave of May Bartram and it is here in this place of death that he realizes that he too is dead having missed the chance to seize life when the beast had sprung at him in the shape of her passionate love. The moment of self-understanding is commensurate with the Gothic's moment of freezing horror when the entrapped victim looks into the eyes of the thing in pursuit that he has dreaded most. In the miserable Marcher's case, the thing is his own denied life. "This horror of waking---this was knowledge, knowledge under the breath of which the very tears in his eyes seemed to freeze....It was as if, horribly, he saw, in the truth, in the cruelty of his image, what had been appointed and done. He saw the Jungle of his Life and saw the lurking Beast; then, while he looked, perceived it, as by a stir of the air, rise, huge and hideous, for the leap that was to settle him."

248. _____. "The Friend of the Friends." The Novels and Tales of Henry James, New York Edition. New York: Charles Scribner's Sons, 1907.

REPRINT EDITION: The Complete Tales of Henry James, ed. Leon Edel, Philadelphia, J.B. Lippincott, 1961.
RESEARCH SOURCES: Kerr, Howard, "James's Last Early Supernatural Tales: Hawthorne Demagnetized, Poe Depoetized," The Haunted Dusk: American Supernatural Fiction, 1820-1920, Athens, GA, Georgia UP, 1983, pp.135-148; Thomas, Lloyd Spencer, "The Haunts of Language: Superstition and Subterfuge in Henry James's Stories of the Supernatural," Dissertation Abstracts International 36 (1975): 1512A (SUNY at Binghamton).

CRITICAL SYNOPSIS: The tale experiments with a type of Gothic character which American supernatural writers would find alluring, the storyteller whose supernatural experiences may or may not be real. The possibility of hallucinated ghosts and the probability of extrasensory perception are two subjects which the tale explores. The narrator possesses a fragmented diary which contains an account of a young man and a young woman who each experienced before the fact the death of someone they loved. The narrator contrives to bring the two together and becomes a sort of third party in this strange triangle. Having become deeply involved, the narrator also experiences foreshadowings of death and actually sees the young woman on the very night of her death. James did not find a way of making these details of ghostly visitation very frightening, but he was able to explore the psychology of a character caught up in a web of fear, a topic to which he would return in The Turn of the Screw (see 245).

249. _____. "The Jolly Corner." The Novels and Tales of Henry James, New York Edition. New York: Charles Scribner's Sons, 1907.

REPRINT EDITION: Henry James, Selected Short Stories, intro. Quentin Anderson, New York, Rinehart, 1957.
RESEARCH SOURCE: Rovit, Earl, "The Ghosts in Henry James's 'The Jolly Corner,'" Tennessee Studies in Literature 10 (1965): 65-72.

CRITICAL SYNOPSIS: This tale of the double self and the hero's terrifying encounter with the maimed apparition of the man he has never been also contains much that is traditionally Gothic including a forbidden chamber within a haunted house that holds a "multiplication of doors." Having spent most of his life away from America, Spencer Brydon returns to his inherited house on the Jolly Corner in New York City at the age of 56. Investigating his house with his companion, Alice Staverton, he begins to suspect that the house is haunted, but not by any ordinary spectral relative, by the ghost of his rejected American self. This denied American self "'walked'--that was the note of his image of him, while his image of his motive for his own odd pastime was the desire to waylay him and meet him." The supreme moment of terrible knowledge comes when he confronts the rejected other self "glooming" and "looming" at him atop a flight of stairs. The figure of the other self is dim but Brydon can still see that "one hand had lost two fingers, reduced to stumps." James finishes the confrontation scene in high Gothic fashion by having the face slowly exposed until Brydon stares directly at his deformed double, then faints only to revive in the arms of Alice Staverton. The tale is one of James's finest explorations of the guilts of cultural exile and expatriation, and, in its employment of an authentic phantom, it is one of the few pieces of Jamesian Gothic in which the supernatural appearance must be taken as actual.

250. _____. "De Grey: A Romance." Travelling Companions. New York: Boni and Liveright, 1919.

REPRINT EDITION: The Complete Tales of Henry James, ed. Leon Edel, Philadelphia, J.B. Lippincott, 1961.
RESEARCH SOURCES: Merivale, Patricia, "The Esthetics of Perversion: Gothic Artifice in Henry James and Witold Gombrowicz," Publications of the Modern Language Association 93 (1978): 992-1002; Thorburg, Raymond, "Terror Made Relevant: James's Ghost Stories," Dalhousie Review 47 (1967): 185-191.

CRITICAL SYNOPSIS: First published in The Atlantic Monthly for July, 1868, the tale uses two standard Gothic themes, the ancestral curse and vampirism. All women of the De Grey household, whether they are born into it or marry into it, are fated to a premature death. When Margaret falls in love with and marries the son of the De Grey house, Paul, she scoffs at the curse, saying "I revoke the curse, I undo it. I curse it." Her angry denuniciation has the peculiar effect to transferring the curse to the male line and Paul dies quickly thereafter. Since Paul De Grey dies as a result of a fall from a horse, the reader is left to ponder what, if any, supernatural agency determined his death and how much Margaret's intemperate remark against such a supernatural agency had to do with his death.

251. Johnston, Mary. To Have and to Hold. Boston and New York: Houghton, Mifflin, 1900.

REPRINT EDITION: Boston, Houghton, Mifflin, 1969.
RESEARCH SOURCE: Mussell, Kay, "Gothic Novels," Handbook of American Popular Literature, ed. M. Thomas Inge, Westport, CT, Greenwood Press, 1988, pp.157-173.

CRITICAL SYNOPSIS: Historical romance of the early Jamestown settlers with Gothicism concentrated in the character of Lord Carnal, pursuer of the young woman, Jocelyn Leigh. She has been purchased as a bride by Captain Ralph Percy in a marriage wager. Shipwreck, swordplay, mutiny, capture and threatened torture by savages, and a timely rescue by Nantauquas, son of the famous chief, Powhatan, embellish the love story. Lord Carnal is a study in damnation whose evil designs suggest the Gothic lineage of his character.

252. Jones, Justin [Harry Hazel]. The Nun of St. Ursula; or, The Burning of the Convent, A Romance of Mount Benedict. Boston: F. Gleason, 1845.

RESEARCH SOURCE: Chaplin, J.P., Rumor, Fear, and the Madness of Crowds, New York, Ballantine Books, 1959.

CRITICAL SYNOPSIS: A sixty-four page shocker based on an actual incident, the burning and destruction of the Charlestown, Massachusetts nunnery on August 24, 1834, by a mob. The book is part treatise, part Gothic horror tale. The cover illustration depicts the conflagration with lurid power. Instead of the usual anti-Catholic propaganda, the little Gothic offers some unique commentary on mob behavior and the psychology of mass hysteria based on ignorance, superstition, and bigotry. The ruined remains of the Ursuline convent are described in terms which condemn the mass insanity of the mob. "The pride of the Catholics and the abomination of the Protestants! Behold now the crumbling and blackened ruins of that once noble edifice, suffered to stand as a monument to intolerance, of desecration and disgrace, upon the otherwise fair escutcheon of the good old Commonwealth of Massachusetts." The narrative ends with a plea for tolerance with a direct address to all Catholics: "Go on and multiply your churches--but have no secret auxiliaries--and both Protestants and Catholics may yet worship the same God in the same community without jealous rivalry--without wrangling--without rioting." Set against the moral didacticism of the novel is the conventional Gothic plot of the entrapped maiden and her melancholy lover in the story of Frederick Gray and the nun, Cecile Melville, his former fiancée who has entered the convent. Cecile is the immured beauty of a thousand monastic shockers. "Were it possible for a human being to rival the angels in heavenly beauty and loveliness, such a being appeared Cecile Melville prostrate at the altar." Of more interest than the stereotyped virgin and solitary young man is Cecile's Yankee Protestant brother, the sailor John Melville, whose Moslem wife, Zillah, acquired in his travels, has been abducted and forced into the convent. The focal Gothic episode occurs in Chapter 6, "The Secret Spring and the Subterranean Passage." Here, Jack Melville, and the leader of the incendiaries, Slippery Joe, penetrate the convent by way of secret corridors and prepare to set it afire. Cecile and Zillah are rescued from the flames, but all other are consumed to the applause of the mob. While the shocker sensationalizes the horror of the event, it does so with insistent moral overtones about the horrible consequences of sectarian fears and unfounded prejudice

253. _____. Sweeny Todd; or, The Ruffian Barber. Philadelphia: T.B. Peterson, 1865.

RESEARCH SOURCES: Summers, Montague, The Vampire; His Kith and Kin, London, Kegan Paul, Trench, Trubner, 1928, pp.60-61; Summers, Montague, A Gothic Bibliography, New York, Russell & Russell, 19-64, pp.519-521.

CRITICAL SYNOPSIS: The ghoulish chronicle of Sweeney Todd, the demon barber of Fleet Street who made pies out of human flesh, became a hugely successful penny dreadful from the gore-clotted quill of the Victorian underworld hack writer, Thomas Peckett Prest, author of Varney the Vampyre; or, The Feast of Blood (1847) and Sawney Bean, The Man Eater of Midlothian (1851). Jones's American plagiarism is only one of a swarm of Sweeney Todd pamphlets, dime novels, and primitive paperbacks to invade the American Gothic market. Jones's "Ruffian" Barber and Prest's "Demon" Barber are one in the same cadaverous gourmet in this cannibalistic comedy. Summers provides the gory outlines of Todd's grisly gastronomic enterprise. "It will be remembered that Todd's victims disappeared through a revolving trap-door into the cellars of his house. Their bodies, when stripped and rifled, were handed over to be used by Mrs. Lovett, who resided next door and kept a pie shop which was greatly frequented. Once it so happened that the supply ran short for a while, as Todd for some reason was unable to despatch his customers, and mutton was actually used in the pies. Complaints were made that the quality of the pies had deteriorated, the meat had lost its usual succulence and flavor." But the Gothic succulence of the story itself kept its special flavor in this plagiarized version by Jones and in the many other cheap editions and dramatic adaptations appearing throughout the nineteenth century.

254. Judah, Samuel Benjamin Herbert. The Rose of Arragon; or, The Vigil of St. Mark. A Melodrama in Two Acts. New York: S. King, 1822.

RESEARCH SOURCE: Carpi, Daniela P., "Il Soprannaturale nel Teatro Elisibettiano-Giacobiano nel Romanzo Gotico: Tra Metafisico e Sociale," Quarderni di Filologia Germanica (Bologna) 1 (1980): 41-54.

CRITICAL SYNOPSIS: One of the dramatic sources of the early Gothic novel and play is the Elizabethan blood tragedy and its successor, the Jacobean melodrama of lurid murder and morbid excitement. Judah's melodrama in two acts draws upon Elizabethan-Jacobean terrors as well as the Gothic dramas of the late eighteenth century. Reliant on spectacle, exaggerated emotions, and melodramatic resolution of suffering, the play is a Gothic pageant of the complex adventures of the lovers, Rosaline and Amelio, in fifteenth-century Barcelona. No event is more characteristic of the sentimental Gothic drama of the period than the interrupted wedding, an event perpetrated by the vile Condé Laranda, resourceful and ever-present villain. The pair of lovers are abducted, separated, dungeoned, while Rosaline's father, Benorio, falls into similar Gothic snares through the guile of Laranda. Now in total control, Condé Laranda gives a masqued ball on the Eve of St. Mark having told Amelio that unless he is saved from the dungeon before the Eve of St. Mark, he shall surely die by some horrible contrivance. The stage is set for melodramatic resolution when Benorio's soldiers arrive at the masqued ball in the guise of monks. Unmasking themselves and led by Benorio, they kill the Condé, proclaim Amelio the Prince of Barcelona, and finish their vigil by the wedding that had been interrupted earlier. This familiar plotline is heavily elaborated and embellished with dozens of minor complexities, dark doings, and shifts in identity among the characters. Gothic drama on both sides of the Atlantic was designed to provide its audience with maximum horrific spectacle while adhering to the requirements of poetic justice.

255. Judson, Edward Zane Carroll [Ned Buntline]. Morgan; or, The Knight of the Black Flag. A Strange Story of By-Gone Times. New York: Frederick A. Brady, 1858.

RESEARCH SOURCE: Summers, Montague, A Gothic Bibliography, New York, Russell & Russell, 1964, pp.82-83.

CRITICAL SYNOPSIS: A 118 page illustrated dime novel adventure with periodic Gothic elements, scenes, devices, and characters. As is frequently the case with Gothified histories, the cast is a mixture of real and imaginary personages including King Charles II. The plot turns on imaginary incidents in the career of the Welsh buccaneer and privateer, Sir Henry Morgan, raider of the Spanish Main and looter of Panama. Recalled to England to stand charges of piracy, he had been knighted by Charles II. Ned Buntline's Morgan, like his other dime novel villain-heroes, is a colorful mixture of Byronic-Gothic traits. He is alternately cruel and kind, vile and refined, good and evil, a virtuous criminal whose motives remain shrouded in mystery. The dime novel takes Morgan from England aboard his ship, the Watchhawk, to Jamaica and the Barbados where thrilling adventures ensue and Morgan's dual character is much in evidence. Morgan's love rival, the foppish and treacherous Lord Percival, the swooning heiress, Helen Caermarthen, Ethelbert, the hermit and guardian of secret Spanish treasure, his daughter, Coraline, and the black servant, Malak, are character stereotypes derived from the sentimental Gothic. Perhaps the most interesting real character is Solomon the Jew who involves Morgan in his strange schemes for protecting his daughter, Miriam, from the anti-semitism of Lord Percival and his ruffians. Arson, murders, betrayal, misery, and mystery fuel the plot which finally sees the noble qualities of Morgan dislodge his vices and reputation for cruelty. Judson authored more than 400 dime Gothics where the formula for a saleable adventure never varied. In A Gothic Bibliography, Summers lists such typical titles as Mysteries and Miseries of New York (1851), Ella Adams; or, The Demon of Fire, A Tale of the Charleston Conflagration (1861), Red Ralph; or, The Daughter of the Night (1858), and an apparent fictionalization of Lincoln's assassination, The Parricides; or, The Doom of the Assassins, The Authors of a Nation's Loss (1865).

256. _____. Thayendanegea, The Scourge; or, The War-Eagle of the Mohawks. A Tale of Mystery, Ruth, and Wrong. New York: Frederick A. Brady, 1859.

RESEARCH SOURCE: Johannsen, Albert, The House of Beadle and Adams and its Dime and Nickel Novels, foreword John T. Mc Intyre, Norman, OK, Oklahoma UP, 1950, pp.167-176.

CRITICAL SYNOPSIS: A nickel novel thriller by the prolific dime novelist, Ned Buntline. Printed in difficult double columns, the Brady edition was followed by another profitable printing as Dime Library Number 14 in the Beadle and Adams collection. Thayendanegea or "He Who Umpires" is the famous Mohawk chief, Joseph Brant, protégé of Sir William Johnson and terror of the Mohawk and Schoharie Valleys during the Revolution. The dime novel captures something of Brant's ambiguous relationship to the white settlers during the Iroquois savagery since Brant was seen as humane, intelligent, courageous, and possessing high military ability. But Sir William Johnson's dying words to him to "Control your people, Joseph," often went unheeded in the excesses of frontier war. Buntline's Brant is both scourge and seer, an extreme mixture of charity and cruelty, of good and evil. The result is a redskin version of the Gothic villain, a fierce and proud character torn by opposite impulses. Since Ned Buntline's objective is to thrill and harrow the reader and not to delve deeply into the personality of his hero-villain, the emphasis is on bloody incident, slaughter during and after battle, and the climate of terror that "the scourge" brings to the settlers as he makes war "like a statue of bronze." As there should be in any good Gothic, there is a mystery about Thayendanegea's paternity with hints that he is the illegitimate son of Sir William Johnson himself. Buntline's style consists of loud melodramatic splashes of crimson gore as in his description of the skirmish with the patriots at Oriskany: "Hark! A yell--loud, long, more fearful than that of the hungered panther on a track none but the great war eagle of the Mohawks could give that signal cry. The patriots halt, would form, but it is all too late. From behind every tree, and rock, and bush come the leaden messengers of death. Yells as of fiends are heard on every hand. Davis, Van Sluyck, and fifty more bite the dust. Where is the coward, Herkimer?"

257. Keller, David H. "The Folsom Flint" in The Folsom Flint, and Other Curious Tales. Sauk City, WI: Arkham House, 1969.

CRITICAL SYNOPSIS: A speaking skull story which should be compared with F. Marion Crawford's "The Screaming Skull" (see 107). The narrator, an eccentric scientist and electrical theorist, has acquired a skull which has a metal projectile partially lodged in the occiput. Using the projectile as an electrode, he attempts to communicate with skull by means of an electric current. The skull sends back a deadly message informing him that he had been the skull's killer in a prior life and must now forfeit his own to satisfy the skull's revenge.

258. Kelso, Isaac. Danger in the Dark: A Tale of Intrigue and Priest-craft. Cincinnati: Moore, Anderson, Wilstach, & Keys, 1854.

RESEARCH SOURCE: Kievitt, Frank D., "Attitudes toward Roman Catholicism in the Later Eighteenth-Century English Novel, Dissertation Abstracts International 36 (1975): 1481A-1482A (Columbia University).

CRITICAL SYNOPSIS: One type of American Gothic novel followed the lead of the English in its portrayal of Catholic secrecy, treachery, atrocity, and horror. The virulent anti-Catholicism of the Gothicists began with Lewis's sordid and lecherous picture of the church and churchmen in The Monk (1796) and reached its fullest expression in the inquisitorial and monastic horrors of the Gothic chapbooks. Typical titles such as The Midnight Assassin; or, The Confessions of the Monk Rinaldi (1802), Almagro and Claude; or, Monastic Murder Exemplified (1803), and The Abbot of Montserrat; or, The Pool of Blood (1826) inspired American Gothicists to exploit the horrific and propagandistic possibilities of anti-Catholic materials. With its atmospheric gloom and insinuated theme of worldwide Catholic conspiracy, Danger in the Dark is a typical specimen of the continuing anti-Catholic tendency of Gothic fiction. Compare with another item of anti-Catholic propaganda, Maria Monk's Awful Disclosures (see 339).

259. King, Stephen. Carrie. Garden City, NY: Doubleday, 1973.

REPRINT EDITIONS: New York, New American Library, 1974.
RESEARCH SOURCES: Alexander, Alex E., "Stephen King's Carrie: A Universal Fairytale," Journal of Popular Culture 13 (1980): 282-288; Gibbs, Kenneth, "Stephen King and the Tradition of the American Gothic," Gothic New Series 1 (1986): 6-14; Thompson, Bill, "A Girl Named Carrie," Kingdom of Fear: The World of Stephen King, San Francisco, CA, Underwood, Miller, 1986, pp.29-33.

CRITICAL SYNOPSIS: The corridors, locker rooms, class rooms, shower rooms, and gymnasium of Ewen High School in Chamberlain, Maine are the new chambers of horror in King's first Gothic. Commenting on the Gothic themes of the novel in Danse Macabre, King identifies the pubertal fears and peer pressures which lie at the core of the teenage heroine's horror of the high school anti-culture into which she is thrust. Carrie White is a sensitive and intelligent adolescent girl entrapped between a home dominated by a fundamentalist mother and a school ruled by brutal snobs described in Gothic terms by King as "a place of almost bottomless conservatism and bigotry, a place where the adolescents who attend are no more allowed to rise above their station than a Hindu would be allowed to rise above his or her caste." In this hopeless and terrifying environment, Carrie endures a series of horrors and humiliations at least as fearful and self-demeaning as any eighteenth-century Gothic victim held prisoner within the haunted castle. When her first menstruation occurs during a group shower, she thinks that she is bleeding to death, to the derision of her classmates. The group sadism of the bloody shower episode is gruesomely enlarged when Carrie is doused with buckets of pig's blood at the prom. She has always possessed psychic powers and now exerts them in a concentration of telekinetic energy to annihilate the gymnasium, the town, her classmates, and herself in an outburst of violent retaliation. Incredible as this ending might be, it is a most orthodox climax so far as the Gothic tradition is concerned, an avenging spectre of blood bringing mass carnage down upon the castle and power-mad evil occupants. The collapse of the school and town caused by Carrie's special powers successfully symbolizes the impending collapse of a closed society founded on social lies, class arrogance and cruelty, and parental indifference. Gothic fantasy in either the Eighteenth or the Twentieth Century is not lacking in apocalyptic moral vision; it can and does expose the rotten social and religious structures which isolate and bestialize the individual.

260. _____. 'Salem's Lot. Garden City, NY: Doubleday, 1975.

REPRINT EDITION: New York, New American Library, 1983.
RESEARCH SOURCES: Lidston, Robert, "Dracula and 'Salem's Lot: Why Monsters Won't Die," West Virginia University Philological Papers 28 (1982): 70-78; Ryan, Alan, "The Marsten House in 'Salem's Lot," Fear Itself: The Horror Fiction of Stephen King, eds. Tim Underwood and Chuck Miller, San Francisco, CA, Underwood-Miller, 1982,

pp.169-180.

CRITICAL SYNOPSIS: In Bram Stoker's classic vampire novel, <u>Dracula</u> (1897), the threat of vampire proliferation and the emergence of a Vampire empire are ever-present menaces to civilization. The spread of the vampire virus through the New England village of Jerusalem's Lot extends Stoker's idea of vampire world dominion. The hero of the story is the writer, Ben Mears, who comes back to the deserted family home of Marsten House now occupied by vampires who use it as a center for the corruption of the community they have invaded. The forces of conventional religion, represented by Father Callahan, are helpless in the face of the vampire infection, and Mears himself is forced to accept the fact that his hometown is doomed to vampirism. He leaves 'Salem's Lot to warn the surrounding communities of the contamination that is coming. Although there are probably too many vampire assaults in the novel, these scenes are brilliantly salacious in their insistence upon the bond between the sexual and the sadistic impulses buried deep within ourselves. If the vampire may be read symbolically as a figure of unbridled sexual appetite, then a conservative interpretation of 'Salem's Lot would argue that King is commenting on the sexual excesses of American culture and the breakdown in sexual mores.

261. _____. <u>The Shining</u>. Garden City, NY: Doubleday, 1977.

REPRINT EDITION: New York, New American Library, 1978.
RESEARCH SOURCES: Crawford, Gary W., "Stephen King's American Gothic," <u>Discovering Stephen King</u>, ed. Darrell Schweitzer, Mercer Island, WA, Starmont House, 1982, pp.41-45; Sullivan, Jack, "Two Ways to Write a Gothic: <u>Little Angie</u> and <u>The Shining</u>," <u>New York Times Book Review</u> February 20, 1977, p.8.

CRITICAL SYNOPSIS: King's third novel, set at the Overlook Hotel in the Rockies, is struck through with the atmospheric and historical evil so characteristic of the classic Gothics of the Eighteenth Century. Here, the Torrance family is isolated during the winter off-season and menaced by the curse of "the shining," a set of paranormal and psychic powers. The shining ability is most prominent in 5-year-old Danny Torrance, but his presence in the story is over-shadowed by the presence of his homicidal father, Jack Torrance. Torrance is a reformed alcoholic and failed writer who has come to the Overlook Hotel as caretaker. He enters a house with an evil history where a gangland massacre once took place. As is always the case with enclosure and confinement, the house soon possesses Jack Torrance and drives him to insane deeds against his family. When he murderously stalks his wife and children with a mallet, the student of American Gothicism might recall the events of Charles Brockden Brown's <u>Wieland</u> (see 063). Family murder is prevented by the melodramatic arrival of the Overlook's black cook, Dick Hallorann. At the finale, Jack and the hotel collapse in a picture of Gothic apocalypse when the boilers explode. Other elements of Gothic structure in King's violent collage include attack by wasps, bleeding wallpaper, and memories of a pestilential party at the Overlook which draws its details directly from Poe's "The Mask of the Red Death" (see 383). Other echoes of Poe's Gothic tales reverberate throughout <u>The Shining</u>. As the explosion and collapse of the building and its mad master show at the end of the novel, Jack Torrance can no more break the hold that the Overlook exerts upon him than Roderick Usher could free himself from the crumbling mansion that becomes his tomb at the climax of "The Fall of the House of Usher" (see 379).

262. _____. "The Children of the Corn." Night Shift. Garden City, NY: Doubleday, 1978.

REPRINT EDITION: Night Shift, New York, New American Library, 19-79.
RESEARCH SOURCES: Magistrale, Anthony, "Crumbling Castles of Sand: The Social Landscape of Stephen King's Gothic Vision," Journal of Popular Literature Fall/Winter 1985: 45-59; Notkin, Deborah L., "Stephen King: Horror and Humanity for Our Time," Fear Itself: The Horror Fiction of Stephen King, eds. Tim Underwood and Chuck Miller, San Francisco, CA, Underwood-Miller, 1982, pp.131-142.

CRITICAL SYNOPSIS: A chilling story which incorporates three perrenial Gothic motifs: loss of way, hideous entrapment, and displacement from time, all regular conditions of the haunted centers of Gothic action. Vicky and Burt Robeson turn off the Interstate and stray into the isolated Nebraska community of Gatlin. It is the year 1976, but in Gatlin, it is permanently August of 1964. And what is more, there are no young adults left in Gatlin, only a cult of vicious children, who venerate the corn god by sacrificing all those over 19 years of age. Typically, the sacrifice takes the form of cornfield crucifixion with humans propped up as scarecrows. The story abounds in accomplished Gothic effects such as the lost couple's encounter with a vampiric portrait of Christ. "In each of the wide, black pupils of his eyes someone was drowning in a lake of fire. But the oddest thing was that this Christ had green hair...hair which on closer examination revealed itself to be a twining mass of early summer corn." Since this bloodthirsty Christ demands the slaughter of all innocents during the 19th year and since the time frame of the story is month in which the United States accelerated the Viet Nam War at the Bay of Tonkin, the tale invites a serious reading as King's allegorical commentary on America's needless sacrifice of a generation to a perverted ideal during the Viet Nam debacle.

263. _____. "The Ledge." Night Shift. Garden City, NY: Doubleday, 19-78.

REPRINT EDITION: Night Shift, New York, New American Library, 19-79.

CRITICAL SYNOPSIS: A tale of natural terror at 43 stories up. Cressner punishes his wife's lover by forcing him to circumnavigate the ledge running around the highrise penthouse. The victim is told that if the wind takes him, "You'd have time to scream a long, long scream." Poe's prisoner at the brink of the pit in "The Pit and the Pendulum" (see 385) becomes King's prisoner circuiting the highrise ledge.

264. _____. "The Mangler." Night Shift. Garden City, NY: Doubleday, 1978.

REPRINT EDITION: Night Shift, New York, New American Library, 19-79.

CRITICAL SYNOPSIS: The mangler is a Hadley-Watson Model 6 speed ironer and folder, a machine with a hideous will of its own and an appetite to match. The grisly description of one of the mangler's many victims tells the story: [George Stanner's] arm was disappearing under the safety bar and beneath the first roller; the fabric of his shirt had torn away at the shoulder seam and his upper arm bulged grotesquely as the blood was pushed steadily backward. The folder spat out pieces of shirt sleeve, scraps of flesh, a finger." The crude horror of such scenes which depict the worker devoured by the machine carry back to the gruesome fate of the workers in Upton Sinclair's famous novel, The Jungle (1906). King's machines are truly Gothic in the way that they are endowed with a life and superior will of their own.

265. _____. "Sometimes They Come Back." Night Shift. Garden City, NY: Doubleday, 1978.

REPRINT EDITION: Night Shift, New York, New American Library 19-79.

CRITICAL SYNOPSIS: An autobiographical fantasy of King's own experiences as a high school English teacher. The corridors and classrooms of Davis High, where the main character, Jim Norman, "plays to the toughest audience in the world," is the new Gothic setting. "They" are the homicidal delinquents of Norman's teaching past, the monstrous residents of his nightmares. He attempts an exorcism of these demonic hoods by drawing the pentagram and incanting a curse. But the price of psychic freedom is self-mutilation as he is required to sever both index fingers. The final scene of the story carries Faustian overtones and is something of a grisly parody of Faustus's forfeiture of his soul to demons in the last scene of Marlowe's play.

266. _____. "Trucks." Night Shift. Garden City, NY: Doubleday, 1978.

REPRINT EDITION: Night Shift, New York, New American Library, 19-79.

CRITICAL SYNOPSIS: "Outside, all of the headlights suddenly popped on in unison, bathing the lot in an eerie depthless glare. Growling, they cruised back and forth. The headlights seemed to give them eyes, and in the growing gloom, the dark trailer boxes looked like the hunched, squared-off shoulders of prehistoric giants." For the Biblical prophecy, "The Beasts Shall Inherit the Earth," King's story substitutes "The Machines Shall Inherit the Interstate." The trucks in the diner's parking lot off the highway rise up against their human masters in a savage wave of machine madness. Humans trapped in the diner must watch helplessly as their trucks take over the outer world and smash all life. Although the revolt of the machines is not a new idea for Gothic science fiction, King's presentation of the theme carries the frightening prospect that technology is not progressive but regressive instead. The mechanical monsters on the loose in the parking lot are deliberately and repeatedly likened to prehistoric beasts awakened by careless science and warped notions of progress. Amidst the threat of motorized Armageddon, King has time to provide some macabre comedy. Killing a berserk bulldozer is such a moment. "Trucks" relies for its effectiveness on a sound Gothic technique which goes back to the beginnings of the tradition: the potent and hideous animation of inanimate substances or objects. In the old Gothic, the object is a statue or portrait; in the modern Gothic, driverless trucks take on a character and biology of their own.

267. _____. The Dead Zone. New York: Viking Press, 1979.

REPRINT EDITION: New York, Viking Press, 1980.
RESEARCH SOURCES: Egan, James, "'A Single Powerful Spectacle':
Stephen King's Gothic Melodrama," Extrapolation 27 (1986): 62-75;
Neilson, Keith, "The Dead Zone," Survey of Modern Fantasy Litera-
ture, pp.350-354.

CRITICAL SYNOPSIS: The novel borders on both science fiction and
Gothic horror. The "dead zone" is a tumorous sector of John
Smith's brain which has caused a lengthy coma but also endowed him
with special psychic powers including the ability to prophesy the
destinies of persons and nations. The surname Smith recalls Winston Smith, Orwell's single thinking citizen at the mercy of the
fascist monolith in 1984. John Smith's clairvoyance is activated
by the act of touching (symbolizing human sensitivity?), and he
demonstrates the practical applications of his dead zone percep-
tivity by using psychic tactility to identify a rapist for the
police. Ironically, the cerebral deadening of Smith's brain renders him more awake and more alive to truths that are hidden from
normal people, thus giving him a heightened awareness of self and
society. But eventually, Smith's psychic skill proves as much a
curse to him as an asset, for he can see into the future, and the
future is an abyss of destruction and despair. When Smith attends
a party rally and shakes hands with a glib orator, Greg Stillson,
he instantly foresees that Stillson's demagogic career will carry
him to a dictatorial presidency and then on to the precipitation
of nuclear war if his rise to power is not checked immediately.
Smith's moral obligation, then, which he and he alone must perform, is to halt this potential American Hitler before he can develop a power base. The crude thirst for unlimited power cleverly
concealed beneath patriotic clichés and empty democratic slogans
makes a formidable task for Smith, who comes to represent the one
clear-eyed voter amidst an easily deceived and mislead multitude
in this political Gothic. The shadow of one of the arch-villains
of American politics, Senator Joseph McCarthy, creeps across the
portrait of Stillson and is used by King to remind the reader that
the collective misjudgment of the intentions and ambitions of a
tyrant is something not unique to the Germany of the 1930's. It
could happen here.

268. _____. Firestarter. New York: Viking Press, 1980.

REPRINT EDITION: New York, New American Library, 1981.
RESEARCH SOURCES: Herron, Don, "Horror Springs in the Fiction of
Stephen King," Fear Itself: The Horror Fiction of Stephen King,
eds., Tim Underwood and Chuck Miller, San Francisco, CA, Under-
wood, Miller, 1982, pp.57-82; Magistrale, Anthony, "The Social
Landscape of King's Fiction," Landscape of Fear: Stephen King's
American Gothic, Bowling Green, OH, Bowling Green State UP, 1988,
pp.23-40.

CRITICAL SYNOPSIS: The America imaged by Stephen King in his Gothic fiction sometimes takes on terrifying Orwellian qualities when
naturally innocent characters are caught up in bureaucratic or
governmental machinery operated at the pleasure of Big Brother.
The Gothic villain in The Firestarter is the state itself operating under the Orwellian label "The Shop." The Shop's head agent,
Cap Hollister, controls the life and seeks to exploit the demonic
talent of the little girl, "Charlie" (Charlene) McGee. Biological

control of Charlie began prenatally in a 1969 experiment when the Shop artificially altered the chromosomes of her parents to engender a child with powers which might be used as a secret weapon. They had participated in the infamous "Lot Six Experiment," which also changed her father, Andy McGee, by transforming him into a vicious goader of other people. Charlie was born with a pyro-optic ability and is capable of starting fires with a laser-like gaze or glance. The Gothic history of the fiery or lethal optic extends all the way back to Beckford's Vathek (1786) in the Eighteenth Century, but King's adaptation of it, although not new, is to assign this terrible power to the innocent child and to attribute its origins to the impersonal scientific machinations of a government without scruples or conscience and interested only in new weapons systems. Charlie's story conforms to the Gothic pattern of flight, confinement and persecution. To develop her pyro-optical powers and to enhance her fire-starting training, The Shop employs a sinister agent named John Rainbird. His task is to dupe Charlie into believing that starting fires with her eyes is in the national interest and it is perhaps not accidental on King's part that much of his persuasive rhetoric sounds like the glib Watergate conspirator, G. Gordon Liddy, on the witness stand. But like Carrie White (see 259), Charlie McGee resists, rebels, and finally turns her supernatural power on her tormentors to incinerate The Shop in a fiery climax. Beneath the Gothic action of the book, one feels the presence of a deeper and darker message relating directly to the sinister drift of the national life. In The Firestarter, the main function of government is to ignite the average citizen's latent hatred and to turn him into a tool for military violence. Instead of support and service from governmental institutions, the lonely citizen "can expect to find no sanctuary from its agencies and officials, and have every reason to fear their tenacity and penchant for violence."

269. _____. "The Mist." Dark Forces. New York: Viking Press, 1980.

REPRINT EDITION: Skeleton Crew, New York, New American Library, 1985.
RESEARCH SOURCES: Winter, Douglas E., "The Night Journeys of Stephen King," Fear Itself: The Horror Fiction of Stephen King, eds. Tim Underwood and Chuck Miller, San Francisco, CA, Underwood, Miller, 1982, pp.183-229.

CRITICAL SYNOPSIS: In this novella, the arena of Gothic horror is that universal place of aisles and products, the supermarket. An atomic accident occurs at Project Arrowhead releasing a radioactive mist harboring prehistoric creatures and trapping the population of a small Maine town inside the supermarket. Once begun, the blunders of irresponsible science cannot be reversed and all life on earth is imperilled. Technical misconduct and governmental irresponsibility are the present day horrors which King projects in this long story which may also derive its specific atmosphere of terror from the near melt-down at the Three Mile Island atomic power facility in March, 1979.

270. _____. Cujo. New York: Viking Press, 1981.

REPRINT EDITION: New York, New American Library, 1982.
RESEARCH SOURCES: Bleiler, Richard, "Stephen King," Supernatural Fiction Writers, pp.1037-1044; Stump, Debra, "A Matter of Choice: King's Cujo and Malamud's The Natural," Discovering Stephen King,

ed. Darrell Schweitzer, Mercer Island, WA, Starmont House, 1985, pp.131-140; Winter, Douglas E., Stephen King: The Art of Darkness, New York, New American Library-Signet, 1984.

CRITICAL SYNOPSIS: King's canine Gothic, Cujo, has recently been designated "his most pessimistic book, since its central theme is the essential inability of men and women to coexist harmoniously." In every instance, the book's Gothicism symbolizes the degeneration of love into sexual tension and aggression which reduces the man-woman relationship to the drives of a mad dog trying to tear its prey to pieces. The central Gothic episode is also a refabrication of the victim's night of confinement within the chamber of horrors, certainly a variable fixture of the tale of terror. Two families, the Trentons and the Cambers, typify the American way of life by their sexual infidelity and marital warfare. Donna Trenton has taken a lover only in order to maintain the self-lie that she is still young and sexually attractive. With her four year old son, Tad, Donna is caught in her car when it breaks down and is attacked by a rabid Saint Bernard. Thus, King reproduces his motorized version of the horrid chamber infested by the beast or monster. Instead of rescue by the dog, the Saint Bernard's traditional role, the entrapped Trentons undergo the fury of the beast in a ferocious 48 hour ordeal. As is true of so much of King's best Gothic work, the reader can respond to the horror of the situation on two levels. Sheer, simple thrill and pleasure in the fear generated by the monster dog's raid on the cab of the car is certainly a legitimate response. But on the figurative level, what we seem to get again from King are all of the brutish, selfish, and power-mad impulses of the middle class family seeking to "make it" in America turned loose upon itself. At the bottom, the frothing Cujo is ourselves.

271.   . "The Monkey." Fantasy Annual IV, ed. Terry Carr. New York: Pocket Books, 1981.

REPRINT EDITION: Skeleton Crew, New York, New American Library, 1985.
RESEARCH SOURCES: Bosky, Bernadette Lynn, "The Mind's a Monkey: Character and Psychology in Stephen King's Recent Fiction," Kingdom of Fear: The World of Stephen King, San Francisco, Underwood, Miller, 1986, pp.209-238.

CRITICAL SYNOPSIS: A psychological Gothic tale concerning the repressed traumas of childhood. Hal Shelburn's "monkey" is a windup toy buried deep in the debris of his parents' back closet. The toy monkey and its mechanical cymbals are associated with various deaths and family tragedies, and by extension, with Hal's guilty sense of complicity in his subconscious wishing of the agony and death of his mother. "There was the guilt, the certain deadly knowledge that he had killed his mother by winding the monkey up on that sunny after-school afternoon." Hal remembers that when the toy is wound up and the cymbals chime, someone close to him is thereby doomed. Ridding himself of the deadly toy proves as difficult as selling the famous bottle in Stevenson's classic story, "The Bottle Imp," the story which seems to be the primary source for "The Monkey." To control his guilt and to silence his terrible recollections, he must bury the toy monkey in an ever-deeper grave until it cannot get free. Several entombments prove too shallow and the monkey returns to bedevil Hal's consciousness. Finally, he takes the monkey to the center of Crystal Lake during a lightning

storm and consigns the annoying toy to the deep while risking his
own life in the dangerous weather. With this burial of his guilty
memories, he is free from the terrors of childhood and truly ready
to be a father to his own son. Although somewhat mechanical in its
handling of the symbol of repressed guilt, the tale's conclusion
is unusual for King in the main character's triumph over the malign and lethal plaything which has prevented him from growing
up.

272.   _____. Pet Sematary. New York: Doubleday, 1983.

REPRINT EDITION: New York, New American Library, 1984.
RESEARCH SOURCES: Indick, Ben P., "King and the Literary Tradition
of Horror and the Supernatural," Fear Itself: The Horror Fiction
of Stephen King, eds. Tim Underwood and Chuck Miller, San Francisco, CA, Underwood, Miller, 1982, pp.153-167; Magistrale, Anthony,
"Stephen King's Pet Sematary: Hawthorne's Woods Revisited," The
Gothic World of Stephen King, eds. Ray Browne and Gary Hoppen-
stand, Bowling Green, OH, Bowling Green UP, 1987, pp.126-134; Magistrale, Anthony, "Hawthorne's Woods Revisited: Stephen King's
Pet Sematary," Nathaniel Hawthorne Review 14 (1988): 9-13.

CRITICAL SYNOPSIS: The "sematary" is an extension of the old Mic-
mac Indian burial ground near the village of Ludlow, a place of
strange restorative powers and the domain of a malign spirit
called the Wendigo. Dr. Louis Creed, the main character in the
novel, is a recasting of the Faustian or Frankensteinian overreacher whose rational creed drives him to cheat death or circum-
vent the iron design of fate. Calling upon the resurrective forces
of the ancient Indian burial site, he hopes to restore his child
and wife to life. But Creed's selfish probing of mortal limits has
the opposite effect of transforming him into a type of fiend.
Creed's character and his loss of soul strongly resemble the dehumanized father figures of Hawthorne's dark universe, particularly
such reincarnated Gothic villains as Dr. Rappaccini and Ethan
Brand.

273.   _____. "The Raft." Skeleton Crew. New York: Putnam's, 1985.

REPRINT EDITION: New York, New American Library, 1986.
RESEARCH SOURCES: Egan, James, "Antidetection: Gothic and Detective Conventions in the Fiction of Stephen King," Clues: A Journal
of Detection 5 (1984): 131-146; Nolan, William F., "The Good Fabric: Of Night Shifts and Skeleton Crews," Kingdom of Fear: The
World of Stephen King, San Francisco, CA, Underwood, Miller, 19-
86, pp.99-106.

CRITICAL SYNOPSIS: An initiation story, but done in the Gothic
manner so as to permit no survivors from the rite of passage. Four
college students, Deke, Rachel, La Verne, and Randy, swim to a
raft on a deserted Pennsylvania lake to enjoy the last blissful
moments of the summer vacation. A monstrous creature from King's
own version of a black lagoon rises from the depths and devours
each innocent in turn. As in Poe's submarine tale of terror, "A
Descent into the Maelström" (see 382), the fatal experience is
also peculiarly visionary carrying with it a kind of precious
wisdom and maturity. Last to be pulled from the raft and devoured
by the thing are La Verne and Randy who are consumed even as they
make love during their last moments of life. Last to die is Randy,
naked and alone on the shattered raft, but possessing new insight

into the adult world of pain and loss. The raft is our fragile
adolescence and the unseen creature from the dark world below is
the grim Kraken of adulthood. According to King's pessimistic parable, all dreams of youth must perish hideously in the grip of
growing up as each innocent is forcibly dragged down into the dark
underworld of life.

274. Kirk, Russell. Old House of Fear. New York: Fleet Publishing, 1961.

RESEARCH SOURCE: Herron, Don, "Russell Kirk: Ghost Master of Ma-
costa," Discovering Modern Horror, ed. Darrell Schweitzer, Mercer
Island, WA, Starmont House, 1982, pp.21-47.

CRITICAL SYNOPSIS: Of this ample Gothic thriller from the pen of a
leading conservative political writer turned horror novelist, The
New Yorker wrote that Kirk's book held the reader "from the first
muffled cry to the final midnight scream." Kirk is best known for
his analysis of the conservative mind in the 1953 book, The Conservative Mind: From Burke to Santayana. His Gothicism is really
an extension of a scenic tradition begun by Mrs. Ann Radcliffe in
her first work, The Castles of Athlin and Dunbayne (1789) where
wild Scottish landscapes and Gothic terror are combined for the
first time. Kirk's setting is an ancient and lonely manor house in
the Hebrides where an atmosphere of imminent catastrophe hangs
over the old house of fear. Here, the chivalric and noble personage of the young lawyer, Hugh Logan, must contend with danger and
disaster in a hundred different forms including the malign supernatural. To be protected and eventually rescued are the maiden of
the house and her ancient father. Kirk rightfully referred to his
materials as a "Gothick tale" and objected strongly when certain
reviewers attempted to impose conservative political meanings and
fears of the welfare state on this pure and straightforward Gothic
thriller.

275. _____. "Ex Tenebris." Surly Sullen Bell, Ten Stories and Sketches, Uncanny or Uncomfortable. New York: Fleet Publishing, 1962.

RESEARCH SOURCE: Mc Cann, William, "The Fictional Writing of Russell Kirk," Society for the Study of Midwestern Literature Newsletter 15 (1985): 1-5.

CRITICAL SYNOPSIS: Kirk's own words on his propensities for writing and reading the Gothic tale are illuminating. He has described
himself as having "a Gothic mind, medieval in its temper and
structure. I did not love cold harmony and perfect regularity of
organization; what I sought was variety, mystery, tradition, the
venerable, the awful." "In Tenebris," or "in darkness," reflects
these Gothic values. An old woman, Mrs. Oliver, returns at the end
of her life from mysterious India, a land where belief in the supernatural and the ancient ways is paramount. Back in England, she
settles in a desolate cottage in Low Wentworth and is immediately
besieged by modern civilization in the form of a land developer
who would evict her and push the cottage aside in the name of progress. She invokes spectral aid in the form of an apparitional
cleric who furnishes a supernatural solution to the vulgar encroachments of modern life. Both Mrs. Oliver and the mysterious
past are saved and protected from those forces which seek "cold
harmony and perfect regularity of organization."

276. _____. Lord of the Hollow Dark. New York: St. Martin's Press, 19-

79.

RESEARCH SOURCE: Herron, Don, "The Crepuscular Romantic: An Appreciation of the Fiction of Russell Kirk," The Romantist 3 (1979): 1-12.

CRITICAL SYNOPSIS: Written purely to startle and to satisfy the reader's needs for fear, Kirk's third novel has been called "at once a Gothic novel in the tradition of Ann Radcliffe and a mystical romance that conjures up comparison with Arthur Machen." The story has an intriguing literary foundation to accompany the terror. Several guests have come to a remote castle in the Highlands at the behest of the cabalist, Mr. Apollinax, to enjoy the experience of timelessness and spacelessness when the soul is temporarily released from the confines of the body. Curiously, most of the guests who are invited to the psychic party have names taken from the works of T.S. Eliot with other character names such as Manfred Arcane recalling figures from classic Gothic novels. Names such as Alexander Fillan Inchburn, tenth Baron of Balgrummo, seem to be completely satirical. The transcendental moment promised by the Lord of Hollow Darkness, Mr. Apollinax (see Eliot's poem), is a diabolic ruse to steal their souls. The novel is saturated with Kirk's purgatorial vision and sense of a real and imminent hell to which the soul too often condemns itself through its spiritual vulnerability.

277. La Spina, Greye [Fanny Greye Bragg]. Invaders from the Dark. Sauk City, WI: Arkham House, 1960.

CRITICAL SYNOPSIS: Moderately successful werewolf novel rewritten from the version appearing in Weird Tales in 1925 under the title, Shadow of Evil. The heroine, who has been instructed in the arts of thaumaturgic communication and possession by her deceased husband, struggles with a female werewolf for the body and soul of a young man desired by both. Although the premise is strained, the tale does have its moments.

278. Lawrence, Louise. The Wyndcliffe: A Story of Suspense. New York: Harper, 1975.

RESEARCH SOURCE: Nelson, Alex, "Review," New York Times Book Review, May 4, 1975, p.26.

CRITICAL SYNOPSIS: A reasonably intelligent psycho-Gothic which reuses the stock situation of a liaison between the living and the dead. However, suspense plus high talk minus all terror can never become a wholly satisfying Gothic experience for the reader. The main character is a posthumous hero, a Byronic-Shelleyean poet dead for 150 years who now roams alone over Wyndcliffe, ponders the eternal verities, and poses deep metaphysical questions to an always heeding nature. Is he or isn't he the apparition of some great romantic poet or has the heroine, Anna, fantasized her own Heathcliffian mate for her imaginary needs? In any case, the situation allows for trysts and conversations on love, justice, God, the nature of nature, and all the other mysteries of romantic inquiry. But a missing and absolutely necessary Gothic element deprives the story of a terror which mounts to horror. The Byronic phantom lacks perilous qualities and young Anna is never in any real danger in these meetings on the windswept heath. When her brother and sister break the romantic spell and retrieve Anna from her hyperactive dreamlife, the novel has not yet come near a truly terrifying crisis for the heroine. However, the Wyndcliffe scenery is Gothic enough for such climaxes to occur.

279.   Lee, Eliza Buckminster. <u>Delusion; or, The Witch of New England</u>. Boston: Hilliard, Gray, 1840.

CRITICAL SYNOPSIS: A Salem witchcraft Gothic which admirably reproduces the atmosphere of hysteria which led to the legalized murder of nineteen ordinary citizens during the year 1692. The author's serious purpose is set forth in her preface where she vows "not to write a tale of witchcraft, but to show how circumstances may unfold the inward strength of a timid woman, so that she may at last be willing to die rather than yield to the delusion that would have preserved her life." A further remark by the author reveals her intention of adapting the Gothic spirit to native American terrors based on historical fact rather than fantasy. "It is said that we have no ruins of ancient castles frowning over our precipices; no time-worn abbeys and monasteries, mouldering away in neglected repose in our valleys." What the American landscape does have, however, is a stern Puritan tradition of a guilty fear of God and a sense of the Devil's omnipresence. How any group or class of Americans can succumb to evil under the guise of good is the subject of <u>Delusion</u>. The accused witch of the story is the kind and innocent Edith Grafton. During the height of the witchcraft hysteria, she makes the mistake of visiting and ministering to the old woman of the cliff whose "witch's cottage" also houses the old woman's grandchild, Phoebe. While she cares for the sick old lady, little Phoebe, following the example of other children in Salem Village, goes into writhings and contortions which "brings on the demoniac fury of the accusers." Arrested, publicly tried, and condemned, she faces "the hardening power of fanaticism." Only the climax of this tense portrait of a young woman caught in an American version of Gothic entrapment lacks the effectiveness of the rest of the novel. Another accused young woman takes Edith's place in the prison while Edith escapes from the Massachusetts Bay Colony having refused to confess or to succumb to the mass delusion. In the naming of the characters, the psychological treatment of evil, and the descriptions of the persecuted woman there are obvious parallels with the work of Hawthorne.

280.   Leiber, Fritz. <u>The Conjure Wife</u>. New York: Twayne, 1953.

REPRINT EDITIONS: Baltimore, Penguin, 1969; ed. Charles L. Grant, Boston, Gregg Press, 1982.
RESEARCH SOURCE: Frane, Jeff, <u>Fritz Leiber</u>, Mercer Island, WA, Starmont House, 1980.

CRITICAL SYNOPSIS: Leiber's first novel was serialized in <u>Unknown</u> in 1943. It uses an academic setting to dramatize a repetitive Gothic theme, the collision between smug scientific rationalism and the passionate belief in the spiritual and supernatural universe. The novel's anthropologist hero, Norman Saylor, comes into conflict with conjuring faculty wives who practice sorcery to advance their husbands' academic careers. The skeptical professor even discovers that his spouse, Tanzy, is one of these conjure wives and that his success in academe might be the result of her black arts in his behalf. Finally, the rationalist who has always doubted the reality of the supernatural and taught others to view witchcraft as gross superstition is forced to resort to black ma-

gic to save his wife from her malefic confederates. When he becomes a conjuring husband the idea of the superiority of the supernatural over the scientific outlook is affirmed. The downfall
of the rational skeptic who resists or denies the supernatural
realm only to find that it will not abide resistance or denial is
an old one, but given suspenseful and horrifying treatment in this
modernized witchery tale.

281.   . "The Oldest Soldier." Night Monsters. New York: Ace Books,
     1969.

     REPRINT EDITION: Night Monsters, London, Victor Gollancz, 1974.
     RESEARCH SOURCE: Morgan, Chris, Fritz Leiber: A Bibliography,
     1934-1979, Birmingham, UK, Morgenstern, 1979.

     CRITICAL SYNOPSIS: The tale of terror appears to be a variation on
     the theme of the Wandering Jew. The narrator, a man obsessed with
     war and deeply drawn to it, has a strange meeting with an old sol-
     dier who seems to have participated in all of the bloodiest bat-
     tles of history, yet never found glorious death. The deathless
     suffering of the old soldier stands as a warning to the war lover.
     Ghosts who are condemned to wander the corridors of time appeared
     regularly in the Gothic tale in the Eighteenth and Nineteenth Cen-
     turies.

282.   . Our Lady of Darkness. New York: Berkley/Putnam, 1977.

     REPRINT EDITION: London, Millington Books, 1978.

     CRITICAL SYNOPSIS: The novel's main character makes his living by
     writing pulp horror fiction, but he aspires to higher literary
     achievement. He researches the de Castries mystery which leads him
     into an investigation of occultism and parapsychology in San Fran-
     cisco in the early 1900's. Leiber shows an ability to adapt liter-
     ary myth to the requirements of the horror story by introducing
     the disappearance of Ambrose Bierce into the fabric of the plot.
     The novel also deals with the theme of the pursuit of the sinister
     beloved when the writer-hero, Franz Westen, becomes involved with
     a beautiful musician who is, in actuality, one of the city demons.
     Bizarre situations and the loneliness of the struggling writer en-
     courage autobiographical readings of this novel.

283.   . "Dark Wings." Heroes and Horrors. Chapel Hill, NC: Whis-
     pers Press, 1978.

     CRITICAL SYNOPSIS: A tale which combines two Gothic motifs, vam-
     pire assault and the confrontation of long-separated twins. The
     nocturnal meeting of the two sisters climaxes in the terrible re-
     velation that each woman bears the mark of the vampire.

284.   . "Midnight in the Mirror World." Heroes and Horrors. Chapel
     Hill, NC: Whispers Press, 1978.

     RESEARCH SOURCE: Stableford, Brian M., "Fritz Leiber," Supernatur-
     al Fiction Writers, pp.933-939.

     CRITICAL SYNOPSIS: Hawthornesque horror story using the theme of
     the alternate world within the mirror. The lonely main character,
     Giles Nefandor, is so obsessed with mirrors that his house is one
     continuous corridor of reflective devices and dark glasses. Out of

the mirror world emerges the spectre of his abandoned beloved, a young actress whom he had once loved and then rejected when she failed on the stage. The story is sensitively written and concerns the crime of denying love and life for the sake of art. Hawthorne's theme of the isolation of the artist becomes Leiber's more complex theme of the fatality inherent in such inhuman separation from others. The idea for Leiber's story may have originated with his remembrance of Hawthorne's "Monsieur du Miroir." (see 193).

285. Lennan, Katie. Elmwood; or, The Withered Arm. Baltimore: Kelly, Piet, 1876.

CRITICAL SYNOPSIS: The short novel makes use of a common Gothic prop or device, the human limb which can maintain an independent and supernatural life from the remainder of the deceased. Partial disinterment by the withered arm, hauntings, and the climactic visit to the murderer's bedside give this little Gothic its shock power.

286. Levin, Ira. Rosemary's Baby. New York: Random House, 1967.

REPRINT EDITION: New York, Dell, 1979.
RESEARCH SOURCES: Neilson, Keith, "Rosemary's Baby," Survey of Modern Fantasy Literature, pp.1338-1342; Pearson, Maisie, "Rosemary's Baby: The Horns of a Dilemma," Journal of Popular Culture 7 (1968): 493-502.

CRITICAL SYNOPSIS: The famous novel of satanic nativity has much to recommend it as a modern Gothic. The heroine, Rosemary Woodhouse (the surname possibly taken from Jane Austen's well-intentioned Emma Woodhouse in Emma) is victimized when she becomes the unwitting biological host of the devil when she mothers Satan's child. Also appropriate to Gothic circumstances is her place of confinement, the ancient Bramford Hotel in Manhattan. The characters of her husband, Guy, their friend the English Professor, Hutch Hutchins, and the sinister satanist, George Castavet (Stephen Marcato), complete the Gothic cast. Despite her diabolic legacy, Rosemary yields to her maternal instincts and accepts the demon-baby whose "eyes were golden yellow with neither whites nor irises, with vertical black slit pupils." The heroine's satanic pregnancy and final submission to the newborn satan, quite horrifying in themselves, are somewhat undercut by the ironic blend of humor and horror. Stephen King and others have commented that Levin's Gothic cleverly plays off the current theme of the "death of God" by depicting the "birth of Satan."

287. Lippard, George. The Ladye Annabel; or, The Doom of the Poisoner. Philadelphia: R.G. Berford, 1844.

RESEARCH SOURCE: Wyld, Lionel D., "George Lippard: Gothicism and Social Consciousness in the Early American Novel," Four Quarters 5 number 3 (1956): 6-12.

CRITICAL SYNOPSIS: The third edition title reads: A Romance of the Alembic, the Altar, and the Throne (Philadelphia: G.B. Zieber, 1849). This novel could be described as a "goblet of gore" and a "feast of blood" for it is the most luridly and sensationally Gothic of all of Lippard's many works. Lippard, who often displayed a tendency toward social propaganda and democratic ideology in his fiction, abandoned all such didactic flummery in The Ladye Annabel, a consummate Gothic shocker conceived and composed as an American equivalent to the salacious horrors and erotic cruelty of M.G. Lewis's The Monk (1795). In fact, in its sickening excesses and garish mutilations, Lippard's Gothic frequently surpasses The Monk and reaches an emetic extreme seldom found elsewhere in the all the pages of Gothic fiction. David Reynolds, Lippard's biographer, has summed up its plot and content in a single telling sentence: "The book is full of lip-smacking accounts of decomposing corpses, spurting blood, and quivering torsos during torture." Two sadists extraordinaire preside over the novel's sanguinary pageant, the Doomsman, the torturer-executioner of 13th Century Florence, and the fratricidal wizard, Aldarin. The slight plot involves the political rivalry of Aldarin and his brother for power in medieval Florence, but the real action takes place on scaffolds, in crypts and vaults, and within the hideous Red Chamber of Aldarin. The heroine of the title and the handsome Adrian are mere victim props to feed the racks and thumbscrews of the Doomsman and the putrid experiments conducted on human remains performed by Aldarin within the Red Chamber. In accordance with the formula of the crude Gothic chapbooks and bluebooks, something abominable or something supernatural occurs on every blood-spattered page. Like Monk Lewis, Lippard lingers over ossiferous descriptions of torture and fleshly decay devoting many pages to the bodies that litter Aldarin's Red Chamber, "discolored faces, green with decay... the rotting relics of what had once enthroned the giant soul." Gothic deaths also abound along this corridor of blood. For Aldarin, the butcher of hundreds of others, there awaits an appropriate stroke of Gothic justice when he meets death by vivisection. But the good also die in equally dreadful ways as shown when the virtuous Adrian is interred alive with the murderer, Balvardo. Lippard's works along with their tendency toward the repulsive and the loathsome were well known to Poe who responded and reacted to the Philadelphia author's gross Gothicism in interesting ways. The reader can recognize scenes and situations in The Ladye Annabel that will remind of Poe's straighforward use of the pestilential and the horrid in "Berenice" (see 376), "The Mask of the Red Death" (see 383) and "The Pit and the Pendulum" (see 385). But for sheer gore for gore's sake, no other American Gothic artifact of the period can rival Lippard's Gothic masterpiece.

288.   . The Quaker City; or, The Monks of Monk Hall. Philadelphia: T.B. Peterson, 1846.

REPRINT EDITION: ed. Leslie Fiedler, New York, Odyssey Press, 1970.
RESEARCH SOURCES: Ehrlich, Heyward, "The 'Mysteries' of Philadelphia: Lippard's Quaker City and 'Urban' Gothic," ESQ: A Journal of the American Renaissance 18 (1972): 50-65; Ridgely, J.V., "George Lippard's The Quaker City: The World of American Porno-Gothic," Studies in the Literary Imagination 7 (1974): 77-94.

CRITICAL SYNOPSIS: Also published as a serialized Gothic in ten parts running through 1844-1845 by G.B. Zieber of Philadelphia. Its matter and manner should be compared with G.W.M. Reynolds's The Mysteries of London (1847), a sensational penny dreadful or magazine Gothic of the 1840's which uses London low life to produce its thrills. Lippard's complex plot is actually many intersecting and superimposed tales of terror which makes the work nearly impossible to summarize although easy to categorize. E.F.

Bleiler's comment about this peculiar American Gothic is apt. The Monks of Monk Hall is "amusing in small doses, disgusting in large." But a Gothic can succeed with its readers by being both entertaining and repulsive, and, in this respect Lippard's novel succeeds on almost every page. Monk Hall is a titanic subterranean brothel and sinister den of variegated depravity. In this Gothic underground there convene criminals and degenerates of every type presided over and attended to by a monstrous cripple named Devil-Bug. He reigns over the lower world of Monk Hall like a zestful demon ushering the souls of the damned to the infernal regions, but he is not totally depraved either, being devoted to the welfare and protection of his beautiful daughter, Mabel Pyne. Devil Bug is a specialist in the art of homicide. His ingenious murders and mysterious removals worm their way into most of the book's many dark plots and give the novel what little structure it possesses. He is especially keen on live burials of victims and delights so much in his crimes that he becomes a figure of comic evil almost on a par with Dickens's malicious dwarf, Daniel Quilp, in The Old Curiosity Shop (1841). One of the plots involving Devil Bug's talents is the Lorrimer-Byrnewood story of seduction and murder. Byrnewood, a roué, wagers with Lorrimer over the success of a seduction he has now in progress only to discover that his victim is his own sister. Another lurid plot follows the misadventures of Dora Livingstone, her cruel husband, and her lover, Fitz-Cowles. Livingstone makes passionate love to his wife's corpse in one of the most candidly necrophiliac scenes in all of American Gothicism. Other characters, events, and scenes in the subterranean darkness carry the strong Gothic imprint. Devil Bug, apparently for sheer amusement, plots to eliminate Ravoni, a 200 year old necromancer who has established a satanic cult somewhere in the halls of Monk Hall. Lippard's vigorous Gothicism was supposed to have had a serious social purpose. By such shocking exaggerations, he used the Philadelphia underworld to expose the wickedness of the city, but his Gothic imagination was clearly more assertive than his social conscience. Like that other great pulp Gothic, Varney the Vampire, its wild effects are just that, a series of high voltage Gothic jolts to electrify and not to edify the reader.

289. _____. The Entranced; or, The Wanderer of Eighteen Centuries. Philadelphia: Joseph Severns, 1849.

RESEARCH SOURCES: Reynolds, David S., George Lippard: Prophet of Protest, Boston, Twayne, 1982.

CRITICAL SYNOPSIS: Variation on the theme of the Wandering Jew. The time traveller begins his journey in the days of Christ and finally arrives in Europe just as the Revolution of 1848 is beginning. The theme seems to be the elusive, but necessary, quest for social justice in a dark and Gothic world. Another Gothic romance of the same year by Lippard, The Killers, is a grotesque rendition of a contemporary event, the riots and gang warfare that swept through Philadelphia on the election night of October 9, 1849.

290. Long, Frank Belknap. "The Black Druid." Hounds of Tindalos. Sauk City, WI: Arkham House, 1946.

REPRINT EDITION: London, Panther Books, 1975.
RESEARCH SOURCE: Collins, Tom, "Frank Belknap Long," Twilight Zone 1 number 10 (1982): 13-19.

CRITICAL SYNOPSIS: A touch of grotesque comedy of the kind found in Nikolai Gogol's famous short story, "The Cloak," enlivens Long's short story. The main character, Stephen Benefield, is obsessed with Druidic lore and spends all of his time in libaries tracking down information on these ancient cults. When he takes the wrong overcoat from a library coat rack he suddenly takes on the personality of the garment's fiendish owner, apparently one of the Druids. The amusing predicament is resolved by a visit from the Black Druid himself come to claim his misplaced coat. The sly supernatural humor is deftly balanced against the tale's horror and self-shock.

291. _____. The Horror from the Hills. Sauk City, WI: Arkham House, 1963.

REPRINT EDITION: Andover, MA, Digit, 1965.
RESEARCH SOURCES: Collins, Tom, "Frank Belknap Long on Literature, Lovecraft, and the Golden Age of 'Weird Tales,'" Twilight Zone Magazine January, 1982, pp.13-19; Daniels, Les, "Frank Belknap Long," Supernatural Fiction Writers, pp.869-874.

CRITICAL SYNOPSIS: Written under the tutelage of H.P. Lovecraft, the first publication of the short novel was in two parts in Weird Tales, January-March, 1931. The novella belongs to the genre of Gothic science fiction in the way that the plot reuses the traditional Gothic prop of the animated statue. Horror begins when the curator of a museum, Algernon Harris, receives a strange artifact, the idol of the Great Chaugnar Faugn. Brought from Asia by the archeologist, Clark Ulman, the idol comes alive and moves about as soon as it is put into the museum's collection and eventually goes on a vampiric rampage against the scientists who try to confine it. At last, a psychic occultist, Mr. Little, has to be called in to counter the destructive threat of this miniature version of the Juggernaut. The message of the novel, the helplessness of science to classify and contain its own discoveries, seems plain enough. Faced by the supernatural, the empirical must give way to the powers of the occult.

292. _____. "Woodland Burial," Whispers III. Garden City, NY: Doubleday, 1981.

RESEARCH SOURCE: Schweitzer, Darrell, "Frank Belknap Long," Science Fiction Voices, #5, San Bernardino, CA, Borgo Press, 1981, pp.41-48.

CRITICAL SYNOPSIS: A tale of cadaverous revenge told in the taut manner of one of Poe's homicidal monologues. The murdered victim rises from the grave to summon his assassin to justice. Written especially for Stuart David Schiff's anthology of horror tales, Whispers, this is one of Long's purest Gothic stories unmixed with ironic humor or science fiction elements.

293. Longfellow, Henry Wadsworth. "The Skeleton in Armor," "Haunted Houses," "The Phantom Ship," "The Haunted Chamber." The Poetical Works of Henry Wadsworth Longfellow, With Bibliographical and Critical Notes. Boston: Houghton, Mifflin, 1886.

REPRINT EDITION: The Poetical Works of Longfellow, intro. George Monteiro, Boston, Houghton, Mifflin, 1975.

RESEARCH SOURCE: Eng, Steve, "Supernatural Verse in English," Horror Literature: A Core Collection and Reference Guide, ed. Marshall B. Tymn, New York, R.R. Bowker, 1981, pp.401-452.

CRITICAL SYNOPSIS: The Gothic strain in Longfellow's verse runs fairly deep. Generally, the terror is sentimentalized or serves the moral about life that Longfellow would impart. "The Skeleton in Armor" (Volume I, 55-60) has the ballad properties to be found in sagas of the demon lover. A maiden has been taken away to a tower by a viking warrior. When she dies, he falls upon his spear to be with her in death. Although his soul ascends, his armored skeleton continues to wander the earth. A fine Gothic sound effect is heard in the poem in "the werewolf`s bark." The poem, "Haunted Houses" (Volume III, 26-27), is moralized, sentimentalized Gothic. The moral states that "All houses wherein men have lived and died are haunted houses" filled with "quiet, inoffensive ghosts as silent as the pictures on the wall." "The Phantom Ship" (Volume 3, 22-24) is based on an episode which Longfellow chanced upon in Mather's Magnalia Christi Americana. After the ship of Master Lamberton of New Haven is lost at sea, God annually sends the mourners a "ship of air" to commemorate the tragedy. "The Haunted Chamber" (Volume III, 74-75) has distinct Hawthornesque overtones and makes use of one of Hawthorne's obsessive Gothic metaphors, the heart as dungeon or chamber of horrors. Moreover, the haunted heart is universal. "Each heart has its haunted chamber where the silent moonlight falls" making visible "the phantoms of the past." Poignant sorrow rather than gory shock is the predominant mood of Longfellow's Gothic. In this respect he uses the Gothic to achieve emotional coloration in these somber poems concerning the desolation of memory.

294. Lortz, Richard. Dracula's Children. Sag Harbor, NY: Permanent Press, 1981.

CRITICAL SYNOPSIS: A second generation vampire novel which requires some knowledge of Stoker's Dracula (1897) for the appreciation of its fantastic plot. In some ways, the book is a Gothic sequel to Lortz's earlier Lovers Rising, Lovers Dead (1977).

295. Lovecraft, Howard Phillips. "The Rats in the Walls." Weird Tales, August, 1923.

REPRINT EDITION: Great Tales of Terror and the Supernatural, eds. Herbert A. Wise, Phyllis Fraser, New York, Modern Library, 1944. RESEARCH SOURCE: Shreffler, Philip A. "Lovecraft and an American Literary Tradition," H.P. Lovecraft Companion. Westport, CT, Greenwood Press, 1977, pp.19-32.

CRITICAL SYNOPSIS: One of Lovecraft's most celebrated stories and thoroughly Gothic in its every aspect. The narrator is one Delapore, ancestor of an "accursed house." Returning to England from Virginia, he purchases Exham Priory, "a jumble of tottering mediaeval ruins covered with lichens and honeycombed with rooks' nests, perched perilously upon a precipice." Discerning that the Priory has been erected over the ancient site of a monstrous Druidic temple, he determines to explore the subterranean history of the place in order to absolve in some obscure way the fiendish reputation of his family. The narrator is further fascinated by the Priory's legend of the rats, an "unforgettable rodent army" which had once ravaged the Priory and its surroundings. Soon Delapore's dreams are filled with the nauseous sounds of giant rats chewing and clawing behind the massive walls of the Priory. Following the classic Gothic pattern of descent to the horror of all horrors, Delapore and his companion, Captain Norrys, descend through layer after layer "deeper than the deepest known masonry of the Romans [which] underlay this accursed pile." His cryptic journey downward is also a monstrous journey backward in time and leads to the horrific climax of the tale, Delapore's regression to cannibal savagery. By following his growls, grunts, and shouts, the rescuers eventually find him "crouching in the blackness over the plump, half-eaten body of Captain Norrys," both his mind and his civilized self forever gone. All of these gruesome events are reported from memory by the mad Delapore from within his padded cell. This Gothic tale contains several memorable effects such as Lovecraft's verbalization of the regression of Delapore at the climax. He begins by speaking in modern English, moves back to Elizabethan English, then to Latin, then to some Celtic dialect, and finally to the grunts of a wolfish animal tearing at dead prey.

296. _____. "The Outsider." Weird Tales, April, 1926.

REPRINT EDITION: The Best of H.P. Lovecraft, ed. Robert Bloch, New York, Ballantine Books, 1982.
RESEARCH SOURCE: Fulwiler, William, "Reflections on 'The Outsider,'" Lovecraft Studies 1 number 2 (1980): 3-4.

CRITICAL SYNOPSIS: The Gothic themes and the central moment of shocked revelation are not new, but handled with special intensity in this stylish imitation of Poe. The narrator lives alone in a great, dark castle and has never beheld himself, spoken a single word aloud, or ventured beyond "the putrid moat." He resolves at last to scale the castle tower and look upon the world beyond--and to venture forth into that world if he can. Following a fearful ascent, he sallies forth to come upon another castle with windows and gates open and a grand feast in progress. For the outsider, this must be that festive world of revelry, bliss, and companionship that he has missed. But his appearance amidst the company scatters every man and woman in an utmost state of horror and revulsion, "a herd of delirious fugitives." The outsider too is nauseated by a shape framed in a golden-arched doorway, "a leering, abhorrent travesty on the human shape; and in its moldy disintegrating apparel an unspeakable quality that chilled me even more." Mesmerized by the terrible thing, the narrator stretches forth his fingers only to touch the surface of a mirror. The Gothicism of the tale derives from four recognizable sources: Oscar Wilde's "The Birthday of the Infanta," Browning's nightmare poem, "Childe Roland to the Dark Tower Came," and two Poe fantasies, "Berenice," (see 376) and "The Fall of the House of Usher" (see 379). In pure Gothic rather than psychological terms, the story features that same unbearable encounter with self that informs so much American Gothic literature.

297. _____. "The Call of Cthulhu." Weird Tales, February, 1928.

REPRINT EDITION: The Best of H.P. Lovecraft, ed. Robert Bloch, New York, Ballantine Books, 1982.
RESEARCH SOURCES: Carter, Lin, Lovecraft: A Look Behind the Cthulhu Mythos, New York, Ballantine Books, 1972; Wheelock, Alan S., "Dark Mountain: H.P. Lovecraft and 'The Vermont Horror,'" Vermont

History 45 (1977): 221-228.

CRITICAL SYNOPSIS: Lin Carter refers to "the peculiar, almost documentary, technique" of this first of the Cthulhu Mythos stories in the Lovecraft canon. The central theme of the Mythos, that the earth was once home to a prehuman race called the Old Ones and that their power over man operates in unbroken cycles, is set forth in this primal story. The scholarly narrator who is apparently part philologist and part cabalist acquires a three part clay tablet in hieroglyphic text which shows the bas relief portrait of a horrid octopoid being. The slim plot involves the narrator's attempt to comprehend his find and to classify it scientifically, a futile attempt as it proves. Lovecraft's pessimistic moral of the inadequacy of the human intellect to understand either itself or higher worlds forever beyond its reach is asserted in the tale's opening sentences. "The most merciful thing in the world is the inability of the human mind to correlate all its contents. We live on a placid island of ignorance in the midst of black seas of infinity, and it was not meant that we should voyage far." The narrator investigates "The Horror in the Clay," "The Tale of Inspector Legrasse," and "The Madness from the Sea" and learns of the universal cult and call of the Cthulhu, a mad chant which always accompanies their blood rituals. The incantation is Lovecraft's syllabic parody of Anglo-Saxon and runs: "Ph-nglui mglw'nafh Cthulhu R'lyeh wgah'nagl fhtagn." With the Mythos as well as its language and history now established, Lovecraft would build on this tale to create a sequence of interconnected Gothic pieces under the rubric, "the Cthulhu stories." Among the best are "At the Mountains of Madness" (Astounding Stories, February, 1936) and "The Nameless City" (Weird Tales, November, 1938).

298.   _____. "The Dunwich Horror." Weird Tales, April, 1929.

REPRINT EDITION: The Dunwich Horror and Others, Collected Lovecraft Fiction Series, I, ed. S.T. Joshi, Sauk City, WI, Arkham House, 1985.
RESEARCH SOURCES: Burleson, Donald R., "Humor Beneath Horror: Some Sources for 'The Dunwich Horror' and 'The Whisperer in Darkness,'" Lovecraft Studies 1 number 2 (1980): 5-15; Joshi, S.T., H.P. Lovecraft, Mercer Island, WA : Starmont House, 1982.

CRITICAL SYNOPSIS: First publication in Weird Tales, April, 1929. This horror tale is almost always mentioned first when Lovecraft is discussed, although it is not necessarily his best Gothic effort. Sited in the region of the two Massachusetts towns, Athol and Wilbraham, it makes scenic use of actual places, namely the Bear's Den and Wilbraham Mountain. The Dunwich Horror is the terrible twin or demonic brother of the main character, Wilbur Whateley, the spawn of the devil-god, Yog-Sothoth. From Cold Spring Ravine, the Horror issues forth to raid, terrify, and ravage the rural countryside. The Horror is a version of a recurrent figure of inhuman superhuman power throughout the Lovecraft canon. According to the anti-Bible, the hideous NECRONOMICON of the mad Arab, Abdul Alhazred, the appearance of the Horror demonstrates again that "the Old Ones were, the Old Ones are, and the Old Ones shall be. Man rules now where they ruled once; they shall soon rule where man rules now." To counter this reconquest of the earth by a dark inhumanity, the tale introduces the student of occult sciences, Dr. Armitage, who seeks to save the planet and the race from the Old Ones. Unfortunately, the tracking down of the thing and the destruction of the horror atop Sentinel Mount make for a thematically dissonant climax because all prior events in the tale indicate a final victory for evil over puny human resistance. The expulsion of the Horror and his return to Yog-Sothoth is neither expected nor warranted for the lover of Lovecraft's ghoulish climaxes.

299. _____. "The Shadow Out of Time." Astounding Stories, June, 1936.

REPRINT EDITION: The Best of H.P. Lovecraft, ed. Robert Bloch, New York, Ballantine Books, 1982.
RESEARCH SOURCE: Shea, J. Vernon, "On the Literary Influences Which Shaped Lovecraft's Works," H.P. Lovecraft: Four Decades of Criticism, ed. S.T. Joshi, Athens, OH, Ohio UP, 1980, pp.113-139.

CRITICAL SYNOPSIS: First published in Astounding Stories, June, 1936. This tale makes use of the terror inherent in one of the tenets of Lovecraftian mythology and pre-history, that human beings were preceded on earth by a superior race and that humans remain inferior to these higher orders. Accounts of the myth are to be found in the grimoires (manuals for invoking demons) such as Lovecraft's dreaded Necronomicon of the mad Arab Abdul Alhazred. In the novella, the amnesiac investigator, Nathaniel Wingate Peaslee, records his findings for his son, Professor Wingate Peaslee, as he returns home from an incredible underground experience in the Great Central desert of Australia. "Of all living persons, he is the least likely to ridicule what I shall tell of that fateful night." The fateful night refers to that evening of July 17, 1935 when he probed into "that primal basalt crypt" deep in the Australian interior, the archeological evidence of the earth's domination by a race of Great Ones. Lovecraft's subterranean décor is a clear and direct refabrication of the abyssmal interiors of Beckford's Gothic novel, Vathek (1786), a book that remains one of Lovecraft's principal sources for the voyage to the center of the earth. Vast black caverns, mountains of debris, "cyclopean buried ruins" and a "fungoid moon" sinking reddeningly all recall the details of the Vathekian downward journey. Peaslee's manuscript to his son terminates in a series of anguished questions, each question confirming the cosmic pettiness of the human race as it creeps along beneath the mocking shadow out of time.

300. _____. "The Shadow Over Innsmouth." Everrett, PA: Visionary Press, 1936.

REPRINT EDITION: The Best of H.P Lovecraft, ed. Robert Bloch, New York, Ballantine Books, 1982.
RESEARCH SOURCE: Mosig, Dirk, "Lovecraft: The Dissonance Factor in Imaginative Literature," Gothic: The Review of Supernatural Horror Fiction 1 (1979): 20-26.

CRITICAL SYNOPSIS: Done in collaboration with August Derleth and published again by Arkham House in 1945, the tale furnishes an example of a fine story ruined by a mechanical and ineffectual climax. The fishing village of Innsmouth north of Boston attracts the interests of the antiquarian narrrator-investigator who is struck by the strange piscatory head shapes and expressions of its inhabitants, described as the "Innsmouth look." He proceeds to investigate, using the Marsh family and its patriarch, Captain Obed Marsh, as a focal point for explaining the fishy appearance of the Innsmouthians. As they grow up, the inhabitants of the village lose their human traits, grow gills, and are driven to return to the sea in the shape of a reef off the shore. The narrator's science uncovers the fact that the Marsh ancestor had come back from a south sea voyage in the condition of a fish, that he had colonized the reef with sea beings that had interbred with the locals. Alarmed by his discovery of the pollution of the human breed, the narrator alerts Federal authorities who order the reef and its inhabitants destroyed by the "Hiroshima solution," the dropping of a bomb. The story is eerie, gripping, and powerful up to this point where it attempts to become political statement. Suicidally guilty over his part in this genocidal act, the narrator considers shooting himself, but finally atones for his deed by planning to swim to the reef and surrender himself to the wonders of the deep: "We shall swim out to that brooding reef in the sea and dive down through the black abysses to Cyclopean and many-columned Y'hanthlei, and in that lair of the Deep Ones we shall dwell amidst wonder and glory forever."

301. _____. "The Thing on the Doorstep." Weird Tales, January, 1937.

REPRINT EDITION: In The Best of H.P. Lovecraft, ed. Robert Bloch, New York, Ballantine, 1982.
RESEARCH SOURCES: Burleson, Donald R., "H.P. Lovecraft," Supernatural Fiction Writers, pp.853-859; Emmons, Winfred S., "A Bibliography of H.P. Lovecraft," Extrapolation 3 (1961): 2-25.

CRITICAL SYNOPSIS: First appeared in Weird Tales, January, 1937. Uses an idea which fascinated Lovecraft, the family legend of the reincarnated ancestral monster who possesses various bodies of relatives as hosts in an eternal chain of horrible outbreaks. The wizard, Ephraim Waite, invades the body of his daughter, Asenath Waite, using his residence within her body as a type of host for the repetition of his evil deeds. The tale is somewhat marred by the narrator's tendency for dark moralizing: "There are horrors beyond life's edge that we do not suspect, and once in a while man's evil prying calls them just within our range." Such moralizing clashes harshly with one of Lovecraft's better putrid climaxes, the discovery in the bedroom of "mostly liquescent horror."

302. _____. The Case of Charles Dexter Ward: A Novel of Terror. Beyond the Wall of Sleep. Sauk City, WI: Arkham House, 1943.

REPRINT EDITION: New York, Ballantine Books, 1982.
RESEARCH SOURCES: Selley, April, "Terror and Horror in 'The Case of Charles Dexter Ward,'" Nyctalops 3 number 1 (1980): 8-14; St. Armand, Barton Levi, "H.P. Lovecraft: New England Decadent," Caliban 12 (1975): 127-155.

CRITICAL SYNOPSIS: The novel first appeared in Weird Tales, 1941. The young antiquarian, Charles Dexter Ward, is a pale student of the unhallowed arts and usually seen as something of a pen portrait of Lovecraft himself. Ward becomes infatuated with his necromancer ancestor, Joseph Curwen, whose eighteenth century farm near Pawtucket has been used as a laboratory for experiments in the reanimation of corpses. Determined to make contact with his ancestor, Ward exhumes the remains and discovers a journal written in cipher which contains the secrets of necromancy. Secluding himself in his attic study, Ward succeeds in raising his ancestor from the dead but his Faustian meddlings redound upon him when

Curwen murders Ward, then takes his place in the twentieth century. The case is solved and order restored by a character who had
become a standard figure in Victorian Gothics, the scientist-
physician whose training and beliefs still do not prevent him from
acknowledging the existence of the malignant supernatural. Dr.
Willett investigates Ward's case and even makes a version of the
underground journey when he delves into the vast subterranean
vaults beneath Curwen's Pawtucket farm. True to his conception of
the horror story, Lovecraft provides no final assurance that the
evil Curwen will not find a way to come back in some later time
cycle to switch fates with an over-inquisitive relative. The wicked ancestor who can penetrate the time barrier had been Maturin's
subject in his Gothic novel, Melmoth the Wanderer (1820), a book
praised by Lovecraft in Supernatural Horror in Literature as a
"vivid horror-masterpiece."

303.   . The Lurker at the Threshold. Sauk City, WI: Arkham House,
       1945.

REPRINT EDITION: The Best of H.P Lovecraft, ed. Robert Bloch, New
York, Ballantine, 1982.
RESEARCH SOURCES: Lévy, Maurice, Lovecraft: A Study in the Fantastic, trans. S.T. Joshi, Detroit, Wayne State UP, 1988; Nic, Howard, "Mr. Derleth Entertains," Horizons 25 (1982): pp.22-25.

CRITICAL SYNOPSIS: Long short story of diabolism mainly from the
pen of August Derleth with Lovecraftian interpolations. Most of
the required Gothic apparatus is present, but somewhat mechanically assembled. The great estate at Arkham offers sealed and
haunted towers, Runic columns and ruins, Indian witchcraft, and a
foul fiend of an ancestor in the persons of Quamis and Abijah Billington. The narrator, Ambrose Dewart, expects to possess the mansion, but the mansion soon possesses him. A noteworthy Gothic
effect is created around the device of the forbidden circular window. To gaze through it is to gaze upon the forbidden landscape of
all evil. The "lurker" is a revived monstrosity from Lovecraft's
Cthulhu cast, the demiurge, Yog Sothoth. His lurking presence,
however, is not well integrated with the other horrific effects.
Although this tale has been called "the best of the Derleth pas-
tiches," it is distinctly inferior to the pure Lovecraft.

304.   . The Dream-Quest of Unknown Kadath. Arkham Sampler, Fall-
       Winter, 1948.

REPRINT EDITION: New York, Ballantine, 1982.
RESEARCH SOURCES: Burleson, Donald R., The Dream Quest of Unknown
Kadath, Survey of Modern Fantasy Literature, pp. 431-435; Cannon,
Peter, "The Influence of Vathek on H.P. Lovecraft's The Dream-
Quest of Unknown Kadath," H.P. Lovecraft: Four Decades of Criti-
cism, ed. S.T. Joshi, Athens, OH, Ohio UP, 1980, pp.153-157.

CRITICAL SYNOPSIS: Commentaries on this short fantasy novel of infernal descent trace its lineage to Lovecraft's acknowledged admiration for the works of Lord Dunsany. or they liken the dark
voyage of the dreamer, Randolph Carter, to Marlow's Congo journey
to an encounter with his evil self in the form of Kurtz in Conrad's Heart of Darkness (1898). But a closer look at the dream imagery and surreal style suggests Lovecraft's use of Beckford's demonic quest story, Vathek (1786). Specific horror events such as
Carter's perilous descent of the 700 steps to "The Gate of Deeper

Slumber," his arrival at the onyx castle of Kadath, and his mysterious encounter with the Great Stone Face peering at him from Mount Ngranek suggest the topographies of Beckford's Gothic novel. The plot is also something of a visionary inversion of the quest for the heavenly city of God. The traveler through nightmare, Randolph Carter, begins the voyage with a glimpse of the fabulous city of the sun in one of his dreams. Carter determines to pursue his fantasy to its limits, even if this means a denial of the vision of beauty contained in the dream. The dark voyage unfolds the entire range of Lovecraft's private mythos and projects a somber and pessimistic theme which is prominent throughout his work: man's precarious and inferior position in the cosmos. Carter encounters various primordial deities or anti-deities in the form of Zoogs, Gugs, Ghasts, Gaunts, and ultimately "the Crawling Chaos" itself in the dark reunion with Nyarlathotep, the principle of universal disorder and despair. As in Vathek, Lovecraft's "oneiric Ulysses" descends into an underworld and is brought face to face with a dark demigod devoted to man's confusion and despair. If the Gothic world is a lightless world from which the inquiring hero is never allowed to return, then this novella of cosmic nightmare is surely one of Lovecraft's most successful fantasies of the soul's midnight.

305. _____. "The Survivor." Weird Tales, July, 1954.

REPRINT EDITION: The Shuttered Room, and Other Tales of Horror, London, Panther Books, 1970.
RESEARCH SOURCES: Buhle, Paul, "Dytopia as Utopia: Howard Phillips Lovecraft and the Unknown Content of American Horror Literature," Minnesota Review 6 (1976): 118-131; Burleson, Donald R., "H.P. Lovecraft: The Hawthorne Influence," Extrapolation 22 (1981): 261-269.

CRITICAL SYNOPSIS: First published in Weird Tales, 1954. The tale offers terror in the Hawthornesque mode and is at points a conscious tribute to the Gothic genius of Hawthorne. The narrator inherits the ancient Charriere mansion in Providence and determines to explore the house's secret past in order to dispel disturbing rumors about the former owner, Jean-François Charriere. Like one of Hawthorne's fiendish scientists or doctors, Charriere seems to have carried on sinister experiments in his quest for an elixir of immortality. The narrator's exploration of the house's hidden past and dark interior eventually produces a serpent-man or man-serpent, the hideously transformed but still living Jean-François Charriere. The motif of serpentine transformation was available to Lovecraft through Hawthorne's "Egotism; or, The Bosom Serpent" (see 191) and Holmes's Elsie Venner (see 216).

306. _____. "The Shuttered Room." The Shuttered Room and Other Pieces. Sauk City, WI: Arkham House, 1959.

REPRINT EDITION: The Shuttered Room, and Other Tales of Horror, London, Panther Books, 1970.
RESEARCH SOURCE: Mc Innis, John Lawson III, "H.P. Lovecraft: The Maze and the Minotaur," Dissertation Abstracts International 36 (1975): 2207A (Louisiana State University).

CRITICAL SYNOPSIS: Pastiche by Lovecraft completed by August Derleth. Abner Whately returns to the town of Dunwich to settle the estate of his grandfather, Luther. A letter from Luther Whately urges him to dismantle the Whately mill and to destroy the occupant of its shuttered room, telling him he must kill anything he finds in the mill section of the house "No matter how small it may be. No matter what form it may have." Doubting all of this, Abner's skepticism is wrenched into horror-struck belief when entry to the shuttered room exposes a piscatory creature "that was neither frog nor man with blood still slavering from its batrachian jaws." In the face of the room's secret, Abner's disbelief and reason both vanish in the realization that "the monster would loom forever on the perimeter of [his] awareness." Lovecraft's Gothic style in this story and elsewhere is naturally florid and arcane, but Derleth's attempt to finish these tales in a high Lovecraftian key has the hollow ring of meretricious imitation.

307. Lytle, Andrew Nelson. A Name for Evil. Indianapolis, MN: Bobbs, Merrill, 1947.

RESEARCH SOURCE: "Review," New Republic, August 25, 1947, p.31.

CRITICAL SYNOPSIS: The reviewer in The New Republic was only partially correct when he said of this sturdy Gothic that "the horror is described rather than conveyed." Moving into a rundown southern mansion a young couple tries to restore both the condition of the house and the once-great family name, but with tragic results in the violent dissolution of the house. Both the style and the climax suggest Poe in this modern Usherization. The Gothic attracted the reserved praise of Edmund Wilson in his review in The New Yorker.

308. Mannering, Guy. Rosalvo Delmonmort. Boston: Thomas G. Bangs, 1818.

RESEARCH SOURCE: Petter, Henri, The Early American Novel, pp.210-211.

CRITICAL SYNOPSIS: The novel is a rather artless mixture of the sentimental, the sensational, and the Gothic, but is nevertheless a pertinent historical example of many early American Gothicists' practice of joining the themes and characters of Richardson and Mrs. Radcliffe. For all its clumsy overwriting, the romance does not want for Gothic events and action. Deciphering these events from Guy Mannering's needlessly intricate plot, however, is a major challenge even to the attentive and Gothically oriented reader. By using the pen name, "Guy Mannering," the name taken from Sir Walter Scott's novel of 1815, the author hoped to attract readers with an appetite for Scott's blend of history, mystery, and adventure. The character names read like a roster of Mrs. Radcliffe's casts with the addition of William Godwin's rapacious English aristocrats. Surrounding the illegitimate hero, Delmonmort, are the children of Lord Bonville, Eugenio, Frances, and Lucinda, the cruel seducer and eloper, Lord Bellerton, the rakish Lord Elform, and the helpless maiden, Eliza Clonton. Intertwined with the seduction plot and Delmonmort's rescue of Eliza are the Gothic intrigues of Mandoni, a villain taken intact from Mrs. Radcliffe's Montoni in The Mysteries of Udolpho (1794). He is a poisoner, an agent of domestic disorder, and a black shadow over the lives of Angelina and her father, the Count of Roxillion. Guy Mannering's mismanaged splicing of the two plots exhibits a typical failing of the early Gothic novel in English or American forms. The effort to intersperse the virtuous career of Delmonmort with the wicked career of Mandoni pulls an already unwieldy plot down into the abyss of incoherency. But such narrative catastrophe is not an unusual outcome for amateur Gothicists of Guy Mannering's ilk on either side of the Atlantic.

309. Marasco, Robert. Burnt Offerings. New York: Delacorte Press, 1973.

RESEARCH SOURCE: "Review," Saturday Review, February 26, 1973, p. 67.

CRITICAL SYNOPSIS: This Long Island Gothic employs the technique of teasing terror associated with the school of Mrs. Radcliffe. Marian and Ben Rolfe rent an old summer place for the season. Instead of a vacation they face mounting tension as the old building begins to invade their lives and alter their relationship. This competent and capable Gothic did well with the popular market as evidenced by the approval of the reviewer in The Saturday Review who called Burnt Offerings "a hauntingly creepy book that I suggest you read only in a sunlit room with at least one other person around."

310. Marshall, Edison [Hall Hunter]. Castle in the Swamp; A Tale of Old Carolina. New York: Farrar, Straus, 1948.

REPRINT EDITION: New York, Dell, 1967.
RESEARCH SOURCE: Radcliffe, Elsa J., Gothic Novels of the Twentieth Century, Metuchen, NJ, Scarecrow Press, 1979, p.145.

CRITICAL SYNOPSIS: Reviewers divided sharply over the merits, but not over the gory content, of this "plantation" Gothic. The antebellum castle in the Carolinian swamps is well-staffed with demon blacks, fratricidal whites, and is replete with lust, sadism, and supernatural legendry. Both the surrounding territory and the castle itself are heavily draped in Spanish moss. This novel does not try to be anything except the grossest of Gothic thrillers, and as such and nothing else it must be put down as a resounding success. Other tantalizing titles in the Gothic mold by the same author include The Death Bell (1924) and The Isle of Retribution (1923).

311. Matheson, Richard. I Am Legend. New York: Fawcett, 1954.

REPRINT EDITION: New York, Berkley Press, 1971.
RESEARCH SOURCE: King, Stephen, Danse Macabre, New York, Everest House, 1981, pp.317-330; Neilson, Keith, "I Am Legend," Studies in Modern Fantasy Literature, pp.725-727.

CRITICAL SYNOPSIS: A novel of vampire extermination which combines that activity with the theme of the last man on earth. The last human survivor of a bacterial pestilence which has transformed all the rest of humanity into vampires is Robert Neville. Instead of a pandemic plague which wipes out civilization, this plague causes a proliferation of Draculas who spread over the earth in the year 1976. Neville converts his home into a fortress and ventures forth only by sunlight to pry open caskets and impale as many of the brutes as he can find. His one-man campaign against the vampirization of the planet finally leads him to explore the scientific causes of this infection of all humanity. In the course of his research, he encounters a woman--a sort of toxic Eve--in Ruth who at first appears to be almost normal like Neville. But their attempt at a loving relationship fails because Neville's compulsion to track down and destroy all vampires is too strong. Nor can the race be re-purified by the hatred of one last man whose own lust to kill renders him a creature more foul than any vampire. Keith Neilson writes of Neville's character: "The central irony is that in a world of vampires the 'normal' man is the real 'vampire.' Like the traditional vampire, he kills not only in the name of survival but also for pleasure."

312. _____. Hell House. New York: Viking, 1971.

REPRINT EDITION: New York, Warner Paperbacks, 1985.
RESEARCH SOURCES: Neilson, Keith, "Richard Matheson," Supernatural Fiction Writers, pp.1073-1080; Reed, Julia R., "Hell House," Survey of Modern Fantasy Literature, pp.725-727.

CRITICAL SYNOPSIS: In situation and characterization, this Gothic is imitative of Shirley Jackson's The Haunting of Hill House (see 232). Its style, however, is far more garish, its horror climaxes far more gory. A team of three investigators enter the Emerick Belasco mansion to track down psychic phenomena and to prove or disprove certain theories of postmortem existence. Lionel Barrett is a dispassionate scientist who is sure that all so-called supernatural phenomena are scientifically explainable. Florence Tanner is a spiritualist who believes just the opposite. The third party, Benjamin Franklin Fischer is something of a synthesis of these two opposite attitudes. He is a psychic scientist who trusts to extrasensory perception. In its own perverse way, Hell house defies all three investigators. And as should be the case with an effective Gothic, it is finally the house and not the human characters which precipitates the climax and decides the fates of the occupants. In Danse Macabre, Stephen King credits Matheson with producing "the break from Lovecraftian fantasy that had held sway over serious American writers of horror for two decades or more."

313. _____. "Where There's a Will." Shock II. New York: Dell, 1980.

REPRINT EDITION: Collected Stories, Los Angeles, CA, Scream Press, 1988.
RESEARCH SOURCE: Sharp, Roberta, "The Short Fiction of Matheson," Survey of Modern Fantasy Literature, pp.1645-1651.

CRITICAL SYNOPSIS: A story of live burial and postmortem confrontation. The main character returns to consciousness to find himself enclosed in a coffin thus reproducing what Poe had called the most unendurable nightmare of all, to be alive and conscious within one's grave. The will to transcend the grave causes the victim of live burial to find a way to claw through the casket walls then through the layers of soil to the surface and freedom, ecstatic to have escaped death. But a moment before the mirror shows him all of the grisly consequences of a seven month entombment. "Staring back at him was a face that was missing sections of flesh. Its skin was gray, and withered yellow bone showed through." Seldom has the stock Gothic scene of the monster in the mirror been handled with so much horrid flare.

314. Matthews, Jack. Ghostly Populations. Baltimore: Johns Hopkins UP, 1986.

RESEARCH SOURCE: Johnson, Greg, "Isn't It Gothic?" Georgia Review 42 (1988): 840-849.

CRITICAL SYNOPSIS: Characters desperately trying to hold on to their vulnerable views of reality and losing out to superior forces is the sequential theme in this collection of Gothic tales. Analyzing the essential Gothicism of the collection, Greg Johnson states that "Ghostly Populations offers a guided tour through the haunted regions of memories, dreams, and the past itself, pointing out subtle and possibly unwelcome truths with a chilling, masterful authority." Like certain Poe prisoners, Matthews's characters are often entrapped within some haunted chamber of time or memory from which they can find no egress. The most Poe-esque piece in the collection is the story, "The Betrayal of the Fives." Like a Poe narrator, the speaker attempts to rationalize the experience he recalls, but the logical approach fails. The compulsive opening sentence has the sound of a Poe neurotic who can neither eradicate nor control the memory. "How many times have I gone over the first confrontation!" agonizes the narrator. Three strange beings, perhaps extra-terrestrials, have included the narrator in their "Group of Five." His previous sense of reality is shattered as he ends reduced to an absurd view of life and self, "impaled somewhere in the jagged irregularities of ink, which in its larger, extended perspectives constitutes a single letter on a page." Other tales with strong overtones of Poe's Gothic are: "Return to an Unknown City," "Tour of the Sleeping Steamboat," "The Amnesia Ballet," and "The Ghost of First Crow."

315. Maule, Rachel. Zimulko; or, The Hag of Beetling Cliff. Philadelphia: J.H. Jones, 1849.

CRITICAL SYNOPSIS: Of dime novel or chapbook quality, the story of witchcraft in the wilds offers a thrill per page and a spectacular death. The author's use of the American wilderness is remiscent of both James Fenimore Cooper and John Neal. The thrill quality is remiscent of the dime sensationalism of Ned Buntline's (see 255) forest and frontier Gothics.

316. Mayer, Nathan. The Fatal Secret; or, Plots and Counterplots. A Novel of the Sixteenth Century. Cincinnati: Office of "The Israelite" and "Deborah," 1858.

CRITICAL SYNOPSIS: Gothified history of Elizabethan times written in imitation of Sophia Lee's popular fictionalization of the hidden daughters of Mary Queen of Scots, The Recess: A Tale of Other Times (1785).

317. Mc Corry, Peter. Mount Benedict; or, The Violated Tomb. A Tale of Charlestown the Convent. Boston: Patrick Donahoe, 1871.

CRITICAL SYNOPSIS: Very similar in its sensational anti-Catholic content to Bunkley's The Escaped Nun (see 070) and Jones's The Nun of St. Ursula; or, The Burning of the Convent, A Romance of Mount Benedict (see 252), the novel again demonstrates the lurid appeal of mob reaction against the menace of Catholicism. The vogue of the American monastic shocker began with Maria Monk's Awful Disclosures in 1836 (see 339).

318. Mc Cullers, Carson. Reflections in a Golden Eye. Boston: Houghton, Mifflin, 1941

REPRINT EDITION: New York, Bantam Books, 1962.

RESEARCH SOURCES: Johnson, Thomas Slayton, "The Horror in the Mansion: Gothic Fiction in the Works of Truman Capote and Carson Mc Cullers," Dissertation Abstracts International 34 (1973): 2630A (University of Texas at Austin); Malin, Irving, New American Gothic, Carbondale, IL, Southern Illinois UP, 1962; Mc Dowell, Margaret B., "Mc Cullers and the Gothic Mode," Carson Mc Cullers, Boston, Twayne, 1980. pp. 48-51.

CRITICAL SYNOPSIS: Violent, sexually shocking, psychologically bizarre, and often coldly cruel, the novel possesses those qualities usually associated with "Southern Gothic." All of the characters are her own versions of monsters and cripples, domestic demons or psychological cripples. And the world of the novel is a closed, rigidly contained, and unnatural environment which warps or tortures the individuals which it holds prisoner. Confusion of sexual identity, brutalizing loneliness, sadistic anger, and intense fear of self contribute to the novel's hard Gothic fabric. The locale is an army base in the south during peacetime. It is a stifling world of artificial authority, meaningless orders and regulations, and complete social decadence where the officers and their wives act out their little power roles. More poignantly, it is a world where natural love in any form is prohibited by the brutish demands of the grotesque people in authority. The principal horror of all this can be seen in the hostile relationship of Captain Wendell Penderton and his monstrous wife, Leonora. Penderton is homosexual and also impotent, but he is hardly a pathetic figure in all of his verbal and physical brutality. In a particularly violent scene, he lashes Leonora's horse, Firebird, nearly to death simply because the dumb creature will not obey his command. Leonora too is a grotesque figure of cold taunting power and deadly beauty. To humiliate Penderton, she removes her clothes at one of their cocktail parties and flouts her nudity by tempting her lover, Major Morris Langdon, while Penderton watches. Mc Cullers seems to have converted a traditional Gothic character, the innocent and entrapped maiden, into the helpless enlisted man, Private Elgee Williams, who is compelled to trim shrubs around the Penderton home. Attracted by the private's handsomeness, but disgusted by his natural sexuality, the officer persecutes him. All other relationships are equally tense, sadistic, and fraught with hatred. Private Williams is shot by Penderton in Leonora's bedroom, but his death does nothing to arrest Leonora's vicious sexuality or to awaken the lost humanity of Penderton. The somber darkness of the novel's atmosphere in general and the appalling spiritual deaths of all of the characters make this book one of the darkest and most disturbing murals on the wall of the American Gothic.

319. _____. The Member of the Wedding. Boston: Houghton Mifflin, 1946.

REPRINT EDITION: New York, Bantam Books, 1969.
RESEARCH SOURCES: Eisinger, Chester E., "The Gothic Spirit in the Forties," Pastoral and Romance: Modern Essays in Criticism, ed. Eleanor Terry Lincoln, Englewood, NJ, Prentice-Hall, 1969, pp. 289-296; Hassan, Ihab, "Carson Mc Cullers: The Alchemy of Love and Aesthetics of Pain," Modern Fiction Studies 5 (1959): 311-326; Phillips, Robert S., "The Gothic Architecture of The Member of the Wedding," Renascence 16 (1964): 59-62.

CRITICAL SYNOPSIS: The theme of profound hopelessness arising out of what Lawrence Graver calls "jubilant hope founded on misplaced idealism, and disillusionment accompanied by a new wisdom about the limits of human life" gives A Member of the Wedding its Gothic tenor. The story belongs to the 12 year old tomboy, Frankie Addams, a member of her brother Jarvis's wedding but actually "a member of nothing in the world." From the margins of her adolescent world, Frankie watches the wedding preparations with increasing self-isolation. Her efforts to involve herself or to connect with the bliss of Jarvis and Janice only deepen the melancholy of her fantasy world. Even rechristening herself· F. Jasmine Addams and compulsively talking with any stranger she meets about the impending wedding prove futile. Her sole link to hard reality is by way of her kitchen companionship with the black servant, Berenice Sadie Brown. With one real eye and one turquoise false eye, the black woman is a sort of sybil figure who imparts wisdom even as she recounts her four marriages to Frankie, one of which cost her a gouged out eye. But for Frankie Addams, there is no way back from hopelessness and from her "old feelings that the world was separate from herself." The novel leaves her in a condition of dreamlessness, a member finally of nothing but her sad community of one. As it is elsewhere in the work of Carson Mc Cullers, the Gothic provides the means of achieving mood in ways that are somewhat reminiscent of the saddest and somberest stories of Hawthorne.

320. Mc Grath, Patrick. Blood and Water, and Other Tales. New York: Poseidon Press, 1988

RESEARCH SOURCE: Johnson, Greg, "Isn't It Gothic?" Georgia Review 42 (1988): 840-849.

CRITICAL SYNOPSIS: With its purple phrasing and over-exotic landscaping, the titular story, "Blood and Water," is a masterful lampoon of Poe's "The Fall of the House of Usher." There is the dilapidated mansion of Phlange with its "drear crypts" and mad master, Sir Norman. His sister and possible partner in incest, Lady Percy, is a suicidal caricature of hosts of Gothic ladies. The rationalist who tries to restore order to the house, the family Doctor, is a victim of Sir Norman's mad fury and winds up decapitated. The story's final scene appears to be campish parody of violence, gore, necrophilia, vampirism, and incest squeezed into one loud splash of blood. After her bathtub suicide (hence the title, "Blood and Water"), Sir Norman enters to embrace his sister in one triumphant necro-sangui-incestuous clasp. In "The Fall of the House of Usher," sister falls atop brother as the House falls over both as the narrator runs for his life. But in the upstairs bathroom at Phlange, we are suspended forever in a moment of Gothic bliss as "Sir Norman drops the head and presses his lips to the wound on the wrist of the corpse. And thus we leave him as the gloom of twilight steals upon the chamber and the flies begin to gather on the Doctor's eyes." Other tales in the collection exhibit the same mock Gothic qualities in their particular parodies of Poe's language and lethal situations. Among the most effective tales are: "The Skewer" where Sigmund Freud makes a guest appearance as a ghastly gremlin of sexual repression, "Marmilion" where premature burial takes place inside a brick chimney, and "Ambrose Syme," the endearing biography of a Greek and Latin classicist in a public school (Ravengloom) who also happens to be a homicidal homosexual who murders young boys as quickly as he translates the odes of Horace. These tales need not be read as parodies of Poe, however, since their tone and style is straight and unadulterated thrill Gothic.

321. Mc Henry, James. The Spectre of the Forest; or, The Annals of the Housatonic, A New England Romance. New York: E. Bliss & E. White, 1823.

CRITICAL SYNOPSIS: An historical romance with a thick overlay of Gothic plotting and properties. The freebooter, Sir Henry Morgan, who had sometimes been depicted in a heroic light as in Ned Buntline's Morgan; or, The Knight of the Black Flag (see 255), is here painted in the blackest hues of villainy. Other actual historical personages who figure into the story include Charles II and Count Frontenac. The action ranges from Block Island and Long Island Sound, to Stratford, Connecticut, to Quebec, to Pittsburgh, with frequent forest and wilderness intervals for the characters. Abraham Wilkins, a fugitive from the England of Charles II, arrives in Stratford, Connecticut, where he helps to rescue a Mrs. Parnell from the clutches of Morgan who is operating from his pirate stronghold on Block Island. Morgan's fury and pursuing vengeance against her and her offspring constitute the Gothic background. The narrative focuses on the adversities of Mrs. Parnell's son, George Parnell, now the object of Morgan's victimization and pursuit after the death of Mrs. Parnell. While hiding from Morgan in the depths of the forest, he encounters the spectre, an apparition in fur who knows George Parnell's history and offers to become his supernatural guide. The complicated narrative now winds through the atrocities of King Philip's War, then northward to Quebec and Parnell's meeting with Count Frontenac, then to the wilderness of western Pennsylvania, and finally home again to Stratford, where with the aid of his spectral protector he exonerates his beloved, Esther Devenant, who is on trial for witchcraft as a result of Morgan's machinations. The spectre of the forest reveals himself to be Esther's father and a champion of liberty in the person of William Goffe, English Puritan and signer of the death warrant of Charles I. Out of this complicated web of history, mystery, and wilderness adventure, Hawthorne perhaps derived the material for his political parable, "The Gray Champion" (see 181). American historical fiction of the 1820's reflected the extensive Gothic origins of the historical novel in its complicated plotting and mixture of love and terror.

322. Mc Killip, Patricia. The House on Parchment Street. New York: Atheneum, 1973.

REPRINT EDITION: New York, Macmillan, 1978.
RESEARCH SOURCE: Wymer, Thomas L., "Patricia Mc Killop," Supernatural Fiction Writers, pp.1067-1072

CRITICAL SYNOPSIS: Combines Gothic settings with adolescent longings and fears. The old house on Parchment Street in London is the habitat of Cromwellian ghosts including the phantom of a priest who was killed during the religious violence of the English Civil War. The mysterious house is visited by three young people who find themselves involved in the entrapped lives of the house's ghostly crew. The impetuous and somewhat aggressive Carol, her artistic cousin, Bruce, and their poetic friend, Alexander, comprise a sort of committee of investigators as they probe the mysteries and ghosts of what amounts to a monument to history. When they come to the house, they have no knowledge of each other or of the past, but their Gothic residency changes all of this. Their mutual quest and the ghostly appearances sensitize the three young people and succeed in making them grow into their potential humanity. Using conventional Gothic events and happenings, Mc Killop has written a three-way Bildungsroman or novel of education.

323.   Melville, Charles K. The Forest Witch; or, The Terror of the Odjib-wes. Providence: General Intelligence and Publishing, 1874.

RESEARCH RESOURCE: Blackbeard, Bill, "Pulps and Dime Novels," Handbook of American Popular Literature, ed. M. Thomas Inge, Westport, CT, Greenwood Press, 1988, pp.217-250.

CRITICAL SYNOPSIS: Of dime novel Gothic quality, the tale features a white woman who has rejected her civilization to live with the Indians. Warfare, torture, exquisite villainy, and a full quota of thrills and shocks mark every page of the narrative. Commenting on the history of this type of frontier Gothic, Bill Blackbeard writes: "The term dime novel was coined to describe the pocket-sized original novels (measuring 6" x 4") of one hundred pages or so published by the New York firm of Beadle and Adams for the reading convenience of Civil War soldiers. Published monthly from the 1860s on, and originally intended for adult and young readers, with such titles as The Rival Scouts, The Outlaw Brothers, The Deer-Hunters, and The Dacotah Queen, the Beadle's Dime Novels line was chiefly concerned with western and frontier adventure until well into the 1870s, when such titles as The Phantom Hand; or, The Heiress of Fifth Avenue of 1877 anticipated the urban detective thrillers that would rival the western stories in popularity in the 1880s and after."

324.   Melville, Herman. Moby-Dick; or, The Whale. New York: Harper, 1851.

REPRINT EDITION: ed. Charles Feidelson, Indianapolis, MN, Bobbs-Merrill, 1964.
RESEARCH SOURCES: Boudreau, Gordon V., "Of Pale Ushers and Gothic Piles: Melville's Architectural Symbology," ESQ: A Journal of the American Renaissance 18 (1972): 67-82; Magistrale, Anthony, "'More Demon Than Man': Melville's Ahab as Gothic Villain," Extrapolation 27 (1986): 203-207; Mc Aleer, John J., "Poe and the Gothic Elements in Moby Dick," Emerson Society Quarterly 27 (1962): 34; Nelson, Lowry Jr., "Ahab as Gothic Hero," Moby-Dick as Doubloon, eds. Hershel Parker and Harrison Hayford, New York, W. W. Norton, 1970, pp.296-308.

CRITICAL SYNOPSIS: In a famous review of Hawthorne's "Mosses from an Old Manse," Melville attributed to Hawthorne a Gothic outlook which had "the power of blackness." A shared Gothic vision in the form of "the power of whiteness" pervades Melville's demonic quest romance, Moby-Dick. As a reader, Melville had been attracted to the Gothic school, purchasing and devouring such classics of the Gothic as Beckford's Vathek (1786), Walpole's Castle of Otranto (1764), and the romances of Mrs. Radcliffe. These works of horror literature enabled Melville to transmute the haunted castle into the haunted forecastle of his Gothic epic, Moby-Dick. A monster roaming the deep, a monomaniacal villain of mysterious origins and potent eye, and a fatal voyage are but a few of the recognizable Gothic elements to be seen in the book's structure. Terror turns into horror and reason succumbs to madness as the "fiery hunt" for the white whale pulls all save the young wanderer, Ishmael, into the maelström. If the matter of the novel is highly Gothic, the manner or style is equally suggestive of Gothic imagery, metaphor, and symbol. Ishmael's midnight soliloquy, "Look not too long in the face of fire, O man!" and Ahab's Satanic shout of defiance, "Speak not to me of blasphemy, man. I'd stike the sun if it insulted me," echo the titantic and destructive passions of the Gothic heroes and villains, Manfred, Vathek, Ambrosio, and Melmoth. Central to the Gothicism of Moby-Dick is the characters' involvement with elemental, cosmic evil, the degree of evil that activates the characters of high Gothic fiction and propels them toward their spectacular dooms. Only Ishmael, like the astonished narrator at the end of "The Fall of the House of Usher," avoids the vortex as he escapes from Ahab's destroyed "castle" to recount his incredible story. "The tale that Ishmael lives to tell," writes Anthony Magistrale, "ultimately succeeds in transcending the restrictive Gothic world of the late Eighteenth Century. The genre's scope is enlarged by Melville to include a tragic dimension. Through an adaptation of standard Gothic apparatus Moby-Dick attains the power and dimensionality of classical tragedy."

325. _____. Pierre; or, The Ambiguities. New York: Harper, 1852.

REPRINT EDITION: New York, Grove Press, 1957.
RESEARCH SOURCE: Arvin, Newton, "Melville and the Gothic Novel," New England Quarterly 22 (1949): 33-48.

CRITICAL SYNOPSIS: When Melville tried to write a Gothic romance in the formal sense, the result was the interesting fiasco, Pierre, an exhausting and over-written novel by an exhausted and written-out writer. Melville critics almost universally agree that Pierre is a bad book in its every feature, but for the explorer of the Gothic, this judgement might require qualification. Arvin is correct in pointing out that "Pierre is the Childe Harold or Lara of a hundred romantic poems and novels; Isabel glides straight out of Monk Lewis and Mrs. Glendinning is the haughty dowager or worldly matron of The Italian and The Mysteries of Udolpho [of Mrs. Radcliffe.] Secondhand too are the Gothic properties Melville borrowed, the Magic Portrait (the 'chair' portrait of Pierre's father) and the Magic Instrument (the guitar that Isabel 'plays' without touching its strings)." The plot too exhibits the dark turbulence and chaotic passions so characteristic of traditional Gothic romance. Sub-themes of incest, homicide, suicide, insanity, and fatal guilt supply the narrative's Gothic ambience. Pierre, an aspirant writer and heir to a great estate in upstate New York, deserts his fiancée, Lucy Tartan, after he becomes infatuated with the dark and mysterious Isabel. His passion deepens into incestuous desire once he is persuaded that she is his sister. Torn by guilt, he realizes that he has violated the ideals of father and family, but more painfully, that he has betrayed his own absolute standards of ethical truth. The novel ends in emotional cataclysm and the dual suicide of Pierre and Isabel as Pierre declares himself "the fool of Truth, the fool of Virtue, the fool of Fate." This stock Gothic plot allows Melville the opportunity for some astounding Gothic metaphors and herein lies the real literary value of the novel. Pierre has many Hamletlike moments when the protagonist sees into the self with a kind of entropic clarity, using the Gothic metaphor of dark descent to express the experience: "Deep, deep, and still deep and deeper must we go, if we would find out the heart of man; descending into which is as descending a spiral stair in a shaft, without any end, and where that endlessness is only concealed by the spiralness of the stair, and the blackness of the shaft." In Gothic form, Pierre is certainly a failure, but in Gothic vision and the metaphoric embodiment of that vision its imaginative success is assured.

326. _____. "Bartleby the Scrivener." The Piazza Tales. New York: Dix & Edwards, 1856; London: Sampson Low, 1856.

REPRINT EDITION: Herman Melville: Selected Tales and Poems, ed. Richard Chase, New York, Holt, Rinehart, and Winston, 1960.
RESEARCH SOURCES: Cook, Richard M., "Evolving the Inscrutable: The Grotesque in Herman Melville's Fiction," American Literature 49 (1978): 544-559; Ryan, Stephen T., "The Gothic Formula of 'Bartleby,'" Arizona Quarterly 34 (1978): 311-316.

CRITICAL SYNOPSIS: A common Gothic fate is the walling up alive of the victim, but in this sadly amusing and haunting story of Wall Street, the fate is self-inflicted by the enigmatic and phantasmic figure of the law copyist, Bartleby. Bartleby is engaged by the narrator, a sane and practical Wall Street lawyer, to copy out legal documents. But once established within the office, Bartleby proceeds to withdraw from all routine, to refuse all work, and to deny all social intercourse. What is more, he erects various walls, both physical and psychological, between himself and the world, and does so to the befuddlement of the narrator. In fact, the narrator's losing attempt to penetrate these walls and to communicate with Bartleby is at the moral center of the story. Yet, the narrator is sensitized to the riddle of human suffering by the very presence of this strange figure in his otherwise normal world of work. Melville uses the Gothic metaphor of the ruined pillar to describe Bartleby's isolation. "But he seemed alone, absolutely alone in the universe, like the last column of some ruined temple, he remained standing mute and solitary in the middle of the otherwise deserted room." Each attempt to get Bartleby to work or even to speak receives the same nullifying response, "I would prefer not to," which reverberates through the tale like the "Nevermore" of Poe's raven. When the narrator sees Bartleby for the final time, he has become a vagrant occupant of the New York City "Tombs" and is a famished figure surrounded by walls as he takes up a final position "fronting the dead wall." When the narrator kneels to touch the wasted figure, Bartleby expires, his death apparently hastened by the narrator's humane touch. This is a peculiar, yet very moving story, with the Gothic images of enclosure applied to a profound condition of metaphysical loneliness and spiritual desolation that is literally forever beyond the reach of human pathos.

327. _____. "The Bell-Tower." The Piazza Tales. New York: Dix & Edwards, 1856; London: Sampson Low, 1856.

REPRINT EDITION: Herman Melville: Selected Tales and Poems, ed. Richard Chase, New York, Holt, Rinehart, and Winston, 1960.
RESEARCH SOURCES: Mac Pherson, Jay, "Waiting for Shiloh: Transgression and Fall in Melville's 'The Bell Tower,'" Gothic Fictions: Prohibition/Transgression, ed. Kenneth W. Graham, New York, AMS Press, 1989, pp.245-258; Shetty, Nalini V., "Melville's Use of the Gothic Tradition," Studies in American Literature: Essays in Honour of William Mulder, Delhi, India, Oxford UP, 1976, pp.144-153.

CRITICAL SYNOPSIS: An odd, Kafkaesque story of the building of a great tower and the tower's subsequent destruction of its creator. Melville might well have been inspired by the theme of toweromania, the compulsion to erect mighty towers and to retire to their pinnacles in contemptuous isolation, that is such a prominent event in Beckford's Gothic novel, <u>Vathek</u> (1786). Bannadonna, the tower-builder and mechanician, completes and then retires to his proud tower, furnishing the belfry with the great state bell and an ingenious automaton to strike the hours. On the day of dedication the multitude below waits in awe for the striking of the hour but all is sinister silence as they gaze up. The magistrates climb the tower to investigate only to find Bannadonna crushed and mangled in the gearworks beneath the great bell with the mechanical figure of the striker "still impending over Bannadonna, as if whispering some post-mortem terror." At his funeral, the great bell works loose and falls. Within a year, an earthquake levels Bannadonna's mighty monument to himself. The parable of perverted aspiration concludes with the austere moral: "So the blind slave obeyed its blinder lord; but in obedience slew him. So the creator was killed by the creature." The themes of the overreacher who brings about his own destruction and the fatality inherent in soulless modern technology seem clear enough.

328. _____. "Benito Cereno." <u>The Piazza Tales</u>. New York: Dix & Edwards, 1856; London: Sampson Low, 1856.

REPRINT EDITION: <u>Four Short Novels of Herman Melville</u>, New York, Bantam Books, 1963.
RESEARCH SOURCES: Boudreau, Gordon V., "Herman Melville: Master Mason of the Gothic," <u>Dissertation Abstracts</u> 28 (1968): 5007A–5008A (University of Indiana); Kosok, Heinz, <u>Die Bedeutung der Gothic Novel für das Erzählwerk Herman Melvilles</u>, Hamburg, West Germany, Cram, de Gruyter, 1963.

CRITICAL SYNOPSIS: Ships and their sinister crews or cargos are often Melville's substitute for the traditional haunted castle of Gothic fiction. The fact is especially true for the dilapidated Spanish slave vessel, the San Dominick, seemingly under the command of Benito Cereno but actually under the control of the mutinous and guileful black, Babo. The slave ship is Melville's version of a Gothic castle gone afloat. Even when it is first seen, the ship is less an oceangoing craft than it is a haunted abbey whose halls are patrolled by murderous monks. "The ship when made signally visible on the verge of the leaden hued swells, with the shreds of fog here and there raggedly furring her, appeared like a white-washed monastery after a thunderstorm, seen perched upon some dun cliff among the Pyrenees. Peering over the bulwarks were what really seemed in the hazy distance throngs of dark cowls; while, fitfully revealed through the open portholes, other dark moving figures were dimly descried, as of Black Friars pacing the cloisters. Her keel seemed laid, her ribs put together, and she launched, from Ezekiel's Valley of Dry Bones." This is the Gothic perspective as Captain Amasa Delano, an American innocent, prepares to board the slave ship. Now under the control of Babo and the 300 blacks, the slaves will perform an elaborate charade before the eyes of Delano to create the illusion that the slaves are still under white control. Suspense builds slowly, almost painfully, as the blacks led by Babo carry out the hoax of servitude for the benefit of the short-sighted Captain Delano. Gothic melodrama hovers on the edge of macabre comedy when the servile Babo shaves his master, Benito Cereno, using the flag of Spain as a barber's cloth. The Gothicism of the tale works to enhance its political and moral allegory. Like the maidens of Radcliffean romance, Captain Amasa Delano confuses illusion with reality. The naive Americanness in his attitude toward blacks and slavery contains elements of moral simplicity which blinds him to the real facts and also prevents him from seeing through social masks to the real evil behind these masks. When the revolt is finally exposed and the ship retaken, Delano is shocked into recognition, a horrified realization that Melville highlights through the use of a culminating Gothic image of the exposed figurehead of the San Dominick, as the "fag-end in lashing out, whipped away the canvas shroud about the beak, suddenly revealing, as the bleached hull swung round towards the open ocean, death for the figurehead, in a human skeleton." Other equally striking Gothic effects or remade devices of horror permeate this short novel.

329. _____. Billy Budd, Foretopman. The Works of Herman Melville, ed. Raymond Weaver. London: Wells, 1922.

REPRINT EDITION: Melville's Billy Budd and the Critics, ed. William T. Stafford, San Francisco, CA, Wadsworth Publishing, 1961. RESEARCH SOURCE: Mandel, Ruth B., "Herman Melville and the Gothic Outlook," Dissertation Abstracts 30 (1970): 3015A-3016A (University of Connecticut).

CRITICAL SYNOPSIS: The last work of Melville's life contains his most brilliant resetting of the Gothic's primary symbol, the haunted castle. Here, the castle is a British man-of-war, the Indomitable, during the year of revolutionary crisis, 1797. This is the year of the great naval mutinies at the Spithead and the Nore. Impressed aboard the warship, the innocent and handsome Billy Budd encounters his moral and spiritual opposite in the person of John Claggart, master-at-arms and master as well of the ship's underworld, the lower gundecks, where he enjoys "official seclusion from sunlight." On the mythic level, Claggart's hatred for Billy is the primal confrontation of Satan and Adam; on the Gothic level, this character collision resembles the persecuted maiden's rendezvous with the fearful villain in the lightless castle labyrinth. Exercising consummate guile and sadistic power, Claggart intrigues to bring Billy Budd up on a charge of mutiny before Captain Vere, a decent and honorable man but quite helpless in the face of Claggart's absolute and superhuman depravity. In Captain Vere's presence, Claggart foully accuses Billy of mutiny. Unable to speak, Billy strikes Claggart and kills him, a mutinous act and committed in wartime. To uphold "justice" and maintain military discipline, Vere is forced to hang Billy Budd at sea. The victory of evil and the annihilation of goodness in a dark and fallen world, an ending sometimes found in the best of high Gothic fiction, is asserted most effectively in this short novel. That Melville's imagination reached back to several high Gothic villains in drawing the portrait of John Claggart is established through direct and indirect references to those earlier Gothic Satans, Walpole's Manfred in The Castle of Otranto (1764), Lewis's Ambrosio in The Monk (1795), Maturin's Melmoth in Melmoth the Wanderer (1820), and most particularly, Mrs. Radcliffe's Montoni and Father Schedoni in The Mysteries of Udolpho (1794) and The Italian (1797). In chapter 11, which profiles Claggart's personality in depth, Melville mentions Radcliffean villainy in answering the chapter's opening query, "What was the matter with the master-at-arms?" The answer: "And yet the cause, necessarily to be assumed as the sole one assignable, is in its very realism as much charged with that prime element of Radcliffean romance, the mysterious, as any that the ingenuity of the author of the Mysteries of Udolpho could devise."

330. Menzies, Sutherland. "Hugues, The Wer-wolf, A Kentish Legend of the Middle Ages." Lady's Magazine and Museum, September, 1838.

REPRINT EDITION: Gothic Tales of Terror, ed. Peter Haining, New York, Taplinger, 1972.
RESEARCH SOURCE: Summers, Montague, "A Note upon the Werewolf in Literature," The Werewolf, New Hyde Park, NY, University Books, pp.262-277.

CRITICAL SYNOPSIS: According to the authority on werewolfery, Montague Summers, this tale might be considered the prototype of lycanthropic Gothic since it precedes by one year Captain Marryat's Phantom Ship with its inset tale of Krantz the werewolf. Menzies's story also makes use of that gory device of Gothic fiction, the severed hand which continues to live after being cut off. Hugues Wulfric is the last of the line of an ancient Norman family feared and despised by the Saxon peasants of Kent because they are thought to be werewolves. Hugues himself is a pitiable, sensitive, and even lovable man who forms an amorous attachment with Branda, the niece of a local flesher or butcher, Willieblud. Costuming himself as a wolf, Hugues forages for meat by assaulting Willieblud's wagon until "instead of handing him his joint of beef or mutton, Willieblud raised his cleaver and lopped off the paw," then displays to Branda's horrified gaze "a freshly severed human hand enveloped in wolfskin." While Branda attends to her mutilated lover, the phantom hand becomes the nemesis of Willieblud, finally driving him to drown himself in the River Stour. One year later and "minus a hand," Hugues leads Branda to the altar. Thus, one of the first werewolf tales in all of literature proves to be a love story adorned in Gothic trappings.

331. Merritt, Abraham. The Moon Pool. New York: Putnam, 1919.

RESEARCH SOURCE: Bleiler, E.F., Supernatural Fiction Writers, pp. 835-843.

CRITICAL SYNOPSIS: First published in All-Story, June 22, 1918, this horror tale remains Merritt's best known horror piece. Horror is generated by the beast which rises from the dark depths to seize its human prey, a Gothic situation which might be traced back in epic and folklore to the mere or pool of Grendel's mother in Beowulf. The Moon Pool itself is an ancient archeological site somewhere in Micronesia, When the scientific narrator descends through an underground vault to investigate the mysteries of the pool, he arouses the monster that his science cannot contain. Together with "The Conquest of the Moon Pool," a sequel, the story was reshaped into a short novel. Merritt is not without literary ability in the field of supernatural fiction, but the comment of E.F. Bleiler that he is "very dated" is probably just.

332. _____. Burn, Witch, Burn! New York: Liveright, 1933.

RESEARCH SOURCE: Yoke, Carl B., "A. Merritt," Supernatural Fiction Writers, pp.835-843.

CRITICAL SYNOPSIS: A firstrate thrill novel which appeared originally in Argosy, October through November, 1932, and later
thrilled audiences as the film, The Devil Doll (1936). The book
could be called "Manhattan" Gothic since its settings are the
apartment houses, shops, and hospitals of the City. Although Merritt's main purpose was to tell a chilling tale, there are some
serious moral and cultural themes imbedded in the Gothic framework. Among these are the ineptitude of modern science in the face
of timeless evil, the fragile nature of our humanness which is
perhaps even more fragile in the impersonal metropolis, and finally the occult relationship between illusory beauty and evil horror. The plot is skillfully manipulated if somewhat incredible. A
confident psychiatrist, Dr. Lovell, investigates a series of
strange deaths and tries to bring medical logic to bear on their
causes. The deaths are connected with the shop of a dollmaker, Madame Mandalip, a subway sorceress who animates her dolls with her
own murderous will, then sends them forth to seek victims on the
sidewalks of New York. One of these victims in a close associate
of the gangster, Julian Ricori, a reversal of the thirties stereotype of the brutal gunman. Ricori is hard-headed, soft-hearted,
and as imaginative as Poe's detective, Monsieur Dupin. As Carl
Yoke points out, "He mitigates the hard and unfeeling nature of
science and embodies the theme of the novel--humanness." Where Madame Mandalip is a figure of cold evil and is portrayed like one
of Baudelaire's Parisian giantesses, and where Dr. Lovell is a
figure of cold logic and scientific skepticism, Ricori is the sensitive and scorned common man who knows absolute evil when he sees
it. Lowell and Ricori are saved from Madame Mandelip's murderous
designs when a doll made in the image of Nurse Walters, one of her
victims, rebels against her mistress's lethal command, stabs the
witch and burns the doll shop. While evil is destroyed at last, it
is not science which has subdued the witch's power, but the human
and humane impulse which rises up even in the doll form of Nurse
Walters to affirm the superior power of common humanity in the
contest with two inhuman forces, uncaring science and natural evil
masquerading as beauty.

333.   _____. Creep, Shadow! Garden City, NY: Doubleday, Doran, 1934.

CRITICAL SYNOPSIS: The short novel first ran in Argosy Magazine,
September-October, 1934. This Gothic novel generates its terror
from a premise of Jungian psychology that there is an abyss or
dark reservoir of racial memory in us all and that our civilized
selves are built on a savage foundation of ancestral personalities
and sublimated animal instincts. Such a collective unconscious can
and does cast its creeping shadow over our rational selves dooming
us to repeat our ancient fates. The novel's modern lovers, the anthropologist, Alan Caranac, and Dahut de Keradel, are possessed by
two prehistoric shadow selves, Alain de Carnac and the bloodthirsty Princess Dahut of the underwater City of Ys. The aggressor is
the wicked woman residing within the mind and body of the beautiful Dahut while Alan is both the object of her love and a victim
of her revengeful schemes since it was Alan in his previous personage of Alain who had tempted her to the destruction of her City
of Ys. She becomes a fatal version of the restorative earth goddess, Isis, who raised the murdered Osiris from the Nile. Their
love-hate relationship is at the center of this complex fantasy
which ends when the Princess drowns after a magical incantation
releases the sea again as it had originally been released in
flooding the walls and towers of Ys. The two Dahuts are opposite

sides of the life force, the creative and destructive maternal principle which renews itself in cyclical experiences of love and death. Merritt's conscious use of mythic and archetypal themes yields a Gothic fantasia capable of thrilling readers on several levels of mystery.

334. _____. "The People of the Pit." The Fox Woman and Other Stories. New York: Avon, 1949.

   REPRINT EDITION: Short Stories Series, eds. R. Reginald, Douglas Melville, Salem, NH, Ayer, 1978.

   CRITICAL SYNOPSIS: The story first appeared in the pulp magazine, All-Story, on January 5, 1918. The last words of the dying narrator make up the narrative. In a bleak, polar setting he had fallen into an icy abyss containing another race of beings, the people of the pit. His horrifying experiences at their hands constitutes his narrative, a story without a moral and a journey into the center of the earth without an explanation. Nor is the narrator's return to the surface ever fully explained. Although Merritt may not have read Poe's novel of polar descent, The Narrative of Arthur Gordon Pym (see 378), there are still many parallels between the two works.

335. Mertz, Barbara [Barbara Michaels]. House of Many Shadows. New York: Dodd, Mead, 1974.

   REPRINT EDITION: Greenwich, CT, Fawcett-Crest, 1974.
   RESEARCH SOURCE: Radcliffe, Elsa, Gothic Novels of the Twentieth Century, Metuchen, NJ, Scarecrow Press, 1979, pp.150-152.

   CRITICAL SYNOPSIS: A formulaic but intelligently plotted and fast paced modern Gothic romance. To recover from a head injury, the heroine, Meg, decides to redecorate an old house. Within its winding corridors she encounters both the lover she had always desired and the spectre she had always dreaded. The treatment of the maiden's encounter with the supernatural is both real and realistic. Mertz is a professional historian of Roman and Egyptian history, a fact which shows in her many recreational Gothics such as Prince of Darkness (1969) and The Sea-King's Daughter (1975).

336. Mildred, E.W. The Ghost House; or, The Story of Rose Lichen. New York: A.D.F. Randolph, 1893.

   CRITICAL SYNOPSIS: A tidy Gothic tale, but not too terrifying or violent out of deference for the lady readers of this typical tea table thriller. Like her predecessors among the heroines of Mrs. Radcliffe, Rose Lichen is thrust into a search for her origins and identity in the usual ghostly environment. Her anxious encounters with a malign spirit world are, of course, the product of her imagination. Radcliffean Gothic narrative always permits vigorous supernatural activity until the final pages and such is the formula followed in this pleasantly chilling woman's Gothic.

337. Millhiser, Marlys. The Mirror. New York: Putnam, 1978.

   REPRINT EDITION: Greenwich, CT, Fawcett-Crest, 1982.
   RESEARCH SOURCE: Friend, Beverly, "Time Travel as a Feminist Didactic in Works by Phyllis Eisenstein, Marlys Millhiser, and Octavia Butler," Extrapolation 23 (1982): 50-55.

CRITICAL SYNOPSIS: One of the best psychological Gothics to emerge in the 1970's, the novel makes provocative use of the device of the mirror as the repository of memory and prison of time. Prior usages of the mirror in American Gothic fiction occur throughout Hawthorne's tales (e.g. see 223, "Monsieur du Miroir") and evoke the theme of alternate selves caught in an identity crisis of some type. The work might also be considered in the tradition of the double or secret sharer because the sinister mirror of the title is responsible for a personality exchange between two women. The two principal characters of the story are the young woman, Shay Garrett, and her grandmother, Brandy Mc Cabe. But the leading Gothic character is the device of the mirror itself, a family heirloom apparently brought forth only on wedding days. When both women gaze into the mirror on the day of Shay's wedding, the glass produces a transference, projecting Shay backward to the year 1900 and giving her the body of her grandmother; reciprocally, the grandmother is projected forward from her wedding day in 1900 to the year 1978 and is given Shay's body. Thus, time displacement and incarceration within collective family memory form the basis for the novel's unique presentation of the a Gothic entrapment. Deprived of the security of their own generation and time frame by the Gothic mirror, both women are faced with bad or loveless marriages, a classic situation of the domestic Gothic. From the perspective of 78 years, Shay can see through the glass darkly into the future but can do nothing to change it. Likewise, the grandmother-become-granddaughter can see what lies ahead for Shay but is helpless against the denying power of the mirror which holds both women's lives in thrall. While time entrapment is not a new theme for either Gothic or science fiction, the novel's addition of body exchange to the theme results in a subtle and engrossing treatment of an old theme. Millhiser has also written another superior psychological Gothic, Nella Waits: A Novel of the Supernatural (New York: Putnam, 1974).

338. Mitchell, Isaac. The Ayslum; or, Alonzo and Melissa, An American Tale Founded on Fact. Poughkeepsie, NY: Joseph Nelson, 1811.

REPRINT EDITIONS: New York, AMS Press, 1978.
RESEARCH SOURCES: Davidson, Kathy N., "Isaac Mitchell's The Asylum; or, Gothic Castles in the New Republic," Prospects: An Annual Journal of American Cultural Studies 7 (1982): 281-299; Pearson, Edmund, "Isaac Mitchell's The Asylum; or, Alonzo and Melissa (1811)," Queer Books, Garden City, NY, Doubleday, 1928; Pearson, Edmund, "Romance: Early American Style," Bookman 68 (September, 19-28): 1-8; Petter, Henri, Early American Novel, pp.316-319; Reed, Edward, "The Asylum," The Nation, December 8, 1904, p.458.

CRITICAL SYNOPSIS: Haunted castles in colonial Connecticut and Long Island? Medieval horrors in the midst of the struggling new republic? Apparently, the Gothic novel in pristine condition could sink its roots anywhere, as this fascinating specimen of early American Gothic shows. The mouldering, feudal monuments of Mrs. Radcliffe's romances along with her hysterical heroine have been transported intact across the Atlantic, then reconstructed in the colonies during the American Revolution. Mitchell clearly knew how to turn the screws of terror when he placed his menaced maiden, Melissa Bloomfield, in the obligatory fainting posture while immured in her father's Connecticut castle. "Groping to find the stairs, as she came near their foot, a black object, apparently in human shape, stood before her, with eyes which resembled glowing

coals, and red flames issuing from its mouth. As she stood fixed
in inexpressible trepidation, a large ball of fire rolled slowly
along the extended hall and burst with an explosion which seemed
to rock the building in its deepest foundations. Melissa closed
her eyes and fell senseless to the floor." Melissa has been cas-
tled by her irate father for refusing his choice of husband, the
repulsive Mr. Beauman, and preferring instead the fervent patriot,
Alonzo. Separated from Melissa, this ardent young man translates
love into patriotic ardor and goes off to join the naval war
against the British. Captured at sea, he is aided by none other
than Benjamin Franklin, who makes his first and only appearance in
the pages of a Gothic novel. The climax and reunion occur in
Charleston, South Carolina, and are worthy of any of Mrs. Radcliffe's sentimental finales. The despairing Alonzo casts himself
upon Melissa's grave believing that he has won his revolution but
lost his beloved in the process. She is not dead, of course, but
has managed to slip away from Gothified Connecticut to interrupt
Alonzo's lamentations with her tearful reunion speech, her reformed father by her side. In its several editions, including at
least one plagiarized conversion into a Gothic chapbook under the
altered title, The Unfeeling Father, by Daniel Jackson, Jr. (see
228), Mitchell's colonialized Gothic romance won the approval of
American Radcliffean readers. It further reflects American Gothicism in its transitional phase from the high-minded horrors of
Charles Brockden Brown to the spooky excitement of James Fenimore
Cooper's romances of the forest. First published under the title,
"Alonzo and Melissa," in the Poughkeepsie Political Barometer,
June 5 through October 30, 1804.

339. Monk, Maria. Awful Disclosures of Maria Monk of the Hotel Dieu Convent of Montreal; The Secrets of the Black Nunnery Revealed. Au-
rora, MO: Menace Publishing, 1836.

REPRINT EDITION: Columbia, SC, Camden Publishing, 1939.
RESEARCH SOURCES: Billington, R.A., "Maria Monk and Her Influ-
ence," Catholic Historical Review 22 (1937): 283-296; Tarr, Sister
Mary Muriel, Catholicism in Gothic Fiction, Washington, DC, Cath-
olic University of America Press, 1946; Ann Arbor, MI, University
Microfilm International, 1980; Thompson, Ralph, "The Maria Monk
Affair," Colophon Part 17 number 6 (1934).

CRITICAL SYNOPSIS: The monastic shocker exposing the horrors of
the convent life and terrors of Popery had long been known in English Gothic fiction. Maria Monk's purportedly autobiographical exposé of the "sinful ways of the nunneries" continues the tradition
of sensational anti-Catholic horror which can be traced back to
Monk Lewis's The Monk (1796) and such anonymous shilling shockers
as Almagro and Claude; or, Monastic Murder Exemplified in the
Dreadful Doom of an Unfortunate Nun (1803). Maria Monk's shocker
was marketed as an authentic account of the author's immurement
within a Montreal convent where she saw before her miraculous
escape "nuns executed for refusing to obey the lustful will of
priests and witnessed the strangling of two small babies. She discovered a large hole in the basement of the Hotel Dieu in which
the bodies of those murdered were thrown and the secret passage
connecting the convent with a neighboring priest's home." The book
and its sequel which continues the tale of her persecution while a
fugitive nun, revived the lurid themes of the earlier anti-
Catholic shocker and exploited the same mass fears of Popery which
had led to the infamous destruction of an Ursuline convent in

Charlestown, Massachusetts by a mob in 1834. Just as this type of Gothic had been commercially successful with the British Gothic audience, so Awful Disclosures sold out in repeated editions until more than 300,000 copies had spewed from American presses before the Civil War.

340. Moore, Catherine Lucille [Lewis Padgett]. "The Devil We Know." Unknown, August, 1941.

REPRINT EDITION: The Best of C.L. Moore, ed. Lester Del Rey, Garden City, NY, Doubleday, 1975.
RESEARCH SOURCE: Mathews, Patricia, "C.L. Moore's Classic Science Fiction," The Feminine Eye: Science Fiction and the Women Who Write It, ed. Tom Staicar, New York, Ungar, 1982.

CRITICAL SYNOPSIS: Gothic tale done in collaboration with her husband, Henry Kuttner. Revives the Faust legend of the Satanic pact and projects it into a futuristic world.

341. _____. "Daemon." Famous Fantastic Mysteries, October, 1946.

REPRINT EDITION: The Best of C.L. Moore, ed. Lester Del Rey, Garden City, NY, Doubleday, 1975.
RESEARCH SOURCE: Gunn, James, "Henry Kuttner, C.L. Moore, Lewis Padgett, et al.," Voices for the Future, ed. Thomas D. Clareson, Bowling Green, OH, Bowling Green UP, 1976.

CRITICAL SYNOPSIS: The story takes up the theme of soullessness in the dying plight of the Brazilian mariner, Luiz. Because he is deprived of soul, Luiz has daemonic vision or the ability to see the conditions of the souls of his fellow creatures. Each soul appears in its symbolic color on a sort of moral spectrum running from the purity of white to the baseness of red. The red soul of the tale is Captain Stryker, Luiz's tormentor and a fallen angel figure who abandons Luiz on a deserted Caribbean island. This is a Gothic tale of moods rather than high moments of horror.

342. _____. "Shambleau." Shambleau and Others. New York: Gnome Press, 1953.

REPRINT EDITION: The Best of C.L. Moore, ed. Lester Del Rey, Garden City, NY, Doubleday, 1975.
RESEARCH SOURCES: Letson, Russell, "C.L. Moore," Supernatural Fiction Writers, pp.891-898; Shroyer, Frederick, "C.L. Moore, 1911-; Henry Kuttner, 1915-1958," Science Fiction Writers: Critical Studies of the Major Authors from the Early Nineteenth Century to the Present Day, ed. E.F. Bleiler, New York, Scribner's, 1982, pp.161-167.

CRITICAL SYNOPSIS: The Victorian conception of the female vampire as a psychic and erotic aggressor as found in Joseph Sheridan Le Fanu's Carmilla (1878) is the basis for the characterization of Shambeau whose soul-threatening grip upon the hero, Northwest Smith, is also an act of sexual transfer. Shambeau is the very incarnation of sadistic and loveless sex. Her hold upon Smith illustrates the general view of the vampire as a symbol of self-destructive sexual force. "Even a loathsome embrace," states Devendra P. Varma in Voices from the Vaults, "marks the naked cruelty of passion. The vampire's embrace plumbs the bottomless pit of damnation; yet it ravages the heights of heaven with rage and rapture." On the mythic level of the tale, Shambleau represents the irresistible attractiveness of all that is repellent in our natures. Confirming the symbolic reading, Smith cannot ward off the vampire's persistent attacks because to do so would be to deny his deepest and most powerful secret appetites. The horror theme of the vampire as alternate self is handled here with suggestive skill.

343. Morgan, Susan Rigby Dallam. The Haunting Shadow. Baltimore: Cushing and Brother, 1848.

    CRITICAL SYNOPSIS: Short Gothic tale of the supernatural and ancestral lover who assists the heroine in the defense of her heritage. The form of the tale is anecdotal reverie with Gothic effects employed sparingly to induce an aura of wonder rather than the sheer fright of the crude shocker.

344. Morrow, W.C. "The Monster Maker." The Ape, the Idiot, and Other People. Philadelphia: Lippincott, 1897.

    CRITICAL SYNOPSIS: Several tales in the collection extend the Frankenstein theme of perverse science or artificial creation. The selfish and bestial nature of the intellect carries over from "The Monster Maker" to other tales such as "His Unconquerable Enemy" and "A Story Told by the Sea."

345. Mott, Lawrence. "The Black Thing of Hatchet Lake." White Darkness, and Other Stories of the Great North West. New York: Outing Publishing, 1907.

    REPRINT EDITION: Short Story Reprint Series, Salem, NH, Ayer Publishing, 1974.

    CRITICAL SYNOPSIS: A Montana Gothic featuring the animal or reptilian spook, a supernatural beast akin to the Wendigo. There are overtones here of several of H.G. Wells's tales of terror concerning beasts from the depths or the wilds such as "Sea Raiders," an octopus story, and "Aegypornis Island," about the incubation of a prehistoric bird.

346. Moxley, Frank Wright. Red Snow. New York: Simon and Schuster, 1930.

    CRITICAL SYNOPSIS: Combines horror with the science fiction motif of the earth's last survivor, an idea initiated by Mary Shelley in The Last Man (1826). The red snow which begins to cover the earth on August 17, 1935, is only one sign of the impending apocalypse and bloodbath which eradicates civilization, leaving behind only the last man, Phaeton Howard Andrews. After witnessing racial war and the decay of all civilization by reversion to primitive behavior among the remaining survivors, Andrews is apparently saved by the sun god when he is carried into the heavens by Helios in the last year of earth, 2027 A.D. The blanket of crimson snow or global rain of blood is a powerful natural symbol for individual and national failings as the dark dawn of fascism crept across the world of the thirties.

347. Munn, H. Warner. The Werewolf of Ponkert. Providence, RI: Grandon, 1958.

    REPRINT EDITION: New York, Centaur Books, 1976.

RESEARCH SOURCE: Bush, Lawrence C., "The Realms of H. Warner Munn," The Romantist, 4-5 (1980-81): 41-42.

CRITICAL SYNOPSIS: Historical werewolf legend with a special dimension. Usually, when a man becomes a wolf, the bestial side totally displaces the human and sensitive side. But when Wladislaw Brenryk, a fifteenth century Transylvanian, is forced into a pack of werewolves after being bitten and infected, he retains his human feelings by loathing all that he has become. Indeed, his humane sensitivity is heightened by his lupine transformation. At the heart of the tale is the Werewolf of Ponkert's losing struggle to regain and retain his lost humanness, a battle which sees Brenryk forced to kill and consume his own wife. In this werewolf story and others such as "The Werewolf's Daughter," Munn sought to extend the crude lycanthropic material several degrees beyond physical shock.

348. Murfree, Mary Noailles [Charles Egbert Craddock]. The Phantoms of the Foot Bridge, and Other Stories. New York: Harper, 1895.

RESEARCH SOURCE: Cary, Richard, Mary Noailles Murfree, New York, Twayne, 1967.

CRITICAL SYNOPSIS: Several of her Tennessee mountaineer stories are local color examples of Smoky Mountain Gothic. Her topographies as well exude the primitive remoteness and lurking supernaturalism of a nature that is characteristic of Gothic landscaping. The novella, The Mystery of Witch-Face Mountain, opens with a Gothic description of a mammoth face, seemingly alive, which appears, then disappears on the mountain side: "Sometimes in the uncanny electric flicker smitten from a storm-cloud, a gigantic, peaked sinister face is limned on the bare, sandy slope, so definite, that one is amazed that the perception of it came no earlier, and is startled when it disappears." "The Phantoms of the Footbridge" is a more straightforward horror-and-ghost story which centers on the theme of the apparitional return. Millicent's return is precipitated by the lovers' rivalry between the Byronic John Dundas and the rough mountaineer, Emory Keenan, whose shot-riddled body is discovered in a deserted hotel. These characters and events are integrated with a realistic narrative so as to produce a regional or local color type of Gothic tale, a native sub-genre of the tale of terror which was also practiced by Thomas Nelson Page, Bret Harte, and Mark Twain.

349. Neal, John. Logan; or, The Mingo Chief. Philadelphia: H.C. Carey & I. Lea, 1822.

REPRINT EDITION: New York, AMS Press, 1978.
RESEARCH SOURCE: Lang, Hans-Joachim, "Critical Essays and Stories by John Neal," Jahrbuch für Amerikastudien 7 (1962): 204-293.

CRITICAL SYNOPSIS: Like Ned Buntline's dime novel villainous Indian hero, Thayendanegea (see 256), Neal's Logan is a mixture of noble and nefarious qualities. Based loosely on the life of James Logan (1725-1780), a chief of the Mingos whose family had been butchered by white settlers, the Mingo chief dedicates himself to a revenge so awesome that Neal chose a line about Satan from Milton's Paradise Lost as a fitting epigraph for the novel: "Evil!-- be thou my good." Logan's struggle against Governor Dunmore is painted in the most sanguinary and melodramatic terms. "Logan's

was the disposition and appetite of the parent vulture, that
perches above her young and flaps over them, while their clotted
beaks are searching into their first banquet of blood and flesh."
As bloodthirsty in defeat as in victory, Logan becomes a dissipated and degraded monster of the forests, reveling in the terror he
brings to the frontier. Neal's descriptions of haunted Indian burial grounds and the mass slaughter of frontier warfare endow the
book with all the qualities of a new subgenre of the tale of terror, the redskin Gothic. Blood flows profusely in every battle
scene. "They fell upon their enemy at midnight. Not one, not one
man, woman, or child, was left to tell the tale,--not one! They
swept over them like a whirlwind of fire; and the dust of their
skeletons, the cinders of their tribe, were scattered to the four
corners of the earth. The depth of an American forest, and a sheet
of boundless water, reddened with the long trailing flaky storm of
burning ashes that went in a high wind from the place of sacrifice." Such is the red Gothic fury of Logan.

350.   . Rachel Dyer, A North American Story. Portland, ME: Shirley and Hyde, 1828.

REPRINT EDITION: Delmar, NY, Scholars' Facsimiles, 1964.
RESEARCH SOURCES: Grove, Gerald R., Sr., "John Neal: American Romantic," Dissertation Abstracts International 35 (1974): 1045A-
1046A (University of Utah); Lease, Benjamin, "John Neal and Edgar
Allan Poe," Poe Studies 7 (1974): 38-41; Ringe, Donald A., American Gothic, pp.119-120.

CRITICAL SYNOPSIS: A novel of the Salem witchcraft hysteria and
something of a study of the psychology of mass panic and mob delusion. The main figure is the tormented minister, George Burroughs,
whose character and conduct symbolize all that is best and worst
in the Puritan conscience. Caught up in the witch hunting hysteria, Burroughs nevertheless defends the accused women against rumor, fear, innuendo, and the mad fits of the accusing children.
One of the accused witches is Rachel Dyer, a Quaker woman whose
heretical faith makes her automatically suspect. Eventually, a
false witness charges Burroughs with wife murder. The public trial
of Burroughs is the Gothic highpoint of the book. Like a later
Puritan clergyman, the Reverend Arthur Dimmesdale in Hawthorne's
The Scarlet Letter (see 197), Burroughs is gifted or cursed with
unusual powers of oratory. His self-defense, an articulate denun-
ciation of the bigotry and fear which precipitated the witch trials themselves, looks ahead to the scaffold scenes in The Scarlet
Letter. Donald Ringe sums up the mass fear that overwhelms even
the ordinary and skeptical people in the courtroom. "A violent
storm arises as the trial progresses, the light grows progressively darker, and thunder and lightning seem to shake the earth. So
wrought up do the people become and so conditioned are they to believe in the imminent appearance of supernatural beings, that when
Burroughs denies that he killed his wives, the nearly hysterical
onlookers, in a remarkable mass delusion, actually see the dead
women come to confound him." Such self-generated spectral evidence
goes directly to the mental terrors and moral horrors of the American Gothic.

351. Nicolson, John Urban. Fingers of Fear. New York: Covici Friede, 19-
37.

CRITICAL SYNOPSIS: This genuinely Gothic novel reads like a composite modernization of the early horror romance with the supernatural contraptions and locales extrapolated from Walpole's Castle of Otranto (1764) and the bloody events and gruesome or repulsive eroticism transferred from the pages of Lewis's The Monk (1795). These traditonal Gothic trappings are mingled with searing images of the depression thirties when American was a wasteland of no escape from urban and rural horrors. The main character, Selden Seaverns, comes to the aid of his distressed friend, Ormond Ormes, by the unlikely means of writing a saleable essay on the influence of Elizabethan literature on colonial America. There may be an insular joke here on the economic desperation of the period when almost everything was tried in a jobless America. As a sort of formal Gothic world within the larger informal Gothic world, we have Ormes's home in the Berkshires inhabited by his psychopathic relatives both living and dead. Within its rotted walls, portraits walk from their frames and homicidal screams fill the air. Many of the horrors have a distinctly repulsive and pornographic content rather similar to the Schauerromantik Gothics with their ugly and outrageously supernatural tenor and tempo. In one scene, a nude woman feasts voluptuously on a servant after biting him to death. Another nude is graphically described as she copulates with the portrait of the Orme patriarch. The disclosure of horrendous family secrets, a standard revelation scene in Gothic fiction, is done with equal emphasis on the sickening when the family safe is opened to reveal a cache of dead babies. Another horror image of the depression perhaps? English Gothic readers at the close of the Eighteenth Century demanded almost exactly the same revolting inventory from the chapbooks. The "grossing out" of the Gothic reader, as Stephen King has called it, may not be literary art but it is one face of the American Gothic which is as real and insistent as the moral terrors of Hawthorne or the refined horror of Henry James.

352. Norris, Frank. Mc Teague: A Story of San Francisco. New York: Doubleday and Mc Clure, 1899.

REPRINT EDITIONS: ed. Donald Pizer, New York, W.W. Norton, 1978; ed. Kenneth Rexroth, New York, New American Library, 1981.
RESEARCH SOURCE: Pizer, Donald, "Evolutionary Ethical Dualism in Frank Norris's Vandover and the Brute and Mc Teague," Publications of the Modern Language Association 76 (1961): 552-560.

CRITICAL SYNOPSIS: There is a logical line of development and strong relationship between the supernatural brutality of Gothic fiction and American naturalist fiction of the 1890's. In fact, the repetitive plot pattern of the degeneracy of human beings into beasts such as Mc Teague might be designated as part of a hybrid genre, the naturalist Gothic. For crazed spectres, incarcerating castles and mansions, and authoritarian villains, we now have the omnipotent brutalizing force of the environment acting in conjunction with the innate brute or primitive force lurking just below the social self. The naturalist Gothic internalizes all of the horrors that had been external in the older Gothic novel to render a sordid, yet powerful and even tragic, picture of the beast's triumph over the higher self. In Norris's novel, the San Francisco dentist, Mc Teague, is both villain and hero in one physically powerful body. The object of his love, then of his animal lust, and finally of his bestial ferocity, Trina Sieppe, is the persecuted maiden of Gothic fiction now naturalized. The novel grimly records their mutual destruction by biological and environmental forces over which they have no control. After their marriage, Mc Teague and Trina sink slowly but inevitably into poverty. Mc Teague's animal instincts exhibit themselves as violent greed and rage over Trina's lottery winnings of $5000. In a savage outburst, he kills her and flees from the vengeful pursuit of Trina's cousin, Marcus Schouler. The novel's ending is appropriately Gothic in a naturalistic sense. Pursued into the wastes of Death Valley by Schouler, Mc Teague overwhelms Schouler but as he kills him, Schouler handcuffs himself to the bewildered brute. Thus Mc Teague is shackled to the corpse of his victim in the middle of the desert, a crude but effective tableau of horror. The final image of Mc Teague chained to a dead man and doomed to die slowly of hunger and thirst is Norris's brilliant adaptation one of the Gothic's most conventional moments of horror, the cadaverous embrace. "Mc Teague was locked to the body; all about him, vast, interminable, stretched the measureless leagues of Death Valley."

353. _____. Vandover and the Brute. Garden City, NY: Doubleday, Page, 1914.

REPRINT EDITION: Lincoln, NE, Nebraska UP, 1978.
RESEARCH SOURCE: Cooperman, Stanley, "Frank Norris and the Werewolf of Guilt," Modern Language Quarterly 20 (1959): 252-258.

CRITICAL SYNOPSIS: The downfall of Vandover into brutishness is a naturalistic variation on the Jekyll-and-Hyde theme. This novel of lycanthropic degeneracy draws upon the idea behind Zola's La Bete Humaine (1890), that there is a crouching beast within us that is infinitely stronger than we think. No elixir is needed to cause the change in Vandover from artist into brute, only the natural forces of our bestial selves rising to push aside all civilized safeguards. When young Vandover returns from Harvard to San Francisco, he aspires to the artist's life of sensitivity and beauty, but the environment and his own self-indulgent character soon conspire to brutalize and bestialize him. Beginning with wolflike charades for his friends, Vandover is gradually deteriorated by interior forces into a subhuman wolfish creature to the point where the lycanthropic identity is so real to him that he is for all practical purposes a wolfman. Crude drives and sordid appetites eat away at the human being until there is nothing left to Vandover except a brutish hulk. Norris's treatment of the ascendancy of the beast within demonstrates how naturalism can be considered the successor to Gothicism in the illumination of the monstrosities of the darker self. Some critics have read Vandover's brutish transformation as reflective of the onset of venereal disease with lycanthropy used as an acceptable metaphor for the ruination of manhood by sexual profligacy.

354. Oates, Joyce Carol. "Where Are You Going? Where Have You Been?" Epoch, Fall, 1966.

REPRINT EDITIONS: The Modern Tradition: Short Stories, ed. Daniel F. Howard, Boston, Little, Brown, 1976; Stories of Young America, New York, Fawcett-Crest, 1976.
RESEARCH SOURCES: Chell, Cara, "Un-Tricking the Eye: Joyce Carol Oates and the Feminine Ghost Story," Arizona Quarterly 41 (1985): 5-23; Jeannotte, M. Sharon, "The Horror Within: The Short Stories of Joyce Carol Oates," Sphinx: A Magazine of Literature and Society 2 number 4 (1977): 25-36; Wegs, Joyce M., "'Don't You Know Who I Am?': The Grotesque in Oates's 'Where Are You Going? Where Have

You Been?" Critical Essays on Joyce Carol Oates, ed. Linda M. Wagner, Boston, G.K. Hall, 1979, pp.87-92.

CRITICAL SYNOPSIS: A story of initiation into adulthood, sex, and death as well as a fable of identity, this narrative is a superb example of the modern Gothic tale. Every modern element in the story has a recognizable equivalent deriving from traditional Gothic material. Additionally, two Gothic poems of wonder and terror by Emily Dickinson, "Because I Could Not Stop For Death" and "I Heard a Fly Buzz When I Died" contribute to the tale's theme and atmosphere. In the first Dickinson poem, death is personified as the gentle and courteous suitor who invites a young lady to take a ride with him. In the second Dickinson poem, death takes on the shape of an enormous fly, agent of decay, who stands ready to claim both body and soul at the moment of death when the dying narrator had expected salvation. The adolescent heroine, Connie, combines the experiences of salvation and damnation found in the Dickinson poems. She is a modern Cinderella or Sleeping Beauty who comes from childhood into adulthood when the spectre of sex and death insistently intervenes. She lives in a world of hard rock music, fast food, and fast boys, the virginal blond innocent heroine and potential victim who will be captivated, menaced, and finally seized and carried off by a friendly fiend. The fiend is the demonic villain of the Gothic tradition reincarnated as a California Hell's Angel, the prince of darkness himself in "tight faded jeans, stuffed into black scuffed boots....He took off the sunglasses and she saw how pale the skin around his eyes was, like holes that were not in shadow but instead in light. His eyes were like chips of broken glass that catch the light in an amiable way. ...His teeth were big and white. He grinned so broadly his eyes became slits and she saw how thick the lashes were, thick and black as if painted with a tarlike material." This devil figure whose name is ARNOLD FRIEND (with "R's" removed, AN OLD FIEND), comes calling while Connie is home alone on a Sunday afternoon. She resists but there is no denying this lord of the flies as he takes her virginity and perhaps her life. The price that Connie pays for growing up is rape and destruction, a Gothic end to childhood's end. Consciously conceived as a tale of demonic encounter, the story is among Oates's best modernizations of Gothic pleasure and tension.

355. _____. Them. New York: Vanguard Press, 1970.

REPRINT EDITION: New York, Fawcett-Crest, 1979.
RESEARCH SOURCES: Hodge, Marion Cecil Jr., "What Moment is not Terrible? An Introduction to the Works of Joyce Carol Oates," Dissertation Abstracts International 35 (1975): 5407A (University of Tennessee); Johnson, Greg, "Isn't It Gothic?" Georgia Review 42 (1988): 840-849; W.,G., "Gothic City," Newsweek, September 29, 19-69, pp.119-122.

CRITICAL SYNOPSIS: The reviewer in Newsweek referred to this novel, the third in a Gothic trilogy consisting of A Garden of Earthly Delights (1967) and Expensive People (1968), as "a charnel house of Gothic paraphernalia: blood, fire, insanity, anarchy, lust, corruption, death by bullets, death by cancer, death by plane crash, death by stabbing, beatings, crime, riot, and even unhappiness." Them is the murky chronicle of the Wendall family, another example of the American Gothic family beset by anxieties, tormented by aggressive drives, and driven to extinguish itself.

Loretta Wendall, the matriarch of the house, is discovered in bed with her dead and bleeding lover; Jules Wendall, the son of the house, kills, burns, and is shot by his lover; Maureen Wendall, the menaced maiden of the novel, is savagely beaten by her brutal step-father. The action of the novel spans thirty years beginning in the grinding depression of Detroit in 1937 and ending with the inner city riots of 1967. In its relentless picture of social horror, Them demonstrates in full Oates's own belief about the uses of the Gothic. "Gothicism, whatever it is, is not a literary tradition so much as a fairly realistic assessment of modern life." What Oates has written of Gothic literature in general can apply to her own work in the vein of horror and terror: "In Gothic literature, 'wonderful regions'--ruined castles, accursed houses, the poisoned garden of Rappaccini--are dimensions of the psyche given a luridly tangible form, in which unacknowledged (or rigorously suppressed) wishes are granted freedom." Explosive social pressures, the extinction of the individual by the material icons of mass culture, the terrors of conformity, the artificiality of innocence, and the thin line between nightmare and reality in American life are all problem themes well-suited to her Gothic procedures.

356.   _____. "The Dungeon." Night-Side. New York: Vanguard Press, 19-77.

REPRINT EDITION: Night-Side, New York, Fawcett Crest, 1980.
RESEARCH SOURCES: Bloom, Kathleen Burke, "The Grotesque in the Fiction of Joyce Carol Oates," Dissertation Abstracts International 40 (1979): 2059A (Loyola University of Chicago); Pinsker, Sanford, "Isaac Bashevis Singer and Joyce Carol Oates: Some Versions of Gothic," Southern Review 9 (1973): 895-908.

CRITICAL SYNOPSIS: Overtones of Poe's Gothic prisons and prisoners mark this compelling tale. The unnamed narrator delivers a fragmented monologue in the form of bits and pieces of a journal concerning his affair with Eleanora. "Dungeon" refers metaphorically to the dark pit of sexuality toward which the narrator's imagination is constantly drawn. Sexual fears intermingled with inseparably sharp desires lacerate the narrator whose emotional predicament is done in the idiom of the Gothic prisoner crawling helplessly in the darkness. "I am swimming through a tunnel of filth, holding my head high, my mouth shut, grim. Terrified....Now the Forbidden slips easily into my consciousness, teasing & prickling my skull. Shall I send my Invisible Army over to maul & rape you?" Poe's dungeon story, "The Pit and the Pendulum" (see 385) ends with the miraculous emancipation of the victim; Oates's analogue leaves the narrator writhing eternally in the dungeon of sex.

357. O'Brien, Fitz-James. "A Terrible Night." Harper's Magazine, October, 1856.

REPRINT EDITION: The Supernatural Tales of Fitz-James O'Brien, ed. Jessica Amanda Salmonson, Garden City, NY, Doubleday, 1988.
RESEARCH SOURCE: Clareson, Thomas D., "Fitz-James O'Brien," Supernatural Fiction Writers, pp.717-722.

CRITICAL SYNOPSIS: Some of O'Brien's stories anticipate the ghoulish shocks of Bierce's horror tales at the end of the century. "A Terrible Night" might have served Bierce as a model in both its tone and situation. The horror situation here is somnambulistic homicide, or what the physician on the case terms, "somnolentia," a psychotic sleep in which the patient performs deeds of unspeakable violence. The narrator, a friend of Dick Linton, the lover of Bertha Linton, his sister, consents to spend a night in a cabin with Dick, a "terrible night" as it turns out. The cabin is the property of a half-breed who bears watching by the two men. In the middle of the night, the narrator sees the half-breed hovering over him with a knife and shoots him, only to discover that these were the sleeping hallucinations of a terrible night and that he has killed Linton. The horror of mental collapse is skillfully related inviting comparisons with the deceived murderers of Poe.

358. _____. "The Lost Room." The Poems and Stories of Fitz-James O'-Brien, Collected and Edited With a Sketch of the Author by William Winter. Boston: J.R. Osgood, 1881.

REPRINT EDITION: Perturbed Spirits, A Book of Ghost and Terror Stories, ed. R.C. Bull, London, Arthur Barker, 1954.
RESEARCH SOURCE: Wolle, Francis. Fitz-James O'Brien: A Literary Bohemian of the Eighteen-Fifties, Boulder, CO, Colorado UP, 1944.

CRITICAL SYNOPSIS: A haunted chamber invaded by allegorical figures representing the narrator's darkest memories suggests the influence of Hawthorne on this imaginative story. The supernatural invaders challenge the narrator to a game of dice to see who will possess the room. The narrator's loss of the room in the game of chance might suggest loss of mind, but such is not the case. O'Brien opts for a supernatural and inexplicable climax when the room dissolves to be forever lost.

359. _____. "What Was It? A Mystery." The Poems and Stories of Fitz-James O'Brien, Collected and Edited with a Sketch of the Author by William Winter. Boston: J.R. Osgood, 1881.

REPRINT EDITION: New York, Irvington, 1972.
RESEARCH SOURCES: Lovecraft, H.P., Supernatural Horror in Literature, New York, Dover, 1973, p.66; Moskowitz, Sam, "The Fabulous Fantasist--Fitz-James O'Brien," Explorers of the Infinite, Cleveland and New York, World Publishing, 1963.

CRITICAL SYNOPSIS: This undeservedly ignored master of horror fantasy won the praise of H.P. Lovecraft who called "What Was It?" "the first well-shaped short story of a tangible but invisible being and the prototype of de Maupassant's Horla." O'Brien's special talent tended toward subtle and delicate Gothic effects. The "It" of the title is a strange being who haunts seemingly because that is what spirits are supposed to do. Can a ghost perish of starvation? What does one feed a ghost to keep it ectoplasmically alive? When the "It" disintegrates from hunger, a plaster death mask reveals the most sensitive of faces.

360. _____. "The Diamond Lens." The Diamond Lens and Other Stories. New York: Scribner, 1885.

REPRINT EDITIONS: The Diamond Lens and Other Stories, intro. Gilbert Seldes, New York, William E. Rudge, 1932; New York, AMS Press, 1970.
RESEARCH SOURCE: Wolle, Francis, "Fitz-James O'Brien in Ireland and England, 1828-1851," American Literature 14 (1942-43): 234-239.

CRITICAL SYNOPSIS: First publication in The Atlantic Monthly, January, 1858. Regarded by rediscoverers of O'Brien's work as his finest story, the piece is an excellent example of Gothic science fiction. The narrator, a student of microscopy, makes spiritual contact with the instrument's inventor, the ghost of Anton van Leeuwenhoek. If he would behold the infinitesimal wonders of the microscopic world, he is told by van Leeuwenhoek that he must obtain a 140 carat diamond and install it in the microscope. But to get such a diamond lens requires the narrator to kill. Beneath the diamond lens the beautiful form of Animula encased in a waterdrop becomes visible and he soon falls in love with the microscopic maiden. Leaving the room momentarily, he returns to find his miniature love in the throes of death because the waterdrop has evaporated beneath the lens. Although he has been compared to Poe and Bierce, O'Brien obviously has a Gothic style uniquely his own. His stories merit a better fate than the footnote that literary historians have made of them.

361. O'Connor, Flannery. "Good Country People." A Good Man is Hard to Find, and Other Stories. New York: Harcourt, Brace, 1953.

REPRINT EDITION: A Good Man is Hard to Find, and Other Stories, New York, Harcourt, Brace, Jovanovich, 1976.
RESEARCH SOURCES: Kahane, Claire, "The Maternal Legacy: The Grotesque Tradition in Flannery O'Connor's Female Gothic," The Female Gothic, ed. Juliann E. Fleenor, Montreal, Eden Press, 1983, pp. 242-256; Schleifer, Ronald, "Rural Gothic: The Stories of Flannery O'Connor," Modern Fiction Studies 28 (1982): 475-485.

CRITICAL SYNOPSIS: First appeared in Harper's Bazaar, June, 1951. Symbolic amputation or psychic crippling forms the grotesque climax of this cruel story. The heroine, Joy (also called Hulga), is a one-legged woman of thirty-two and confined to the tedium and mindlessness of her mother's, Mrs. Hopewell's, tenant farm. Joy, is sensitive, intelligent, highly educated but hopelessly condemned to a deadly existence for life because of her missing leg and her mother's simplistic love which refuses to see her as an adult. The farm is visited by a nineteen year old Bible salesman, Manley Pointer, one of Flannery O'Connor's best perverted creations, a devil figure almost without peer in her gallery of amiable fiends. He professes innocence, charitable Christianity, sincerity, and a desire to love the one-legged Joy. But his real motive is to obtain her false leg as a gruesome trophy for his collection of "interesting things" such as a woman's glass eye. The scene in the hayloft where Pointer gets her to remove her artificial leg and then carries it off in his Bible valise is a kind of spiritual rape which renders Joy helpless in the face of absolute evil. "She saw him grab the leg and then she saw it for an instant slanted forlornly across the inside of the suitcase with a Bible at either side of its opposite ends." In this moment of horror, O'Connor has duplicated the chilling dismemberments of the mind and soul that befall many of Ambrose Bierce's victims.

362. _____ . "A Good Man is Hard to Find." A Good Man Is Hard to Find and Other Stories. New York: Harcourt, Brace, 1953.

REPRINT EDITION: Flannery O'Connor, The Complete Stories, New York, Farrar, Straus, Giroux, 1971.
RESEARCH SOURCE: Martin, Carter W., "The Gothic Impulse," The True

Country: Themes in the Fiction of Flannery O'Connor, Nashville, TN, Vanderbilt UP, 1968, pp.152-188.

CRITICAL SYNOPSIS: First appeared in Modern Writing I, 1953. Much of O'Connor's work has been called "Georgia Gothic" or "rural Gothic," and rightly so, if one meaning of Gothic is the disintegration of the self under the pressures of outmoded culture and human delusion. Carter Martin sums up the quality of O'Connor's Gothic as flowing from her "preoccupation with the ugliness of reality," a preoccupation which prompts her to use such traditional Gothic patterns as the fatal or final journey to convey the grotesqueness of that reality. Most of her characters experience the terror of isolation in some self-destructive form, division from family, from community, and often from God. "A Good Man Is Hard To Find" is a generic tale of terror in these three senses. Driving from Atlanta to Florida, a family supervised by the grandmother stops at Red Sammy's diner where they hear news of the Misfit, an escaped murderer. Trying to find an old southern mansion in the backwoods to show her grandchildren, John Wesley and June Star, the grandmother's car turns over in a gulch. A car approaches, "a big black battered hearselike automobile," and her demonic encounter begins. The savage irony of the story's title is brought home when the grandmother tries to persuade the Misfit that he is a good man, even to convert him to her naive Christianity. Shots ring out as the Misfit snarls "'No pleasure but meanness,'" and the grandmother sinks to the ground with the horrible outcry that denies her simplistic faith in Christ and the resurrection: "'Maybe he didn't raise the dead,' the old lady mumbled and feeling so dizzy that she sank down in the ditch with her legs twisted under her." This is a favorite O'Connor climax, the convergence of a violent event and a terrible epiphany for a character who had thought that the world belonged to God but found in a last moment that it belongs to the devil instead.

363. _____. "A Late Encounter with the Enemy." A Good Man is Hard to Find, and Other Stories. New York: Harcourt, Brace, 1953.

REPRINT EDITION: A Good Man is Hard to Find and Other Stories, New York, Harcourt, Brace, Jovonovich, 1977.
RESEARCH SOURCE: Snow, Ollye T., "The Functional Gothic of Flannery O'Connor," Southwest Review 50 (1965): 286-299.

CRITICAL SYNOPSIS: The grotesque and sardonic comedy of the story relates to Poe's parody of the sturdy military man, General John A.B.C. Smith in "The Man That Was Used Up; A Tale of the Late Bugaboo and Kickapoo Campaign." The 105 year old General Tennessee Flintrock Sash "lived with his granddaughter, Sally Poker Sash, who was sixty-two years old and who prayed every night on her knees that he would live until her graduation from college." And live he does, this senile relic in wheelchair and full dress uniform. He lives until the moment of her diploma from the local state teachers' college where the General has been wheeled on stage as a ceremonial exhibition of a glorious Confederate past. But the general himself has eliminated all memory and not just because of senility but out of an active desire to be free of the trash of history. At the commencement he fights a last fatal battle against the onslaught of memory as the graduation speakers invoke the past and as his decrepit daughter crosses the stage to receive her degree. "He was running into a regular volley of [words] and meeting them with quick curses. As the music swelled toward him, the entire past opened up on him out of nowhere and he felt his body riddled in a hundred places with sharp stabs of pain and he fell down, returning a curse for every hit....Then a succession of places, Chickamauga, Shiloh, Marthasville rushed at him as if the past were the only future now and he had to endure it." Ambushed and overrun by memories, he dies gallantly in his wheelchair on the graduation stage. With much of the story told from the point of view of the cantankerous old man, the humor cleverly counterbalances the horror of his death in battle at the hands of his rebellious memories.

364.   _____. "A Stroke of Good Fortune." A Good Man is Hard to Find, and Other Stories. New York: Harcourt, Brace, 1953.

REPRINT EDITION: Flannery O'Connor, The Complete Stories, New York, Farrar, Straus, Giroux, 1971.
RESEARCH SOURCES: Browning, Preston M. Jr., "Flannery O'Connor and the Demonic," Modern Fiction Studies 19 (1973): 29-41; Nisly, Paul W., "Wart Hogs from Hell: The Demonic and the Holy in Flannery O'-Connor's Fiction," Ball State University Forum 22 (1981): 45-50.

CRITICAL SYNOPSIS: The story was published in Shenandoah, Spring, 1953. Almost the entire action takes place on a dark staircase, that place of Gothic ascent and descent which joins the terrors of the turret with the horrors of the dungeon in traditional Gothic buildings. As the thirty-four year old Ruby climbs the stairs in the old apartment building, she reviews all of the anxieties and desires of her life. Her deepest dread is fear of pregnancy followed next by a fear of doctors, cancer, and premature old age. As she climbs the dark staircase a vague pain torments her but she has been assured of a move or a change by the palmist, Madame Zoleeda. She nearly falls over a child's toy pistol and pauses to catch her breath at the top apartment of Laverne Watts, who tells Ruby that she looks pregnant and that she ought to see a doctor. Thus, the two worst fears of her life await her at the top of the stairs. The moment of high horror is a remade Gothic sound effect. Leaning over the staircase "she gave a long hollow wail that widened and echoed as it went down. The stair cavern was dark green and mole-colored and the wail sounded at the very bottom like a voice answering her--Baby, good fortune." The foetus growing inside her is her "stroke" of good fortune. The story demonstrates O'Connor's ability to rework the encounter with the phantom on the staircase into a horrifyingly ironic self-entrapment.

365.   _____. The Violent Bear it Away. New York: Farrar, Straus, Cudahy, 1960.

REPRINT EDITION: Three by Flannery O'Connor, New York, New American Library, 1981.
RESEARCH SOURCES: Bowen, Robert O., "Hope vs. Despair in the New Gothic Novel," Renascence 13 (1961): 147-152; Brinkmeyer, Robert H. Jr., "Borne Away by Violence: The Reader and Flannery O'Connor," Southern Review 15 (1979): 313-321; Gentry, Marshall B., "The Demonic O'Connor: The Violent Bear It Away and 'The Lame Shall Enter First,'" Flannery O'Connor's Religion of the Grotesque, Jackson, MI, University Press of Mississippi, 1986, pp. 142-159; Paulson, Suzanne M., "Apocalypse of Self, Resurrection of the Double: Flannery O'Connor's The Violent Bear It Away," Literature and Psychology 30 (1980): 100-111.

CRITICAL SYNOPSIS: O'Connor's Gothic bears frequent comparison with Brockden Brown's Wieland (see 063), another Gothic which uses religious insanity as a foundation for its terrors. The novel in three parts is the dark and tangled saga of young Francis Mason Tarwater, a boy kidnapped by his mad uncle, Mason Tarwater, who conceives of himself as an Old Testament prophet and the custodian of God's word and will. Old Tarwater intends to train his nephew to be a baptizing prophet and to this end he carries him off to his remote cabin at Powderhead for prophet-training. Opposing this mad scheme is the novel's sceptic and agnostic, George Rayber, another uncle, who devotes himself to saving young Tarwater. Young Tarwater is pulled two ways by the psychotic religion of old Mason and the godless logic of Rayber in his losing struggle "to live his life as he had elected it." Gothic events are frequent and easily traceable to earlier horror episodes in the tradition. While burying his uncle, Tarwater is interrupted by a mysterious voice which instructs him to leave the grave half open and to defy his uncle's injunction that he become a baptizer. Tarwater later drowns the idiot child, Bishop, in an act of violent mock baptism. He is himself the victim of violent homosexual rape. Descriptions of young Tarwater's lacerations of soul are explicitly Gothic as in this figure: "In the darkest, most private part of his soul, hanging upsidedown like a sleeping bat, was the certain undeniable knowledge that he was not hungry for the bread of life." All ends in visionary madness for Tarwater when he meets the negro, Buford Munson, at his uncle's grave, smears his forehead with grave dirt and sets forth for the dark city with the glint of mad prophecy on his countenance.

366. _____. "Everything That Rises Must Converge." Everything That Rises Must Converge, intro. Robert Fitzgerald. New York: Farrar, Straus, Cudahy, 1965.

REPRINT EDITION: Everything That Rises Must Converge, intro. Robert Fitzgerald, New York, New American Library, 1967.
RESEARCH SOURCE: Nisly, Paul Wayne, "Flannery O'Connor and the Gothic Impulse," Dissertation Abstracts International 36 (1974): 892A-893A (University of Kansas).

CRITICAL SYNOPSIS: First published in New World Writing, 1961. The night journey to self-discovery, collapse of faith, and violent death at the hands of a sinister stranger reveal the technical expertise of the story's Gothicism. As Julian Godhigh and his mother ride the bus downtown, they encounter a massive black woman and her little son, Carver. This is a fatal encounter of white and black, of racial past and racial present, of self-fantasy and self-reality. Until this last ride, Mrs. Godhigh had "lived according to the laws of her own fantasy world, outside of which he had never seen her set foot." Across from her in the bus sits her nemesis, "a ponderous figure, rising from the red shoes upward over the solid hips, the mammoth bosom, the haughty face....She carried a mammoth red pocketbook that bulged throughout as if it were stuffed with rocks." When these weak and strong mother figures rise, they inevitably converge. When Mrs. Godhigh offers the little black boy a condescending penny, the black woman explodes and the great red purse descends, prostrating Mrs. Godhigh in the street. The supreme moment of Gothic horror belongs to Julian Godhigh as he stands over his dead mother. Having believed that he was free of the mother's domineering grip, he discovers to his horror that he has no identity outside her identity. This grim

Gothic climax is linked to a fundamental theme in O'Connor's fiction, the spiritual expiration of a youthful character. The image
of the accusing eye, somewhat reminiscent of Poe's old man in "The
Tell-Tale Heart," (see 386) is one of O'Connor's best Gothic
touches. "One eye, large and staring, moved slightly to the left
as if it had become unmoored. The other remained fixed on him,
raked his face again, found nothing and closed."

367. O'Connor, William Douglas. The Ghost. New York: G.P. Putnam, 1867;
London: Sampson Low, 1867.

CRITICAL SYNOPSIS: A well-sustained piece of spookery which combines the ways and means of the Gothic with a Civil War theme in
the reunion of the lonely heroine and her deceased soldier-lover.

368. Page, Thomas Nelson. "The Spectre in the Cart." Bred in the Bone.
New York: Charles Scribner's Sons, 1904.

REPRINT EDITION: Short Stories Reprint Series, Salem, NH, Ayer
Publishing, 1971.
RESEARCH SOURCE: Gross, Theodore, Thomas Nelson Page, New York,
Twayne, 1967.

CRITICAL SYNOPSIS: A powerful, brutal story with strong racial
overtones and well-wrought Gothic effects. The ghostly and ghoulish tale even calls into question Page's own white supremacist
views. It is tempting, but probably incorrect given Page's views
on race, to see in the story a parable of racial tension and violence. The narrator is Stokeman, a southern lawyer who had always
been "a scornful sceptic in matters relating to the supernatural."
When the narrator's white friend, John Holloway and his wife, are
viciously murdered, suspicion immediately falls upon two blacks,
old Joel Turnell and his fiery, white-hating son, Absalom Turnell.
Absalom is a revolutionary in the style of the leader of the slave
revolt, Nat Turner. "He called on the negroes to 'wade in blood to
their lips.'" Despite no evidence for the Holloway murders, Absalom and Joel, are prosecuted by the lawyer and executed, the father going to his death with a servile smile and the son with a
defiant snarl. Justice is speeded up by a lynch mob in a scene
that overflows with coldly real horror. The tale ends with a
ghastly meeting on a moonlit road between the two black men that
the narrator brought to "justice" and the lawyer. As he approaches
the great sycamore hanging tree on horseback he spies "something
white on the road....Coming along the unused road up the hill from
the Holloways, was old Joel, sitting in a cart, looking at me, and
bowing to me politely, just as he had done that morning on the way
to the gallows, while dangling from the white limb of the sycamore, swaying softly in the wind, hung the corpse of Absalom." The
tale ends with this apocalyptic vision as the narrator is granted
a moment of horrible understanding by way of this ghostly encounter. He will never scorn the supernatural again although his views
of the dangerous and inferior nature of blacks apparently remains
unshaken.

369. Paulding, James Kirke. Koningsmarke, The Long Finne: A Story of the
New World. New York: Charles Wiley, 1823.

REPRINT EDITIONS: ed. Ralph M. Alderman, Madison, WI, Wisconsin
UP, 1962; New York, AMS Press, 1971.
RESEARCH SOURCES: Herold, Amos L., "Paulding's Literary Theor-

ies," Bulletin of the New York Public Library 66 (1962): 236-243; Ringe, Donald, American Gothic, pp.114-116.

CRITICAL SYNOPSIS: Although referred to by Donald Ringe as displaying "a strong Gothic strain throughout...in the person and actions of a black slave, Bombie of the Frizzled Head," in tone and incident the book is far closer to Diedrich Knickerbocker's burlesque History of New York (1809) by Paulding's friend and contemporary, Washington Irving. Most of the characters' names from Heer Peter Piper, the Governor of Elsingburgh in New Sweden, to Master Gottlieb Schwaschbuckler, to Wolfgang Langfanger, to Ludwig Varlett, to Shadrach Moneypenny, to the young Finn, Koningsmarke, recall the dramatis personae of Irving's Sleepy Hollow or New Amsterdam. The black witch, Bombie, induces some fear and mystery and her treacherous betrayal of the settlement of Elsingburgh into the hands of the Indians creates a few moments of suspense and strife for Konigsmarke and his beloved Christina. But for the most part, Paulding's object is literary and social satire, not Gothic horror, which he himself had forsworn in an essay on the "National Literature" (1820): "The agency of ghosts, fairies, goblins, and all that antiquated machinery which till lately was confined to the nursery, is not necessary to excite our wonder or interest our feelings." Besides the presence of Bombie the sorceress, the narrative has occasional strokes of Gothicism, but a Gothicism that is always undercut by Paulding's comic realism and the narrow escapes of his picaresque young Finn. The disquisition on the Inquisition, the torture of Claas Thompson by the Indians, and the hard jawed parody of popular narratives of Indian capture are entertaining bits of satiric terror in this early American mock historical romance.

370. _____. The Vroucolacas, A Tale. Graham's Magazine, June, 1846.

RESEARCH SOURCE: Aderman, Ralph, "James Kirke Paulding's Contributions to American Magazines," Studies in Bibliography 17 (1964): 141-151.

CRITICAL SYNOPSIS: A vampire tale, but done in the risible manner of Paulding's friend, Washington Irving. The tale is preceded by an authenticating preface designed to establish the scientific existence of vampirism. A young man plays the role of Vroucolacas or vampire, and very convincingly too, in order to terrify a resistant father into allowing him to marry his daughter. The premise of a vampire charade is amusing and somewhat unusual when applied to so foul and fiendish a creature as the vampire.

371. _____. The Puritan and His Daughter. New York: Baker and Scribner, 1849.

REPRINT EDITION: New York, AMS Press, 1978.
RESEARCH SOURCE: Herold, Amos L., James Kirke Paulding: Versatile American, New York, Columbia UP, 1926; New York, AMS Press, 1966.

CRITICAL SYNOPSIS: This historical romance appeared one year before Hawthorne's The Scarlet Letter (see 197) and is a more direct assault on religious bigotry and the irrational violence bred by the Salem witchcraft trials. Just as Hawthorne's Hester Prynne is tried for adultery, the Puritan's daughter, Miriam Habingdon, is tried for sorcery during the 1694 witchcraft hysteria and con-

demned to death. She is rescued from the scaffold by Langley Tyr-
ingham, the son of a Virginia Cavalier. Although more historical
and sentimental than Gothic, the presentation of the witch hunting
mania evokes the Gothic atmosphere of irrational dread and mass
fear.

372. Peattie, Elia Wilkinson. The Shape of Fear and Other Ghostly Tales.
New York: Macmillan, 1898.

CRITICAL SYNOPSIS: Tales include "The Room of the Evil Thought,"
"A Spectral Collie," "Story of an Obstinate Corpse," and "A Gram-
matical Ghost," all well crafted and reliant upon the standard
Gothic machinery. As the titles suggest, the comic or "sportive"
Gothic continued to be appealing and popular.

373. Percy, Walker. Love in the Ruins; The Adventures of a Bad Catholic
at a Time Near the End of the World. New York: Farrar, Straus, Giroux, 1971.

REPRINT EDITION: New York, Bard-Avon, 1978.
RESEARCH SOURCES: Ciuba, Gary M., "The Apocalyptic Vision in the
Fiction of Walker Percy," Dissertation Abstracts International 47
(1986): 1321A (Fordham University); Ryan, Steven Tom, "Chaotic
Slumber: Picaresque and Gothic in Contemporary American Novels,"
Dissertation Abstracts International 37 (1976): 2187A (University
of Utah).

CRITICAL SYNOPSIS: Biting futuristic fantasy with periodic Gothic
touches. The narrator is an alcoholic psychiatrist, Dr. Thomas
More, inventor of the ontological lapsometer. This device is capable of inducing artificial psychic change when attached to a subject, thus giving More the power to shape and reshape personalities. More is visited and tempted by Art Immelmann, a Mephisto-
philean figure who is finally exorcised when More prays to his
saintly namesake, the humanist Sir Thomas More. Various other
Gothic aspects of the fantasia include a deserted Howard Johnson's
Hotel which contains only the three women in More's life, Moira,
Lola, and the dominant Nurse Ellen Oglethorpe, Honey Island Swamp,
the spawning place of a Bantu uprising against white racism, and
the love clinic, a pointed satire on birth control centers and the
sexual experiments of Masters and Johnson and other followers of
Dr. Kinsey. This is intelligent and amusing satire with overtones
of social horror concerning the absurd directions of runaway research and absolute sexual liberation.

374. Poe, Edgar Allan. "Metzengerstein." Saturday Courier, January, 1832;
Tales of the Grotesque and Arabesque. Philadelphia: Lea & Blanchard 1840.

REPRINT EDITION: Edgar Allan Poe, Selected Writings, ed. David
Galloway, Baltimore, Penguin Books, 1975.
RESEARCH SOURCES: Forclaz, Roger, "Poe et le Roman Noir," Le Monde
d'Edgar Poe, Berne, Switzerland, Peter Lang, 1974; Thompson, G.
R., "Poe's 'Flawed' Gothic: Absurdist Techniques in 'Metzengerstein' and the Courier Satires," Emerson Society Quarterly 60 (19-
70): 38-58.

CRITICAL SYNOPSIS: This early tale is often categorized as a spoof
on Germanic shockers or a hoax on the more horrific brand of Gothic thrillers. No direct comedy or overt satire, however, can be

detected in the tale's events although the style may imply a covert burlesque of heavy-handed Gothic rhetoric. One of Poe's sources, Walpole's Castle of Otranto (1764), is obvious at many points. His more immediate source, however, is the Teutonic shocker or Schauerroman of dreadful title and absurd supernatural catastrophe. Udo the Man of Steel; or, The Ruins of Drudenstein (17-99) and similar wild romances influenced Poe. The story line involves a feud between the households of Frederick, Baron Metzengerstein and Wilhelm, Count Berlifitzing. For added mystery, Poe brought in the theme of metempsychosis, or equine metempsychosis, since the transmigration of soul here is from human into horse. Count Berlifitzing is burned to death trying to save his horses from a mysterious stable fire. The fire seems to be the fulfillment of an ancient prophecy which dooms the Berlifitzings: "A lofty name shall have a fearful fall when, as the rider over his horse, the mortality of Metzengerstein shall triumph over the immortality of Berlifitzing." But one horse escaped the flames, "all smoking and foaming with rage, from the burning stables of the Castle Berlifitzing." When the animal is brought to Baron Metzengerstein, he develops "a perverse attachment to his lately acquired charger," or more accurately, the strange stallion with its "human-looking eye" now holds the Baron in sway. When a second mysterious fire levels the Palace Metzengerstein, the demon horse emerges like a nightmare come-to-life and ridden into the sky by a demon rider to proclaim the fall of the house of Metzengerstein. The final sentences of the story foreshadow the cadences and clauses of the final sentences of "The Fall of the House of Usher" (see 379): "The fury of the tempest immediately died away, and a dead calm sullenly succeeded. A white flame still enveloped the building like a shroud, and, streaming far away into the quiet atmosphere, shot forth a glare of preternatural light; while a cloud of smoke settled heavily over the battlements in the distinct colossal figure of--a horse." Is this story a conscious burlesque of Gothic excesses and crudities, or simply a straightforward, hair-raising, money-making thriller designed to gratify an audience that preferred its horrors in traditional wrappings? Did Poe have artistic control over his materials or did the Gothic control him at this stage of his writing life? The debate continues.

375. _____. "Morella." Southern Literary Messenger, April, 1835; Tales of the Grotesque and Arabesque. Philadelphia: Lea & Blanchard, 18-40.

REPRINT EDITION: Complete Tales and Poems of Edgar Allan Poe, New York, Vintage-Ballantine, 1984.
RESEARCH SOURCE: Richmond, Lee J., "Edgar Allan Poe's 'Morella': Vampire of Volition," Studies in Short Fiction 9 (1972): 93-94.

CRITICAL SYNOPSIS: Psychic survival and the omnipotent "posthumous heroine," two Gothic ideas which Poe developed extensively in the later story, "Ligeia," form the core of "Morella." The narrator, who "never spoke of passion, nor thought of love" detests his erudite wife, Morella, while she is alive. The foundation for this hatred seems to be her intellectual and physical vitality. It is the very life quality in her that repels him. Dying in childbirth, she vows that she will return and that he will love her in death as passionately as he had hated her in life, a prophecy that is weirdly fulfilled. "'The days have never been when thou couldst love me--but her whom in life thou didst abhor, in death thou

shalt adore.'" When Morella's child, a reincarnation of the mother, is baptized, the narrator impulsively whispers the name
"Morella" to the priest. Immediately the first Morella's spirit
invades the spirit of her daughter as "she turned her glassy eyes
from earth to heaven, and falling prostrate on the black slabs of
our ancestral vault, responded--'I am here.'" When the narrator
inters his dead daughter there are no charnel traces at all in the
empty tomb of the first Morella. Morella's reanimation through the
body of her daughter can be interpreted as a victory for divine
imagination over earthly rationality, an aesthetic conflict to
which Poe would return in "Ligeia" (see 377).

376. _____. "Berenice." Southern Literary Messenger, October, 1835;
Tales of the Grotesque and Arabesque. Philadelphia: Lea & Blanchard, 1840.

REPRINT EDITION: Tales and Sketches, Collected Works of Edgar Allan Poe, ed. Thomas O. Mabbott with Eleanor D. Kewer and Maureen
C. Mabbott, Cambridge, MA, Harvard UP, 1978.

RESEARCH SOURCES: Blythe, Hal and Charlie Sweet, "Poe's Satiric
Use of Vampirism in 'Berenice,'" Poe Studies 14 number 2 (1981):
23-24; Frank, Frederick S., "Poe's Gothicism: An Analytic Bibliography," Sphinx: A Magazine of Literature and Society 4 number 4
(1985): 277-301; Sloane, David E.E., "Gothic Romanticism and Rational Empiricism in Poe's 'Berenice,'" American Transcendental
Quarterly 19 parts 1-2 (1973): 19-26; Sloane, David E.E. and B.F.
Fisher IV, "Poe's Revisions in 'Berenice': Beyond the Gothic,"
American Transcendental Quarterly 24 (1974): 19-25.

CRITICAL SYNOPSIS: Some critics have found "Berenice" to be a pre-
cise lampoon of the horror tale at its Schauerromantik extremes,
the kind of grisly story that pleased the readers of Blackwood's
Magazine but would have offended the clientele of Godey's Lady's
Book. Certainly, the narrator's (Egaeus's) extraction of Berenice's teeth while she lies in a cataleptic coma is a deed of the
same repulsive quality as lovers devouring each other's flesh in
Maturin's Melmoth the Wanderer or the savage mutilations of the
school of Monk Lewis. Poe's Gothic concentration is on sadism, ab-
normality, and the act of bizarre disfigurement. The fact that
Egaeus draws the teeth of Berenice while he is in an amnesiac
state does not lessen the ghastliness of his psychotic urge to
possess the teeth. In his warped mind, only the drawing of her
teeth can restore his lost sanity: "I felt their possession could
alone ever restore me to peace, in giving me back to reason." Poe
stops short of any graphic detailing of the dental violation of
Berenice's corpse. A lacuna or gap follows Egaeus's determination
to have Berenice's teeth, followed by an epilogue in which a servant enters the library of Egaeus to inform him of "a violated
grave--of a disfigured body enshrouded, yet still breathing, still
palpitating--still alive." The terrible sound of the thirty-two
teeth of Berenice spilling from a strongbox and scattering on the
floor remains one of Poe's ugliest, yet most unnerving, Gothic
sound effects.

377. _____. "Ligeia." Baltimore American Museum, September, 1838;
Tales of the Grotesque and Arabesque. Philadelphia: Lea & Blanchard, 1840.

REPRINT EDITION: The Complete Tales and Poems of Edgar Allan Poe,

New York, Vintage-Ballantine, 1984.
RESEARCH SOURCES: Griffith, Clark, "Poe and the Gothic," Papers on
Poe: Essays in Honor of John Ward Ostrom, Springfield, OH, Chan-
try Music Press at Wittenberg University, 1972, pp.21-27; Heller,
Terry, "Poe's 'Ligeia' and the Pleasures of Terror," Gothic: The
Review of Supernatural Horror Fiction 2 (1980): 39-48; Lewis,
Paul, "The Intellectual Functions of Gothic Fiction: Poe's 'Ligeia' and Tieck's 'Wake Not the Dead,'" Comparative Literature Stu-
dies 16 (1979): 207-221; Matheson, Terrence J., "The Multiple Murders in 'Ligeia': A New Look at Poe's Narrator," Canadian Review
of American Studies 13 (1982): 279-289; Salzburg, Joel, "The Gothic Hero in Transcendental Quest: Poe's 'Ligeia' and James' 'The
Beast in the Jungle,'" ESQ: A Journal of the American Renaissance 18 (1972): 108-114; Thompson, G. R., "'Proper Evidences of
Madness': American Gothic and the Interpretation of 'Ligeia,'"
ESQ: A Journal of the American Renaissance 18 (1972): 30-49.

CRITICAL SYNOPSIS: Like Chaucer, Poe too has a cluster of tales
which constitute a "marriage group," but a marriage group with
Gothic rather than comic properties. The marriage unit in Poe consists of "Morella," "Eleonora," and "Berenice," with "Ligeia" to
be considered the culmination of Gothic marital fantasy. Counter-
ing the tale's simplicity of plot is its complexity of equivocal
meanings. So complex is Poe's use of the Gothic in "Ligeia" that
it has become the prototype for many critics of the ambiguous mode
which characterizes so much American Gothicism in general. The
purpose of such psychological ambiguity is to display disturbing
mental qualities which are opposite to the aspiring innocence, optimism, and rationality of the American mind. The American Gothic
as presented by Poe takes as its central subject "the precariously
logical human mind which is capable of gross misperception, unreal
construction, and instant irrationality. The vision of the human
mind that emerges from the complex literary technique and philos-
ophy in these Gothic works is one of despair over the ability of
the mind ever to know anything, either about the ultimate reality
of the world or about the mind itself." (G.R. Thompson) In "Ligeia," "the hideous drama of revification" which climaxes in the
heroine's return from the dead to displace the body of her rival,
Lady Rowena, is all completely recalled through the flawed consciousness of an opium addicted narrator. Ligeia, his first wife,
is a woman of immense mystical learning and a dark, Egyptianate
beauty, actually more of a pyramid shrine goddess and an "idea"
than any femininized earthly form. When she dies, vowing to return
through an act of supermortal will, the narrator remarries Ligeia's antithesis, the Lady Rowena, and takes up residence in an
English abbey. Brooding upon Ligeia, he soon comes to hate Rowena,
"loath[ing] her with a hatred belonging more to demon than to
man." His opium-fed obsession apparently causes both the death of
Rowena and the cadaverous resurrection of Ligeia as he sits alone
with Rowena's shrouded body in the bridal chamber of the abbey
turret. Suddenly, the corpse of Rowena stirs, then "advances bold-
ly and palpably into the middle of the apartment." When the grave
clothes fall away, the figure that had been Rowena has now become
the figure of Ligeia restored to life by the colossal exertion of
her will. Is the return of Ligeia an instance of genuine supernatural survival or the diseased hallucination of a deluded observ-
er? Had there ever been a real woman named Ligeia with an existence outside the narrator's mind? Did the narrator murder Rowena
in the mad belief that her body would furnish a host for the wandering spirit of Ligeia? And what is the final mental state of the

narrator, a crazed victim's horror or restored lover's rapture? As the unexplained or ambiguous climax of "Ligeia" indicates, Poe's Gothic is both psychologically realistic and multi-leveled, falling both within the Gothic tradition and at the same time rising far above it.

378. _____. The Narrative of Arthur Gordon Pym of Nantucket: Comprising the Details of a Mutiny and Atrocious Butchery on Board the American Brig Grampus, on Her Way to the South Seas, in the Month of June, 1827. New York: Harper, 1838.

REPRINT EDITION: ed. Harold Beaver, Baltimore, Penguin Books, 1975.
RESEARCH SOURCES: Fiedler, Leslie, "The Blackness of Darkness: E. A. Poe and the Development of the Gothic," Love and Death in the American Novel, New York, Criterion, 1960, pp.370-382; Frank, Frederick S., "The Gothic at Absolute Zero: Poe's Narrative of Arthur Gordon Pym," Extrapolation 21 (1980): 21-30; Frank, Frederick S., "Polarized Gothic: An Annotated Bibliography of Poe's Narrative of Arthur Gordon Pym," Bulletin of Bibliography 38 (1981): 117-127; Kopley, Richard, "The Narrative of Arthur Gordon Pym," Survey of Modern Fantasy Literature, pp.1092-1095; Mainville, Stephen, "Language and the Void: Gothic Landscapes in the Frontiers of Edgar Allan Poe," Genre 14 (1981): 347-362.

CRITICAL SYNOPSIS: Once the most neglected of Poe's writings, his only novel has enjoyed since 1950 an intense and prolonged critical renaissance. It is informative to interpret The Narrative of Arthur Gordon Pym as a Gothic novel gone afloat. In a stroke of ambitious genius, Poe has reset the central metaphor of all Gothic fiction, the dark, confining castle. By globalizing the Gothic environment, Poe allows his suicidal hero to grope and wander through an enlarged underworld in which the spectral contraptions, architectural enigmas, cadaverous surprises, and horrific confrontations of the haunted castle's interior now assume hemispheric dimensions. Cannibalism, butchery, premature entombment, and mass death line the long Gothic sea tunnel which brings Pym to the torrid and concave South Pole and to his rendezvous with the enormous white figure at the novel's equivocal climax. Pym's dark voyage begins in Nantucket and apparently ends in the white blur of the universe of pure imagination at the edge of some impossible milky abyss. Enroute to the absolute south aboard the ships Grampus and Jane Guy, he experiences confinement in "a labyrinth of lumber," mutiny and shipwreck highlighted by a cannibal feast, the feeding of his companion, Augustus Barnard, to the sharks, an unnatural avalanche on the island of Tsalal (or "Last Land"), and finally his reception by the mysterious snow image as he sails "beyond the veil" of terror and over a hot polar sea without a particle of ice. At the much-discussed ending, Pym appears to make a departure from the globalized Gothic castle back into a lost paradise of premortality and pure dream. Maiden-centered Gothics often conclude with the persecuted maiden's escape from the castle and a return to domestic bliss; in Poe's Pym, the Gothic prisoner of the world-castle escapes into a white world of cosmic bliss or primal suspension of being. Poe's revised and innovative Gothic vision in The Narrative of Arthur Gordon Pym, and in the related sea tale, "A Descent into the Maelström," (see 382) renders his special adaptation of the antiquated apparatus of the Gothic worthy of much deeper study.

379. _____. "The Fall of the House of Usher." Burton's Gentleman's Magazine, September, 1839; Tales of the Grotesque and Arabesque. Philadelphia: Lea & Blanchard, 1840.

REPRINT EDITION: Selected Writings of Edgar Allan Poe, ed. David Galloway, Baltimore, Penguin Books, 1975.
RESEARCH SOURCES: Butler, David W., "Usher's Hypochondriasis: Mental Alienation and Romantic Idealism in Poe's Gothic Tales," American Literature 48 (1976): 1-12; Frank, Frederick S., "Poe's House of the Seven Gothics: The Fall of the Narrator in 'The Fall of the House of Usher,'" Orbis Litterarum 34 (1979): 331-351; Kendall, Lyle H. Jr., "The Vampire Motif in 'The Fall of the House of Usher,'" College English 24 (1963): 450-453; St. Armand, Barton Levi, "The 'Mysteries' of Edgar Poe: The Quest for a Monomyth in Gothic Literature," The Gothic Imagination: Essays in Dark Romanticism, ed. G.R. Thompson, Pullman, WA, Washington State UP, 1974, pp.65-93; Thompson, G.R., "Poe and the Paradox of Terror: Structures of Heightened Consciousness in 'The Fall of the House of Usher,'" Ruined Eden of the Present: Hawthorne, Melville, and Poe, ed. G.R. Thompson and Virgil L. Lokke, West Lafayette, IN, Purdue UP, 1981, pp.313-340.

CRITICAL SYNOPSIS: No other Poe story has been more critically scrutinized, although the Gothicism has often been belittled or criticized as its weakest feature. Literally every character, event, and detail of setting, has its precedent in Gothic fiction, especially the sublime gloom of Ann Radcliffe's novels and the supernatural tension of the school of Monk Lewis. The setting reflects the fallen and menacing nature of the Gothic world, a nightmare world that is "out of space--out of time," while the very title of the story itself is the commonest form of Gothic titles, mentioning a castle, mansion, abbey or house which encloses and victimizes its feverish occupants. The basic story line conforms to what is almost the rudimentary Gothic plot. The unnamed narrator sojourns within a dark house located in a desolate landscape. He is received by the mysterious and spectral master of the house and he catches fleeting glimpses of Roderick Usher's phantasmic sister, Madeline. The House itself seems persistently alive, perhaps more alive than the crazed owners whose lives are infected by some strange ancestral curse and crime. An almost palpable atmosphere of madness, darkness, gloom, foreboding, destruction, and death closes in upon the narrator, whose rational defenses collapse when the House sinks into the tarn or mountain lake. The super-Gothic climax is noteworthy because Poe seems consciously to have turned to the architectural apocalypse that terminates the first Gothic novel, Walpole's The Castle of Otranto (1764). Rising from a cadaverous sleep within a copper-sheathed sarcophagus, Roderick's sister, Madeline, falls atop her brother while the horrified narrator flees aghast as the stones of the House crumble, dissolve, and fall like the fall of Otranto's battlements in the first Gothic. The narrator just barely escapes back across the tarn from the primal disorder of the Gothic world, but a "blood-red moon" wedging itself into the widening crack on the facade of the House signals that he too has been engulfed by the madness within. This great Gothic tale operates on many levels and can be so read. It evokes responses ranging from sheer pleasure in supernatural horror to an intellectual inquiry into the symbolic significance of its Gothic machinery.

380. _____. "William Wilson." Burton's Gentleman's Magazine, October,

1839; Tales of the Grotesque and Arabesque. Philadelphia: Lea & Blanchard, 1840.

REPRINT EDITION: Selected Writings of Edgar Allan Poe, ed. Edward H. Davidson, Boston, Houghton, Mifflin, 1956.
RESEARCH SOURCES: Carlson, Eric, "'William Wilson': The Double as Primal Self," Topic (Washington and Jefferson College, PA), 16 number 30 (1976): 35-40; Sullivan, Ruth, "William Wilson's Double," Studies in Romanticism 15 (1976): 253-263.

CRITICAL SYNOPSIS: The narrator, the first of two William Wilsons, recalls the presence in his life of an angelic double who has haunted him since his schooldays. The first Wilson is by nature a dissolute and perverted character, given to all the vices and vicious pleasures and fond of dominating others. The second William Wilson, a shadow self and a figure of conscience, constantly calls him to account or warns the first Wilson against his evil ways. To escape his conscience, the narrator first leaves Dr. Bransby's school, then Eton and Oxford, and finally roams the continent in search of degenerate pleasures. In Rome, the narrator plans a seduction of the Duchess Di Broglio, but the plan is thwarted when the second self intervenes. "In an absolute frenzy of wrath, I turned at once upon him who had thus interrupted me, and seized him violently by the collar....and thus, getting him at mercy, plunged my sword, with brute ferocity, repeatedly through and through his bosom." Thus, the diabolic self or perverse identity tries to rid itself of moral and humane constraints. The ending is highly ambiguous because the narrator strongly fancies that he has become the other Wilson and that he has killed himself, leaving him "dead to the World, to Heaven, and to Hope!" The theme of the Doppelgänger or secret sharer, and more specifically, the attack upon the righteous twin by the sinful twin, had been James Hogg's subject in a Gothic novel of the dual life, The Private Memoirs and Confessions of a Justified Sinner (1824).

381. _____. "The Man of the Crowd." Burton's Gentleman's Magazine, December, 1840; Tales by Edgar A. Poe. New York and London: Wiley and Putnam, 1845.

REPRINT EDITION: Edgar Allan Poe, Selected Writings, ed. David Galloway, Baltimore, Penguin Books, 1975.
RESEARCH SOURCES: Mazurek, Ray, "Art, Ambiguity, and the Artist in Poe's 'The Man of the Crowd,'" Poe Studies 12 (1979): 25-28; Shelden, Pamela J., "Poe's Urban Nightmare: 'The Man of the Crowd' and the Gothic Tale," Studies in the Humanities (Indiana, PA), 4 number 2 (1975): 31-35.

CRITICAL SYNOPSIS: Could be interpreted as a Gothic double story or a parable of primal loneliness and incommunication. Or could be interpreted as a biographical vignette of Poe's own artistic loneliness in an indifferent American culture. The figure of the street derelict viewed through the cafe window by the narrator is horrifying in a special sense if the man of the crowd is seen as the narrator's alterego. Acting on an impulse he himself cannot explain, the narrator singles out a stranger whom he decides to follow through the London streets in "a craving desire to keep the man in view--to know more of him." After overtaking him, the narrator "gazed at him steadfastly in the face. He noticed me not, but resumed his solemn walk, while I, ceasing to follow, remained absorbed in contemplation." The narrator has an eerie, uncanny, and finally unspoken sense of having met himself, or a desolate and criminal side of himself condemned to wander forever through the urban wasteland. Although it is a minor tale, "The Man of the Crowd" projects a major theme of Poe's Gothic called by David Galloway "the feeling of ontological insecurity, a terror which demands to be taken at something more than its face value."

382.   . "A Descent into the Maelström." Graham's Magazine, May, 1841; Tales by Edgar A. Poe. New York and London: Wiley and Putnam, 1845.

REPRINT EDITION: Complete Tales and Poems of Edgar Allan Poe, New York, Vintage-Ballantine, 1984.
RESEARCH SOURCES: Budick, E. Miller, "Poe's Gothic Idea: The Cosmic Geniture of Horror," Essays in Literature 3 (1976): 73-85; Egan, Kenneth V. Jr., "Descent to an Ascent: Poe's Use of Perspective in 'A Descent into the Maelström,'" Studies in Short Fiction 19 (1982): 157-162; Frank, Frederick S., "The Aqua-Gothic Voyage of 'A Descent into the Maelström,'" American Transcendental Quarterly 29 (1976): 85-93; Sweeney, Gerard M., "Beauty and Truth: Poe's 'A Descent into the Maelström,'" Poe Studies 6 (1973): 22-25.

CRITICAL SYNOPSIS: The great whirlpool into which the narrator first falls and then deliberately descends is the fluidic equivalent of the pit, crypt, cavern, or subterranean dungeon of older Gothic fiction as Poe relocates the fatal experience from underground to underwater in this aqua-Gothic tale. Since Poe balances the events of the tale between Gothic terror and transcendental vision within the unexpected heaven of the vortex, the story can be read as a parable of imaginative discovery or aesthetic vision. Three Norwegian fishermen, all brothers, are pulled into the lethal mouth of the great maelström. Two of the brothers take sensible and pragmatic steps to save their lives, one by clinging to the ringbolt of the fishing smack and the other by lashing himself to the mainmast, but are immediately annihilated for their rational actions. The third brother, the narrator of the tale, undergoes a sea change after his fall into the whirlpool that can only be described as a religious experience. When he decides to hope no more, he gets rid of a great deal of the terror that unmans him; as he descends, the whirlpool grants him a vision of the higher beauty that lies beyond or within the terror. As he goes deeper, he sees deeply into the mysteries of nature and self. Hence the physical descent corresponds symbolically to a metaphysical ascent as the romantic artist relaxes his grip on his own ego and is granted by the maelström both insight and salvation. The Gothic transpositions effected by Poe are ingenious. The conventional episode of descent and enclosure, for example, which usually takes a Gothic character toward madness, the ultimate horror of horrors, or a death too terrible to imagine, here results in an expansion of self and a heightened vision of cosmic unity.

383.   . "The Mask of the Red Death." Graham's Magazine, May, 1842; Broadway Journal, July, 1845.

REPRINT EDITION: Selected Writings of Edgar Allan Poe, ed. Edward H. Davidson, Boston, Houghton, Mifflin, 1956.
RESEARCH SOURCES: Graham, Kenneth W., "'Inconnue dans les Annales de la Terre': Beckford's Benign and Demonic Influence on Poe," Sphinx: A Magazine of Literature and Society 4 number 4 (1985):

226-240; Kelly, Thomas B., "Poe's Gothic Masques," Dissertation Abstracts International 32 (1972): 5187A-5188A (University of Connecticut); Roppolo, Joseph, "Meaning and 'The Masque of the Red Death,'" Tulane Studies in English 13 (1963): 59-69.

CRITICAL SYNOPSIS: The tale's unity of horror in the stark realization that "Death conquers all" places "The Masque of the Red Death" in a class by itself as perhaps the outstanding achievement in Poe's Gothic art. The artistry of the tale is due in no small measure to the economy of its language. Of the plague called the "Red Death" that decimates the land, the narrator avers that "Blood was its Avatar and its seal--the redness and the horror of blood." As for point of view, it is possible that the voice of the story is none other than the Red Death himself. Of the illusory safety of the great abbey and the idle revels of Prince Prospero and his "thousand hale and light-hearted friends," the narrator ominously remarks "All these and security were within. Without was the 'Red Death.'" As the pestilence creeps over the land, Prince Prospero feels secure enough in the seclusion of the great abbey which he "had provided with all the appliances of pleasure." The interior of the abbey is even more fabulous and extravagant than Beckford's Fonthill which may have inspired the décor. There are seven profusely decorated and multi-colored apartments including "the western or black chamber" containing a gigantic ebony clock. When Prince Prospero gives a lavish masquerade ball, an uninvited guest appears wearing a mask and costume "resembling the countenance of a stiffened corpse." The Red Death has penetrated all mortal barriers to summon Prince Prospero to his appointment with doom and decay. When Prince Prospero pursues and confronts the masked figure in the black chamber and attempts to stab it, the figure turns upon him in the manner of a Gothic phantom, felling the Prince in his tracks. The redness of horror and the blackness of death become as one overpowering force as each reveller sinks into death in the presence of the ghastly conqueror. The final paragraph of this great story contains seven clauses each commencing with "And" and each resounding with a clocklike peal of doom. The seventh "And" is like the crashing down of a black curtain of doom on the futile drama of life: "And Darkness and Decay and the Red Death held illimitable dominion over all."

384.   _____. "The Black Cat." United States Saturday Post, August, 18-43; Tales of Edgar A. Poe. New York and London: Wiley and Putnam, 1854.

REPRINT EDITION: Edgar Allan Poe, Selected Writings, ed. David Galloway, Baltimore, Penguin Books, 1976.
RESEARCH SOURCES: Heller, Terry, "The Pure Fantastic Tale of Terror," The Delights of Terror: An Aesthetics of the Tale of Terror. Urbana, IL, Illinois UP, 1987, pp.100-107; Stoehr, Taylor, "Unspeakable Horror in Poe," South Atlantic Quarterly 78 (1979): 317-332.

CRITICAL SYNOPSIS: Like "Berenice" (see 376) and "The Tell-Tale Heart" (see 386), the story is a psychopathic retrospective. These stories dramatize from within certain odd and grotesque mental states which the narrator thoroughly comprehends but cannot control. Awaiting execution for his crimes, a mad narrator "unburdens [his] soul," but the narrative itself is less a confessional than an awestruck appreciation of his own perversity. In fact, it is the remorseless and matter-of-fact quality of the voice telling

the story (in his words, "a series of mere household events")
which endows the tale with its chilling horror. He remembers vividly the two murders, one feline and the other human. Out of a
perverse impulse, he had hanged his pet black cat, Pluto, preceding the murder with the removal of the cat's eye, a sadistic act
that brought him ineffable pleasure and which he recalls with almost surgical satisfaction: "I took from my waistcoat-pocket a
penknife, opened it, grasped the poor beast by the throat, and deliberately cut one of its eyes from the socket!" After the murder
of Pluto, he acquires a new cat and a new wife, both soon to become victims of his strange rages. When his wife interferes with
his killing of cat number two, he "buried the axe in her brain"
and walled the body up in the cellar "as the monks of the Middle
Ages are recorded to have walled up their victims." When the police search the cellar, the cry of a cat from behind the plaster
leads the police to the corpse "clotted with gore," its head
adorned with the shrieking black cat whose howl had disclosed the
place of burial that consigns the narrator to the hangman. The vocal and informative corpse or the accusing voice from within the
tomb had long been a commonplace event of the shock novel, but the
reassignment of the exposing outcry to the cat is a unique twist.

385. _____. "The Pit and the Pendulum." The Gift, 1843; Broadway Journal, May, 1845.

REPRINT EDITION: The Fall of the House of Usher and Other Tales,
ed. R.P. Blackmur, New York, New American Library, 1977.
RESEARCH SOURCES: Clark, David Lee, "Sources of Poe's 'The Pit and
the Pendulum,'" Modern Language Notes 44 (1929): 349-356; Hirsch,
David H., "The Pit and the Apocalypse," Sewanee Review 76 (1968):
632-652; Lévy, Maurice, "Poe and the Gothic Tradition," ESQ: A
Journal of the American Renaissance 18 (1972): 19-28; Mooney, Stephen L., "Poe's Gothic Waste Land," Sewanee Review 70 (1962): 261-
283.

CRITICAL SYNOPSIS: Poe's brilliant condensation of Inquisition
Gothic elevates Gothic horror to its point of maximum anguish. The
dismal dungeons and exquisite tortures of innumerable Gothic tales
are brought to an intense focus on time, darkness, agony, and release from time in one of the great horror stories of world literature. The voice of the unnamed victim facing death from above by
the gradually descending razor-sharp blade of the pendulum and
death just as horrible from below in the yawning pit is a final
utterance of Gothic agony. Stylistically, the tale is punctuated
by a series of metronymic sentences whose very cadence suggests
the swing of a pendulum: "I was sick--sick unto the death with
that long agony;" "then silence and stillness and night were the
universe;" "Down--steadily down it crept. Down--certainly, relent-
lessly down! Down--still unceasingly --still inevitably down!"
Having been tried and condemned by the Inquistion in Toledo, the
narrator faints to find himself in the dank blackness of a dungeon. He explores his fetid cell and narrowly avoids falling into
a pit when he trips and falls on the torn hem of his robe. This
fortunate fall foreshadows his miraculous escape. After "a sleep
like that of death," he awakes to find himself tied face upward on
a wooden frame and watched intently by ravenous, red-eyed rats.
Gazing upward, he beholds the vibrating and slowly descending
"crescent of glittering steel," a fiendish guillotine of time. The
giant pendulum eventually reaches him and severs his bonds, free-
ing him momentarily. Gothic victims are frequently subjected to

the subterranean squeeze, but Poe's version of this horrible pre-dicament is enhanced by a magnificent special effect. As the an-gles of the cell walls begin to flatten out, the walls themselves glow red hot. Driven by the heat and contraction to the brink of the pit, the prisoner gives "one long, loud and final scream of despair" before the salvational embrace of the French General Lasalle pulls him back from the pit's edge. This great Gothic tale is Poe's quintessential parable of the human condition. As Stephen Mooney has remarked, "Poe's typical theme is alienation; his plot, survival; and his character, anxiety personified."

386. _____. "The Tell-Tale Heart." The Pioneer, January, 1843; Broad-way Journal, August, 1845.

REPRINT EDITION: Great Tales and Poems of Edgar Allan Poe, New York, Pocket Books, 1984.
RESEARCH SOURCES: Frank, Frederick S., "Neighborhood Gothic: Poe's 'Tell-Tale Heart,'" Sphinx: A Magazine of Literature and Society 3 number 4 (1981): 53-60; Tucker, B.D., "'The Tell-Tale Heart' and the 'Evil Eye,'" Southern Literary Journal 13 (1981): 92-98.

CRITICAL SYNOPSIS: This parricidal monologue in which the nameless murderer eliminates his "old man" reuses two of the most powerful utilities of the Gothic novel, the lethal or supernatural optic and the chilling or dreadful acoustic. In earlier Gothic fiction, the potent eye is a standard weapon of the Gothic villain, but here the deadly eye is transferred to the features of the tale's passive character, the recumbent old man, whose very presence in the dark old house infuriates the narrator. That horrid acoustic of earlier Gothic fiction, the sound from the depths or the lugub-rious tolling of a midnight bell, now becomes a magnified heart-beat, a cardiac clock which drives the murderer into a screamed confession. For seven nights, the narrator creeps stealthily into the old man's bedroom to spy on the sleeper, but on the eighth visit he lifts his lantern to find the eye "was open--wide, wide open--and I grew furious as I gazed upon it." In a savage bur-lesque of nursery routine, the narrator tips the heavy bed over the old man, thus putting the father to bed for the final time, then carefully dismembers the body, placing the pieces under the floor planking. In what might be called a cardiovascular climax, the pulsations of the old man's heart from beneath the floor grow louder and louder. The burdens of time, guilt, and carnality re-presented by the pounding of the heart compel the narrator to scream out his hopeless confession. In many ways, "The Tell-Tale Heart" is the ultimate American Gothic story since it is about the loneliness of the self entrapped within a cerebral labyrinth of half-understood impulses. In spite of all of his rational postur-ings, the body finally deprives the mind of choice and the narra-tor feels that he "must scream or die." He kills to gain relief from the accusing optic and he confesses to gain relief from the painful acoustic, but he ends where he begins as an organic pri-soner of space and time in the dark dungeon of his own basest drives.

387. _____. "The Oval Portrait." Graham's Magazine, April, 1842; Broadway Journal, April, 1845.

REPRINT EDITION: Selected Writings of Edgar Allan Poe, ed. Edward H. Davidson, Boston, Houghton, Mifflin, 1956.
RESEARCH SOURCES: Sheick, William J., "The Geometrical Structure

of 'The Oval Portrait,'" Poe Studies 11 (1978): 6-8; Thompson, G.R., Poe's Fiction: Romantic Irony in the Gothic Tales, Madison, WI, Wisconsin UP, 1973; Whitt, Celia, "Poe and The Mysteries of Udolpho," University of Texas Studies in English 17 (1937): 124-131.

CRITICAL SYNOPSIS: The tale is one of the few places in the works of Poe where a Gothic novelist is actually named. The opening paragraph contains an evocative reference to Mrs. Radcliffe in the narrator's allusion to the gloomy and abandoned chateau, one "of those piles of commingled gloom and grandeur which have so long frowned among the Apennines, not less in fact than in the fancy of Mrs. Radcliffe." The story is slight and more a sorrowful reverie than a shocker. Wounded and delirious, the narrator has forced his way into the castle to seek refuge and recovery. Lying in bed he inspects a volume of pictures noticing one in particular "of a young girl just ripening into womanhood." He is much taken by the mysterious expression, the oval frame, and the painting's "absolute life likeliness." How is it that art comes to be more alive than life itself? When he reads the artist's account of the painting he realizes in horror where the life energy and vitality of the portrait have come from, for in painting his wife, the artist had vampirized or drained the life force from his subject and transferred it to the canvas. For the artist "had grown wild with the ardor of his work....the tints which he spread upon the canvas were drawn from the cheeks of her who sat beside him." The deadliness inherent is absolute aesthetic devotion to the ideal craft creates an alternate portrait of the artist as parasite or vampire.

388.   _____. "The Facts in the Case of M. Valdemar." American Whig Review, December, 1845; Tales by Edgar A. Poe. New York and London: Wiley and Putnam, 1845.

REPRINT EDITION: Complete Tales and Poems of Edgar Allan Poe, New York, Vintage-Ballantine, 1984.
RESEARCH SOURCES: Burt, Donald C., "Poe, Bradbury, and the Science Fiction Tale of Terror," Mankato State College Studies 3 (1968): 76-84; Kennedy, Veronica M.S., "Gothic: Ghastly, Gruesome, and Romantic," Armchair Detective 9 (1976): 276-277; Lind, S.E., "Poe and Mesmerism," Publications of the Modern Language Association 62 (1947): 1077-1094.

CRITICAL SYNOPSIS: The tale unites horror and medical science fiction. The narrator is a scientific mesmerist who has conducted an experiment upon the person of M. Valdemar, a dying man. The purpose of the experiment is to discern what might follow if a moribund subject were to be placed in a trance on the threshold of death and the mesmeric state extended into death. The mesmerist would also discover from the experiment "to what extent, or for how long a period, the encroachments of Death might be arrested by the process." For nearly seven months M. Valdemar is suspended in hypnosis while his body, although emaciated by the disease that caused his death, apparently resists decomposition. Seeking to triumphantly complete his experiment, the mesmerist brings M. Valdemar out of the trance only to see the subject decay instantaneously into a mass of putrid yellowish ichor. "His whole frame at once--within the space of a single minute, or less, shrunk-- crumbled--absolutely rotted away beneath my hands. Upon the bed, before that whole company, there lay a nearly liquid mass of loathsome--of detestable putrescence." Faithful to his principle of one singular effect, Poe gives the tale a repulsive charnel climax while avoiding the drawing of any moral facts in the case of the overreaching hypnotist.

389. _____. "The Cask of Amontillado." Godey's Lady's Book, November, 1846; The Works of the Late Edgar Allan Poe, ed. Rufus W. Griswold. New York: J.S. Redfield, 1850.

REPRINT EDITION: Edgar Allan Poe, Selected Prose and Poetry, ed. W.H. Auden, New York, Rinehart, 1976.
RESEARCH SOURCES: Shelden, Pamela J., "'True Originality': Poe's Manipulation of the Gothic Tradition," American Transcendental Quarterly 29 (1976): 75-80; Stepp, Walter, "The Ironic Double in Poe's 'The Cask of Amontillado,'" Studies in Short Fiction 13 (1976): 447-453.

CRITICAL SYNOPSIS: The primal Gothic journey is the journey through underground passageways to the horror of horrors. Poe stages his version of this journey in the subterranean walk made by Montresor and Fortunato in this comedy of revenge. The grimness of the revenge is entirely undercut by the tone of the recollecting revenger, Montresor, who recalls a night fifty years ago when he walled up alive the phony wine expert and insulter of his family's coat-of-arms, Fortunato. The vivid memory of how he buried Fortunato alive and how Fortunato insisted upon walking into his own tomb is savored by Montresor like a fine wine. His revenge was his masterpiece of timing, cleverness, prior planning, and absolute justice, a memory which grows finer with age like a rare wine. Poe not only transmuted traditional Gothic materials but he also brilliantly condensed the décor or cryptic environment of the lengthy horror novel into "a close circumscription of space." The belabored mechanism of the Gothic recess or niche which immures the victim or holds the skeleton of the murdered baron is now reserved for Fortunato. This natural coffin is shown to the victim as Poe condenses a whole Gothic novel's elaborate system of chambers into a single paragraph: "Within the wall thus exposed by the displacing of the bones, we perceived a still interior crypt or recess, in depth about four feet, in width three, in height six or seven." The aesthetic act of revenge, which in no sense should be confused with mere homicide, proceeds in five legal stages: the indictment of the drunken fool, Fortunato; his trial as they descend to the Amontillado wherein he is given numerous chances to evade Montresor's justice; the sentencing when Montresor flashes the trowel and declares "'Be it so'"; the execution where Montresor displays his Masonic skill in walling shut the recess; and the memorialization and epitaph. The epitaph, "In pace requiescat" ("Rest in peace") does not refer to the victim, but to the calm and sane Montresor who has enjoyed fifty years of such peaceful rest after the removal of the insulting adversary and alcoholic fraud. Ordinarily, in the magazine fiction of Poe's day, the awful fate of premature burial would be described from the point of view of the sufferer, but with his customary brilliance, Poe chose to depart from the norms of Gothic narrative and shift the point of view from the wallee to the waller.

390. _____. "The Predicament." The Works of the Late Edgar Allan Poe, ed. Rufus W. Griswold. New York: J.S. Redfield, 1850.

REPRINT EDITION: Complete Tales and Poems of Edgar Allan Poe, New

York, Vintage-Ballantine, 1984.
RESEARCH SOURCE: Lewis, Paul, "Laughing at Fear: Two Versions of
the Mock Gothic," Studies in Short Fiction 15 (1978): 411-414.

CRITICAL SYNOPSIS: As shown in such Gothic works as Beckford's Vathek (1786), horror and hilarity can sometimes be combined to
achieve absurdist fantasy. The gruesome buffoonery of "The Predicament" is Poe's Beckfordian contribution to Gothic farce. Poe parodies the lethal entrapment and slow death of innumerable Gothic
victims in the predicament of Signora Psyche Zenobia. The supreme
passion and overriding compulsion of this character's life is the
climbing of towers, turrets, steeples, pinnacles, any and every
Gothic apex that he/she comes upon. Coming to Edinburgh, Signora
Psyche Zenobia is ravished by the view of "a Gothic cathedral--
vast, venerable, and with a tall steeple which towered into the
sky." Yielding to an attack of toweromania, the "uncontrollable
desire to ascend the giddy pinnacle," he/she scurries to the top
and to complete the ecstasy, inserts his/her head through the
winding aperture in the dial plate of the steeple's clock. The
toweromaniac should have checked the time because an unforeseen
predicament now arises. To Signora Psyche Zenobia's dismay, "the
huge, glittering, scimitar-like minute-hand of the clock had, in
the course of its hourly revolution, descended upon my neck. There
was, I knew, not a second to be lost." Poe's prisoner in "The Pit
and the Pendulum" (see 385) escapes the descending blade at the
last moment, but Signora Psyche Zenobia has no such lucky salvation. What follows is his/her analytic description of his/her
gradual decapitation. To pass the time, he/she recites Cervantes,
watches one of her eyes stare up from the gutter, and continues to
talk on even after the head has been separated from the body. No
timely rescue finishes Signora Psyche Zenobia's fate, no last
moment extrication from horrible death from a piece of machinery,
just the headless torso continuing its melancholy tale from the
top of his/her last tower.

391. Price, Edgar Hoffmann. "Bones for China." Strange Gateways. Sauk
City, WI: Arkham House, 1967.

CRITICAL SYNOPSIS: A Popular and prolific pulp Gothicist whose
best tales have a Lovecraftian aura in both their situations and
vocabulary. Several stories have World War II China as their setting. In "Bones for China," the main character, Yang, sets himself
the mission of returning his grandsire's bones to Chinese soil
even though Ming T'ien is under assault by the Japanese. In the
manner of Gothic fiction's animated skeletons, the bones reacti-
vate themselves to direct their reburial and to assist the patriotic Yang to throw off the yoke of the conquerors.

392. Pritchard, Melissa. Spirit Seizures. Athens, GA: Georgia UP, 1987.

RESEARCH SOURCE: Johnson, Greg, "Isn't It Gothic?" Georgia Review
42 (1988): 840-849.

CRITICAL SYNOPSIS: The initial story in the collection, "Spirit
Seizures," bears a relationship to Poe's "Ligeia" (see 377) in its
use of the theme of psychic occupancy of one body by another. The
setting is an Illinois farm in July, 1877, home of the young woman, Lurancy Vennum. Isolated and surrounded by memories, she
feels that she is constantly in contact with the world of the dead
until her body is actually invaded by the spirit of the thirteen

year old girl, Mary Roff. From the the spirit world, the following Ligeian question emanates: "And what is bodily flesh but a house so lightly mortised as to permit an occasional strike of soul to flash through like summer lightning?" The other tales in the collection also draw upon Gothic motifs in the work of Poe and Hawthorne. These are: "La Bete: A Figure Study," "A Private Landscape," "Companions," "Rocking on Water, Floating on Glass," and "A Dance with Alison."

393. Purdy, James. "Color of Darkness." Color of Darkness, Eleven Stories and a Novella. New York: New Directions, 1957.

REPRINT EDITION: Westport, CT, Greenwood Press, 1975.
RESEARCH SOURCE: Malin, Irving, New American Gothic, pp.75-76.

CRITICAL SYNOPSIS: The grotesque breakdown of human relationships stands at the center of the story and perhaps at the center of the American Gothic. Purdy's Gothicism, like that of Sherwood Anderson, focuses on those moments of horrible self-awareness when the character sees into the depths of his own loneliness and isolation. The narrator is the father of the little boy, Baxter. They live with the housekeeper, Mrs. Zilke, although living in the same house does not imply communication between the father, son, and ersatz mother. The narrator cannot recall the color of his dead wife's eyes just as he cannot seem to form any emotional bond with his own little son although the pretense of fatherhood is complete. When the father removes his wedding ring for the first time since her death, the boy suddenly sees and retaliates against the father's emotional charade by putting the ring in his mouth and refusing to give it up. The climax sees a furious rejection of the father, first in verbal form and then in the physical act of kicking the father in the groin, a sort of castrating blow. "'Shut your goddamn face,' the boy spat out at his father. The father nodded from the floor where he twisted in pain." The story offers wonderful touches of morbid comedy such as little Baxter in bed clutching his big toy crocodile.

394. _____. Malcolm. New York: Farrar, Straus, Cudahy, 1959.

REPRINT EDITION: London, Wiedenfeld & Nicolson, 1987.
RESEARCH SOURCES: Baldanza, Frank, "Northern Gothic," Southern Review 10 (1974): 566-582; Malin, Irving, New American Gothic, pp. 46-48.

CRITICAL SYNOPSIS: A common crisis in James Purdy's conception of Gothic is loss or rejection of the father. This absurdist fantasy, surreal in many of its episodes, involves four searches for the lost father, each one a sort of separate legend of abused or warped love. The novel opens and closes with the boy quester, Malcolm, in a posture of desolation sitting on a bench and awaiting the father who never comes. He has been sent by the astrologer, Cox, to four different addresses where his father and even love itself might be found. Malcolm's four quests show him four couples in a variety of sadistic relationships. Cora Naldi and Estel Blanc, a retired mortician and a funeral singer, seem almost to be a gruesome parody on the Gothic motif of necrophilia. The second couple, Kermit and Laureen Raphaelson are equally grotesque, for Kermit is a midget who bullies his normal-sized wife. In the third pair, Girard Girard, the great financier, is utterly degraded by his Wagnerian wife, Madame Melba. The last couple that Malcolm

visits, Jerome and Eloisa Brace, step straight from the pages of
the Marquis de Sade in their sadomasochistic persecution of each
other. Malcolm's vain search for the father reveals only a deformed world of moral freaks.

395. _____. The Nephew. New York: Farrar, Straus, Cudahy, 1960.

REPRINT EDITION: London, Wiedenfeld & Nicolson, 1987.
RESEARCH SOURCE: Brantlinger, Patrick, "Missing Corpses: The De-
constructive Mysteries of James Purdy and Franz Kafka," Novel 20
(1986): 24-40.

CRITICAL SYNOPSIS: Two insular American Gothic themes, the muted
nightmare of misplaced love and entrapment by memory, distinguish
this melancholy novel of hopeless nostalgia. The titular character, the nephew Cliff, never appears directly in the book but is
very much a presence in the intense reveries of his aunt, the retired teacher, Alma, and her brother, Boyd Mason. The nephew, a
soldier, is listed as missing in action. Hence, Alma decides to
delve deeply into her nephew's life and then compose a fitting memorial. She assumes that her nephew was a heroic and masculine
American boy who loved both his family and his country in the Norman Rockwell manner. But her research project reveals otherwise
and a variety of dark and disturbing facts about Cliff begin to
surface. Hints of homosexuality in his biography finally prompt
her to abandon a project in misplaced affection, a labor of love
which eventually engulfs the entire small community in the sadness
of broken assumptions about one of its favorite sons. Several reviewers commented on the Gothic colorations of The Nephew. Gothics
sometimes refuse to resolve their mysteries at the end. The reviewer in Commonweal noted this Gothic effect when he wrote that
The Nephew is "a problem novel in which the problem is never
solved." Similarly, the New Republic reviewer spoke of "the dreamy
horror of the prose," thus identifying yet another Gothic feature.

396. Quinn, Seabury. "The Dead Hand." The Phantom Fighter, and Memoirs of
Jules de Grandin. Sauk City, WI: Mycroft and Moran, 1966.

REPRINT EDITION: Adventures of Jules de Grandin, New York, Popular
Library, 1976.
RESEARCH SOURCE: Crawford, Gary W., "The Modern Masters," Horror
Literature: A Core Collection and Reference Guide, ed. Marshall B.
Tymn, New York, R.R. Bowker, 1981, pp.338-339.

CRITICAL SYNOPSIS: The grandiose and infallible detective, Jules
de Grandin is stamped from the same pattern as Poe's Monsieur Dupin. In this typical Gothic piece, Katherine O'Brien, assistant to
the magician, Professor Mysterio, is able to pursue her criminal
career as a thief even after her death. Operating independently of
her body, the dead hand steals on, a supernatural mystery that can
neither be explained nor solved until Grandin's entry.

397. Read, Harriette Fanning. The Haunted Student: A Romance of the Fourteenth Century. Washington, DC: Published by the Author, 1860.

RESEARCH SOURCE: Peterson, Clell T., "Spotting the Gothic Novel,"
Graduate Student of English 1 (1957): 14-15.

CRITICAL SYNOPSIS: An erotic liaison between a solitary student
and an amorous spectre was a Gothic love theme already in use as

seen in Irving's "Adventure of the German Student" (see 227). This Gothic pamphlet is a redoing of the theme with the student drawn from the medieval Faust legend. The tale includes in some form most of the mandatory features of a Gothic story as "spotted" by Clell T. Peterson. These are: dark and exotic passions; repeated fainting; missing relatives belatedly produced; fantastic coincidence; a southern European locale; supernatural visitations; creepy settings both within and without; subterranean exploration; mysterious documents; garrulous ghosts. Peterson's checklist applies item-by-item to The Haunted Student.

398. Rechy, John. City of Night. New York: Grove Press, 1962.

REPRINT EDITION: New York, Grove Press, 1984.
RESEARCH SOURCE: Gross, Louis S., "The Transformed Land: Studies in American Gothic Narrative," Dissertation Abstracts International 47 (1986): 1323A (University of Pennsylvania).

CRITICAL SYNOPSIS: A novel of displaced identity and an Americanized version of the legend of the Wandering Jew. The main character wanders hopelessly through the metropolitan and rural wasteland of the United States in search of the utopian America of myth and folklore. Everywhere he goes, he is confronted with misery, loneliness, loss of direction and self-esteem, social despair, sexual violence, and all of the sordid underside of the American dream. From its beginnings, the American Gothic is highly skeptical of certain components of the American dream, namely the culture's exuberant ideals of liberty and justice for all, rationality, opportunity for self-development, and the promise of unlimited success. The young man condemned to wander through a dark metropolitan maze forms the basis for Gothic discovery in Charles Brockden Brown's Arthur Mervyn (see 064) and Hawthorne's "My Kinsman, Major Molineux." (see 202)

399. Remington, Eugene. The Victim of the Mysterious Mark; or, The Magic Mirror. Lowell, MA: Wheeler, 1880.

CRITICAL SYNOPSIS: Imitative of Hawthorne's use of the mirror as a Gothic device which contains the reflection of a Gothic self as in "Monsieur du Miroir" (see 193) or as a repository of the dark and guilty past as in the mirrors within The House of the Seven Gables (see 200). In the case of this Gothic, the image actually leaves the mirror to exact a vengeance from beyond the grave.

400. Rice, Anne. Interview with the Vampire. New York: Alfred A. Knopf, 1976.

REPRINT EDITION: New York, Ballantine Books, 1978.
RESEARCH SOURCES: Gross, Louis S., Redefining the American Gothic: From Wieland to the Day of the Dead, Ann Arbor, MI, UMI Press, 1989, pp.3, 49; Lawler, Donald L., "Interview with the Vampire," Survey of Modern Fantasy Literature, pp.776-780; Roberts, Bette B., "Anne Rice's Interview with a Vampire," New Mexico Humanities Review 2 (1979): 45-63.

CRITICAL SYNOPSIS: Probably the premium vampire Gothic of the 1970's in a decade which saw several firstrate updatings of the Dracula prototype (see 418, Saberhagen's The Dracula Tape and 509, Chelsea Quinn Yarbro's trilogy, Blood Games, Hotel Transylvania, and The Palace). Stoker's Dracula (1897) had sought solely to ter-

rify and to provoke dark shudders, not to teach or stimulate debate over the anguishes of modern life. Rice's vampire novel is
rather sternly philosophic and insistently didactic in its preoccupation with the emptiness of modern life, the value vacuum
caused by the departure of God. The vampire protagonist, Louis,
who grants the taped interview to a young man, has the tragic insight that accumulates from being alive for over two centuries.
Since he first became a vampire in 1791, he has witnessed the de-
sacralization of the universe, the eclipse of God, and the rise of
faith-destroying and mystery-destroying technological cultures. In
the philosophic dichotomy between being and nothingness, Louis
senses the triumph of nothingness over all meanings and creeds.
Much of his vampirizing (he enjoys the erotic pleasure that arises
during murderous assault) seems to have as its purpose the production of proof in a God, a supernatural, and a universally mysterious quality to life, but all is futile. He is damned to nothingness by a world which acknowledges neither the vampire or the
saint. Roaming from Paris to New Orleans to Transylvania in search
of roots, he is denied a demonic identity in a skeptical and godless world. The other characters, Lestat, the maker of vampires,
Armand, the vampire of Paris, and Claudia, Louis's vampire daughter, are similarly displaced in a world void of sacred values. He
makes a violent entrance into the Cathedral of his namesake, St.
Louis, in New Orleans, hoping that his supernatural presence will
be matched by God's supernatural presence. In a gesture of metaphysical frustration, he annihilates the Théatre des Vampires in
Paris. But it seems that Satan and his creatures cannot exist
without God, and God, in Louis's view, has vacated the universe
leaving a value vacuum of nothingness. The blood, horror, and perverse erotic energy of the novel are considerable, but it is the
existential predicament of the vampire which gives the book its
ultimate terror.

401. Richards, Elizabeth Barnes. <u>Elisiner; or, The Mysteries of an Old
Stone Mansion</u>. Worcester: Adams & Brown, 1864.

CRITICAL SYNOPSIS: A tea-table romance with mild Gothic overtones
in the form of the "East Gable" of the Old Stone Mansion and the
apparitions of dead memory which reside in its attic tower. The
heroine, Elisiner Hovert, legatee of Ralph Pyrome, moves into the
great old house with her friend, Foresetta Walsingworth, where
they often retire to the attic tower to reminisce about the family
past. Elisiner recalls particularly her friendship with Clarence
Neuvorne, the man she should have married instead of the more eli-
gible Byron Elwell, her deceased husband. Her painful memories
within the attic tower involve her betrayal of true love in order
to marry for position and her cold attitude toward her parents
whom she seems to have deserted to enjoy the legacy of the great
house by being named the sole heir through her uncle, Deacon Pyrome. When Elisiner finally realizes these "sins" of the past, she
marries Clarence Neuvorne and is reunited with her mother and father after clearing them of all debt. The mansion itself is very
much a symbolic place haunted by guilty memories of Elisiner's
egotism. In this respect, <u>The Old Stone Mansion</u> resembles Hawthorne's <u>House of the Seven Gables</u> (see 200) and Henry James's
<u>Jolly Corner</u> (see 249) in which the architectural sites provide a
supernatural education for the sinner who has acted selfishly and
denied the better self.

402. Rinehart, Mary Roberts. <u>The Circular Staircase</u>. Indianapolis, IN:

Bobbs-Merrill, 1908; New York: Dell, 1908.

REPRINT EDITION: Laurel, NY, Lightyear Press, 1976.
RESEARCH SOURCES: Cohn, Jan, "Mary Roberts Rinehart," American Wo-
men Writers: A Critical Reference Guide from Colonial Times to the
Present, New York, Frederick Ungar, 1979, pp.182-185; Mussell,
Kay, Women's Gothic and Romantic Fiction: A Reference Guide, West-
port, CT, Greenwood Press, 1981, p. 35.

CRITICAL SYNOPSIS: With her many novels of mystery and detection,
Mary Roberts Rinehart not only dared to be popular with her readers but also suggested through her craft how the roots of the detective novel lay in the Gothic tradition. The Circular Staircase
has a trio of characters familiar to Gothic fiction. A spinster
aunt plans a pleasant summer vacation in an old manse in the countryside. Accompanied by her nephew and her niece, the three are
soon confronted with a series of mysterious crimes and strange doings. All eventually proves to be the work of an embezzler who has
been using the house and its secret compartments to serve as a
cache for his stolen money and securities. By mingling mystery and
lightly macabre comedy, Rinehart found her formula for literary
success in this early work.

403. _____. The Case of Jennie Brice. Indianapolis, IN: Bobbs-Merrill
1913.

REPRINT EDITION: Laurel, NY, Lightyear Press, 1976.
RESEARCH SOURCE: Overton, Grant, The Woman Behind the Door. . .
Mary Roberts Rinehart, New York, Farrar and Rinehart, 1930.

CRITICAL SYNOPSIS: An elaborate ruse and publicity stunt turn into
a real murder case in this clever thriller. Anxious for a sensational story, a newspaper reporter convinces a disappointed playwright to report the disappearance of the leading lady in a recent
struggling theatrical production. A missing leading lady should
boost attendance and sell papers. The leading lady is also the
playwright's unwanted wife and the soon-to-be victim of a strange
murder. These dark intrigues are performed against the background
of severe flooding in Pittsburgh. A la her formula, the gruesome-
ness of situation is balanced by adept touches of comedy.

404. _____. The Wall. New York: Grosset & Dunlap, 1938.

RESEARCH SOURCE: Cohn, Jan, Improbable Fiction: The Life of Mary
Roberts Rinehart, Pittsburgh, PA, Pittsburgh UP, 1980.

CRITICAL SYNOPSIS: Gothic detective novel. Other books by Rinehart
which combine mystery and detection with both humor and Gothic
touches are Dangerous Days (1919), The Door (1930), and The Frightened Wife (1953).

405. Rives, Amelie. The Ghost Garden. New York: Stokes, 1918.

CRITICAL SYNOPSIS: A formulaic but readable Gothic. The plot is an
assemblage of all of the typical props and stock characters. The
Virginia mansion named "Her Wish" is built literally on the tears
of the victims of Melany Horsemanden, a beautiful lady without
mercy. Her ghost now presides over the house where it has resided
for nearly two centuries. When the northern gentleman, Evan Radford, visits Her Wish, he is greeted by another Melany, Melany

Warrenger, with whom he falls in love. But the second Melany is
constantly threatened by her ancestral namesake and like other
Gothic maidens requires a protector. Radford takes up residence at
Her Wish in order to guard Melany against against the ghost but is
soon possessed himself by the cold and powerful spirit of Melany
Horsemanden. On the eve of their wedding day, a weird urge draws
Radford to the grave of the first Melany where his body is found
at graveside the next morning. Refusing to accept his death, the
second Melany performs a fantastic resurrection. But having been
pulled through the curtain of death, Evan Radford does not want to
come back and longs only to die back into the control of the wicked Melany. Only one means of release will suffice. Her Wish must
be burned to the ground in a grand funeral pyre for the separated
lovers. The novel is well stocked with all the Gothic gadgetry including cellar creaks and attic groans, shuddering shutters, portraits with eyes, and a garden of evil shadows. In her study,
Gothic Novels of the Twentieth Century, Elsa J. Radcliffe enumer-
ates eight elements that might yield a good Gothic. These are: (1)
the supernatural; (2) a quest or a wrong to be righted; (3) a setting that includes an old dwelling; (4) a fantasy of wealth suddenly acquired; (5) mystery, suspense, and intrigue; (6) a fantasy
of romantic love in some form, often including a love-hate, trust-
fear ambivalence; (7) romanticism of the past and a historical
setting; (8) confrontations between the forces of good and evil.
All eight are effectively present to some degree in this workbook
Gothic.

406. Robinson, John Hovey. Marietta; or, The Two Students, A Tale of the
Dissecting Room and "Body-Snatchers." Boston: Jordan & Wiley, 18-
46.

RESEARCH SOURCES: Frank, Frederick S., "Isaac Crookenden," The
First Gothics: A Critical Guide to the English Gothic Novel, New
York, Garland, 1987, pp.64-69; Johannsen, Albert. "John Hovey Robinson," The House of Beadle and Adams and its Dime and Nickel Novels, foreword John T. Mc Intyre, Norman, OK, Oklahoma UP, 1950,
pp.241-243.

CRITICAL SYNOPSIS: A 46 page illustrated shocker by one of the
masters of the dime Gothic in America. Robinson's diverse skills
and enormous output as a purveyor of cheap gore fiction are on a
par with the English Gothic chapbookers such as Isaac Crookenden
whose garish shilling shockers, The Skeleton; or, The Mysterious
Discovery (1805) and The Spectre of the Turret; or, Guolto Castle
(1811) screamed their way to commercial success. The Boston body
snatchers, Mr. Gaunt and Mr. Thick, have filled an order for a
corpse for the medical experimenter, Dr. Levator, who gazes fondly
on the body of Marietta even as he prepares to dissect it. So
strong is his necrophiliac desire that he places a ring on the
body's finger and removes a ring worn by Marietta as a keepsake.
Placing love above medical science, he returns the cadaverous Marietta to Gaunt and Thick, asking them to re-bury her. Before they
can re-sell her body to another doctor, it is stolen from their
ghoulish stockpile by Levator's associate, Dr. Frene. Dr. Frene's
experiment in galvanic resuscitation is a shocking success when he
brings the dead Marietta back to life with an electrical charge.
Meanwhile, Gaunt and Thick have delivered the corpse of a syphi-
litic prostitute to Dr. Levator, a greedy mistake which brings
about the downfall of the body snatchers. The climax occurs inside
their makeshift morgue, a large old building which contains not

just the corpses they sell but also a stable of prostitutes. Lodged in Mr. Thick's apartment is the prostitute Cecil, who fights off her molestor and then sets fire to the building even as the doctors approach to claim more bodies. While the flames consume the vile pair, the good doctors cut their way to safety through the walls. The electrically resurrected Marietta is now free to marry Dr. Levator, the man to whom she became posthumously engaged by the exchange of rings while lying on the dissecting table. Horrible, improbable, shocking, and crammed with charnel gore, Robinson's Marietta is a superb specimen of the American dime Gothic at its wildest extremes. Various details of the metropolitan underworld littered with bodies also recall the urban Gothic of George Lippard in The Quaker City; or, The Monks of Monk Hall (see 288).

407.   . Angela; or, The Convent of Santa Clara, A Tale of Portugal. New York: Samuel French, 1850.

RESEARCH SOURCE: Watt, William Whyte, Shilling Shockers of the Gothic School: A Study of Chapbook Gothic Romances, New York, Russell & Russell, 1967.

CRITICAL SYNOPSIS: A close imitation of the English Gothic's monastic shockers, the novel was also published in The Flag of Our Union, "An Elegant, Moral, and Refined Miscellaneous Family Journal." The persecutions, misfortunes, denials of heritage, and convent incarcerations of Angela Benevetta are the work of the sinister Senor Mondelli, a better-than-average reincarnation of the Gothic villain. Angela's rescue from her dismal cell and the elimination of Mondelli are accomplished by Arthur De Grange and his loyal companion, Don Montisco, but not before the customary dreadful delays, dark corridors, and losses of freedom and way. While the hero, heroine, and villain are utterly stereotypical, several of the grotesque minor characters elevate the Gothic thrill level of the narrative. The brigand captain, Sabocha, a character who is unpredictably benign or malicious, and the monstrously deformed son of Senor Mondelli to whom Angela is forcibly betrothed, are familiar figures from the standard Gothic cast. In his many horror and terror novels, Robinson made almost no effort to Americanize his materials or to vary the formula for pleasurable fear, and was quite content to exploit the still vigorous market for Gothicism in its original shapes and forms. His heroines are unaltered from their English forerunners. William Whyte Watt's trenchant description of the shilling shocker heroine fits Robinson's Angela, who is "swept about like a leaf in the autumn wind by her own feelings. It is her business to get into trouble, and then to pine away with the aid of her plaintive music and poetry and an inherent ability for sighing and weeping, leaving the almost hopeless task of extrication to the unfortunate hero."

408.   . Black Ralph, the Forest Fiend! or, The Wanderers of the West, A Tale of Wood and Wild. Boston: National Publishing Company, 1851.

CRITICAL SYNOPSIS: A dime novel Gothic western which appears to plagiarize its indian-hating hero from Robert Montgomery Bird's Nick of the Woods (see 050). All of the sensational and Gothic elements of the German Räuberroman or "robber romance" are clearly present in Americanized form. Robinson's handling of the avenging and nearly superhuman hero also has connections with Charles Wilkins Webber's Gothic western, "Jack Long; or, The Shot in the Eye" (see 484).

409.   . Catholina; or, Walled Up Alive. New York: Frederic A. Brady, 1851.

CRITICAL SYNOPSIS: Alternately titled The Niche in the Wall, the 90 page monastic shocker is a composite plagiarism from various anti-Catholic novels and sham memoirs concerning the victims of ecclesiastical treachery and lechery such as The Nun of St. Ursula (see 252). Robinson also had access to such English Gothic titles as The Fugitive Countess; or, The Convent of St. Ursula (1807), The Libertines; or, Monkish Mysteries (1800) and Catherine Selden's sensational account of the dreadful agonies of the coercive monastic life, The English Nun, published by William Lane's Minerva Press in 1797 and often reprinted or plagiarized. The special use made by Poe of the common Gothic doom of live burial within a catacomb wall may be observed in "The Cask of Amontillado" (see 389).

410.   . The Ruined Abbey; or, The Gipsies of Forest Hill, A Romance of Old England. Boston: F. Gleason's Publishing Hall, 1852.

CRITICAL SYNOPSIS: A 100 page double-columned dime shocker. Probably a composite plagiarism taken from the hordes of shilling shockers and cheap chapbooks as well as Victorian bloods which still glutted the bookstalls of both nations. Several possible models among the English Gothic chapbooks and longer Gothics are The Ruins of Avondale Priory (1796), The Ruins of Rigonda; or, The Homicidal Father (1808), and The Ruins of Selinunti; or, The Val de Mazzara (1813). Since many of the British Gothics are themselves plagiarized from the works of Lewis and Mrs. Radcliffe, what we may have in Robinson's Ruined Abbey is a plagiarism of a plagiarism.

411.   Roby, Mary Linn. The Broken Key. New York: New American Library, 1973.

RESEARCH SOURCE: Modleski, Tania, Loving with a Vengeance: Mass-Produced Fantasies for Women, Hamden, CT, Archon, 1982.

CRITICAL SYNOPSIS: The author of more than twenty recreational Gothics, many of these published by the New American Library. Together with the Gothic detective story, The Broken Key, her Dig a Narrow Grave (1971), Pennies on Her Eyes (1969), This Land Turns Evil Slowly (1971), The Tower Room (1974), and When the Witch is Dead (1972) successfully exploit all of the formulas and apparatus of Radcliffean thrill fiction. Nothing too awful befalls her inquisitive heroines such as Sara in The Broken Key. Inheriting a cottage in remote Cornwall, she also inherits all of the thrills accompanying the missing and murdered master of the nearby Penrith manor. Although superficially plotted and completely without the sexual violence which seems to be a requirement of the erotic Gothics of the late 1970's, The Broken Key and her other books seem to support Tania Modleski's feminist thesis that such forms of women's mass-produced entertainment use "the Gothic as a powerful mode for exploration of and vicarious amelioration of female victimization in patriarchy."

412. Rogers, Rosemary. <u>Wicked, Loving Lies</u>. New York: Avon, 1976.

> REPRINT EDITION: New York, Avon, 1982.
> RESEARCH SOURCES: Mussell, Kay, "Gothic Novels," <u>Handbook of Amer-</u>
> <u>ican Popular Literature</u>, ed. M. Thomas Inge, Westport, CT, Green-
> wood Press, 1988, pp.161-162; Thurston, Carol and Barbara Doscher,
> "Supermarket Erotica: 'Bodice-Busters' Put Romantic Myths to Bed,"
> <u>Progressive</u> (April, 1982): 49-51.

> CRITICAL SYNOPSIS: A popular erotic Gothic or "bodice-buster" as
> two critics have recently labelled this type of historical romance
> in Gothic costume. The endangered maiden ("endangered" is an un-
> derstatement), Marisa, is a sexual volleyball for every libidinous
> male in the novel. Torrid passages gleam garishly from every page.
> "Marisa's lips felt bruised and swollen, and her breasts seemed to
> burn from the casual, all-too-knowing caresses she had been forced
> to endure. It was all she could do to lean docilely in this man's
> hard embrace and pretend that he had subdued her spirit." This
> scene in repeated ad infinitum as Marisa's trials take her from
> the safety of a Spanish nunnery to captivity in a Moorish harem to
> "war-torn Tripoli and the savage wilderness of untamed America and
> a spectacular climax" as the cover blurb proclaims. Enroute she is
> desired and pursued by any number of sexually starved men includ-
> ing both Comanche warriors and the Emperor Napoleon himself who
> would have her as his mistress. One of her pursuers and violators,
> the "sea rogue" Dominic Challenger, is almost believable as a re-
> incarnation of the Gothic hero-villain in his salacious brutali-
> ty. There are no slow seductions in the erotic Gothic. Confined to
> Captain Challenger's cabin, "Marisa tried to wriggle away, but he
> held her pinioned, concentrating first on one quivering breast and
> then on the other until she felt her whole body burning with em-
> barrassment." This book and others like it revels in all of the
> sexual Gothicism of the Marquis de Sade's <u>Justine</u> (1791) where the
> abused heroine becomes almost a caricature of the naive Gothic
> maiden thrust into a spiked labyrinth of lust, cruelty, aberrant
> sex, torture, and high-spirited depravity. But a stroll through
> any commercial bookstore in any suburban shopping mall anywhere in
> the United States will quickly validate the popularity of such
> erotic Gothics with readers of both sexes.

413. Ross, William Edward Daniel. <u>Haunting of Clifton Court</u>. New York:
Popular Library, 1972.

> REPRINT EDITION: New York, Thomas Bouregy, (under the title, <u>Ghost</u>
> <u>Symphony</u>), 1985.
> RESEARCH SOURCE: Radcliffe, Elsa J., <u>Gothic Novels of the Twenti-</u>
> <u>eth Century</u>, Metuchen, NJ, Scarecrow Press, 1979, p.190.

> CRITICAL SYNOPSIS: Follows the maiden-centered Gothic formulas,
> but rather too slavishly. The updated Radcliffean heroine, Anne,
> has a passion for antiques which is perhaps cured by her harrowing
> experiences on the Merridith estates outside Boston. Her prime
> spectral adversary is Vanessa Clifton, the haunter of Clifton
> Court where Ann cares for the antiques in the shop on the estate.
> As in so many cheap and commercialized Gothics, a potentially sus-
> penseful situation is ruined by what Elsa J. Radcliffe calls "the
> contrived solution of the mystery which makes a complete dope out
> of the heroine."

414. Roth, Philip. <u>The Breast</u>. New York: Farrar, Straus, Giroux, 1982.

REPRINT EDITION: Baltimore and New York, Penguin Books, 1985.
RESEARCH SOURCES: Sabiston, Elizabeth, "A New Fable for Critics:
Philip Roth's The Breast," International Fiction Review 2 (1975):
27-34; Siegel, Mark, "The Breast," Survey of Modern Fantasy Literature, pp.169-172.

CRITICAL SYNOPSIS: Horrible and uncontrollable transformation established itself as an American Gothic motif as early as Charles
Brockden Brown's Wieland; or, The Transformation (see 063). Roth's
grotesque and occasionally comic novella carries Gothic transformation to absurd extremes when the hero, David Allan Kepesh, a college English professor, undergoes a mammary metamorphosis changing
from a man into a female breast. Like the famous prior victim of
horrid change, Gregor Samsa in Frank Kafka's The Metamorphosis,
Kepesh's transformation is physiological only. Mentally, intellec-
tually, emotionally, he remains human, perhaps more totally human
than when he lived in a human body. While lying in his private
room at the Lennox Hill Hospital this mammarized former man has
time to contemplate the impenetrable mysteries of the absurd and
lonely human condition with himself acting as the chief symbol of
that absurdity and loneliness. Visited by his former mistress,
Claire Ovington, the breast retains all the normal male sexual
urges without the attendant means of satisfying them. Examined by
the psychiatrist, Dr. Klinger, he is unable to communicate the data necessary for successful psychoanalysis. Even the knowledge
that this thing has happened to other characters in literature
does not help and he is forced to conclude that he must be mad or
hallucinating. The physical reality of the transformation and the
reasons for it remain too horrible to accept. Roth's breast fantasy indicates again how a victim's Gothic circumstances can sometimes accommodate serious philosophical themes. In the loneliness,
helplessness, and isolation of his bizarre situation, "Kepesh represents the human condition: man trapped in a grotesque and absurd situation from which there is no release but death and of
which there is no satisfactory explanation."

415. Rowson, Susannah. The Inquisitor, or the Invisible Rambler. Phila-
      delphia: William Gibbons, 1793.

      RESEARCH SOURCES: Brandt, Ellen B., Susannah Haswell Rowson: Amer-
      ica's First Best-Selling Novelist, Chicago, Serba, 1975; Brown,
      Herbert Ross, The Sentimental Novel in America, 1789-1860, Durham,
      NC, Duke UP, 1940; New York, Octagon, 1975; Parker, Patricia L.,
      "Susannah Rowson," American Writers Before 1800: A Biographical
      and Critical Dictionary, Westport, CT, Greenwood Press, 1983, pp.
      1247-1250; Piacentino, Edward J., "Susannah Haswell Rowson: A Bib-
      liography of the First Editions of Primary Works and Secondary
      Sources," Bulletin of Bibliography 43 (1986): 13-16.

      CRITICAL SYNOPSIS: Charles Brockden Brown's contemporary, Susannah
      Rowson (1762-1824) authored ten novels during the Gothic period.
      These books respond to the didactic seriousness of Richardson's
      Clarissa (1748) and the sentimental-domestic Gothic of Mrs. Ann
      Radcliffe. Her Charlotte Temple (1791) is a novel of seduction and
      violation and contains periodic reminders of the distressed situa-
      tion of the Gothic heroine. The Inquisitor shows her most direct
      use of the popular Gothic tradition. Via a magic ring, the main
      character renders himself invisible in order to be able to assist
      virtue in distress or punish vice. As he moves about or "rambles

invisibly" through society, he finds deceit, seduction, adultery, oppression, and institutional violence. The novel contains an insert called "Sketch of a Modern Novel" which satirically describes the composition of a good sentimental Gothic. "Remember to mix a sufficient quantity of sighs, tears, swooning, hysterics, and all the moving expressions of heart-rending woe."

416.   Russell, Ray. "Sanguinarius." Haunted Castles: The Complete Gothic Tales of Ray Russell. Baltimore: Maclay & Associates, 1985.

RESEARCH SOURCES: Barber, Paul, How Shall the Dead Arise: The Folklore of Vampires, Burial, and Death, New Haven, CT, Yale UP, 1988; Masters, R.E.L. and Edouard Lea, "Two Monsters Extraordinary," Perverse Crimes in History, New York, Julian Press, 1963, pp.8-31.

CRITICAL SYNOPSIS: Sometimes called a porno-Gothicist, Russell writes powerful tales of terror which make use of both the traditional trappings of the genre as well as its historical horrors. Several monsters extraordinaire of history are members of the cast of Russell's Psychopathia Sexualis. "Sanguinarius" is a graphic account of the hideous career of Countess Elisabeth Bathory, the Hungarian Blutgräfin or "blood countess" who is supposed to have dined on the blood of more than 650 victims within her Castle of Csejthe. Another Russell tale of sado-erotic pleasure is "Sagittarius," a repulsive portrait of the infamous child molester and murderer, the Marshal of France, Gilles de Rais. Along with these gory pseudo-biographies of sexual monsters, Russell has proven himself capable of the subtler tale of terror as in the story, "Comet Wine." Here, the author studies the alleged connection between artistic genius and disease using the rooms of the Russian composer, Rimsky Korsakov, as the setting for the strange emergence of the musician Cholodenko's virtuoso composition which is apparently brought on by a horrible illness.

417.   Russell, W. Clark. The Death Ship: A Strange Story. London: Hurst & Blackett, 1888.

REPRINT EDITION: New York, Arno Press, 1976.

CRITICAL SYNOPSIS: Ghostly ships and spectral crews deriving from the legend of the Flying Dutchman had long proved a worthwhile subject for nautical Gothic. The naval writer, W. Clark Russell took his hero, Geoffrey Fenton, to sea, then had him picked up from shipwreck by none other than the Flying Dutchman under the command of Captain Vanderdecken. Fenton's contact with the sinister crew provides him with the strange history of the lost vessel since it sailed from the Netherlands in 1653. Realizing his danger or the possibility that he had drowned when he fell overboard, Fenton struggles to escape the death ship. The book has scary spots, but both the suspense and the voyage of the doomed ship are too drawn out to produce a taut nautical Gothic.

418.   Saberhagen, Fred. The Dracula Tape, The Dracula Tape Series. New York: Warner Publishing, 1975-82.

REPRINT EDITION: New York, Tor Books, 1989.
RESEARCH SOURCES: Lawler, Donald L., "The Dracula Tape Series," Survey of Modern Fantasy Literature, pp.410-417; Stewart, Alfred D., "Fred Saberhagen: Cybernetic Psychologist," Extrapolation 18

(1976): 42-51; Wilgus, Neal, "Saberhagen's New Dracula: The Vampire as Hero," Discovering Modern Horror Fiction, ed. Darrell Schweitzer, Mercer Island, WA, Starmont House, 1985, pp.92-98.

CRITICAL SYNOPSIS: First novel in the pentology consisting of Holmes, The Dracula File, An Old Friend of the Family, Thorn, and Dominion. "The contemporary reader who seeks entertainment in Gothic adventure fantasy will not be disappointed in Saberhagen's sequels to the Dracula legend." Sequel is an important term in this assessment since a full appreciation of Saberhagen's modern vampire chronicle depends upon a recollective knowledge of Stoker's classic, Dracula (1897). Stoker's vampire count is known only through the other characters' letters and journal entries in that epistolary Gothic. In a tape prepared for Minna's Harker's grandson, Saberhagen's Dracula speaks for himself so as to enlighten the reader and to refute the vile portrayal of his character and activities offered by Stoker's Dr. Van Helsing, Jonathan Harker, and Seward. Saberhagen's Count Dracula is a rehabilitated vampire whose heroic task is the vindication of vampires and vampirism from human fears and prejudices. He corrects such beliefs as the notion that vampires crave and need only human blood or that they cannot endure the rays of the sun. And he reveals at length how the account of his career in Stoker is a misrepresentation or ignorant distortion of Dracula's relationship to Minna and Lucy Westenra. Lucy, for example, did not perish from being sucked to death by the Count, but was the unwitting victim of Dr. Van Helsing's crude and superstitious science. Also, the zooanthrope, Renfield, was actually engaged on a secret campaign to rape and kill Minna. Saberhagen's premise of telling the story from the monster's point of view is not a new technique (see, for example, John Gardner's Grendel or Brian Aldiss's Frankenstein Unbound), but allowing Dracula to speak in his own defense does put a new slant on the Count's curious career. On the negative side, however, the de-Gothified and urbane vampire of Saberhagen foregoes the old power to terrify and to awe.

419. Sands, Robert Charles. The Executioner; or, The Man Who Burnt the Rev. John Rogers, Being a True, Impartial, and Most Extraordinary Account of What Happened to the Man Who Burnt the Rev. John Rogers, as related by his son, James Rogers. Philadelphia: William Beastall, 1835.

CRITICAL SYNOPSIS: A 63 page American Gothic chapbook in the lurid style of the English shilling shockers. The man is a Cain figure or an outcast like the "Wandering Jew who insulted our Divine Redeemer." As a young man, he had been fascinated by the public mutilation and execution of heretics during the persecutions of Bloody Mary Tudor (1553-1558). Fleeing from his crime aboard a ship bound for the Americas, he tells young Rogers, "I attended all executions and was very sure never to be absent when any tragic scene was to be acted at Tower Hill, or at Tyburn. I gained a fearful but intense delight." On February 14, 1554, this delight reaches its apex when he is given the opportunity of lighting the fire at the stake of the Marian martyr, the Reverend John Rogers. But his horrible appetite for the blood of the martyrs has now left him without the sanctuary of conscience in the both the old world and the new. Seeking rest and never finding it and apparently unable to die, the man who burnt the Reverend John Rogers disappears into the American wilderness, leaving behind his lurid account of unpardonable crimes with Rogers's son. A moral theme like the parable of the unpardonable sin in Hawthorne's "Ethan Brand" (see 199) might have infused the writer's purpose, but the chapbooker instead opts both throughout and at the end for the sheer horror of the executioner's deeds and doom. Sheer horror and nothing else had always been the primary aim of the English shilling shockers as well.

420. Scollard, Clinton. The Cloistering of Ursula; Chapters from the Memoirs of Andrea, Marquis of Uccelli, and Count of Castelpulchio, illus. Harry C. Edwards. Boston: L.C. Page, 1902.

CRITICAL SYNOPSIS: Scollard was an admirer of Poe and friend of the vagabond poet, Bliss Carman. His patriotic poetry and Christmas pieces were once literary fixtures in American parlors. A prolific author, he wrote several romances of Renaissance Italy where the Gothic note can be clearly heard. The convent as a place of terrible confinement and as an interruption to marital bliss is the basis for The Cloistering of Ursula. The strong and sinister anti-Catholicism of the monastic shocker, however, is played down as are the darker passions.

421. Seeley, Mabel. The Listening House. Garden City, NY: Doubleday, 1938.

CRITICAL SYNOPSIS: Reviewers gave this well-crafted Gothic very high grades. The reviewer for The Saturday Review recognized the novel's Gothicism and savored it: "The book is a bloodcurdling affair drenched with old evil, and grisly incidents. The sleuthing is able, but it's the background and people that make it hum. Especially good."

422. Seton, Anya. Green Darkness. Boston: Houghton, Mifflin, 1972.

RESEARCH SOURCES: Mussell, Kay, Women's Gothic and Romantic Fiction, Westport, CT, Greenwood Press, 1981, pp.130-131; Seton, Anya, "Writer's Requisites," The Writer 80 (August, 1967): 19.

CRITICAL SYNOPSIS: A very popular historical Gothic of sixteenth-century England. Since the publication of Dragonwyck (1944), Seton has demonstrated that women's Gothic and Romantic fiction, as Kay Mussell classifies her work, need not be dismissed as lowbrow sentimental trash. Both literary craftsmanship and deep research are obvious strengths of Green Darkness, her Gothic mystery of the times of the Tudors. The central figures of the story are the Marsdons, an Elizabethan family whose leading son, Stephen Marsdon, had died under mysterious circumstances in 1585. Marsdon had been a Benedictine monk, but seems to have had a mysterious link with a young Protestant woman, Celia de Bohun, whose disappearance coincided with his death. Their secret love had been played out against a violent backdrop of Catholic-Protestant strife during the reigns of Edward VI, Mary, and Elizabeth. Such is the family mystery that hangs over the modern day Marsdons, as the novel, following the patterns of a good historical Gothic, depicts the dark past impinging upon the bright present. In 1968, Stephen Marsdon's descendant, Richard Marsdon, inherits the mystery when he returns to Medfield place with his new wife, Celia. The Gothic atmosphere consists of vague hauntings and a sense of uneasiness about the great house. It is Celia who most keenly and terribly feels the presence of her historical namesake, Celia de Bohun. Lying in a coma induced by her fears, Celia Marsdon goes back four

centuries to relive the life of the earlier Celia and to realize
her present self through her former self. Reconciliation with a
personal and a national past brings home the point which Hawthorne
would understand in his handling of history: there is an inevitable presentness about the past which can both terrify and glorify
our natures. This is not an exclusively Gothic premise, of course,
but a Gothic context does lend forcefulness to it in this novel
and others by Anya Seton.

423. Sheed, Wilfred. The Blacking Factory and Pennsylvania Gothic; A
Short Novel and a Long Story. New York: Farrar, Straus, 1968.

CRITICAL SYNOPSIS: The passionate and poignant loneliness of both
body and soul link Pennsylvania Gothic with Anderson's Winesburg
Ohio (see O14). The Philadelphia boyhood of Charlie Trimble, his
memories of his father's suicide, and his effort to find a safe
emotional self through his odd relationship with an old woman
named Skinner are the threads of the story. "Gothic" here as elsewhere in later American examples implies mood and tone rather than
a formal set of characteristics, a mood of profound loneliness and
a tone of profound sadness that seem to underlie the coming of age
in America.

424. Shelton, Frederick William. Crystalline; or, The Heiress of Fall
Down Castle. New York: Charles Scribner, 1854.

CRITICAL SYNOPSIS: A fairytale permeated with many of the same
Gothic elements to be found in one of the earliest Gothics, Clara
Reeve's Old English Baron (1977). There are further striking resemblances to one of the Gothic chapbooks, The Recluse of the
Woods; or, The Generous Warrior, A Gothic Romance (1809), versions
of which circulated until well into the mid-century. "Gothic" in
this context refers to chivalrous and magical times, not to supernatural horror. The territory of Crystalline is the ruined Castle
of Valrosarium. At its base, living in poverty with her disgraced
father, Sir Ralph, lives Crystalline, destined by prophecy to become "the heiress of Fall Down Castle." Holy, serious, good, and
compassionate, the expectant heroine spends many hours in an
apartment of the ancient castle tower contemplating her destiny
and wondering how fortune will be made to reverse itself. Clara
Reeve's hero, Edmund Twyford, had run afoul of scheming brothers
who plotted to deny him his rightful proprietorship of Castle Lovel. Crystalline runs afoul of a scheming neighbor, Violante, who
arranges to have the heroine falsely accused and imprisoned over
the alleged theft of a ruby ring. The magic ring had come to her
by falling from a tree, the gift of the "little people," or so it
seems. But a thieving magpie, la gazza ladra of fable and folklore, had been used by Violante to enmesh Crystalline in the theft
of the ruby ring. A spectacular trial scene and the arrival of a
stranger knight resolve all of Crystalline's difficulties, expose
Violante's treachery, and restore her as heiress of Fall Down Castle which now rises miraculously to its former grandeur. This type
of simple Gothic fable with its fantastic resolution of genealogical and heriditary problems for the heroine no doubt furnished the
reader of that age with a pleasant hour's diversion.

425. Shepard, Sam. Buried Child, Seven Plays by Sam Shepard, ed. Richard
Gilman. New York: Bantam, 1981.

RESEARCH SOURCE: Blau, Herbert, "The American Dream in American

Gothic: The Plays of Sam Shepard and Adrienne Kennedy," Modern Drama 27 (1984): 520-539.

CRITICAL SYNOPSIS: From the ancient Greek tragic dramatists to Ibsen and Strindberg to O'Neill, the disintegration of the family from without and within has been depicted as Gothic melodrama. Shepard's plays continue this dark legacy and establish in the 1970's a distinct line of native American Gothic theatre. His plays, The Tooth of Crime, Curse of the Starving Class, Action, and the Pulitizer Prize winning Buried Child are anti-visionary in the fundamental sense because they penetrate behind "the loose and elusive features of the American dream....The dream so fractured, however, that it looks surreal or Gothic, like a stained glass window in a suburban tract where Edgar Allan Poe still lives." Profound family disharmony, neurotic breakdown, the substitution of violence for love, and the concealed crimes of incest and infanticide render Buried Child one of the darkest of Shepard's Gothic spectacles. Dramatic action is totally confined to one room of the farmstead where the young people, Shelly and Vince, have returned to confront their elders and the family's crime-stained past. The elders are Grandfather Dodge and Grandmother Halie, prisoners of an intolerable present and an even more intolerable set of memories. The sons of the house, the wooden-legged Bradley and the pathetic Tilden refuse even to maintain the lie of a family. All of these characters are true American grotesques motivated solely by mutual hatred and memories of a murdered baby, the child of incest. Episodes and stage devices are also strongly Gothic. There is the mouldering picture upstairs which looks like Grandfather Dodge but which he rejects as an image of himself. There is Bradley's brutal clipping or scalping of his sleeping grandfather. Most prominently in the concluding scene there is the mud-clotted Tilden returned from the unmarked grave in the cornfield with the rotted remains of the buried child in his arms. In its hideous exposure of the reverse side of the American dream, no play of the seventies makes such conspicuous use of the Gothic as Buried Child.

426. The Sicilian Pirate; or, The Pillar of Mystery, A Terrific Romance. New York: E. Duyckinck, 1815.

CRITICAL SYNOPSIS: In both chapbook and lengthier form, the outlaw romance or robber romance incorporated many Gothic features. While the publishing brothers, Evert Augustus and George Duyckinck, were helping to give American literature a national identity of its own, they also frequently reissued Gothic imports or followed the Gothic trends. The Sicilian Pirate is a derivative romance taken from such sources as Francis Lathom's The Mysterious Freebooter (1806) and Edward Montague's The Demon of Sicily (1807). The American participation in the Tripolitan or Barbary Wars (1801-05) created a native interest and market for outlaw Gothics of this type.

427. Siddons, Anne Rivers. The House Next Door. New York: Simon and Schuster, 1978.

REPRINT EDITION: New York, Ballantine, 1982.
RESEARCH SOURCES: Burgess, Anthony, "'Boo,'" New York Times Book Review February 11, 1973, pp.2, 24, 26; Mussell, Kay J., "'But Why Do They Read Those Things?': The Female Audience and the Gothic Novel," The Female Gothic, ed. Juliann E. Fleenor, Montreal, Cana-

da, Eden Press, 1983, pp.57-68; Pace, Eric, "Gothic Novels Prove Bonanza for Publishers," New York Times June 18, 1973, pp.31-34.

CRITICAL SYNOPSIS: Popular, clever Gothic, but unlike so many of these garden club Gothics, written with great intellectual skill and full of characters who function as individuals without escaping their yuppie stereotypes. The publisher's dust jacket reads like an inventory for a successful and saleable suburban horror story: "The house next door to Colquit and Walter Kennedy is haunted by an all-pervasive evil, an evil that takes away whatever the occupants hold dearest. Colquit and Walter are about to become witnesses to an overwhelming force that will strip away the veneer of civilization that surrounds and protects them." Everyone who lives in this stylish piece of modern architecture is subsequently destroyed by the model home. The Harralsons, the Greenes, the Sheehans, indeed, every modern suburbanite couple undergoes the same fate from "an all-engulfing force they cannot comprehend." It falls to the Kennedys to warn the real estate world that though it may look like the suburban showplace, the house next door is secretly a wall-to-wall Gothic horror. The final sentence in the novel comes from the lips of another prospective buyer and hits upon the malignant sentience of Gothic buildings, a sentiment which goes back to the beginnings of the genre and to the maiden's rapt gaze upon the facade of gloomy castle. The girl buyer: "Isn't it super? Just look at it. It looks like it's growing right up out the ground, doesn't it?" Her nervous husband: "It looks like it's alive." It is.

428. Simms, William Gilmore. Carl Werner, An Imaginative Story; With Other Tales of Imagination. New York: George Adlard, 1828.

RESEARCH SOURCES: Ringe, Donald, American Gothic, pp.7-8; Ridgely, J.V., William Gilmore Simms, New York, Twayne, 1962.

CRITICAL SYNOPSIS: All of varieties of Gothic find a significant place in the historical romances of William Gilmore Simms. In his criminal heroes and sensational tales of blood, "he relied upon the Gothicizers and upon Godwin and Bulwer for instruction in the literary probing of secret guilt." According to J.V. Ridgely, "These rogues betray far more relationship to the traditional Gothic villain than to the poor-whites or criminals of the South Simms knew." Driven by egotism Carl Werner conspires to discover what lies beyond the curtain of death by making a pact with a dying friend to communicate with him from the other side. The cadaverous messenger returns, but turns out to be a deceiving demon in the guise of the dead friend. In this early tale and elsewhere, Simms would frequently permit an element of the authentic supernatural to darken his romances. An attempt to commune with the dead is also Poe's subject in "The Facts in the Case of M. Valdemar" (see 388).

429. _____. Martin Faber, The Story of a Criminal and Other Tales. New York: Harper, 1837.

REPRINT EDITION: Salem, NH, Ayer, 1975.
RESEARCH SOURCES: Deen, Floyd H., "The Genesis of Martin Faber in Caleb Williams," Modern Language Notes 59 (1944): 315-317; Ringe, Donald, American Gothic, pp.126-127.

CRITICAL SYNOPSIS: Often compared to William Godwin's Caleb Wil-

liams; or, Things As They Are (1794), the Gothic elements of the
story also have curious parallels in several of Hawthorne's tales,
most notably "Roger Malvin's Burial" (see 195), with its powerful
Gothic motif of the unburied corpse deep in the wilderness. Driven
by sexual passion, Faber has committed an awful crime, then concealed the murdered body of the woman he seduced, Emily Andrews,
in the depths of the forest within a large rocky cleft. Almost in
the manner of a Dostoyevskian criminal, Faber has a psychological
need to confess his crime to a virtuous individual and to lead
that individual to the corpus delicti. To these ends, he confesses
in general terms to his friend, William Harding, thus burdening
the conscientious Harding with the terrible knowledge of Faber's
homicidal secret. The strange relationship of Harding and Faber
forms the core of the Gothic psychodrama. Determining to learn the
name of the victim and the place of her impromptu interment, Harding pursues the guilty Faber, even painting a series of pictures
showing Faber's crime and punishment in lurid detail. The dénouement is highly Gothic in Simms's reuse of the moment of horrid
revelation. Harding arranges to explode the boulder concealing Emily's corpse; the explosion reveals a female skeleton still passionately clutching a cameo of Martin Faber. If the Gothic novel, as E.F. Bleiler has suggested, is "a primitive detective
story," then Simms's Martin Faber is a masterful American example
of crime, detection, and punishment.

430.   . Castle Dismal; or, The Bachelor's Christmas. New York:
Burgess, Stringer, 1844.

RESEARCH SOURCE: Guilds, John C., "The Achievement of William Gilmore Simms: His Short Fiction," Spectrum 2 number 2 (1972): 25-
36.

CRITICAL SYNOPSIS: Although considered an historical novelist of
the antebellum south, Simms often used Gothic scenery and techniques to enliven his historical romances. Occasionally, as in
Castle Dismal, he worked in a purely Gothic vein. Castle Dismal is
the ancient seat of the Ashleys situated somewhere in the Carolina
woods. The narrator, Ned Clifton, proposes a sojourn with his
childhood companions, the Ashleys, heirs to the Castle and its
multitude of rooms. Clifton is a hard-headed and skeptical young
man who publicly scorns all superstition and supernatural lore.
His whole attitude toward things Gothic resembles the feelings of
the rationalist narrator of Poe's "Fall of the House of Usher."
(see 379) The young skeptic is a familiar Gothic character type
and his rude conversion to a belief in the malign supernatural is
a common Gothic plot pattern. After voicing his views on haunted
chambers and houses, Clifton is asked by his hosts to spend one
evening in Castle Dismal's forbidden chamber. Those who have had
their doubts tested by an evening's occupancy have reported
strange visions and other unexplained sights and sounds. Clifton's
chamber vigil brings him a horrid vision of double murder in some
sort of lover's quarrel. A felled tree crushes one of the love rivals and the mysterious woman is drowned by the enraged lover. The
tale ends with the revelation of the murderer to young Clifton
when he meets through the Ashleys a local methodist clergyman. Now
an old man, the minister makes a pulpit confession of his deed
adding that he has somehow been a prisoner of Castle Dismal's forbidden chamber for most of his guilty days. The situation of trial
by terror within an awful chamber goes back to the beginnings of
the Gothic in Clara Reeve's Old English Baron (1777), but Simms's

restoration of it is skillful and suspenseful.

431. _____. Count Julian; or, The Last Days of the Goth. Baltimore: William Taylor, 1845.

RESEARCH SOURCE: Thomas, J. Wesley, "The German Sources of William Gilmore Simms," Anglo-German and American-German Crosscurrents 1 (1957): 127-153.

CRITICAL SYNOPSIS: A Gothified historical romance of medieval Spain done in imitation of Sir Walter Scott and intended to compete with James Fenimore Cooper's European romances such as The Heidenmauer (see 099).

432. _____. "Grayling; or, Murder Will Out." The Wigwam and the Cabin. New York: Wiley & Putnam, 1845.

REPRINT EDITION: New York, AMS Press, 1970.
RESEARCH SOURCE: Wimsatt, Mary Ann, "Simms's Early Short Stories," Library Chronicle 41 (1977): 163-179.

CRITICAL SYNOPSIS: Gothic tales involving the opposition of a rationalist who doubts the reality of the supernatural and another character for whom the supernatural is real and immediate is the theme of "Grayling." The narrator opens his story with a disclaimer against rational skeptics who rule out the existence of the supernatural in their "monstrous matter-of-fact" cold reasoning or reliance on the "cold-blooded demon called Science." The tale has come to the narrator by way of his grandmother although his father, the rational skeptic, discounts every word of it. Ultimately, the narrator sides with the old lady against his father in accepting the supernatural nature of the tale's events. The story tells of a traveller, Major Lionel Spencer, who was robbed and murdered by one Sandy Macnab. The ghost of the murdered Major appears to his friend, James Grayling, naming the killer and demanding justice. Although the father regards the legend of the ghost as preposterous, the narrator defends the reality of the supernatural because any natural explanation of these events is even more incredible. This story was much admired by Poe who introduced the theme of reason humiliated in his own traveler's tale, "The Fall of the House of Usher" (see 379).

433. _____. Matilda; or, The Spectre of the Castle, An Imaginative Story. Boston: F. Gleason, 1846.

RESEARCH SOURCE: Morris, J. Allen, "The Stories of William Gilmore Simms," American Literature 14 (1942): 20-35.

CRITICAL SYNOPSIS: Simms's Gothicism is normally quite subdued and subordinate to his serious historical themes. But in the case of the fifty-eight page paperbacked Matilda, we have a genuine horrid supernatural shocker obviously made for the nickel and dime novel clientele. This American Gothic chapbook opens with the narrator traveling in Germany and discoursing on the reality of ghosts as he prepares to tell his tale "founded upon a passage from an ancient monkish legend." Love from beyond the grave is the narrator's theme, but his real purpose is to station the three characters in the path of spectacular supernatural effects. One of these characters is the sensitive criminal, Carl Werner (see 428), transplanted to the dime novel after an earlier appearance in

Simms's work. He loves Matilda Ottfried, but she, it seems, is more attracted to her brother, Herman. Although Matilda marries Carl, possibly to stave off her incestuous fancies, she pledges to her brother when they part at the abbey that "we will come together in death." Just as the incestuous vow is uttered, "a hollow laugh resounded from the dismembered vault of the aged abbot," one of numerous Gothic acoustics and an infernal laugh that will be heard later. When news of Herman's death comes from Amsterdam, Carl Werner volunteers to maintain a spectre vigil within the cathedral having heard a supernatural voice outside his window declare "Carl Werner--I command thee. Come!" One must not look too closely into the motives of the hero in helping to unite his own wife with his brother's ghost in one lovely, deadly embrace, but such is Carl's nocturnal task. The reader of the dime Gothic wanted bizarre and thrilling audio-visual effects, not a sensible plot. Thus, the spectre vigils furnished the audience with moments of pure Gothic thrill of this sort. During one of his vigils, "He looked up with a shudder. A small blue light crawled along upon the opposite wall, like some slimy reptile, and while Carl watched its progress with solemn interest the laugh was repeated almost beside him. A breath of ice seemed to penetrate him from the east. He turned his eyes in that quarter, and the spectacle that then met his gaze paralyzed every faculty of his body. The former Herman Ottfried was there, sitting beside him on the other end of the gravestone. His eyes were riveted upon the spectre, and the glare which was sent back from those of the earthly visitant, was that of hell." Thus, the horror picture shimmers luridly before the supposedly enrapt reader, giving him his moment of dreadful pleasure.

434. Sister Agnes; or, The Captive Nun. A Picture of Convent Life. New York: Riker, Thorne, 1854.

CRITICAL SYNOPSIS: This anti-Catholic narrative appears to be the immediate source for Josephine Bunkley's The Escaped Nun; or, Disclosures of Convent Life (see 070), published in 1855. All of these American monastic shockers derive their content from Maria Monk's sensational account, Awful Disclosures (see 339). The captive nun, Sister Agnes, is really the Protestant girl, Mary Percy, a victim of Jesuit cunning and deceitfulness. Her chief victimizer is Padre Carlo, a man who has seen his own sister Agatha ruined by the church and the enforced monastic life which have left her "pale, desolate, and dying." Yet, the fascination of the cloistered life and its ornate ritual is strong on Mary Percy, especially as it is exerted through her sly governess, Mademoiselle Dupin, who is in the pay of the Jesuits. Taken to Ireland and forced to enter a convent under the name of Sister Agnes, she soon learns the "real horrors" of the cloister. "The serpent, Rome, fascinates before she destroys her prey." Rebelling against her captivity, she is taken to Rome, accused of heresy, tortured, and declared "mentally ill." Instead of the expected escape from the horrors of Catholicism, the captive nun is murdered by her monastic masters and in monstrous fashion. The novel closes with a warning to "Protestant females ever to beware of Popish aggression." The dismal horror of this explosive ending was a departure from the usual emancipation of the endangered heroine of the monastic shocker and her return to the true sanctity of Protestantism.

435. Smith, Clark Ashton. "The Devotee of Evil." The Abominations of Yon-

do. Sauk City, WI: Arkham House, 1942.

REPRINT EDITION: London, Neville Spearman, 1972.

CRITICAL SYNOPSIS: A malignant machine overpowering its inventor or operator becomes the basis for horrible retribution. The Faustian main character, Jean Armand, succeeds in building a time machine which projects a future universe of pure evil. Armand is punished for his overreaching when his machine leaves him stranded forever in the dimension of utter wickedness.

436. _____ . "The Second Interment." Out of Space and Time. Sauk City WI: Arkham House, 1942.

REPRINT EDITION: London, Neville Spearman, 1971.

CRITICAL SYNOPSIS: First printed in Weird Tales, 1932. A fantasy of premature burial done in imitation of Poe's tale, "The Premature Burial."

437. _____ . "Epiphany of Death." The Abominations of Yondo. Sauk City, WI: Arkham House, 1960.

REPRINT EDITION: London, Neville Spearman, 1972.
RESEARCH SOURCE: Behrends, Steve, "The Song of the Necromancer: 'Loss' in Clark Ashton Smith's Fiction," Studies in Weird Fiction 1 (1986): 3-12.

CRITICAL SYNOPSIS: Flashes of genuine brilliance alternate with the somewhat hackneyed pseudo-Lovecraftian style of this pulp writer. Smith's fantasies deal with lost worlds, those worlds usually overrun with Gothic decay. The weird subterranean story, "Epiphany of Death" (Weird Tales, 1942) is typical of his craft and seems to impart the atmosphere of Poe's vault in the ornate manner of Lovecraft's Cthulhu tales. Making a voyage into the remotest vaults, Tomeron promises his friend Theolus an amazing disclosure during their journey. The revelation involves the reanimation of a corpse by way of Tomeron's metempsychotic powers.

438. _____ . "The Ghoul." Other Dimensions. Sauk City, WI: Arkham House, 1970.

REPRINT EDITION: London, Panther Books, 1977.

CRITICAL SYNOPSIS: Orientalized Gothic fantasy done as a sequel to the episodes of Beckford's Vathek (1786). To protect the corpse of his beloved Armina from being devoured by the ghoul, Noureddin is forced to make a pact whereby he will deliver eight meals of flesh to the creature.

439. _____ . "The Supernumerary Corpse." Other Dimensions. Sauk City, WI: Arkham House, 1970.

REPRINT EDITION: London, Panther Books, 1977.

CRITICAL SYNOPSIS: A domestic Gothic bauble illustrative of Smith's macabre irony. The narrator has done in Trilt, and assumes like one of Poe's murderers, that he is rid of Trilt forever. But Trilt's wife informs him of Trilt's simultaneous death of natural causes at home, where the body lies. Hence, the narrator is embarrassed by the inconvenient presence of two corpses, Trilt's home body and the supernumerary corpse of the Trilt he thinks he has killed. Twin cadavers perhaps adds to the lurid list of Gothic effects.

440. Snow, Jack. Dark Music and Other Spectral Tales. New York: Herald Publishing, 1947.

CRITICAL SYNOPSIS: Snow's method of electrifying the reader is to derive probable terrors from improbable premises. "Dark Music," the first story in this collection of Gothic fantasy, has the ugly hermit, Old Aaron, implant musical devices in the throats of his private flock of bats, thus creating his symphony of "dark music." Two other tales are directly indebted to the Gothic tradition, "Night Wings" and "The Dimension of Terror." "Night Wings" features a tower death when its Icarian hero attempts a midnight flight. "The Dimension of Terror" looks ahead to the "gross out" effects in Stephen King when a new island rises from the sea and populates itself with slimy carnivorous organisms.

441. Southworth, Emma Dorothy Eliza Nevitte . Retribution; or, The Vale of Shadows, A Tale of Passion. New York: Harper, 1849.

REPRINT EDITION: New York, AMS Press, 1978.
RESEARCH SOURCE: Boyle, Regis L., Mrs. Eden Southworth, Novelist. Washington, DC, Catholic University of America Press, 1939.

CRITICAL SYNOPSIS: Complex plotting joined to a simple moral characterize this tea table romance. "I have tried," Mrs. Southworth announced, "to show you how from the sin, domestic infidelity and treachery, spring inevitably the punishment, domestic distrust and wretchedness." The sixteen year old orphan, Hester Gray, is heiress to a great Virginian estate. She is plain, delicate in health, and without friends except for the beautiful and ambitious Juliette Summers, another orphan who is Hester's opposite in every way and somewhat sinister as indicated by "the mesmeric spell in her beautiful eyes." Juliette and Hester both fall in love with General Ernest Dent, a handsome but deceitful if not downright cunning man. The odd death of Hester Gray after a two year marriage to General Dent and the subsequent marriage of Juliette Summers to Dent now thickens the plot as action shifts to Italy where Dent has political connections. Juliette tires of Dent, lives extravagantly, and relieves her boredom through several affairs, one of these with Ipolyto di Nozzalina. She has him murdered in order to vent her passions with the Grand Duke, Augustus William. Juliette's degradation comes to an end when she is executed for her scandalous and homicidal crimes by the German confederacy. Back in Virginia, General Dent, like many of Southworth's bad men gone good, disperses his wealth, liberates the slaves owned by Hester Gray's family, and grows exceedingly fond of little Julie, his daughter by Hester Gray. Somewhat like Hawthorne's Pearl in The Scarlet Letter (see 197), Julie Dent is the child of a father's secret sin, but she shines with every moral virtue when she emancipates the last of the Gray household slaves and moves on to a purer west with her recovered father. Various scenes and character relationships bear the mark of a writer well versed in Gothic plotting and detailing. A few scenes such as Juliette Summers's prayer to Satan to endow her with the power to receive love but never to give love are thoroughly Gothic in tone and manner.

442. _____. The Curse of Clifton. A Tale of Expiation and Redemption. Philadelphia: A. Hart, 1853.

REPRINT EDITION: New York, AMS Press, 1974.
RESEARCH SOURCE: Papashvily, Helen W., All the Happy Endings, New York, Harper, 1956.

CRITICAL SYNOPSIS: A lengthy and leisurely genteel romance with occasional Gothic moods and moments. In an 1855 letter to his publisher, Nathaniel Hawthorne decried the quill-driving sentimentalism of Mrs. Southworth and other lady novelists as "a damned mob of scribbling women. Worse they could not be, and better they need not be, when they sell by the 100,000." Before her death in 1899, Mrs. Southworth had churned out more than sixty novels, some of these excelling Hawthorne's figure of 100,000 by huge sales totalling in the millions of copies. The Curse of Clifton is a sterling example of such objectionable and obnoxious fiction. With its romantic setting of the Alleghenies and Richmond, Virginia, during the 1812 War, its flowery and sentimental dialogue, and its melodramatic conflict of heroic good and melodramatic evil, this novel became an instant best-seller. The plot follows the amorous adversities and domestic trials of Captain Archer Clifton and Lieutenant Francis Fairfax, two war heroes who return to even more bitter battles at home in their troubled courtships. Captain Clifton becomes involved with and later married to the haughty and headstrong Miss Carolyn Gower and this marriage becomes his domestic bane, the curse of Clifton. His friend, Francis Fairfax runs into equivalent marital difficulties in his pursuit of Carolyn's capricious cousin, Zuleime. One character in this domestic novel, the ferocious and complotting Mrs. Clifton of Hardbargain Farm, possesses the Gothic qualifications of the conspiring dowager or vile parent. Her presence on the scene usually calls forth a Gothic description from Mrs. Southworth such as in this early encounter between Captain Clifton and his aunt: "Well--Oh very well would it have been for Archer Clifton could he have rent his gaze from his magnetic idol a moment, and caught a certain pair of evil eyes upon him. Their baleful glare might have shed upon his path some light to see the pitfalls in his way." The style here and elsewhere throughout the book suggests the motives for Hawthorne's ire.

443. _____. Miriam the Avenger; or, The Missing Bride. Philadelphia: T.B. Peterson, 1855.

CRITICAL SYNOPSIS: A lengthy (635 page) sentimental romance with a few Gothic shadows to entice the reader. The novel opens with what sounds like a typical Gothic signature: "Deep in the primeval forest of St. Mary's, lying between the Patuxent and Wicomico Rivers, stands the ancient manor house of Luckenough." Here, Commodore Nikolas Waugh lives with his ward, Miss Edith Lance. Having served honorably in the War of 1812, he has retired to this natural setting to enjoy nature and to raise his ward amidst the Chesapeake scenery. But their plans for a tranquil life are upset by the marauding Captain Thorg, a renegade soldier who burns Luckenough and seems to abduct Edith Lance, carrying her off into the wilderness. Some thirty-two chapters into the novel, Edith will come back into the plot as Miriam the avenger. She has matured into a dark beauty of the Ligeia type with "large liquid eyes, dark, fathomless, and splendid as Syrian midnight skies." No ordinary male, and certainly not Captain Thorg, can repel her almost supernatural charms. The Gothic action is reduced to a few scary moments at the gloomy mansion of Dell Delight and several nightmare scenes such as that in chapter 18, "The Apparition in the Dormitory." Although the plot is meandering and confusing, Mrs. Southworth never forgets to moralize on schedule. At intervals throughout the sufferings of Edith and the vengeance of Miriam, the reader is sternly warned, "After a stormy passage in life comes a long calm, preceding perhaps another storm." None of Mrs. Southworth's legion of readers could argue with this glittering truism.

444.   . The Haunted Homestead and Other Nouvellettes. Philadelphia: T.B. Peterson, 1861.

RESEARCH SOURCE: Mussell, Kay, Women's Gothic and Romantic Fiction, Westport, CT, Greenwood Press, 1981, pp.87-88.

CRITICAL SYNOPSIS: The 65 page novella could well be the prototype for a juvenile Gothic mystery of the Nancy Drew variety. Two other novellas in the collection, The Presentiment and The Spectre Revels, are also viable examples of "schoolgirl Gothic." The friends, Mathilde Legare and Agnes____, fellow students at Newton Academy, spend a Christmas holiday together at the Legare homestead of Wolfbrake, a small estate recently purchased by the Legares in the Alleghenies. Mathilde informs her friend that Wolfbrake is said to be haunted and that a female spectral figure roams the unoccupied wing where Agnes's guest bedroom is (naturally). No wonder then that Agnes should dream of a bedside visitation by a ghostly woman and that the door to the bedchamber should be open when she awakens. When she reports her Gothic experience to Mathilde, her friend obliges with a recitation of the tragic history of Madeline Van der Vaughan, deceased mistress of Wolfbrake and reputed still to roam its corridors. Thus we get that venerable requirement of the Radcliffean romance, the inset tale, cast in the form of a Christmas ghost story. The spectre's anguish must have been the cause of the pool of blood which Agnes thought she saw at the foot of the bed. At this point, Agnes's brother, John, and Mathilde's future husband, Mr. Frank Howard of Boston, a mathematical instrument maker, enter the plot to lay the Wolfbrake ghost to rest. Using masculine logic, they will spend the night in the haunted bedchamber to disprove the existence of any ghost. Sure enough, Mr. Howard quickly discovers that the door opened spontaneously because it was activated by "a mechanical phenomenon known as 'Harmon's Patent,' himself a demented machinist." The spectre at the bedside was an optical illusion produced by moonlight, undulating tree branches and curtains, and all stimulated by Agnes's overwrought imagination and Mathilde's tales of spooks. Chagrined by their foolishness, the girls renounce their Gothic ways and grow up, exactly as Mrs. Radcliffe's naive maidens had done upon discovering that all of the horrid mysteries of the castle had been self-induced.

445.   . The Mystery of the Dark Hollow. Philadelphia: T.B. Peterson, 1875.

CRITICAL SYNOPSIS: Domestic Gothic tale with features of the novel of seduction and maidenly peril. At the foot of Bald Mountain in West Virginia stands Milburn House with its adjacent dark hollow. The beautiful tenant of Milburn House is Blanche Milburn, a sensitive, delicate young woman and fitting prey for the cad of the story, the cold-hearted and opportunistic Victor Forestal. Victor's father, Colonel Forestal, holds Blanche's father "under the lion's paw," since he is deeply in debt to the Colonel who threatens foreclosure and uses his son, Victor, as a sort of agent to drive home his economic power. Victor enjoys his mission thoroughly and enjoys mischief in general. His smooth hypocrisy is in contrast to the good miner, John Watt, the virtuous man of the story. Victor arranges to have Blanche's maidservant, Rose Moss, carried off to the dark hollow, a gloomy cleft of rocky terrain, where he holds the girl for ransom. The plight of Rose brings Blanche to the dark hollow, thus fulfilling Victor's seductive goal. Spurning his demand that she become his mistress, Blanche along with Rose is conveyed to the iniquitous city of New York, where Rose, now mad, is exhibited on stage by Victor as "Wild Zoe." With their fortunes at this low ebb, Mrs. Southworth brings on the hero, the rough miner, John Watt. The entire cast reassembles at Milburn House for resolution and retribution. Watt is not a poor man after all but actually the Earl of Auslyn. He now uses his money and his position to counter the villainy of the Forestals, especially the scheming Victor, who obliges the plot by taking his own life when he learns that all the Forestal money has vanished in the gold panic of 1837. This is a complexly plotted ultra-sentimental romance of money and power wherein decency triumphs at last. Mrs. Southworth gave her reader an uncomplicated exercise of poetic justice and embellished it all with creepy descriptions of the dark hollow which is roughly equivalent to the cavern or cave attached to the castle of so many maiden-centered English Gothics.

446. _____. "The Spectre Lover." The Spectre Lover, and Other Tales. Philadelphia: T.B. Peterson, 1875.

CRITICAL SYNOPSIS: Most of the tales in the collection, which also has several stories by her sister, Mrs. Frances Henshaw Baden, show strong traces of Gothicism. Four in particular, "A Spirit Bride," "The Bosom Serpent," "A Modern Bluebeard," and Mrs. Baden's "Horrid Discovery" are models of E.D.E.N. Southworth's imaginative Gothic talents. The narrator of "The Spectre Lover," Anna Mendelsone, is skeptical of the real supernatural even though the experiences she relates vibrate with "supernatural episodes." Susceptible throughout her life to spectral encounters, she sees the ghost of a seventeenth century cavalier and looks up from her bed to stare into the face of the deceased Mrs. Eastup. "I saw bending over me the form of a little, thin, pale old woman, wrapped from head to foot in a white sheet." These supernatural meetings precede the main action of the tale, her macabre love affair with a diabolical little lad, Henry Smith. She knows him first as a boy and then years later in her lonely retirement cottage on the banks of the Hudson when she is visited by a cavalry officer, Colonel Hartleap, her spectre lover. When Anna introduces the Colonel to her niece, the niece cannot see the man since this "stupendous transfiguration" had been killed in the Civil War. The tale closes with Anna Mendelsone still doubting the supernatural experiences of her entire lifetime. The narrator is an especially interesting case for Gothic short fiction because normally a non-believer is wrenched into a horror-struck acceptance of the supernatural world, but here the pattern is violated.

447. _____. The Hidden Hand; or, Capitola, The Madcap. New York: G.W. Dillingham, 1888.

CRITICAL SYNOPSIS: Sentimental Gothic elements imbue the more than sixty romance novels of Mrs. E.D.E.N. Southworth, perhaps the most durably popular woman's novelist of the 1890's in America. Not strictly speaking a high Gothic romancer, Mrs. Southworth never hesitated to reformulate the timeworn devices of Radcliffean romance. Lachrymose reunions preceded by dire difficulties for parentless heroines, sudden swerves of fortune for pitiful female orphans, and "heaven-sent catastrophes, paired off with equally heaven-sent deliverances," were mingled with Gothic gadgets and places to yield a type of success novel geared to the tastes of her largely feminine readership. Her first novel is typical in every way of her modus operandi. The house in the story to which the orphaned twelve year old Capitola finally returns as the ward of Major Warfield, there to grow up both beautiful and nubile, is called Hurricane Hall. Hard to reach and vaguely situated somewhere in the mountains of Virginia, the seat of the Warfields has the Gothic look in every respect. Naturally, the house and its arrogant and moody master harbor a secret relating somehow to Capitola's birth and identity. Events come to a head on Halloween when Major Warfield's cruel past comes knocking at the gates of the Hall. The Reverend Goodwin arrives bearing the dying deposition of the old midwife, Nancy Grewall. Twelve years earlier, she had assisted a black shrouded woman in a twin birth, a stillborn boy and a healthy girl. But the world was told that only one child had been born of the mysterious mother, and that child the desolate Capitola. Moved at last by the crimes of his past and the desertion of his daughter, the Major alters his character from diabolic to angelic, locates the hapless Capitola selling newspapers on the streets of New York, and brings her home to Hurricane Hall and happiness. By reworking this basic story, Mrs. EDEN Southworth turned out numerous highly salesworthy Gothifications of the Horatio Alger success story.

448. Spofford, Harriet Prescott. Sir Rohan's Ghost. A Romance. Boston: J. E. Tilton, 1860.

RESEARCH SOURCE: Halbeisen, Elizabeth K., "Sir Rohan's Ghost and Azarian," Harriet Prescott Spofford: A Romantic Survival, Philadelphia, Pennsylvania UP, 1935, pp.65-75.

CRITICAL SYNOPSIS: Concerning the Gothic content of this anonymously published novel of the supernatural, Elizabeth Halbeisen remarks that "Hawthorne, if one can picture it, collides with Poe, Monk Lewis and Mrs. Radcliffe....The romantic subject matter-- ghosts in a world of emotion, weird lights, a haunted manor, gypsies, and the inner story--are treated ideally." The story is a delicate mixture of moral guilt and brooding terror not unlike the Gothic shading of one of her mentors in the art of moralized Gothic, Nathaniel Hawthorne. The ghost who victimizes Sir Rohan is both a real Gothic phantom and the symbol of his own betrayed conscience; it is the phantom of sinful memory not to be denied and always on hand to remind him of a terrible crime concealed. His crime, like that of Dimmesdale in The Scarlet Letter (see 197), involves sexual incontinence and concealment. Each time Sir Rohan attempts to settle into some kind of happiness, the ghost intervenes to ruin his bliss. After retiring to his manor in Cornwall, Sir Rohan is visited by an old friend, St. Denys, who brings with him his beautiful ward, Miriam. When Sir Rohan and Miriam fall in love, the stage is set for Gothic justice. Miriam is the child of his original sin for which the ghost has long pursued him. If he persists in his love for Miriam--and he cannot help doing so--then the punishment of incest awaits him. Entrapped within this moral labyrinth, Sir Rohan's soul and self waste slowly away until "Sir Rohan was dead of his ghost." Spofford's tale confirms a fact of the American Gothic stated so tersely by her fellow New Englander, Emily Dickinson, "One need not be a chamber to be haunted."

449.   . "The Amber Gods." The Amber Gods and Other Stories. Boston: Ticknor and Fields, 1863.

REPRINT EDITION: American Voices, American Women, eds. Lee R. Edwards, Arlyn Diamond, New York, Avon Books, 1973.
RESEARCH SOURCE: St. Armand, Barton Levi, "'I Must Have Died at Ten Minutes Past One': Posthumous Reverie in Harriet Prescott Spofford's 'The Amber Gods,'" The Haunted Dusk: American Supernatural Fiction, 1820-1920, eds. Howard Kerr, John W. Crowley, Charles L. Crow, Athens, GA, Georgia UP, 1983, pp.101-119.

CRITICAL SYNOPSIS: The Romantic Gothic tales of Harriet Prescott Spofford have affinities with the frenzied monologues of Poe and the self-absorbed sinners of Hawthorne. The heroine of "The Amber Gods" is Giorgione Willoughby (called "Yone"), an inversion of the dark lady of the Gothic, a sort of blond Ligeia. Perverse, vainglorious, blasphemous, she is a type of malign spirit who serves the strange gods symbolized by the beads of an amber necklace, a sort of Satan's rosary. According to Barton Levi St. Armand, "Since Yone herself is an emblem of life without consequence, her own hollow being is absorbed into the vacant space where the true lover's knot should be. The amber gods are a potent charm, and Yone is the amber witch who conspires with them to draw a magic circle around her cousin, depriving Lu of the man they both love, Vaughan Rose." Bizarre, sensational, and cryptic in its macabre depiction of the fatal lady as a Venusian figure, "The Amber Gods" is a connecting link between the physical Gothicism of Poe and the cerebral Gothicism of Henry James. Going beyond the extrinsic Gothicism of "Ligeia," Spofford's story "startled the American public into a confrontation with, if not a tolerance for, the erotic nature of woman. Even the skeptical Henry James could not help falling briefly under Giorgione Willoughby's Gothic spell."

450. Spring, Samuel. The Monk's Revenge; or, The Secret Enemy, A Tale of the Later Crusades. New York: Williams Brothers, 1847.

CRITICAL SYNOPSIS: Typical dime novel Gothic printed in double columns and obviously derivative in its character names, incidents, and supernatural contrivances. The monk who is not a monk but a noble personage in disguise had long been a favorite situation with the English Gothic writers. Supernatural incident and hideous detail to embellish the career of Father Rinaldo could be obtained from the countless piracies of Lewis's Monk (1795).

451. St. Clair, Henry. "The Cavern of Death." Tales of Terror; or, The Mysteries of Magic. A Selection of Wonderful and Supernatural Stories, Translated from the Chinese, Turkish, and German. Boston: Charles Gaylord, 1833.

CRITICAL SYNOPSIS: There are eighteen tales in this Gothic sampler including Austin's "Peter Rugg, the Missing Man" (see 021). Several of the other pieces are outstanding reproductions of English Gothic trends and themes especially as found in the chapbooks. These include a bestial transformation story, "The Boar Wolf," a castle-and-grotto Gothic, "The Cavern of Death," a Gothic sound effects piece, "The Mysterious Bell," a native American tale of terror, "The Haunted Forest," and a monastic shocker, "The Wreckers of St. Agnes." "The Cavern of Death" is an orthodox Gothic shocker done in the shrill key of the German horror romance or Schauerroman in which the ugly and outrageous supernatural is the order of the day. It begins with Sir Albert "traversing the most desolate part of the Black Forest" on his way to the Castle of Dornheim and also on his way to identity and inheritance. Holding sway over the Castle and also holding sway over the lovely Lady Constance is Lord Frederick of Hertzwald, a villain's villain. Beneath the Castle is that familiar Gothic environment, the cavern of doom and destiny, holding many secrets and just as many cadaverous surprises. Yet, it must be penetrated by the hero if he would recover both the endangered maiden and the truth about himself. As hell-fire wreathes the mouth of the cavern, the voice of the murdered baron Roldolph of Dornheim is heard through "a cataract of blood" telling Albert that he is his father and further instructing him to enter the cavern to bury his bones, then overthrow Frederick and marry Constance. Thus, Albert descends where a thousand Gothic heroes have gone before him into the subterranean darkness. Justice upon the usurping Frederick is served up at a banquet where a supernatural guest assists Albert in the exposure and removal of the villain. The gigantic phantom at the feast takes us back to both the first Gothic, Walpole's Castle of Otranto (1764) and to Banquo's appearance at the table of Macbeth after his murder. "Mirth sparkled in the eyes of every guest, and the light of innumerable torches diffused an artificial day, when suddenly their brightness was eclipsed by the interposition of a dark shadow which skimmed along the table and sometimes seemed to rest hovering over the centre of it. Sir Albert and all the guests looked up, and beheld a most hideous spectre, of a gigantic size, traversing the air above their heads with a slow and melancholy flight. The Castle shook from its foundations: the spectre waved his wings, and immediately a thick mist arose, which in a few moments enveloped all who were present." This kind of supernatural cataclysm that had excited English Gothic audiences for so long could still produce a similar jolt on American Gothic readers long after the English Gothic mania had subsided.

452. Steadman, Mark. Mc Afee County: A Chronicle. New York: Holt, Rinehart, Winston, 1970.

REPRINT EDITION: 3 by 3 : Masterworks of the Southern Gothic, ed. Lewis P. Simpson, Atlanta, GA, Peachtree Press, 1985.
RESEARCH SOURCE: Simpson, Lewis, "Introduction," 3 by 3, pp.vii-xiv.

CRITICAL SYNOPSIS: A series of fifties and sixties portraits somewhat reminiscent of Sherwood Anderson's grotesques or Flannery O'Connor's moral cripples. The portraits reveal the warped souls of the black and white folk of Mc Afee County Georgia, "an imaginary coastal county." Of the twelve portraits, the character studies which best exhibit the prime tendencies of southern Gothic are: "The Dreamer," "Smoaks, Dering, Maggie Poat, and the Shark," "Dorcas and the Fat Lady," and "Anse Starkey at Rest." Lewis Simpson's view that "Southern literary Gothicism...tended to render the image of the South as a symbol of the disorder and depravity of the modern age at its worst" is borne out by the vicious undercurrents of all of the pieces in Steadman's Georgia Gothic mosaic. "Anse Starkey at Rest" is the story of an animal tormentor and one of his favorite victims, Billy Coon, a racoon chained in front of Shotford's store. Punishment comes at the head of a freshly dug grave where Anse finds his own tombstone with the scrawled epitaph, "Mr Anz Starky Die 1962 at Rez." Trying to haul away his own tombstone, he collapses in the road while trying to cover up the inscription. Similar grotesque climaxes mark these tense Gothic tales of the sixties South.

453. Stevens, Francis [Gertrude Bennett]. Citadel of Fear. New York: Carroll & Graf, 1970.

REPRINT EDITION: New York, Carroll & Graf, 1984.

CRITICAL SYNOPSIS: This exotic pulp Gothic was first serialized in Argosy Magazine, 1918. Imitative of the florid manner of the lost kingdom romances of H. Rider Haggard, it tracks the adventures of two American archeologists, O'Hara and Kennedy, in their exploration of the lost Aztec city of Tlapallan. While studying the lost city, one of the two falls under the corrupting spell of the malignant deity, Nacoc-Yaotl, and undergoes a secret character transformation before the expedition returns to the United States. The second portion of the novel which takes place in the United States twelve years after the visit to the citadel of fear is a self-contained Gothic novel in its own right. We have a haunted and mysterious mansion presided over by a sinister being (actually, the corrupted Archer Kennedy) and a host of Gothic happenings and effects. The book aspires to nothing more than simple thrill, fear, and pleasurable shock, and attains these ends with a considerable degree of success. Gertrude Bennett also wrote another highly intelligent Gothic thriller, Exit Screaming, published in 1942 by Doubleday.

454. Stewart, Desmond. The Vampire of Mons. New York: Harper & Row, 1976.

REPRINT EDITIONS: New York, Avon, 1977.

CRITICAL SYNOPSIS: Modern vampire novel set in an English public school and expressing indirectly the conflict of the generations and the latent perversity of youth cults. The setting is Malthus College, Foulden Slew, East Anglia; the main characters are the Swinburne brothers, Clive and Ronald, and the mysterious Darwin Corelli. "Mons" in the title refers to the famous battle of the First World War, where occurred the appearance of the Angels of Mons and to the house where the Swinburnes reside. All of the houses of Malthus College are named after great British battles. The heroic symbolism carrying with it Rupert Brooke's injunction, "the rich, red wine of youth," has its perverse equivalent in the vampirism of war, drainer of the blood of youth. The background is the coming of the Second World War with the apparently unquenchable thirst for blood and blood-letting, what Yeats called "the blood-dimmed tide," now again ready to burst upon the world. In more sophisticated novels of vampirism, the vampire's physical need and craving for human blood is transformed into a metaphor for the irrepressibly destructive and self-destructive appetites of the human creature.

455. Stockton, Frank R. "The Transferred Ghost." Stories By American Au-

thors II. New York: Charles Scribner's Sons, 1884.

REPRINT EDITION: Short Story Reprint Series, Salem, NH, Ayer Publishing, 1974.
RESEARCH SOURCE: Golemba, Henry L., Frank R. Stockton. Boston, Twayne, 1981.

CRITICAL SYNOPSIS: Now remembered almost entirely for the teasing short story, "The Lady or the Tiger," Stockton also produced a number of amusing ghost stories and thus contributed to the lighter vein of American Gothic as first opened by Washington Irving. "The Transferred Ghost" is the first in a pair of stories which includes "The Spectral Mortgage." Stockton's ghosts are annoying rather than alarming. They are supernatural pests who disturb the stuffy tranquillity and smug sense of reality of the humans whom they visit. The young man who convenes with the transferred ghost worries and wonders whether it is proper etiquette to do so since he is about to be married to a living woman. The ghost is old Mr. Hinckman, a hired haunter, who is "transferred" to Russia by his superiors for bungling the job. "The Spectral Mortgage" is about a ghostly womanizer, Buck Edwards, who continues his romancing ways from beyond the grave. Stockton's ghostly amusettes partake of the bemused viewpoint of Irving who brought the sportive supernatural to bear upon that "realm of shadows existing in the very center of substantial realities."

456. Stokes, John. The Forest of Rosenwald; or, The Travellers Benighted. A Melodrama in Two Acts. New York: Dramatic Repository; E. Murden, 1821.

RESEARCH SOURCE: Thorpe, Willard, "The Stage Adventures of Some Gothic Novels," Publications of the Modern Language Association 43 (1928): 476-486.

CRITICAL SYNOPSIS: Performed at the Park Theatre, New York, on April 26, 1820, with the subtitle, "or, The Bleeding Nun." This Gothic drama is based on scenic extracts from M.G. Lewis's shocker, The Monk (1796).

457. Stone, Clarence E. The Phantom Horseman; or, Saved by a Spectre. Amherst, MA: Robert A. Marsh, 1877.

CRITICAL SYNOPSIS: Variation on the headless horseman figure of Washington Irving. The ghostly night rider or demon lover can be traced back to the ballad tradition where the salvation of the girl as she is borne off into the eternal night often means her death. Stone's treatment of the theme avoids the grim ending and uses the Irvingesque notion of a supernatural masquerade as in "The Legend of Sleepy Hollow" (see 223). The Gothic motif of the maiden's final ride which conveys her to salvation or damnation is also powerfully applied in Joyce Carol Oates's "Where Are You Going? Where Have You Been?" (see 354).

458. Stovall, Dennis H. The Spirit of the Haunted House. Corvallis, OR: no publisher indicated, 1899.

CRITICAL RESOURCE: Mussell, Kay, "Gothic Novels," Handbook of American Popular Culture, ed. M. Thomas Inge, Westport, CT, Greenwood Press, 1988, pp.157-158.

CRITICAL SYNOPSIS: An example of a chiller rather than a thriller or shocker, this moderately scary ghost story brings together the essentials of household Gothic: an inquisitive young woman away from home for the first time; an absent and possibly murdered relative; an old, dark house in a remote western setting. This species of Gothic romance seems to corroborate Kay Mussell's view that these books "posit a fictional world in which life itself is precarious, but especially for young women. The worldview of the Gothic novel offers vicarious danger and romantic fantasy of a type that is particularly appealing to female readers."

459.   Stowe, Harriet Beecher. "The Visit to the Haunted House." Oldtown Folks. Boston: Fields, Osgood, 1869.

REPRINT EDITION: New York, AMS Press, 1970.
RESEARCH SOURCES: Halttunen, Karen, "Gothic Imagination and Social Reform: The Haunted Houses of Lyman Beecher, Henry Ward Beecher, and Harriet Beecher Stowe," New Essays on Uncle Tom's Cabin, ed. Eric J. Sundquist, Cambridge, UK, Cambridge UP, 1986, pp.107-134; Yates, Jo Anne, "American Gothic: Sources of Terror in American Fiction Before the Civil War," Dissertation Abstracts International 41 (1980): 1602A (University of North Carolina).

CRITICAL SYNOPSIS: A night sketch or supernatural ramble sometimes printed as a separate story, the text of "The Visit to the Haunted House" shows how deeply and extensively Harriet Beecher Stowe responded to the Gothic genre and how she extended the Gothic apparatus and characterization to accommodate her own disquieting social themes. Viewing Uncle Tom's Cabin as a novel incorporating all of the Gothic devices readapted to the monstrous institution of slavery, Karen Halttunen writes of Stowe's Gothic: "The peculiar appeal of the Gothic genre to Harriet extended beyond these symbolic uses of the haunted house. As a child of Calvinism, she was drawn to the Gothic genre's central fable of inexpiable guilt and unremitting punishment." In painting the horrors of slavery and religious indoctrination through an overwhelming sense of sin, Harriet Beecher Stowe added to the catalogue of American Gothic experience some new dimensions in religious and social terror. A dreadful respect for the inherited Calvinism of her fathers and a profound disillusionment with American ideals of freedom and perfection in her attitude toward slavery found expression in Gothic form in her novel of protest and in her ghostly sketches.

460.   Straub, Peter. Julia. New York: Coward, Mc Cann, & Geoghegan, 1975.

REPRINT EDITION: New York, Pocket Books, 1986.
RESEARCH SOURCES: Cunningham, Valentine, "Julia," New Statesman, February 27, 1976, p.265; Gregory, Jay, "Peter Straub: 'I Looked Into My Imagination and That's What I Found,'" Twilight Zone Magazine May, 1981, pp.13-16.

CRITICAL SYNOPSIS: Reviewers declared the novel to be a satisfying modern Gothic if the triumph of evil and utter defeat of human goodness are the desired ends. Fully conscious of the tradition, Straub tells the story of Julia with "stunning Gothic manipulations" while refusing to spare the reader's sensibilities or desires for poetic justice. "Some scenes are deliberatedly nauseating," commented the reviewer in the Library Journal, "and since evil triumphs completely, the resolution of the story is unpleasant." Julia Lofting is a prime specimen of the Gothic heroine.

240 / STRAUB

After a wretched marriage to her lawyer husband, Magnus Lofting, she purchases and moves into a mansion on Ilchester Place, Kensington, hoping to find the happiness that eluded her in her matrimonial days. She finds the opposite. The Loftings' little daughter, Kate, had died a brutal and bizarre death when one of her parents had sliced open her esophagus in an act of emergency surgery while Kate was choking. Was this a deed of mercy or murder? Now Julia is haunted and bedeviled by an enchanting blond child, a fiendish little girl called Olivia. But none of these events are related in a clear or straightforward account as both the sanity and reliability of the narrator are constantly in question. Rather, they are murky and ambiguous as is the strange death of Julia. What really happened or what the real relationship between mother and murdered daughter had been can never be determined through the dark glass of the narrative. Straub thus achieves a classic sense of Gothic in Julia by recreating the Gothic's central effect of reversal and deception whereby apparent safety is suddenly revealed to be illusory, the beautiful to be the grotesque in disguise, and good to be much weaker than evil.

461. _____. Ghost Story. New York: Coward, Mc Cann, & Geoghegan, 19-79.

REPRINT EDITION: New York, Pocket Books, 1981.
RESEARCH SOURCES: Gagne, Paul L., "Ghost Stories: The Novels of Peter Straub," Cinefantastique 12 (1982): 14-19; King, Stephen, Danse Macabre, New York, Everest House, 1981, pp.244-252; Neilson, Keith, "Ghost Story," Survey of Modern Fantasy Literature, pp.607-611.

CRITICAL SYNOPSIS: Writing of this splendid Gothic, Stephen King has said that "Straub seems to have grasped exactly--consciously--what the Gothic romance is about, and how it relates to the rest of literature....Most Gothics are overplotted novels whose success or failure hinges on the author's ability to make you believe in the characters and partake of the mood. Straub succeeds winningly at this and the machinery runs well." King might have added that Straub's novel is Gothic both on its surfaces and on its interior where the horror is surreal and psychomachic or soul-lacerating. The enclosed setting is the small town of Milburn, New York, a town invaded by deadly forces in the shape of four "women," Eva Galli, Alma Mobley, Alice-Marie Montgomery, Anna Mostyn, and lastly, a demoniac little girl. A society for the study of ghostly phenomena, the Chowder Society, summons a young novelist, Donald Wanderley, to investigate and identify the menacing force. He has to consider such causes as shape-shifting and UFO infiltration, coupled with older evils such as lycanthropy, vampirism, ectoplasmic manifestation, sexual nightmares, and revenancy. The story of the battle to save Milburn is narrated through a variety of voices as they try to comprehend and contend with the infecting evil in beguiling feminine shapes. This description of the plot hardly does justice to Straub's Gothic achievement because, as the novel is constructed, the various voices all have their private notions of reality obliterated. Straub himself has described the goal of his Gothic to be "to play around with reality, to make the characters confused about what was actually real." Total and permanent psychic disorientation of each of the characters is the high Gothic achievement of Ghost Story, a fulfillment of the Devil's words in Hawthorne's "Young Goodman Brown," (see 196) "'Depending upon one another's hearts, ye had hoped that virtue were not all a dream! Now ye are undeceived!--Evil is the nature of mankind. Evil must be your only happiness.'"

462. St. Rosalie; or, The Mysterious Casket. Boston: "Star Spangled Banner" Office, 1849.

CRITICAL SYNOPSIS: American Gothic chapbook possibly plagiarized from several English Gothics in which a dreadful voice issues from a sarcophagus, vault, or coffin. An early English Gothic which introduced the posthumous voice emanating from a tomb or vault was the anonymous Correlia; or, The Mystic Tomb published by the Minerva Press in 1802. Correlia's Gothic idea was widely confiscated, first by the English chapbookers and then by the Americans as in the anonymous St. Rosalie, a 75 page double-columned shocker.

463. Sturgeon, Theodore. "Bianca's Hands." E Pluribus Unicorn. New York: Abelard Press, 1953.

RESEARCH SOURCE: Stableford, Brian M., "Theodore Sturgeon," Supernatural Fiction Writers, pp.941-945.

CRITICAL SYNOPSIS: The tale is a peculiar blend of ugliness and beauty, of terror and tenderness. Although there is physical horror, the tale's Gothicism resides primarily in the psychological mode since an uncertainty about the reality of the events of this love story adheres to its every mood and moment. The mentally and physically deformed Bianca possesses one beautiful asset, her hands, which allure and repel her lover, Ran. Disgusted by Bianca, Ran nevertheless adores her hands. Is the death of Ran by strangulation to be understood as retribution or punishment for his abnormal obsession or is his death to be seen as a grotesque and desperate expression of Bianca's love and reaching out? Coupled with the sado-erotic element, this tale of strange compulsion has all of the ambiguous characteristics of the American horror story. The hand fetish of Ran, for example, recalls the teeth fetish of the frenetic narrator of Poe's "Berenice" (see 376).

464. _____. "The Graveyard Reader." The Graveyard Reader. New York: Ballantine, 1958.

RESEARCH SOURCES: Diskin, Lahna, Theodore Sturgeon, Mercer Island, WA, Starmont House, 1981; Hassler, Donald M., "Images for an Ethos, Images for a Change in Style," Extrapolation 20 (1979): 176-188.

CRITICAL SYNOPSIS: A graveyard meditation and sombre reverie close in conception to the postures of grief, isolation, and disconsolation to be found in certain death pieces by Hawthorne. The main character is seen at his wife's graveside where he realizes as he stares at the as-yet unmarked grave that he never had really known his wife. Her death had come in a car accident as she was apparently running away from their marriage. His mourning is therefore mixed with bitter guilt. As he mourns a stranger approaches, a "graveyard reader" who can decipher what the dead are saying to the living from their fine and private places. The mourner vows to master the craft of grave reading so as to "know" the wife he had never known in life. He studies the art of grave reading intensely and at length, finally erecting a headstone to her. The deeper communication that he had foregone in her life is finally consecrated in death. This is a sensitive love story told in the lugubrious but moving manner of Hawthorne's death pieces. The story's tone may be specifically compared to Hawthorne's "The Wives of the Dead" (see 203).

465. _____. Some of Your Blood. New York: Ballantine, 1961.

REPRINT EDITION: London, Sphere Publishers, 1967.
RESEARCH SOURCES: Lindborg, Henry J., "Theodore Sturgeon," Critical Survey of Long Fiction, ed. Frank Magill, Englewood Cliffs, NJ, Salem Press, 1983, pp.257-258; Menger, Lucy, Theodore Sturgeon, New York: Frederick Ungar, 1981.

CRITICAL SYNOPSIS: Shockingly, the "blood" of the title of this vampire novel refers to menstrual discharge only. The novel is cast ,in the form of an investigative case study of a young soldier's peculiar psychosis by a battery of military psychiatrists. The odd nature of his blood perversion is revealed only gradually as various documents, including his bizarre and witty correspondence, come to light. Despite the queer or even emetic nature of the soldier-vampire's blood quest, the portrayal of the vampire is more sympathetic than horrifying. Brian Stableford reads this vampire novel as a parable which urges the broadest tolerance of human needs and desires. In choosing to enslave his vampire with a desire only for menstrual blood, Sturgeon presents the extremest instance of human desire for sexual fulfillment that he could invent. But by such "eccentric erotic behavior," Sturgeon drives home the point that to be human implies a "sheer diversity of human needs and the manifold ways in which relationships can or must be created in order to accommodate needs." As usual, what is grotesquely shocking or disgustingly Gothic in Sturgeon's work also provokes a sympathy for the human dilemma that goes beyond the sheer shock itself.

466. Styron, William. Lie Down in Darkness. New York: Bobbs-Merrill, 19-51.

REPRINT EDITION: New York, Random House, 1960.
RESEARCH SOURCE: Perry, J. Douglas Jr., "Gothic as Vortex: The Form of Horror in Capote, Faulkner, and Styron," Modern Fiction Studies 19 (1973): 153-167.

CRITICAL SYNOPSIS: Together with Set This House on Fire, the novel is a definitive statement of the central themes and forms of the American Gothic. In form, Lie Down in Darkness is anti-chronological and deliberately as well as complexly disordered, thus presenting a dark and chaotic view of American family life. As Douglas Perry has suggested, the governing structural principle is its amorphousness which he likens to the action of the whirlpool. Styron "uses the Gothic form, with its denial of final absolute affirmation, tragic or otherwise, to capture the irony of our twentieth century existence: the conviction that the search for self-awareness may not only be fatal, but fruitless, because it is equivalent to self-negation." The dark forces at work upon the characters in the novel are entirely centripetal pulling each of them inward to a point of nothingness and deadness. In the process each becomes aware of his or her inability to love, realizes the uselessness and powerlessness of memory, finds himself or herself drawn over the edge and into a center that cannot hold. The very reality of reality grows blurred and the narrative disintegrates into isolated and non-fitting pieces. The nihilistic Gothic which

Charles Brockden Brown had begun in <u>Wieland</u> (see 063) attains what may be its ultimate expression in Styron's chronicle of family breakdown. Although told complexly and made difficult by the surrounding and irrelevant sub-stories, the main story has a stark simplicity. Peyton Loftis, daughter of Milton and Helen Loftis, had committed suicide by jumping from a Harlem rooftop. In the words of her suicide note, she has lain down in darkness "myself all shattered. Perhaps I shall rise at another time, though I lie down in darkness and have my light in ashes." As the fragments of the narrative gradually reveal even in their irrelevance to one another, her relationship with her father has been falsely affectionate just as her relationship with her mother has been falsely cold. In essence, there have been no relationships, no emotional or family ties whatsoever, only the illusion of fatherly love and motherly hate. The novel's detached episodes underscore Peyton's isolation and "darkness." For example, the opening of the novel corresponds with the dropping of the first atomic bomb in August, 1945. The inner world explodes with the outer world. The hearse bearing Peyton's body to the cemetery stalls in traffic causing a traffic jam. Between the emotional absurdities of life and the absolute void of death, Peyton's transported remains are caught forever between angry drivers and honking cars. The image of the stalled hearse lingers, finally taking its place as a terrible figure of the motionless blackness at the center of all things.

467. Ten Years of Torture; or, Sutten's Death-Bed Confession of How He Married Miss Martha Morton, An Accomplished Young Lady of Baltimore, With Hellish Design of Torturing Her to Death. Philadelphia: C.W. Alexander, 1871.

CRITICAL SYNOPSIS: Of dime novel quality, the narrative purports to be "a true account" of lurid and gradual homicide. Marital misery and monstrosity often formed the basis of such sensational confession narratives.

468. Thompson, William Tappan. [Major Jones] John's Alive; or, The Bride of a Ghost. Baltimore: Taylor, Wilde, 1846; Philadelphia: David Mackay, 1883.

CRITICAL SYNOPSIS: Ghoulish, graveyard humor is the hallmark of this 123 page comic Gothic. The seventeen year old John Smith finds himself in bitter contention with the foppish Mr. Thaw for the love of Mary Carson. After brawling with Thaw at a fancy dress ball and being dismissed by Mary, Smith decides to use a macabre ruse to advance his faltering courtship. Hearing of the death of a friend who resembles him, he exhumes the corpse, exchanges his clothing and personal effects with the body, and deposits the body in the Delaware River. Pleased to read of the suicide of John Smith in the next morning's newspaper, he attends his own funeral, then departs secretly for New Orleans to enlist in the army and fight in an expedition against the Seminoles. To allow his death to "sink in," and to ravage Mary Carson's conscience with appropriate guilt, he remains away from Philadelphia for two years, then reappears in spectral form to claim Mary Carson as his bride. Night after night, the ghost of Smith stations itself beneath Mary's parlor window to murmur in a hollow, accusing voice: "John's alive! John's alive!" To drive off the persistent Mr. Thaw, a wedding is planned where the ghost might appear at the appropriate moment to scare Thaw from the altar. When John appears right on schedule, Thaw flees and Mary Carson fulfills the novel's subtitle by becoming the "Bride of a Ghost." From John's "death" to his manifestation at the wedding, the novel cleverly and expertly lampoons many of the stock events of Gothic fiction, especially that type of plot wherein the heroine is maritally matched with a phantom lover. The overheated melodramatic exchanges of the dialogue too suggests that Major Jones knew his Gothics well and founded his satire on that firsthand knowledge.

469. Tryon, Thomas. The Other. New York: Alfred A. Knopf, 1971.

REPRINT EDITION: Greenwich, CT, Fawcett-Crest, 1972.
RESEARCH SOURCE: Barth, Melissa, "The Other," Survey of Modern Fantasy Literature, pp.1169-1172.

CRITICAL SYNOPSIS: Gothic doubles in American literature can be traced back to Poe's fable of the dual existence in "William Wilson" (see 380). Tryon's modernized rendition of the evil twin living inside the good self complicates the theme of "William Wilson" by asking whether it is ever possible to know the true self or to retain control over one's identity. Of the two twins, Niles and Holland Perry, in Tryon's Gothic, we can never be absolutely sure which is the wicked and which is the good brother. Nor is it even possible to identify the narrator for certainty at various stages of the story. Neither the natural or psychological explanation of the violent circumstances is wholly satisfactory nor is a supernatural accounting for all that happens completely reliable either. Tryon's Gothic is a blend of two traditionally opposite Gothic modes and the ambiguous resolution of the narrative in favor of neither approach is an intentional effect. Thus, "the novel gives a new twist to what some critics call the 'explained Gothic,'" abandoning the reader to a maze of possible perspectives. What can be known with certainty is the Gothic nature of the story's gory events. Vining Perry, the father, dies a terrible death involving that most Gothic of architectural props, a trap-door. Cousin Russell is impaled on a pitchfork. Brother Holland perishes while hanging a cat in a well. Brother Niles closely guards his "thing," a box containing the severed finger of Brother Holland. Brother Niles pushes his mother, Alexandra, down the stairs. Sister Torrie's baby is bottled up in a wine cask and served at a family banquet. The inventory of Gothic atrocities and horrid shocks is long, large, and occasionally ingenious. But did any of it really happen and who did what to whom? Such is the insoluble otherness of The Other, a major but mystifying feat in American Gothicism.

470. Turnbull, John D. The Wood Daemon; or, The Clock Has Struck. San Marino, CA: Larpent Collection Number 1514, 1808.

RESEARCH SOURCE: Peck, Louis F., "Dramas," A Life of Matthew G. Lewis, Cambridge, MA, Harvard UP, 1961, pp.68-114.

CRITICAL SYNOPSIS: Along with The Monk, Lewis's Gothic plays were also pirated and plagiarized by Americans. Lewis's The Wood Daemon; or, The Clock Has Struck. A Grand Romantic Melodrama in Two Acts was produced at Drury Lane Theatre in London on April 1, 1807. The pilfered American version follows Lewis's plot without change. The ugly peasant Hardyknute strikes a bargain with the wood daemon to gain handsomeness in return for which he must pay the daemon a human sacrifice on the seventh of August at one o'clock. Hardyknute is visited by a mysterious child Leolyn bearing the symbol of a bloody arrow on his arm, an emblem recognized by

Una as the sign of greatness. As Hardyknute prepares to sacrifice Leolyn to the wood daemon, Una intervenes to work his rescue and Hardyknute is seized by the daemon at the stroke of one for failing to keep his debt of flesh. The sensational melodrama would have had an instantaneous appeal for American audiences because of its baleful theatrics and remarkable contraptions. All of the paraphernalia of Gothic horror are here: winding staircases descending to the impenetrable darkness of the Castle of Holstein, demonic and supernatural authority figures, and fiendish justice.

471. Tyler, Royall. The Algerine Captive; or, The Life and Adventures of Doctor Updike Underhill. Walpole, NH: David Carlisle, 1797.

REPRINT EDITION: ed. Don L. Cook, New Haven, CT, College & University Press, 1970.
RESEARCH SOURCE: Davidson, Kathy N. and Arnold E. Davidson, "Royall Tyler's The Algerine Captive: A Study in Contrasts," Ariel: A Review of International English Literature 7 number 3 (1976): 53-67.

CRITICAL SYNOPSIS: The Preface to this early American novel contains a satiric aside that is addressed to the growing Gothic readership of the new republic. Reflecting on national reading habits, Doctor Updike Underhill comments on the Gothic craze which had caused "Dolly, the dairy maid, and Jonathan, the hired hand, [to throw] aside the ballad of the cruel stepmother, over which they had so often wept in concert, and now amused themselves into so agreeable a terror, with the haunted houses and hobgoblins of Mrs. Radcliffe, that they were both afraid to sleep alone." As a corrective to such imported Gothic fancies, the Doctor offers his memoirs of a real and ferocious adventure while he was an Algerine captive, a native and thoroughly American narrative to counter the demand for foreign fiction, especially foreign Gothic fiction. Underhill's account of being captured and sold into slavery by the Algerians and his narrow escape from an enforced conversion to Islam form the core of his adventures. Although the novel is mainly satiric and picaresque in tone and episode, the influence of the Gothic on this early American stylist is not totally absent. The darker episodes include his voyage aboard a slaver to the African coast and the public impalement of a slave for attempting to escape. "They inserted the iron pointed stake into the lower termination of the vertebrae, and thence forced it up near his backbone until it appeared between his shoulders; with devilish ingenuity contrived to avoid the vital parts." Even in the work of an early American author such as Tyler who resisted the Gothic influence, the Gothic is called into play to denote the promises and perils of the democratic experience.

472. An Unlaid Ghost. A Study in Metempsychosis. New York: D. Appleton, 1888.

CRITICAL SYNOPSIS: The subject is a common one in the literature of spiritualism: how to rid a house of an unwanted and intrusive phantom. As the subtitle suggests, transference of the soul at death into another body, either human or animal, and the detection of such transference by "scientific" investigation continued to fascinate readers of every ilk. Ghost-busting or the "laying" or fettering of such annoying spirits became a type of Gothic plot which remained popular into the twentieth century as indicated by its reuse in Shirley Jackson's The Haunting of Hill House (see

232). But some spirits, like the energetic ghost in this tale, refused to be confined.

473. Valentine, Ferdinand Charles. <u>Horrors! Adapted From the French</u>. New York: S.W. Green's Sons, 1884.

CRITICAL SYNOPSIS: A 165 page miscellany of tales, some truly Gothic and others only strange, bizarre, or suspenseful. Among the horrors is an English adaptation of Théophile Gautier's necrophiliac fantasy, "The Dead Lover" (1836).

474. Van Loon, Elizabeth. <u>The Mystery of Allanwold</u>. Philadelphia: T.B. Peterson, 1880.

CRITICAL SYNOPSIS: a 380 page sensation and suspense novel somewhat imitative of the methods, style, and sentimental coincidences of Mrs. E.D.E.N. Southworth. Plot, locale, and Gothic traits are similar to <u>The Mystery of the Dark Hollow</u> (see 445).

475. Victor, Mrs. Metta Victoria Fuller [Seeley Regester]. "The Skeleton at the Banquet." <u>Stories and Sketches</u>. Boston: Lee and Shepard, 1867.

CRITICAL SYNOPSIS: Seeley Regester wrote a large number of chilling Gothic tales designed for the parlor and the tea table. "The Skeleton at the Banquet" goes back to the beginnings of the Gothic tradition in its presentation of the spectral dinner guest. An additional satisfying Gothic is her long detective story, <u>Figure of Eight</u>, which makes use of cryptography and cipher writing to attain its effects. The narrator finds her uncle, Dr. Meredith, dead under mysterious circumstances. The expiring man has scrawled some sort of cabalistic cipher, a figure of eight, in his last moments, "the spasmodic effort of a perishing will." Deciphering the cipher in order to dicipher the mystery of the murder becomes the task of the narrator, whose investigation produces a skein of Gothic clues and events. A somnabulating governess, Miss Miller, seen prying up stones in the garden in the "Haunted Arbor" chapter, odd rays of light from her uncle's laboratory, the discovery of an iron box filled with gold ingots, and the suspicious retirement of her cousin Inez to "The Tower Chamber" provide true and false leads to the identity of her uncle's killer. <u>Figure of Eight</u> shows the tendency of American Gothic fiction to merge with the detective novel in the decade of the 1870's.

476. Vierick, G.S. <u>The House of the Vampire</u>. New York: Moffat, Yard, 19-07.

REPRINT EDITION: New York, Arno Press, 1976.

CRITICAL SYNOPSIS: Two opposite portrayals of the vampire have worked their way down through the Gothic tradition. The first type is the creation of the first vampire novelist, Dr. John Polidori, whose "Vampyre," Lord Ruthven, in <u>The Vampyre</u> (1819) is a suave, intelligent, handsome attacker of souls, a gentleman vampire living in society in order to live off of it. The second type is the gore-clotted, blood-guzzling, bat-faced, befanged fiend like the vampyre made popular by Thomas Peckett Prest in the Victorian blood, <u>Varney the Vampyre</u> (1847). Stoker's Count Dracula is something of a union of the two extreme portrayals. American vampires often forego physical monstrosity to take on gruesome psychologi-

cal powers. From Vierick's vampire to Anne Rice's Vampire in Interview With The Vampire (see 400), they are corrupters of the
soul or psychiatric case studies in helpless evil. American vampire writers also prefer to tell the horror story from the inside
rather than the outside and will just as often let the vampire
speak for himself. The House of the Vampire is an early twentieth
century example of the Americanized Dracula and a prototype for
the American vampire novel.

477. Walton, Evangeline. Witch House. Sauk City, WI: Arkham House, 1945.

REPRINT EDITION: New York, Ballantine, 1979.
RESEARCH SOURCE: Sullivan, Charles W. III, "The Influence of Celtic Myth and Legend on Modern Imaginative Fiction," Dissertation
Abstracts International 37 (1977): 5979A-5980A (University of Ore-
gon).

CRITICAL SYNOPSIS: Called by E.F. Bleiler "a neo-Gothic thriller,"
the novel has some visible affinities with Hawthorne's The House
of the Seven Gables (see 200), its nearest American Gothic model.
The house is the strange and gloomy legacy of the French warlock,
Joseph de Quincy. His progeny, Joseph and Quincy Lee, not only inherit the mansion; they continue the family tradition of black
rites, occult activities, and the persecution of female Quincy
relatives. Filling the role of Gothic maiden is Betty-Ann Stone,
daughter of Elizabeth Quincy. She is the victim of a variety of
psychic assaults while residing against her will in Witch House,
but the most direct Gothic borrowing occurs in the scene where the
portrait of nefarious Aunt Sarai descends from its mouldy frame to
assail a screaming Betty. Eventually, a fearless psychic investigator and expert in parascientific phenomena, Dr. Gaylord Carew,
is summoned to deal with the spirits who afflict Betty and pollute
Witch House. If the novel is read as Gothic allegory, what we have
is the youthful future rescued from the grip of a dark and superstitious past by the democratic hand of science. But Walton's
Gothic does not attempt to duplicate the moral floorplan of The
House of the Seven Gables or to imitiate verbatim the horror art
of Shirley Jackson in The Haunting of Hill House (see 232). As a
neo-Gothic thriller, it can stand on its own merits.

478. Wandrei, Donald. "The Eye and the Finger." The Eye and the Finger.
Sauk City, WI: Arkham House, 1944.

CRITICAL SYNOPSIS: An Arkham House author specializing in Gothified science fiction. The direct horror of this story can be compared against the subtler use of the same Gothic materials by
Edith Wharton in "The Eyes" (see 491). Try as he will, the main
character cannot rid himself of these two items of some spectral
and invisible anatomy, a levitating eyeball and a beckoning finger. Psychiatry and medical science can offer no aid or relief as
the doctor on the case is finally forced to conclude that the eye
and the finger are supernatural manifestations. The conclusion
drives the protagonist to suicide. The style of the story seems to
be a conscious duplication of Poe's maddest monologues. Wandrei
has also written an excellent collection of Gothic verse, Poems
for Midnight (1964).

479. Ward, Mrs. Elizabeth Stuart Phelps. "The Day of My Death." Men, Women, and Ghosts. Boston: Fields, Osgood, 1869.

CRITICAL SYNOPSIS: A collection of eerie and uncanny tales, many of them relating to the public interest in spiritualism. Predominantly Gothic pieces are "Night Watches" (involving corpse vigils and animations), "In the Gray Goth" (about a dark gorge in the Maine woods), "Kentucky's Ghost" (prospector Gothic recalling Bret Harte), and the somewhat whimsical tale, "The Day of My Death." The narrator, Mr. Fred Hotchkiss, a practical fellow who puts little stock in mediums, spirit rappings, and occult phenomena finds the boarding house where he is staying on Nemo Avenue a literal warehouse of disturbing noises and supernatural sights. At one point, in a scene half Gothic and half comic, his bed animates itself and chases him out of the chamber. When he re-enters he is shocked to find an omen of his death in the form of "some white clothing which lay upon the bed, folded in an ugly way, to represent a corpse, with crossed hands." The fatal signs and noises build to a kind of ghostly crescendo with all of the household objects taking on a life of their own until "the house resounds and reechoes with the blows of unseen hammers and the dinner dishes perform a furious mazourka on the table." Matters reach a climax when the house's resident medium, Gertrude Fellows, forecasts Hotchkiss's death on the second of May at one p.m. when he will "be summoned into a spiritual state of existence." But despite overwhelming evidence to the contrary, Hotchkiss can still not bring himself to believe in a supernatural world or the contingency of spirits. In a comic climax during a dinner party on the day of his death, it is Hotchkiss's healthy Yankee skepticism which apparently saves him from the fatal prophecy. These are cleverly constructed tales relying on undertones of comic irony to offset their serious supernaturalism and using such irony to evade the awful fates that seem in store for their characters.

480. Warren, Robert Penn. Night Rider. Boston: Houghton, Mifflin, 1939.

RESEARCH SOURCES: Dimaggio, Richard S., "The Tradition of the American Gothic Novel," Dissertation Abstracts International 37 (1976): 307A (University of Arizona); Wilson, Angus, "The Fires of Violence," Encounter 4 (1955): 75-78.

CRITICAL SYNOPSIS: Robert Penn Warren's first novel is a "roman noir" or novel of the night time, a tale of dark and bloody ground and the self's immersion in moral and psychological midnight. It is also a study in uncontrollable evil in the central character, Percy Munn. Munn's damnation of himself and others is done against the historical backdrop of the Kentucky Tobacco Wars of 1905-1908 when growers rode against buyers by night. The war between growers and buyers turns the land red with arson, brutality, murder, demagoguery, and other terrors of night violence. Munn is a sort of human embodiment of this destructive spirit, Penn Warren's reincarnation of Hawthorne's "fiend of fire and fiend of night" in "My Kinsman, Major Molineux" (see 202). On the surface of his character, Munn seems to be purely demonic. He craves power, relishes violence, especially the violence of armed mobs, loves the spectacle of fiery destruction wrought by the night riders. But on the interior of his character, he is a meditative and guilty man, painfully aware of the emptiness within his being. Power and violence fill that emptiness, give him his only identity. The sensitive and retrospective side of his nature are awakened by his contact with Willie Proudfit, a sage figure whose wisdom derives from his acquaintance with the darker side of the American self. This Daniel Boone figure symbolizes for Munn the purity and natural selfhood that come only through facing and controlling the night-riding side of American character. Munn's dark heritage cannot, however, be averted by his contact with Proudfit. After plotting the murder of Senator Tolliver, he is tracked down by state troopers in the night time. The concluding Gothic image depicts the soul consumed by inner and outer darkness like the shouts of boys playing some nameless game in the night. Rendered Gothically as a dark descent, the struggle for being in this first novel ends in negativism, despair, and death.

481.   . At Heaven's Gate. New York: Harcourt, Brace, 1943.

REPRINT EDITION: New York, New Directions, 1985.
RESEARCH SOURCES: Casper, Leonard, Robert Penn Warren: The Dark and Bloody Ground, Seattle, WA, Washington UP, 1960; Douglas, Wallace W., "Drug Store Gothic: The Style of Robert Penn Warren," College English 15 (1954): 265-272; Eisinger, Chester E., "The Gothic Spirit in the Forties," Pastoral and Romance: Modern Essays in Criticism, ed. Eleanor Terry Lincoln, Englewood, NJ, Prentice Hall, 1969, pp.289-296.

CRITICAL SYNOPSIS: The innate cruelty and cold refusal to be human of Sue Murdock dominate the novel and highlight the dark theme of definition of self solely through violence and power-seeking. She must apparently punish all others for her own lack of self or shallow inhumanity by her sexual and emotional ferocity. She abuses and then abandons the man who sincerely loves her, Jerry Calhoun, simply because he reminds her of her father, Bogan Murdock. Starting with the eccentric character, Slim Starrett, who is a poet-boxer, she takes up with man after man just as an outlet for her brutality. Like her father, who had enjoyed foreclosing on poor people's property, she brutalizes all with whom she comes into contact. Sue Murdock is a cold and sinister figure of death who wants power for its own sake and who is too depthless to realize that being weak is part of being human. Penn Warren's study of evil in his portrait of the deadly lady contains latent elements of the vampire and lamia legends, demonic creatures incapable of love but needing to feed off the love of others. The book partakes deeply of the Gothic spirit of the nineteen forties, a spirit exemplified by "the world of flight, childhood terror, estrangement, and perverted love."

482. Watterston, George. The Lawyer; or, Man As He Ought Not To Be. Pittsburgh, PA: Zadok Cramer, 1808.

RESEARCH SOURCE: Petter, Henri, The Early American Novel, pp.322-324.

CRITICAL SYNOPSIS: The novel's subtitle suggests the influence of the English radical or "Jacobin" novelists, William Godwin and Robert Bage. Bage's Hermsprong; or, Man As He Is Not (1796), with its characters allegorizing various moral positions and its situations drawing upon some familiar Gothic crises, seems to be Watterston's most immediate model. The story traces the sordid career of the reformed profligate, Morcell, and employs various Gothic devices and situations to illustrate his degenerate life. The Gothicism of the novel goes beyond what Henri Petter calls "superficial tricks in the service of the author's Gothic suspense" to become a means of communicating the malicious potential on the underside of the American character. Raised and educated or miseducated by the the evil Baltimore lawyer, Dorsey, Morcell undertakes a career as a lawyer, but his real profession is criminality, crafty dishonesty, and sexual intrigue. His seduction of Matilda Ansley enables Watterston to contrast the depraved Morcell with her virtuous brother, Edward Ansley, a sort of moral role model for the reformed rake. Morcell's eventual contrition and the growth of conscience in his deeper nature provide for his conversion to humanitarianism and benevolence, an alteration in character which is not justified given the character's psychological attraction to evil and his energetic villainy throughout most of the book. Gothic episodes include the invasion of Morcell's chamber by apparitions, the murder of a man named Rattle in the dark, and Morcell's sexual harassment of Matilda Ansley. The English crime novel, the English Gothic novel, and the English novel of radical ideas all leave a strong imprint on this early American Gothic.

483.   . Glencarn; or, The Disappointments of Youth. Alexandria, VA: Cottom & Stewart, 1810.

RESEARCH SOURCES: Petter, Henri, The Early American Novel, pp.319-322; Ringe, Donald, American Gothic, p.80.

CRITICAL SYNOPSIS: Gothic and sentimental influences from abroad converge in the work of George Watterston. Written to improve the reader's morals or to warn against such social vices as domestic tyranny, Watterston's novels were steeped in Richardsonian seriousness and Gothic melodrama. But the Gothic did not always remain subordinate to the didactic in his work and what began as novel of ethical purpose sometimes quickly became a rousing tale of terror. Glencarn falls into such a pattern of development. In addition, Watterston has revised the original Gothic formula of female virtue in distress by shifting the centers of excitement to male victimization. In a Gothic with a male victim, "the hero can act in situations in which a heroine's resistance must be passive." Young Glencarn is the very embodiment of male virtue in distress. Hated and persecuted by his adoptive father's wife and her loathsome son, the Richardsons, he is slandered, abused, falsely accused, denied his name and birthright, and driven into a world where every experience is a snare or peril. At the College of William and Mary, he follows his natural virtue and saves the life of one, Gray, only to become the object of Gray's insidious plots and perjury. His wanderings take him from Williamsburg to Pittsburgh and eventually to the wild Ohio frontier where he is seized by a gang of bandits in a forest terror interlude. The bandit captain, Wilson, will play a part in the clearing up of Glencarn's true identity at the Gothic dçnouement. Wounded by the robber, Motalbert, and nursed by the tender Sophia Williams, Glencarn returns from his forest sojourn a wiser man. Glencarn's use of ventriloquism to evade his persecutors brings to mind the perverse use of vocal powers in Charles Brockden Brown's Wieland (see 063). Put on trial and victimized by Gray's false testimony, he is the object of a timely rescue by a mysterious stranger. With the downfall of Gray, Mrs. Richardson, and the death of his loathsome stepbrother, Rodolpho, Glencarn comes into his own as the true Richardson heir and the proper husband for Amelia. The pathway to bliss, however, has been strewn with Gothic predicaments and near fatal perils as would be the pattern with the run-of-the-mill domestic Gothic of the 1790's. The moral object lesson relates to the reward of persistent virtue, but the moral pretext is frequently displaced by the Gothic context of Glencarn's multiplying adversities.

484. Webber, Charles Wilkins. "Jack Long; or, The Shot in the Eye." <u>Tales of the Southern Border</u>. Philadelphia: Lippincott, Grambo, 1853.

RESEARCH SOURCES: Davis, David Brion, <u>Homicide in American Fiction, 1798-1860</u>, Ithaca, NY, Cornell UP, 1957, pp.286-290; Marovitz, Sanford E., "Poe's Reception of C.W. Webber's Gothic Western, 'Jack Long; or, The Shot in the Eye,'" <u>Poe Studies</u> 4 (1971): 11-13.

CRITICAL SYNOPSIS: Frontier Gothic is the very stuff of this western thriller. Whether the revenge that the sharp-shooting hunter, Jack Long, takes on ten men who brutally whip him almost to death in front of his wife and children is supernatural revenge is a matter left to the reader. The Gothicity of this story and others in the collection is a firstrate example of Webber's own description of a Gothic western in his preface as dealing with "the wild actualities of life on our most storied, yet least illustrated borders,--those of the Great South West and South." The story is set during the savage Regulator Wars in Shelby County, Texas, in the late 1830's. The Regulator Captain is the marauding and sadistic Hinch, who, having lost a shooting contest to Jack, vows "to dog the inoffensive hunter to the death, or out of the country." To this end, he turns his mob of ten loose on Jack with the hideous "quirt" or rawhide whip and urges them into a flogging frenzy while Jack's family watches. Jack, who is famous for "shooting the varmints' eyes! I never takes 'em anywhere else!" now vanishes, then reappears in the form of a spectral Daniel Boone or ghostly Nick of the Woods (see 050), meting out justice with a shot through the eye of each of his tormentors. Known locally as "the bearded ghost," he is a "tall, gaunt, skeleton-like figure--an' such eyes! A grisly head and shoulders above the bushes, and the heavy rifle laid along their tops, bearing full, with its dark tube, into their faces." Taking his revenge one by one, Jack reserves the execution of Hinch until last, allowing him to think about it as he flees up the Red River. Did Jack Long survive the mob whipping or is it his phantom in buckskin who deals out the ten shots in the eye? The reader can have it both ways and also marvel in the frontier moral of this Gothic western: "The stern hunter had wiped out with much blood the stain of stripes on his free limbs." In earlier Gothics of the American wilderness, it was the skulking redskin who was cast as the evil tormentor; now his role is taken by whitemen more savage than any savage acting under the pretext of law and order.

485. _____. <u>Yieger's Cabinet. Spiritual Vampirism: The History of Etherial Softdown and Her Friends of the "New Light"</u>. Philadelphia: Lippincott, Grambo, 1853.

CRITICAL SYNOPSIS: An acerbic satire on spiritualist groups and cults, mesmerism, Bloomerism, theosophical mysticism, and phrenology, the novel resembles Hawthorne's critique of transcendental idealists and reformers, <u>The Blithedale Romance</u> (1852). The narrator comes to the story by way of the Softdown manuscript, a document reposing in Yieger's cabinet and relating a history of the sinister effects of "Mahomet, Joe Smith, Miller, and all such agitators" on the strange life of the Vermont girl, Etherial Softdown. For those foolish enough to subscribe to their ideas and isms, "these human vampires or sponges may be, therefore, as well absorbents of the spiritual as well as animal vitality. Their parasitical roots may strike into the very centres of life, and their hungry suckers remorselessly draw away the virility of manhood, or the spiritual strength." A product of such social vampirism, "Etherial would grow strong on cannibalism of the soul," first slowly murdering her Quaker husband and then descending into the murky underworld of mesmeric politics and wild evangelicalism. The minor characters in the case study are equally sinister but have strong satiric features. The phrenologist, Dr. E. Willamot Weasel, the zealot, Stewart Manton, "who behaves on stage as if a ghoul had disturbed him at a feast with angels," and the ardent feminists, Regina Straightback and Eusedora Polypheme, "the new lights of the Committee of Disorganization," all represent the dangerous lunatic fringe of American society as Webber perceived it, each "convulsing true Christianity by one dexterous jugglery of cant." Using the framework of the lurid exposç, Webber determined to warn Americans against the presence of these social vampires in their midst and to "unveil a class of crimes which were enabled to work and worm their way nearest to the core of the social state."

486. Weld, Edward. The Ransomed Bride: A Tale of the Inquisition. New York: Burgess, Stringer, 1846.

CRITICAL SYNOPSIS: An 86 page, double-columned monastic shocker with the familiar lurid trappings concerning Jesuit treachery. The victims of Jesuit intrigue are the Xavier family of Grenada whose mansion is confiscated by the Jesuits to be used as a storage place of "secret booty and malign practices." Anti-Catholic propaganda is blatant and frequent. "The Jesuits from the first of our story had had but one object in view, the gratification of a revengeful spirit. They acquired in great measure the mastery they so long held by a thorough knowledge of human nature. Their great study was man, their object to sway him, and yet to rule unsuspected." The agency of power is the Inquisition, the perverse creation of the Jesuits, applied to force Felipe Xavier's sister into an incestuous relationship with him. Crude shockers of this sort circulated and perpetuated the rumors of an international Jesuit conspiracy operating underground in Protestant countries and played upon the widespread phobia for Catholic plotting and intrigue. The dime Gothic was quick to take commercial advantage of such social phobias.

487. Wellman, Manly Wade. "His Name on a Bullet." Worse Things Waiting. Chapel Hill, NC: Carcosa, 1973.

RESEARCH SOURCE: Wagner, Karl Edward, "Manly Wade Wellman: A Biography," August Derleth Society Newsletter 4 number 1 (1980): 4-9.

CRITICAL SYNOPSIS: Wellman excels in a variety of Gothic fantasy, but perhaps his most distinctively American Gothic strain appears in his Civil War pieces in which the emphasis on a sadistic supernatural links him to Ambrose Bierce. The presence of death in the midst of life along with the grisly irony of that presence is felt in all of these battlefield Gothics. In "His Name on a Bullet," a Confederate veteran comes through the entire war unscathed because he possesses a charmed bullet, the only bullet that can cause his death, given to him by a witch. But the gift of life also implies the curse of life since the soldier discovers to his dismay that, like the Wandering Jew, he can never die. To find the peace of death in his old age, he must ask to be shot with the

lead charm. Other Civil War stories which use powerful Gothic motifs are "Fearful Rock" where a Union brigade is assaulted by Confederate dead, "The Valley Was Still" involving a Confederate soldier's rejection of a bargain with Satan and the subsequent annihilation of his regiment, and "Coven" which unites the makeshift
graves of a battlefield with the grave of a vampire. Although
these tales draw heavily upon the devices and situations of Gothic
fantasy, they are narrated with grim realism and an attention to
accurate military history.

488.   . "The Black Drama." Lonely Vigils. Chapel Hill, NC: Carcosa, 1981.

RESEARCH SOURCE: Coulson, Robert, "The Recent Fantasies of Manly
Wade Wellman," Discovering Modern Horror Fiction, ed. Darrell
Schweitzer, Mercer Island, WA, Starmont House, 1985, pp.99-105.

CRITICAL SYNOPSIS: First appeared in Weird Tales, June, 1938. The
tale is an eerie Gothic literary fantasy which brings the
scholarly investigator, Judge Keith Hilary Pursuivant, into contact with the resurrected Lord Byron who did not die in 1824. Byron's supernatural survival is verified by the discovery of "The
Black Drama," a Gothic play whose date of composition is definitely fixed at 1930. Byron was able to achieve his posthumous drama
by a pact with Satan. By accepting the evidence as undeniably
factual, Wellman's investigator confirms the psychic truth of supernatural survival. This sophisticated horror story and others by
Wellman indicate a worth to his work which merits a wider audience
than the horror pulps of the thirties. The eleven Gothified folk
tales in another collection, Who Fears the Devil? (Arkham House,
1963) combine Carolinas and Ozarks folklore with horror themes.

489. Welty, Eudora. "Petrified Man." A Curtain of Green, and Other Stories. New York: Doubleday, Doran, 1941.

REPRINT EDITION: Studies in the Short Story, eds. Adrian H. Jaffe,
Virgil Scott, New York, Holt, Rinehart, Winston, 1968.
RESEARCH SOURCE: Weston, Ruth Deason, "Nothing So Mundane As
Ghosts: Eudora Welty and the Gothic," Dissertation Abstracts In-
ternational 49 (1988): 821A-822A (University of Tulsa).

CRITICAL SYNOPSIS: Feminist criticism has provoked Gothic readings
of several of her stories in which the motif of entrapment is presented as a cultural, regional, or psychological crisis rather
than a physical ordeal. Gothic forms "serve her ultimately feminist theme of the escape of women from various cultural bondages
into a fuller humanity." The theme of "The Petrified Man" is the
hardness and stagnation of all human relationships. The vanity,
vulgarity, and pettiness of the two conversations in a beauty parlor which form the story expose the strangeness, or even the un-
reality, of reality itself. The meandering, gossipy conversation
of the beautician, Leota, as she arranges Mrs. Fletcher's hair
comprises the narrative. Jumping from topic to topic, she informs
Mrs. Fletcher that someone has noticed her pregnancy, that she
takes in roomers, and that she enjoys her days off at the traveling freak show which features among other oddities a petrified
man, a Mr. Petrie who causes everything that he eats to turn into
stone. Her boarders, Mr. and Mrs. Pike, recognize the stone freak
as a convicted California rapist and turn him in for the reward.
Leota's second conversation deteriorates into violent frustration

over her failure to identify the rapist herself and reap the reward. The story ends with her spanking of the Pikes' brat, Billy
Boy, as he rushes about the beauty parlor and the group of
wild-haired ladies gloating sarcastically over Leota's frustration: "'If you're so smart, ·hy ain't you rich?'" No one in this
small town can or will escape the petty prison of ego, meanness,
and self-delusion. In a horrifying sense, they are all petrified
people in a petrified world.

490. Wharton, Edith. "Afterward." Tales of Men and Ghosts. New York: Appleton, Century, 1910.

REPRINT EDITION: Great Tales of Terror and the Supernatural, eds.
Herbert A. Wise, Phyllis Fraser, New York, Random House, 1944.
RESEARCH SOURCE: Zilversmit, Annette, "Edith Wharton's Last
Ghosts," College Literature 14 (1987): 296-309.

CRITICAL SYNOPSIS: First published in Century Magazine, January,
1910. If understated horror and subdued terror can produce a more
powerful Gothic response than direct and blatant gore, "Afterward"
should be the ghostly prototype for this sort of response. The
prosaic title refers to what will befall the residents of lonely
and solitary Lyng House, a mansion in Dorsetshire. The legend says
that those who live in the house will be visited by a ghost, but
will not realize it until "afterward." Ghostly visitation is only
one of the "supernatural enhancements" available at Lyng House.
The Gothic catalogue is very complete as Wharton offers a concealed crime concerning money, a husband who disappears and never
returns, secret rooms and mysterious noises, and spectral manifestation in the shape of "The stranger!--the stranger in the garden....It was he who had called for her husband and gone away with
him." Events are perceived through the consciousness of Mary Boyne
whose husband, Ned, has apparently cheated his partner, Elwell,
driving him to suicide. Having retired to Lyng House on this ill-
gotten money, their tranquil life is disturbed by Elwell's ghost
and Ned's permanent removal by the phantasmic stranger. The tale
concludes with an image of collapsing walls and live burial. Realizing only "afterward" that the man in the garden was Elwell's
ghost, Mary Boyne's rational defenses crumble into helpless hysteria. "'Oh, my God! I sent him to Ned--I told him where to go! I
sent him to this room!' she screamed. She felt the walls of books
rush toward her, like inward falling ruins." The refined Gothicism
of the story and Wharton's sensitive portrayal of Mary Boyne show
the extensive influence of Henry James's The Turn of the Screw
(see 245), a work Wharton had complimented for its "imaginative
handling of the supernatural."

491. _____. "The Eyes." Tales of Men and Ghosts. New York: Appleton,
Century, 1910.

REPRINT EDITION: The Ghost Stories of Edith Wharton, New York,
Scribner's, 1973.
RESEARCH SOURCE: Mc Dowell, Margaret B., "Edith Wharton's Ghost
Stories," Criticism 12 (1970): 133-152.

CRITICAL SYNOPSIS: First published in Scribner's Magazine, June,
1910. The lethal Gothic optic and later the accusing eye of the
old man in Poe's "The Tell-Tale Heart" (see 386) are direct aids
to Wharton's imagination in this tale of guilt and ghosts. The
subjective nature of the ghostly eyes is not revealed until the

end of the tale where it is skillfully related to the moral of a self denied or a self unseen. The main character, Andrew Culwin, tells his ghost story as a kind of confessional to several inquisitive friends. Thus, it serves as an epilogue or epitaph to his life of deceit and self-evasion. As a young man, he had proposed to Alice Nowell, but had done so more out of pity and propriety than love. The act was decent, but the motive was fraudulent. A pair of decrepit eyes now materializes to stare him down with their gruesome glare. Here is one of the oldest devices of the Gothic appearing in detached form like Macbeth's airborne dagger of guilt. In middle life, Culwin again performs a good deed for a sordid reason. He defends a young writer whose work is obviously worthless and lies about the quality of the work to the writer. Just as he had abused the laws of love, he now violates the laws of friendship. Through these experiences, the supernatural eyes grow more hideous. The final scene is a mirror confrontation revealing the awful eyes to be his own, now radiant with the terrible light of the truth of his self-betrayal. Like her other supernatural pieces, this story is Gothic in a special sense: her ghosts have the convincing reality felt only in the presence of the soul's spectres broken loose from the dungeons of memory.

492. _____. "All Souls." Xingu and Other Stories. New York: Scribner's, 1916.

REPRINT EDITION: The Collected Short Stories of Edith Wharton, ed. R.W.B. Lewis, New York, Scribner's, 1968.
RESEARCH SOURCES: Chu, Li-min, "The Ghostly Stories of Edith Wharton," Bulletin of National Taiwan University 26 (1977): 417-448; Sullivan, Jack, "Psychological, Antiquarian, and Cosmic Horror," Horror Literature, ed. Marshall B. Tymn, New York, R.R. Bowker, 1981, pp.221-275.

CRITICAL SYNOPSIS: The tale's opening paragraphs contain a statement which fixes Edith Wharton's predilection for the Gothic both as a reader and as a writer. Defending the existence of ghosts, the narrator endorses the validity of all Gothic experience. "As between turreted castles patrolled by headless victims with clanking chains, and the comfortable suburban house with a refrigerator and central heating where you feel, as soon as you're in it, that there's something wrong, give me the latter for sending a chill down the spine! And by the way, haven't you noticed that it's generally not the highstrung and imaginative who see ghosts, but the calm matter-of-fact people who don't believe in them, and are sure they wouldn't mind if they did see one?" Sara Clayburn, the narrator's cousin, is the owner of a modernized and redecorated eighteenth century colonial foursquare, Whitegates, a house with all the appliances and conveniences. Her recollection of her strange experience commences on October 31, when a storm snowbounds the house. A fall on the ice and ankle injury immobilize the heroine who spends a terrifying evening in what seems to her to be an utterly deserted house. As she inspects room after empty room in their "inexorable and hostile silence," she senses "that the house had retained in full daylight its nocturnal mystery, and was watching her as she was watching it; that in entering those empty orderly rooms she might be disturbing some unseen confabulation on which beings of flesh-and-blood had better not intrude." The next day, All Souls, the servants are puzzled and baffled by the report of her experience since they had not left the house. Exactly one year later, Sara has a similar Gothic experience at Whitegates with a strange woman coming up the drive. The narrator speculates that Sara must have seen a "fetch," a witch who summons and escorts others to the coven or witches' convocation on All Souls' Eve. Whatever the cause of her terror, Sara Clayburn shrinks at ever returning to the haunted Whitegates. This excellent Gothic tale establishes Edith Wharton's formula for the effective ghost story. Even though a plausible explanation is given for a character's supernatural experiences, the natural reason seems less convincing than unaccountable horror felt by the character.

493. _____. "Bewitched." Here and Beyond. New York: D. Appleton, 19-26.

REPRINT EDITION: The Collected Short Stories of Edith Wharton, ed. R.W.B. Lewis, New York, Scribner's, 1968.

CRITICAL SYNOPSIS: First published in Pictorial Review, March, 19-25. This is a superlative New England Gothic tale which erases the fine line of demarcation between the natural and supernatural as well as the normal and the abnormal in human behavior. The isolated locale and the restricted point of view add to the Gothic suspense. Two women, one living and the other dead, struggle to possess Saul Rutledge. Ironically, Rutledge's living wife, Prudence, is frigid and corpse-like with "marble eyeballs" and bony, bloodless hands. The dead woman, Ora Brand, is a passionate succubus figure who attaches herself to Saul Rutledge from beyond the grave. Thus, the story employs two conceptions of Gothic femininity which strongly recall the marmoreal figure of Poe's Ligeia or the superhuman will of Poe's Morella. Saul Rutledge had once courted Ora Brand before marrying Prudence. Now, to prevent a courtship from beyond the grave and to deny Saul all erotic fulfillment, the stony, sexless Prudence opposes the spectral lover, even demanding that a stake be driven through the buried body of Ora to stop her from enjoying a posthumous liaison with her husband. The story climaxes in the graveyard where footprints are seen in the snow, shots are fired, and a spectral woman in white looms up in the darkness. Combining the bleak Gothic atmosphere of Hawthorne's New England with Poe's chilling sense of an animated supernatural, Edith Wharton shows her mastery of Gothic storytelling in the bone-chilling horror of this winter's tale.

494. _____. "A Bottle of Perrier." Certain People. New York: Curtis Publishing, 1926.

REPRINT EDITION: The Collected Short Stories of Edith Wharton, ed. R.W.B. Lewis, New York, Scribner's, 1968.

CRITICAL SYNOPSIS: First published in The Saturday Evening Post, March, 1926. The young archeologist, Medford, visits his new friend, Henry Almodham, at a crusader fortress in the middle of the Egyptian desert, but Almodham is not to be found. Only his servant, Gosling, is on hand. Mystery builds as Gosling, in the true tradition of the English butler, ministers to all of Medford's needs. Unable to understand why his host should be missing, Medford begins "to wonder if Almodham had not simply withdrawn to some secret suite of that intricate dwelling, and were waiting there for his guest's departure....Aerial chambers, jutting out at capricious angles, baffled him with closely shuttered windows, or here and there with the enigma of painted panes. Behind which window was his host concealed, spying, it might be, at this very mo-

ment on the movements of his lingering guest?" When Medford finally confronts Gosling with the possibility of Almodham's secret
presence, the butler breaks down and confesses that his master indeed is present, his body at the bottom of the well. Denied his
"'oliday" in Wembley, Gosling had pushed Almodham over the castle
parapet. This superb mood piece concludes with a low-hanging lunar
beacon. "The moon, swinging high above the battlements, sent a
searching spear of light down into the guilty darkness of the
well."

495. _____. "Miss Mary Pask." Here and Beyond. New York: D. Appleton,
1926.

REPRINT EDITION: The Collected Short Stories of Edith Wharton, ed.
R.W.B. Lewis, New York, Scribner's, 1968.
RESEARCH SOURCE: Robillard, Douglas, "Edith Wharton," Supernatural
Fiction Writers, pp.783-788.

CRITICAL SYNOPSIS: A sinister tale of possible self-deception or
equally possible spectral encounter. The story's success lies in
the manner in which the natural and supernatural worlds intersect
to create a suspenseful ambiguity that lingers even after the climax and the rational accounting for the narrator's strange meeting. The narrator, an unnamed man, has long known two sisters, the
married Grace Bridgeworth and the spinster, Miss Mary Pask. Visiting the Brittany seacoast while he recuperates from fever, he
also decides to visit Miss Mary Pask in her solitary cottage having been asked to do so by her sister, Grace. The sunset journey
through the fog and darkness to the Bay of the Dead is a splendid
little Gothic interlude. Enroute, the narrator suddenly recalls
that Miss Mary Pask is dead, that a gap in memory perhaps induced
by the fever has made him forget her recent death. Why then does
the narrator persist in his night journey and is the figure in
white garments who receives him a ghostly Mary Pask or a projection of his fevered memory? "The white figure flitted spectrally
to the chimney piece, lit two more candles, and set down the third
on a table. 'It's an event--quite an event! I've had so few visitors since my death, you see.'" Although her sister provides evidence that Mary Pask is still very much alive and the victim of a
"cataleptic trance," there is equal evidence that she had died and
that the spectral encounter was all-too-real. The subtle terror of
the story rests delicately on the tension set up between the two
possibilities, neither of which is fully acceptable.

496. White, J.B. The Mysteries of the Castle; or, The Victim of Revenge. Charleston, SC: J. Hoff, 1807; San Marino, CA: Larpent Collection number 1054, 1807.

RESEARCH SOURCE: Evans, Bertrand, Gothic Drama from Walpole to
Shelley, Berkeley, CA, California UP, 1947.

CRITICAL SYNOPSIS: A Gothic melodrama taken from Miles Peter Andrews's Gothic spectacular of 1795, The Mysteries of the Castle; A
Dramatic Tale in Three Acts. The English play is an operatic adaptation of Mrs. Radcliffe's The Mysteries of Udolpho (1794). The
American version alters the title of the British source, but very
little else.

497. Williams, Harper. The Thing in the Woods. New York: Robert Mc Bride,
1924.

CRITICAL SYNOPSIS: Well-received by reviewers who liked the relo-
cation of the Gothic to the Pennsylvania Dutch country, the novel
establishes and maintains a certain supernatural uncanniness without too much added or insinuated explanation and without becoming
so fantastic as to impair credibility. Seeking a tranquil life
away from the city, young Dr. Austin Haverill finds quite the opposite when he moves to a little community in central Pennsylvania. There is something in the woods, but just what it is or how it
came there can be known only at a terrible price. There have been
several attacks by some unidentified creature and a local chemist,
Dick Lessing, was badly mauled while working in his laboratory.
Suspicion falls on a surly, ugly man, Aaron Menning, whose face is
badly disfigured by smallpox and whose reputation for animal cruelty is widely known. Aaron's wild brother, Jake, had died mysteriously and was hastily buried before an inquest could be conducted. Suspecting a possible outbreak of lycanthropy, Dr. Haverill
investigates and delves deeply into the Menning family background. While uncovering the Westphalian origins of the Mennings,
he is suddenly attacked by a foul-smelling, frothing, beclawed
man-beast. When the thing in the woods is finally killed, all of
the dark truth comes to light. It was not Jake but brother Aaron
who had died mysteriously, the victim of one of Jake's werewolf
frenzies. Mother and son have conspired to conceal the truth about
the thing in the woods and to hide the lycanthropic family malady
from their neighbors. Now that both of her sons are dead, the mother can disclose the dark truth and receive the sympathy of her
neighbors. The Gothic pivot of the novel is its well-made suspense
leading up to Dr. Haverill's dark enlightenment. This is neither a
great nor a major American novel, but it is an extremely satisfying and satisfactory werewolf Gothic.

498. Williams, Tennessee. The Two Character Play. New York: New Directions, 1969.

RESEARCH SOURCES: Dersnah, James L., "The Gothic World of Tennessee Williams," Dissertation Abstracts International 45 (1985): 31-
31A (University of Wisconsin); Gillen, Francis, "Horror Shows Inside and Outside My Skull: Theater and Life in Tennessee Williams's Two Character Play," Forms of the Fantastic, eds. Jan Hokenson, Howard Pearce, New York, Greenwood Press, 1986, pp.227-
231.

CRITICAL SYNOPSIS: With their characters immersed in strained sexual relationships and imprisoned within destructive dreams and
self-delusions, many of the plays and short stories of Tennessee
Williams fall within the American Gothic tradition. A primitive
destructiveness that cannot be ignored lurks just beneath the civilized veneer of many of his characters. The human interrelation-
ship comes to a deadly intimacy in The Two Character Play, a type
of Gothic psychodrama which obliterates the fragile line between
living one's life and merely performing one's life. The two characters are Felice and Clare who act out roles in a drama within a
drama within a drama in something like a triple removal from self-
reality. As elsewhere in Williams, the achievement of permanent
self-identity is synonymous with death, a primal terror felt when
the play is forced to a final curtain by one of the characters
with revolver in hand. Although we might wish it otherwise, intimacy is death in this demonic, ghostly, and elliptical rendition
of human tensions and failures. Similar defeats and terrors of the

spirit may be found in the stories in <u>One Arm, and Other Stories</u> (1848). In a pioneering study of Tennessee's Williams's ties with Gothicism, James Dersnah notes that "he has used Gothic terror not as mere sensationalism, but to convince his audience that life is more lonely, dreadful, and mysterious than we commonly believe."

499. Williamson, Jack. <u>Darker Than You Think</u>. Alhambra, CA: Fantasy Press, 1948.

REPRINT EDITIONS: London, Sphere Books, 1976; illus. David G. Klein, New York, Bluejay Books, 1984.
RESEARCH SOURCES: Elms, Alan C., "Darker Than He Thought: Jack Williamson's Fictionalization of his Psychoanalysis," <u>Extrapolation</u> 30 (1989): 205-218; Myers, Robert E., <u>Jack Williamson: A Primary and Secondary Bibliography</u>, Boston, G.K. Hall, 1980; Williamson, J.N., "Introduction," <u>Masques: All New Works of Horror and the Supernatural</u>, Baltimore, Maclay, 1984.

CRITICAL SYNOPSIS: The original version of this Gothic fantasy of lycanthropic love and gruesome transformation was published for <u>Unknown</u> in 1940 by Street and Smith Publications. The ascendancy of a society of werewolves and the displacement of human beings as the dominant species in the evolutionary struggle constitute the plot and theme. But the real value of the novel lies in its oneric or dreamlife imagery and the psychological variations which Williamson brings to such old-fashioned Gothic motifs as bestial transformation and sexual evil. The storyline tracks the bizarre involvement of an investigative reporter, Will Barbee, with the alluring if lethal female werewolf, April Bell. Dr. Mondrick, "a big-shot anthropologist at Clarendon University," and his blind wife, Rowena are other recognizable Gothic character types. His skeptical scientific rationalism will be utterly destroyed by the rise of homo lycanthropus as the beasts conspire to reinherit the earth. Several chapters stand out as independent Gothic episodes in the sense that they refurbish an established Gothic moment or event. "The Kitten Killing," "The Thing Behind the Veil," "The Trap in the Study," "The Huntress in the Dark," "Private Hell," "The Most Frightful Shape," and the final chapter, "Into the Shadows," each denote some traditional Gothic device, theme, or character condition. The theme of the beast within our so-called civilized selves and erupting without warning is frequently given literal form as when Will Barbee is turned into a python to do the bidding of April Bell. In reptilian fury, Barbee's snake self attacks Nick Spivak, "his hollowed face stiffened with horror. Behind the glasses, his red eyes popped. He opened his mouth to scream, but a savage blow from the side of Barbee's long head paralyzed his throat. The breath hissed out of his collapsing chest. The coils drew tighter and his chest caved in. 'Tighter, Barbee,' the white bitch was whispering. 'Kill him while you can.'" The dark theme of evolution in reverse is fixed by Barbee's final metamorphosis into a pterosaur, a gigantic flying dinosaur, and then into "huge gray wolf." Picking up the exciting scent of April Bell, he follows her into the shadows of prehistoric time.

500. Windsor, William. <u>Ghost Gleams: Tales of the Uncanny</u>. London: Heath, Crampton, 1921.

RESEARCH SOURCE: Hawkins, Jean, "Ghost Stories and Tales of the Supernatural," <u>Bulletin of Bibliography</u> 5 (1909): 142-145, 168-171.

CRITICAL SYNOPSIS: A typical twenties anthology of short Gothic fiction and an international mix of classic horror stories.

501. Wolfe, Gene. The Shadow of the Torturer. New York: Simon & Schuster, 1980.

REPRINT EDITION: New York, Timescape/Pocket Books, 1984.

CRITICAL SYNOPSIS: The first volume of a sequence of Gothic fantasies under the title, The Book of the New Sun, Wolfe's medievalized Gothic extravaganza can be compared with Mervyn Peake's Gormenghast trilogy (1967). The novel records the strange adventures of the torturer's apprentice, Severian. In true Gothic fashion, it commences at a dark gate and terminates at another dark gate. "Having carried you, reader, from gate to gate," Severian moves on into darker terrain. Between the gate of the necropolis citadel and the final gate, the Gothicism of the novel is relentless, surreal, spellbinding. We have the "corpse door," the ancient guild of professional torturers associated with "our Matachin Tower," the education of a torturer's apprentice, the corpse-eaters who relive the lives of their victims by gastronomic mutation, the chatelaines, Theckla and Barbea, the founder's feast of St. Catherine of the Torturers, House Absolute, House Azure, and Thrax, the city of windowless rooms. There is something of Spenserian nightmare allegory in all of this as well as in the names Wolfe gives to his characters: Eata, Vodalus, Master Gurloes, Odo, Mennas, Eigel, and the bleeding dog, Triskele. The torturer's guild imprisons Severian, apparently for performing an illegal act of that most sacred deed, the excruciation. Although the fantasy sometimes dissolves into incoherency and disarray, the book's Gothic rendition of a "post-historic world" is genuinely fearful. Like Peake's Gormenghast Gothics, the whole of the dark puzzle can be realized only through a patient pushing together of its jagged and disparate parts. The strange episodes themselves deliberately work against any solid plot structure, an anti-structure that is certainly a traditional Gothic design.

502. Wood, Sally Sayward Barrell Keating. Julia and the Illuminated Baron; A Novel Founded on Recent Facts Which Have Transpired in the Course of the Late Revolution of Moral Principles in France. Portsmouth, NH: Oracle Press, 1800.

RESEARCH SOURCES: Loshe, Lillie Deming, The Early American Novel, New York, Columbia UP, 1907; New York, Frederick Ungar, 1966; Ringe, Donald, American Gothic, p.80; Petter, Henri, The Early American Novel, pp.315-316

CRITICAL SYNOPSIS: Charles Brockden Brown's Gothic contemporary, Mrs. Sally Sayward Barrell Keating Wood, succeeded in combining the radical novel of ideas with the popular novel of terror. The expected events and techniques of her Radcliffean Gothic models, seduction, abduction, castle confinement, cunning villainy, maidenly hysteria, mortuary sojourns, and midnight encounters, are joined to the lurid politics of the French revolutionary period. For most of the novel, the heroine's true identity is concealed from herself and her persecutors until the complicated genealogical gears finally yield freedom and marriage for Julia. The reader has to pass through a perplexing maze of genealogical complications and delusions, but such was the very stuff of the eighteenth century Gothic novel. Separated from her lover, Henry Ormond, she has to fend off assaults by the master plotter, the Count de Launa (belatedly revealed to be Julia's uncle). Because he is a member of the secret society of Illuminati, he is an "illuminated baron," a sinister member of a sinister organization dedicated to assassination and international intrigue. The Count de Launa shows himself the master of Gothic perversity when he openly declares: "I am to myself a god and to myself accountable; I pursue my own pleasure!" After being ensnared almost endlessly in his plottings, Julia finally and melodramatically emerges from her trials to reside in America, a land free of castles, curses, and conspiratorial aristocrats. In murky and confused form, the myth of young America's struggle with intrinsic evil is already present in this early sample of American Gothic. The historian of the American novel, Alexander Cowie, gave the book an important place in the rise of an American Gothic: "Her first story, the Gothic _Julia_, remains Mrs. Wood's most distinctive achievement."

503. _____. Dorval; or, The Speculator. Portsmouth, NH: Ledger Press by Nutting & Whitlock, 1801.

RESEARCH SOURCES: Coad, Oral S. "The Gothic Element in American Literature Before 1835," _Journal of English and Germanic Philology_ 24 (1925): 72-93; Cowie, Alexander, _The Rise of the American Novel_, pp.21-37.

CRITICAL SYNOPSIS: To the well-established patterns of female victimization and superhuman criminality, Mrs. Wood adds the native American element of the lust for undeveloped land. The villain is the arch-schemer and devious land speculator, Dorval. The object of his commercial chicanery is the obtaining of property rights in Georgia where he seems to be engaged in the creation of a private empire founded on these illegitimate speculations. Cunning, unpredictable, exploitative, and cruel, Dorval is an American Gothic superman whose control over an evil web of crime and corruption resembles the villainy of Charles Brockden Brown's city criminal, Welbeck, in _Arthur Mervyn_ (see 064). Not content with the rape of the land, Dorval also pursues and terrorizes Aurelia Morely, a transplanted Radcliffean virgin. Another survival from the original cast of Mrs. Radcliffe's Gothic novels includes Aurelia's lover, Burlington, who is absent for much of the complicated plot until the exposure and overthrow of Dorval are called for. Although still entangled in the conventions of British Gothicism, what gives _Dorval_ its interest as a specimen of early American Gothic is its handling in symbolic terms of one of the less savory characteristics of the American character, the lust for land and the violation of new world frontiers by ruthless enterprise. What emerges in blurred form is an image of America as a fallen world, not a new Eden but a Gothic landscape infested and endangered.

504. _____. Amelia; or, The Influence of Virtue. Portsmouth, NH: Oracle Press, 1802.

CRITICAL SYNOPSIS: A sentimental romance which shows distinct traces of Gothic plotting and machinery. Like Richardson's persecuted heroines, Pamela Andrews and Clarissa Harlowe, Mrs. Wood's heroine is the object of a ruthless and profligate master accepting both the taunts of his mistress and his bastard offspring. Amelia's integrity and virtue in the face of domestic danger and distress provided another new dimension of the Gothic to complement the natural terrors for the new citizens of the republic.

505.   _____ . "Storms and Sunshine; or, The House on the Hill." Tales of the Night, by a Lady of Maine. Portland, ME: Thomas Todd, 1827.

RESEARCH SOURCE: Wagenknecht, Edward, Cavalcade of the American Novel, pp.6-7.

CRITICAL SYNOPSIS: Several of these night pieces derive their themes, settings, and characterization from the props of Gothicism. The house on the hill is the inherited Maine estate of the Arnold family and reputed to be haunted. Arriving from England on January 1, 1791, Henry Arnold and his daughters, Emma and Cornelia, travel through the wilderness and struggle to make the deserted house a habitable home after their arrival. The family saga is beset with difficulties and danger, some of these suggestively supernatural in the Radcliffean manner. Disasters, misfortunes, illness, and isolating storms, one of which brings a stranger, Henry Tudor, into the story, test the endurance of the Arnold family in the new world. To compound matters, the deed to the house on the hill has long been missing, thus casting a shadow over the Arnolds' rightful ownership, but the discovery of a secret panel behind a portrait brings the deed to light and clears their claim to the estate. All of these secret trappings and melodramatic twists of fortune are the very substance of the domestic Gothic tale.

506.   Wood, Mrs. Seth S. Doctor Phoenix' Skeleton; or, The Man With a Mystery. Fortress Monroe, VA: S.S. Wood, 1887.

CRITICAL SYNOPSIS: A cold-blooded "factual" account or true case study of deception, concealment and murder. This type of factual or true-to-life Gothic flourished in the 1870's and 1880's. Compare with The Five Fiends; or, The Bender Hotel Horror (see 137).

507.   Wright, Richard. Native Son. New York: Harper, 1940.

REPRINT EDITION: New York, Harper & Row, 1986.
RESEARCH SOURCES: Kaminsky, Marc, "Richard Wright," Encyclopedia of World Literature, ed. Wolfgang B. Fleuischmann, New York, Frederick Ungar, 1971, pp.545-547; Payne, Ladell, "A Clear Case: Richard Wright, 1908-1960," Black Novelists and the Southern Literary Tradition, Athens, GA, Georgia UP, 1981, pp.54-79.

CRITICAL SYNOPSIS: The Gothic mode was an ideal mode for depicting the horrors of the black experience in America. The grim chronicle of one black life tormented and destroyed by its entrapment within the castle of racism allows the novel to be read as the ultimate expression of the terror and hopelessness of blacks' bedeviled relationship to a haunted society from which there was neither redress nor escape. The main character, Bigger Thomas, is a tragic victim of a depression America and of urban despair made more depressing and horrifying by the taint of racism. The grim irony of his status as a "native son" is made clear through various Gothified scenes and episodes, since Bigger Thomas is a man without a country, and even more tragically, without a self. Coming of age in the Chicago slums, he murders and decapitates a white woman, is pursued by the police and captured in the dark on a tenement rooftop, is tried and defended by a Communist lawyer, and condemned to death after a sensational and racist trial. The murderers and murders in Poe's tales must have inspired Wright in the making of Bigger Thomas's character as did Poe's immobilized or prematurely buried victims enclosed by pits and catacombs. Specific details recalling Poe's Gothic are to be found in almost every violent scene and setting in the novel. The grisly horror of Bigger's mutilation of Mary Dalton's corpse, his flight through the dismal Chicago streets and past "the ghostly lamps" of the inner city, his physical and mental torture at being conveyed to that final chamber of horrors, the whiteman's courtroom are among Wright's brilliant adaptations of traditional Gothic events and places. The three divisions of the novel, "Fear," "Flight," and "Fate," also confirm the underlying Gothic structure. But the Gothic moods of cultural and spiritual displacement, coercive isolation from identity, moral desolation and dehumanization leading to a horror of self are countered by the other vision of Bigger Thomas as noble and heroic victim of a world he did not make and a community he cannot enter. When Bigger Thomas is cornered and captured at the conclusion of the "Flight" section, the Gothic horror of the moment gives way to another image of Bigger ennobled and larger than the demons of race who surround him. The Gothic elevates into the tragic at the moment of seizure: "They let go of his feet; he was in the snow, lying flat on his back. Round him surged a sea of noise. He opened his eyes a little and saw an array of faces, white and looming. Two men stretched his arms out as though about to crucify him; they placed a foot on each of his wrists, making them sink deep down in the snow. His eyes closed, slowly, and he was swallowed in darkness."

508. _____. "The Man Who Lived Underground." Eight Men. Cleveland and New York: L.B. Fisher Publishing, 1944.

REPRINT EDITION: The Modern Tradition: An Anthology of Short Stories, ed. Daniel F. Howard, Boston, Little, Brown, 1976.
RESEARCH SOURCES: Engel, Leonard W., "Alienation and Identity: Richard Wright's 'The Man Who Lived Underground,'" West Virginia University Philological Papers 32 (1986-1987): 72-78; Walker, Ian, "Black Nightmare: The Fiction of Richard Wright," New Studies in the Afro-American Novel Since 1945, ed. A. Robert Lee, London, Vision Press, 1980, pp.11-28.

CRITICAL SYNOPSIS: Pursued by the racial fury of the ruling white world above, Fred Daniels descends through a manhole into the "wet gloom" of the city sewer system where he determines to live underground. This is a powerful tale which makes almost a formal use of one of the traditional Gothic environments, the dank and dangerous underworld that lies beneath the lighted superstructure of the Gothic building. Seeking the safety of the labyrinth like many previous Gothic victims fleeing from their persecutors, he finds unspeakable horrors instead. Wright's use of the Gothic tradition involves all the smells, sights, and sounds of Gothic enclosure. Fetid water rises around him; rats stare at him, "wet with slime, blinking beady eyes and baring tiny fangs;" cadaverous shocks and surprises await him at every turn as when he extends a hand to touch "a tiny nude body of a baby snagged by debris and half-submerged in water." The decayed infant becomes an icon of human suffering almost worthy of Dante. "The eyes were closed as though in sleep; the fists were clenched as though in protest; and the mouth gaped black in a soundless cry." Daniels's subterranean journey as he gropes through the maze shows him that there is no escape from the nightmare of racism. Yet, when he pecks out his own name on a typewriter that he finds and when he papers the walls of his cave with money he has stolen, he feels that "he has triumphed over the world aboveground! He was free! He wanted to run from this cave and yell his discovery to the world." Emerging briefly from his subterranean hideout, he finds that his sense of freedom is all illusion. When he tries to return to the underground, a policeman's bullet terminates the nightmare for Daniels. The concluding image of the man in the whirlpool is a brilliant statement in Gothic terms of the helplessness, hopelessness, and special hell of blacks condemned to suffer eternally in an American racial Hades. "Then his mouth was full of thick, bitter water. The current spun him around. He sighed and closed his eyes, a whirling object rushing alone in the darkness, veering, tossing, lost in the heart of the earth."

509. Yarbro, Chelsea Quinn. Hotel Transylvania. New York: St. Martin's Press, 1978.

RESEARCH SOURCE: Leiber, Fritz, "On Fantasy: 'Dracula's Heritage & Other Matters,'" Fantasy Newsletter 25 (1980): 4-6, 30.

CRITICAL SYNOPSIS: The first of five novels in the St. Germain Series which follows the deathless career of the vampire from Nero's Rome to the Bolshevik Revolution and Hitler's rise to power. The other novels are The Palace (1978), Blood Games (1979), The Path of the Eclipse (1981), and Tempting Fate (1982). Like other modern vampires such as Saberhagen's Dracula (see 418), Yarbro's St. Germain is a completely non-malevolent being who inspires admiration and pity rather than horror and revulsion. He has lived through 3000 years of the nightmare called history, an eye witness to catastrophe, atrocity, and man-made horror. Sensitive, studious, artistic and far more humane and civilized than any of the humans he lives among or the civilizations he observes, St. Germain is a mutation of the feeling hero in an unfeeling world. Although he is a vampire and does require blood sustenance, he never attacks or victimizes in the classic manner of his literary forerunners, Varney the Vampyre and Count Dracula. Blood is received, never demanded or taken, by St. Germain as in his deep love for Madelaine de Montalia. Whether or not the vampire, that soul-sucking creature of the night who is traditionally portrayed as the quintessence of evil and foul power over others, should be altered into the role of heroic healer and moral model for a vicious humanity is worth questioning. What happens to the Gothic effect when the Dracula image of fearsome fiend dons the crusading cape of Superman? The result is a shifting of the horror back onto ourselves and away from the convenient monsters created by a refusal to see ourselves at our worst.

Appendix One
Annual Chronology
of American Gothics

1786
The House of Night (Freneau)

1793
The Inquisitor; or, The Invisible Rambler (Rowson)

1797
The Algerine Captive (Tyler)

1798
Wieland; or, The Transformation (Brown)

1799
Arthur Mervyn; or, The Memoirs of the Year 1793 (Brown)
Edgar Huntly; or, The Memoirs of a Sleep-Walker (Brown)
Ormond; or, The Secret Witness (Brown)

1800
Julia and the Illuminated Baron (Wood)

1801
Dorval; or, The Speculator (Wood)

1802
Amelia; or, The Influence of Virtue (Wood)

1803
Ribbemont; or, The Feudal Baron (Dunlap)

1804
A Journey to Philadelphia; or, Memoirs of Chares Coleman (Adelio)

1806
Adventures in a Castle (Anon.)

1807
Fountainville Abbey (Dunlap)
The Mysteries of the Castle; or, The Victim of Revenge (White)

1808
The Lawyer; or, Man As He Ought Not to Be (Watterston)
Secret History; or, The Horrors of St. Domingo (Hassall)
The Wood Daemon; or, The Clock Has Struck (Turnbull)

1810
Glencarn; or, The Disappointments of Youth (Watterston)
The Prisoners of Niagara; or, The Errors of Education (Holman)

1811
The Asylum; or, Alonzo and Melissa (Mitchell)
Ilonzo and Melissa; or, The Unfeeling Father (Jackson, D.)

1815
The Sicilian Pirate; or, The Pillar of Mystery (Anon.)

1816
Adelaide (Botsford)

1818
Rosalvo Delmonmort (Mannering)

1819
The Legend of Sleepy Hollow (Irving)
The Spectre Bridegroom (Irving)

1820
Yamoyden; A Tale of the Wars of King Philip (Eastburn & Sands)

1821
The Forest of Rosenwald; or, The Travelers Benighted (Stokes)
Paul Felton (Dana)
The Spy; A Tale of Neutral Ground (Cooper)

1822
Dolph Heyliger (Irving)
Logan; or, The Mingo Chief (Neal)
The Rose of Arragon; or, The Vigil of St. Mark (Judah)

1823
Koningsmarke, The Long Finne (Paulding)
The Spectre of the Forest; or, The Annals of the Housatonic (Mc Henry)

1824
The Adventure of My Aunt (Irving)
Adventure of the German Student (Irving)
Peter Rugg, the Missing Man (Austin)

1825
Lionel Lincoln; or, The Leaguer of Boston (Cooper)

1827
The Legend of the Devil's Pulpit (Bryant)
Storms and Sunshine; or, The House on the Hill (Wood)

1828
Carl Werner; An Imaginative Story (Simms)
Fanshawe (Hawthorne)
Rachel Dyer, A North American Story (Neal)

1830
The Hollow of the Three Hills (Hawthorne)
The Indian Spring (Bryant)

1832
The Heidenmauer; or, The Benedictines, A Legend of the Rhine (Cooper)
Metzengerstein (Poe)
My Kinsman, Major Molineux (Hawthorne)
Roger Malvin's Burial (Hawthorne)
The Skeleton's Cave (Bryant)
The Wives of the Dead (Hawthorne)

1833
Tales of Terror; or, The Mysteries of Magic (St. Clair)

1834
Calavar; or, The Knight of Conquest (Bird)

1835
Alice Doane's Appeal (Hawthorne)
Berenice (Poe)
The Culprit Fay (Drake)
The Devil in Manuscript (Hawthorne)
The Executioner; or, The Man Who Burnt the Rev. John Rogers (Sands)
Graves and Goblins (Hawthorne)
The Gray Champion (Hawthorne)
The Haunted Mind (Hawthorne)
The Hawks of Hawk Hollow (Bird)
Morella (Poe)
The White Old Maid (Hawthorne)
Young Goodman Brown (Hawthorne)

1836
Awful Disclosures of Maria Monk (Monk)
The Castle of Altenheim; or, The Mysterious Monk (Anon.)
The Man with the Cloaks; A Vermont Legend (Austin)
The Minister's Black Veil (Hawthorne)
The Wedding Knell (Hawthorne)

1837
The Man of Adamant (Hawthorne)
Martin Faber, The Story of a Criminal (Simms)
Monsieur du Miroir (Hawthorne)
Nick of the Woods (Bird)
The Prophetic Pictures (Hawthorne)

1838
Edward Randolph's Portrait (Hawthorne)
Hugues, the Wer-Wolf; A Kentish Legend of the Middle Ages (Menzies)
Ligeia (Poe)
The Narrative of Arthur Gordon Pym (Poe)

1839
The Fall of the House of Usher (Poe)
Old Esther Dudley (Hawthorne)
William Wilson (Poe)

1840
Delusion; or, The Witch of New England (Lee)
The Man of the Crowd (Poe)

1841
A Descent into the Maelström (Poe)
Monaldi (Allston)
The Skeleton in Armor (Longfellow)

1842
Ben Blower's Story; or, How to Relish a Julip (Hoffman)
The Mask of the Red Death (Poe)

1843
The Birthmark (Hawthorne)
The Black Cat (Poe)
Egotism; or, The Bosom Serpent (Hawthorne)
Fire Worship (Hawthorne)
Howard; or, The Mysterious Disappearance (Ingraham)
The Pit and the Pendulum (Poe)
The Tell-Tale Heart (Poe)

1844
Castle Dismal; or, The Bachelor's Christmas (Simms)
The Ladye Annabel; or, The Doom of the Poisoner (Lippard)
Rappaccini's Daughter (Hawthorne)

1845
Count Julian; or, The Last Days of the Goth (Simms)
The Drop of Blood; or, The Maiden's Rescue (Bailey)
The Facts in the Case of M. Valdemar (Poe)
Father Felix (Cannon)
Grayling; or, Murder Will Out (Simms)
The Nun of St. Ursula; or, The Burning of the Convent (Jones)
The Oval Portrait (Poe)

1846
The Cask of Amontillado (Poe)
Matilda; or, The Spectre of the Castle (Simms)
The Quaker City; or, The Monks of Monk Hall (Lippard)
The Ransomed Bride; A Tale of the Inquisition (Weld)
The Spectre Steamer (Ingraham)
The Vroucolacas (Paulding)

1847
The Countess; or, The Inquisitor's Punishments (Engolls)
The Monk's Revenge; or, The Secret Enemy (Spring)
The Mysteries of Troy (Hazelton)

1848
The Chieftain of Churubusco; or, The Spectre of the Cathedral (Halyard)
The Haunted Bride; or, The Witch of Gallows Hill (Halyard)
The Haunting Shadow (Morgan)

1849
The Entranced; or, The Wanderer of Eighteen Centuries (Lippard)
Retribution; or, The Vale of Shadows (Southworth)
St. Rosalie; or, The Mysterious Casket (Anon.)
Zimulko; or, The Hag of Beetling Cliff (Maule)

1850
Angela; or, The Convent of Santa Clara (Robinson)
The Predicament (Poe)
The Puritan and his Daughter (Paulding)

1850 (continued)
The Scarlet Letter (Hawthorne)

1851
Black Ralph; or, The Forest Fiend! (Robinson)
Catholina; or, Walled Up Alive (Robinson)
Ethan Brand (Hawthorne)
The House of the Seven Gables (Hawthorne)
Moby-Dick; or, The Whale (Melville)

1852
The Iron Tomb; or, The Mock Count of New York (Bowline)
Pierre; or, The Ambiguities (Melville)

1853
The Curse of Clifton (Southworth)
Jack Long; or, The Shot in the Eye (Webber)
Yieger's Cabinet. Spiritual Vampirism (Webber)

1852
The Ruined Abbey; or, The Gipsies of Forest Hill (Robinson)

1854
Crystalline; or, The Heiress of Fall Down Castle (Shelton)
Danger in the Dark; A Tale of Intrigue and Priestcraft (Kelso)
Sister Agnes; or, The Captive Nun (Anon.)

1855
The Escaped Nun; or, Disclosures of Convent Life (Bunkley)
The Missing Bride; or, Miriam the Avenger (Southworth)

1856
Bartleby the Scrivener (Melville)
The Bell-Tower (Melville)
Benito Cereno (Melville)
A Terrible Night (O'Brien)

1857
The Haunted Castle; or, The Abducted Niece (Bradbury, O.)

1858
The Angel and the Demon; A Tale of Modern Spiritualism (Arthur)
The Fatal Secret; or, Plots and Counterplots (Mayer)
Morgan; or, The Knight of the Black Flag (Judson)

1859
Thayandanegea, the Scourge; or, The War-Eagle of the Mohawks (Judson)

1860
The Haunted Student; A Romance of the Fourteenth Century (Read)
Sir Rohan's Ghost (Spofford)

1861
Elsie Venner; A Romance of Destiny (Holmes)
The Haunted Homestead (Southworth)

1862
The Marble Faun; or, The Romance of Monte Beni (Hawthorne)
Victoria; or, The Heiress of Castle Cliffe (Fleming)

1863
The Amber Gods (Spofford)
Pauline's Passion and Punishment (Alcott)
A Whisper in the Dark (Alcott)

1864
Elisiner; or, The Mysteries of an Old Stone Mansion (Richards)
Hallow Ash-Hall; A Story of a Haunted House (Francis)

1865
A Marble Woman; or, The Mysterious Model (Alcott)
Sweeny Todd; or, The Ruffian Barber (Jones)

1867
The Abbot's Ghost; or, Maurice Treherne's Temptation (Alcott)
Dad's Dog-School (Harris, G.W.)
The Ghost (O'Connor, W.D.)
The Skeleton at the Banquet (Victor)

1868
De Grey: A Romance (James)
The Phantom of the Forest; A Tale of Dark and Bloody Ground (Bennett)
The Romance of Certain Old Clothes (James)

1869
The Day of My Death (Ward)
Perilous Play (Alcott)
The Visit to the Haunted House (Stowe)

1871
Mount Benedict; or, The Violated Tomb (Mc Corry)
Ten Years of Torture; or, Sutten's Death-Bed Confession (Anon.)

1872
Septimius Felton; or, The Elixir of Life (Hawthorne)

1873
A Night of Terror (De Ponte)

1874
La Belle Dame Plantations (Cable)
The Five Fiends; or, The Bender Hotel Horror in Kansas (Anon.)
The Forest Witch; or, The Terror of the Odjibwes (Melville, C.)
The Last of the Valerii (James)

1875
A Ghost Story (Clemens)
The Mystery of the Dark Hollow (Southworth)
The Spectre Lover (Southworth)

1876
Elmwood; or, The Withered Arm (Lennan)
Gabriel Conroy (Harte)
The Ghostly Rental (James)

1877
The Phantom Horseman; or, Saved by a Spectre (Stone)

1878
A Ghost of the Sierras (Harte)

1879
Archibald Malmaison (Hawthorne, J.)
A Haunted House (Armstrong)
Jean Ah-Poquelin (Cable)

1880
The Mystery of Allanwold (Van Loon)
The Stillwater Tragedy (Aldrich)
The Victim of the Mysterious Mark; or, The Magic Mirror (Remington)

1881
A Ghost Story (Harris, J.C.)
The Lost Room (O'Brien)
What Was It? A Mystery (O'Brien)

1882
The Ancestral Footstep (Hawthorne)
The Dolliver Romance (Hawthorne)
Dr. Grimshawe's Secret (Hawthorne)
The Portrait of a Lady (James)

1883
John's Alive; or, The Bride of a Ghost (Thompson)

1884
Horrors! Adapted from the French (Valentine)
The Transferred Ghost (Stockton)

1885
The Diamond Lens (O'Brien)

1887
A Modern Mephistopheles (Alexander)
Dr. Phoenix' Skeleton; or, The Man with a Mystery (Wood, Mrs. Seth)
The Soul of the Great Bell (Hearn)

1888
The Death Ship (Russell, W.C.)
The Hidden Hand; or, Capitola the Madcap (Southworth)
Ken's Mystery (Hawthorne, J.)
An Unlaid Ghost. A Study in Metempsychosis (Anon.)

1891
Chickamauga (Bierce)
The Damned Thing (Bierce)
The Eyes of the Panther (Bierce)
The Giant Wistaria (Gilman)
The Golden Arm (Clemens)
The Middle Toe of the Right Foot (Bierce)
The Moonlit Road (Bierce)
A New England Nun (Freeman)
An Occurrence at Owl Creek Bridge (Bierce)
One of the Missing (Bierce)
Vampires. Mademoiselle Réséda (Cruger)
The Witch of Prague (Crawford)

1892
The Ghosts of Stuckeley Castle (Harte)
Sir Edmund Orme (James)
The Yellow Wallpaper (Gilman)

1893
The Death of Halpin Frayser (Bierce)
The Ghost House; or, The Story of Rose Lichen (Mildred)
Owen Wingrave (James)
The Secret of Macarger's Gulch (Bierce)
Toppleton's Client; or, The Spirit in Exile (Bangs)

1894
At the Ghost Hour (Heyse)
The Mystery of the Hacienda (Harte)
The Spectre Cook of Bantletop (Bangs)
The Upper Berth (Crawford)
The Water Ghost of Harrowby Hall (Bangs)

1895
The Altar of the Dead (James)
The Dead Valley (Cram)
In the Court of the Dragon (Chambers)
The Mask (Chambers)
The Phantoms of the Footbridge (Murfree)
The Yellow Sign (Chambers)

1896
The Friend of the Friends (James)
Singed Moths (Dawson)

1897
The Ghost of Guir House (Beale)
The Monster Maker (Morrow0

1898
The Blindman's World (Bellamy)
The Shape of Fear (Peattie)
The Turn of the Screw (James)

1899
The Conjure Woman (Chesnutt)
Mc Teague: A Story of San Francisco (Norris)
The Monster (Crane)
The Spirit of the Haunted House (Stovall)

1900
To Have and to Hold (Johnston)

1901
The Amalgamated Brotherhood of Spooks (Bangs)
The Sacred Fount (James)

1902
The Cloistering of Ursula (Scollard)

1903
The Beast in the Jungle (James)
The Hall Bedroom (Freeman)
His Apparition (Howells)
Luella Miller (Freeman)
The Shadows on the Wall (Freeman)
The Southwest Chamber (Freeman)
Though One Rose from the Dead (Howells)
The Vacant Lot (Freeman)

1903 (continued)
The Wind in the Rose Bush (Freeman)

1904
The Harbor-Master (Chambers)
In the Closed Room (Burnett)
The Spectre in the Cart (Page)

1905
The Bell in the Fog (Atherton)
The Dead and the Countess (Atherton)
Death and the Woman (Atherton)
The Mortgage on the Brain (Harper)
The Striding Place (Atherton)
The Tyranny of the Dark (Garland)

1907
The Black Thing of Hatchet Lake (Mott)
The House of the Vampire (Vierick)
The Jolly Corner (James)
Perdita (Hawthorne, H.)
The White Cat (Burgess)

1908
The Circular Staircase (Rinehart)
The Intoxicated Ghost (Bates)

1909
One Summer Night (Bierce)

1910
Afterward (Wharton)
The Eyes (Wharton)

1911
The Dead Smile (Crawford)
For the Blood is the Life (Crawford)
The Haunted Pajamas (Elliott)
The Screaming Skull (Crawford)

1913
The Case of Jennie Brice (Rinehart)
The Forbidden Floor (Harvey)

1914
Vandover and the Brute (Norris)

1916
All Souls (Wharton)

1918
Citadel of Fear (Stevens)
The Ghost Garden (Rives)
The People of the Pit (Merritt)

1919
Dey Ain't No Ghosts (Butler)
The Moon Pool (Merritt)
Sinister House (Hall)
Winesburg, Ohio (Anderson)

1921
Ghost Gleams, Tales of the Uncanny (Windsor)
The Thing From the Lake (Ingram)

1922
Billy Budd, Foretopman (Melville)
The Curious Case of Benjamin Button (Fitzgerald)
Louquier's Third Act (Gerould)

1923
The Rats in the Walls (Lovecraft)
The Shadowy Third (Glasgow)
The Witch of Coös (Frost)

1924
The Thing in the Woods (Williams, H.)

1925
An American Tragedy (Dreiser)
Bewitched (Wharton)
Vale of the Corbies (Burks)

1926
A Bottle of Perrier (Wharton)
The Dark Chamber (Cline)
The Eater of Darkness (Coates)
Miss Mary Pask (Wharton)
The Outsider (Lovecraft)

1927
The Hand (Dreiser)
The Place Called Dagon (Gorman)

1928
The Call of Cthulhu (Lovecraft)

1929
The Dunwich Horror (Lovecraft)
Skull-Face (Howard)

1930
As I Lay Dying (Faulkner)
It Walks by Night (Carr)
Red Snow (Moxley)
A Rose for Emily (Faulkner)

1931
Dry September (Faulkner)
The Horror from the Hills (Long)
Sanctuary (Faulkner)

1932
Burn, Witch, Burn! (Merritt)
The Second Interment (Smith)

1933
The Werewolf of Paris (Endore)

1934
Creep, Shadow! (Merritt)

1934 (continued)
Silent Snow, Secret Snow (Aiken)

1935
The Feast in the Abbey (Bloch)

1936
Absalom, Absalom! (Faulkner)
The Shadow Out of Time (Lovecraft)
The Shadow Over Innsmouth (Lovecraft)

1937
The Burning Court (Carr)
Fingers of Fear (Nicolson)
The Thing on the Doorstep (Lovecraft)

1938
The Black Drama (Wellman)
The Listening House (Seeley)
The Wall (Rinehart)

1939
Night Rider (Warren)

1940
Native Son (Wright)
Sapphira and the Slave Girl (Cather)

1941
The Case of Charles Dexter Ward (Lovecraft)
The Devil We Know (Moore)
Petrified Man (Welty)
Reflections in a Golden Eye (Mc Cullers)
The White Wolf (Gregory)

1942
The Devotee of Evil (Smith)
Epiphany of Death (Smith)

1943
At Heaven's Gate (Warren)
Yours Truly, Jack the Ripper (Bloch)

1944
The Eye and the Finger (Wandrei)
The Man Who Lived Underground (Wright)

1945
The Lurker at the Threshold (Lovecraft & Derleth)
No Light for Uncle Henry (Derleth)
Witch House (Walton)

1946
The Black Druid (Long)
Daemon (Moore)
The Member of the Wedding (Mc Cullers)

1947
The Dark Fantastic (Echard)
Dark Music (Snow)

1947 (continued)
A Name for Evil (Lytle)
Revelations in Black (Jacobi)

1948
Castle in the Swamp; A Tale of Old Carolina (Marshall)
Darker Than You Think (Williamson)
The Dream Quest of Unknown Kadath (Lovecraft)
One Foot in the Grave (Grubb)
Other Voices, Other Rooms (Capote)

1949
The Headless Hawk (Capote)
The House of Breath (Goyen)
Shut a Final Door (Capote)
A Tree of Night (Capote)

1950
Castle of Iron (De Camp)

1951
Hangsaman (Jackson, S.)
Lie Down in Darkness (Styron)

1953
Bianca's Hands (Sturgeon)
The Conjure Wife (Leiber)
Good Country People (O'Connor)
A Good Man is Hard to Find (O'Connor)
A Late Encounter with the Enemy (O'Connor)
Shambleau (Moore)
A Stroke of Good Fortune (O'Connor)

1954
The Bird's Nest (Jackson, S.)
The Black Prince (Grau)
I Am Legend (Matheson)
The Survivor (Lovecraft)

1955
The Vanishing American (Beaumont)

1957
Color of Darkness (Purdy)

1958
Canavan's Back Yard (Brennan)
The Graveyard Reader (Sturgeon)
The Sundial (Jackson, S.)
The Werewolf of Ponkert (Munn)

1959
The Haunting of Hill House (Jackson, S.)
Malcolm (Purdy)
Psycho (Bloch)
The Shuttered Room (Lovecraft)

1960
A Fine and Private Place (Beagle)
The Howling Man (Beaumont)

1960 (continued)
Invaders from the Dark (La Spina)
The Nephew (Purdy)
The Violent Bear It Away (O'Connor)

1961
The Beetle Leg (Hawkes)
Everything That Rises Must Converge (O'Connor)
Old House of Fear (Kirk)
Some of Your Blood (Sturgeon)

1962
City of Night (Rechy)
Ex Tenebris (Kirk)
The Lonesome Place (Derleth)
We Have Always Lived in the Castle (Jackson, S.)
Who's Afraid of Virginia Woolf? (Albee)

1963
The Man Who Collected Poe (Bloch)

1965
The Possibility of Evil (Jackson, S.)
Tiny Alice (Albee)

1966
The Dead Hand (Quinn)
In Cold Blood (Capote)
Where Are You Going? Where Have You Been? (Oates)

1967
Bones for China (Price)
Rosemary's Baby (Levin)

1968
Black Easter (Blish)
The Blacking Factory and Pennsylvania Gothic (Sheed)
The Rock (Jackson, S.)
The Visit (Jackson, S.)

1969
The Folsom Flint (Keller)
The Goose on the Grave (Hawkes)
Lila, the Werewolf (Beagle)
The Oldest Soldier (Leiber)
The Two Character Play (Williams, T.)

1970
Death's Echo (Hershey)
The Ghoul (Smith)
Mc Afee County: A Chronicle (Steadman)
The Supernumerary Corpse (Smith)
Them (Oates)

1971
The Broken Key (Roby)
Hell House (Matheson)
Love in the Ruins; The Adventures of a Bad Catholic (Percy)
The Other (Tryon)

1972
Green Darkness (Seton)
Haunting of Clifton Court (Ross)
The Mangler (King)
Something Wicked This Way Comes (Bradbury, R.)

1973
Beasts of the Southern Wild (Betts)
Burnt Offerings (Marasco)
Carrie (King)
His Name on a Bullet (Wellman)
The House on Parchment Street (Mc Killip)
Trucks (King)

1974
House of Many Shadows (Mertz)
Sometimes They Come Back (King)
Trewlawny (Holland)

1975
American Gothic (Bloch)
The Dead Father (Barthelme)
The Dracula Tape (Saberhagen)
Julia (Straub)
'Salem's Lot (King)
The Skull of the Marquis de Sade (Bloch)
Wyndcliffe: A Story of Suspense (Lawrence)

1976
The Fury (Farris)
Interview with the Vampire (Rice)
The Ledge (King)
The Vampire of Mons (Stewart)
Wicked Loving Lies (Rogers)

1977
The Children of the Corn (King)
The Dungeon (Oates)
Little Angie (Cave)
Our Lady of Darkness (Leiber)
The Shining (King)
The Unearthly (Daniels, D.)

1978
The Black Castle (Daniels, L.)
Dark Wings (Leiber)
Hotel Transylvanis (Yarbro)
The House Next Door (Siddons)
Midnight in the Mirror World (Leiber)
The Mirror (Millhiser)
The Shot-Tower Ghost (Counselman)

1979
The Dead Zone (King)
Ghost Story (Straub)
Lord of the Hollow Dark (Kirk)

1980
Firestarter (King)
The Mist (King)

1980 (continued)
Where There's a Will (Matheson)

1981
Buried Child (Shepard)
Cujo (King)
Dracula's Children (Lortz)
The Monkey (King)
Woodland Burial (Long)

1982
The Breast (Roth)
Night of Black Glass (Ellison)
The Raft (King)
Stalking the Nightmare (Ellison)

1983
Pet Sematary (King)

1984
Shadow of the Torturer (Wolfe)

1985
Carpenter's Gothic (Gaddis)
Sanguinarius (Russell, Ray)

1986
Ghostly Populations (Matthews)

1987
Spirit Seizures (Pritchard)

1988
Blood and Water (Mc Grath)

Undated Work
Unpunished (Gilman)

Appendix Two
Bibliography of Critical
Sources on American Gothicism

GENERAL STUDIES RELATED TO THE AMERICAN GOTHIC

Bell, Michael Davitt. The Development of American Romance. Chicago: Chicago UP, 1980.

Brown, Herbert Ross. The Sentimental Novel in America, 1789-1860. Durham, NC: Duke UP, 1940; New York: Octagon Books, 1975.

Cawelti, John G. Adventure, Mystery, and Romance: Formula Stories as Art and Popular Culture. Chicago: Chicago UP, 1976.

Cowie, Alexander. The Rise of the American Novel. New York: American Book Company, 1948.

Daniels, Les. Living in Fear: A History of Horror in Mass Media. New York: Scribner's, 1975.

Davis, David Brion. Homicide in American Fiction, 1798-1860: A Study in Social Values. Ithaca, NY: Cornell UP, 1957.

Hart, James D. The Popular Book: A History of America's Literary Taste. New York: Oxford UP, 1950; Westport, CT: Greenwood Press, 1976.

Hazen, Helen. Endless Rapture: Rape, Romance, and the Female Imagination. New York: Scribner's, 1983.

Hokenson, Jan and Howard Pearce. Forms of the Fantastic. Westport, CT: Greenwood Press, 1986.

Hoyt, Charles A. Minor American Novelists. Carbondale, IL: Southern Illinois UP, 1971.

Johannsen, Albert. The House of Beadle and Adams and its Dime and Nickel Novels. Norman, OK: Oklahoma UP, 1950.

Kerr, Howard. Mediums and Spirit-Rappers and Roaring Radicals: Spiritualism in American Literature, 1850-1900. Urbana, IL: Illinois UP, 1972.

Loshe, Lillie Deming. The Early American Novel. New York: Columbia UP, 19-07; New York: Frederick Ungar, 1966.

Mc Carthy, Paul. Long Fiction of the American Renaissance: A Symposium on Genre. Hartford, CT: Transcendental Books, 1977.

Modleski, Tania. Loving with a Vengeance: Mass-Produced Fantasies for Women. Hamden, CT: Archon, 1982.

Mussell, Kay. Fantasy and Reconciliation: Contemporary Formulas of Women's Romance Fiction. Westport, CT: Greenwood Press, 1984.

Nye, Russel B. American Literary History; 1607-1830. New York: Alfred A. Knopf, 1970.

O'Connor, William Van. The Grotesque: An American Genre and Other Essays. Carbondale, IL: Southern Illinois UP, 1962.

Payne, Ladell. Black Novelists and the Southern Literary Tradition. Athens, GA: Georgia UP, 1981.

Petter, Henri. The Early American Novel. Columbus, OH: Ohio State UP, 19-71.

Quinn, Arthur Hobson. American Fiction: An Historical and Critical Survey. New York: Appleton-Century-Crofts, 1936.

Wagenknecht, Edward. Cavalcade of the American Novel. New York: Holt, Rinehart and Winston, 1952.

Wright, Lyle H. American Fiction 1774-1900. 3 vols. San Marino, CA: Huntington Library, 1939; 1969.

REFERENCE SOURCES

Barron, Neil. Horror Literature: A Reader's Guide. New York: Garland Publishing, 1990.

Baym, Nina. Woman's Fiction: A Guide to Novels by and about Women in America 1820-1870. Ithaca, NY: Cornell UP, 1978.

Bleiler, E.F. A Guide to Supernatural Fiction. A Full Description of 1,775 Books from 1750 to 1960. Kent, OH: Kent State UP, 1983.

_____. Supernatural Fiction Writers: Fantasy and Horror. 2 vols. New York: Scribner's, 1985.

Frank, Frederick. Guide to the Gothic: An Annotated Bibliographg of Criticism. Metuchen, NJ: Scarecrow Press, 1984.

_____. Gothic Fiction: A Master List of Twentieth Century Criticism and Research. Westport, CT: Meckler Corporation, 1988.

Hawkins, Jean. "Ghost Stories and Tales of the Supernatural." Bulletin of Bibliography, 5 (1909): 142-145, 168-171.

Hubin, Allen J. The Bibliography of Crime Fiction, 1749-1975. Listing All Mystery, Detective, Suspense, Police, and Gothic Fiction in Book

Form Published in the English Language. Del Mar, CA: Publisher's, 1979.

Magill, Frank N. Survey of Modern Fantasy Literature. 5 vols. Engelwood Cliffs, NJ: Salem Press, 1983.

Mainiero, Lina. American Women Writers: A Critical Reference Guide from Colonial Times to the Present. 4 vols. New York: Frederick Ungar, 1979.

Mussell, Kay. "Gothic Novels." Handbook of American Popular Culture, ed. M. Thomas Inge. Westport, CT: Greenwood Press, 1978, pp.151-169.

_____. Women's Gothic and Romantic Fiction: A Reference Guide. Westport, CT: Greenwood Press, 1983.

_____. "Gothic Novels." Handbook of American Popular Literature. ed. M. Thomas Inge, Westport, CT: Greenwood Press, 1988, pp.157-173.

Parker, Patricia L. American Writers Before 1800: A Biographical and Critical Dictionary. Westport, CT: Greenwood Press, 1983.

Radcliffe, Elsa J. Gothic Novels of the Twentieth Century: An Annotated Bibliography. Metuchen, NJ: Scarecrow Press, 1979.

Siemon, Fred. Ghost Story Index: An Author-Title Index to More Than 2,200 Stories of Ghosts, Horrors, and the Macabre Appearing in 190 Books and Anthologies. San Jose, CA & Monroe, NY: Library Research Associates, 1967.

Tymn, Marshall B. The Year's Scholarship in Science Fiction, Fantasy, and Horror Literature. Kent, OH: Kent State UP, 1980-82; annually in the journal, Extrapolation.

_____. Horror Literature: A Core Collection and Reference Guide. New York: R.R. Bowker, 1981.

Vinson, James and D.L. Kirkpatrick. Twentieth Century Romance and Gothic Writers. Detroit, MI: Gale, 1982.

CRITICAL STUDIES OF THE AMERICAN GOTHIC

Accetta, Michael Angelo. "Gothic Elements in the Early American Novel, 1775-1825." Dissertation Abstracts, 14 (1954): 1394 (University of Pittsburgh).

Banta, Martha. "American Apocalypses: Excrement and Ennui." Studies in the Literary Imagination, 4 (1974): 1-30.

Benton, Richard. "The Problems of Literary Gothicism." ESQ: A Journal of the American Renaissance, 18 (1972): 5-9.

Büssing, Sabine. Aliens in the Home: The Child in Horror Fiction. Westport, CT: Greenwood Press, 1987.

Coad, Oral S. "The Gothic Element in American Literature Before 1835." Journal of English and Germanic Philology, 24 (1925): 72-93.

Dimaggio, Richard S. "The Tradition of the American Gothic Novel." Dissertation Abstracts International, 37 (1976): 307A (University of Arizona).

Dimic, Milan V. "Aspects of American and Canadian Gothicism." Proceedings of the 7th Congress of the International Comparative Literature Association: Literatures of America: Dependence, Independence, Interdependence. Stuttgart, West Germany: Bieber, 1979, pp. 143-149.

Egan, Kenneth. "Apocalypse Against Progress: Gothic and Pastoral Modes in the American Romance." Dissertation Abstracts International, 45 (1985): 2526A-2527A (University of Wisconsin).

Fiedler, Leslie A. Love and Death in the American Novel. New York: Criterion, 1960; New York: Dell, 1966.

Fleenor, Juliann E. The Female Gothic. Montreal: Eden Press, 1983.

Green, Gary Lee. "The Language of Nightmare: A Theory of American Gothic Fiction." Dissertation Abstracts International, 46 (1985): 1279A (University of Oklahoma).

Gross, Louis S. Redefining the American Gothic: From Wieland to the Day of the Dead. Ann Arbor, MI: UMI Press, 1989.

Haining, Peter. Gothic Tales of Terror: Classic Horror Stories from Great Britain, Europe, and the United States 1765-1840. New York: Taplinger, 1972.

Heller, Terry. The Delights of Terror: An Aesthetics of the Tale of Terror. Urbana, IL: Illinois UP, 1987.

Hofstadter, Beatrice. "Popular Culture and the Romantic Heroine." American Scholar, 30 (Winter 1960-1961): 98-116.

Jones, Robert Kenneth. The Shudder Pulps: A History of the Weird Menace Magazines of the 1930s. West Linn, OR: FAX Collector's Edition, 1975; New York: New American Library, 1978.

——. "Popular's Weird Menace Pulps." Selected Tales of Grim and Grue, ed. Sheldon Jaffery. Bowling Green, OH: Bowling Green University Popular Press, 1987, pp.1-8.

Kerr, Howard, John W. Crowley and Charles Crow. The Haunted Dusk: American Supernatural Fiction, 1820-1920. Athens, GA: Georgia UP, 1983.

King, Stephen. Danse Macabre. New York: Everett House, 1981.

Lacombe, Alain. Le Roman Noir Americain. Paris: Union Generale d'Edition, 1975.

Lloyd-Smith, Allan Gardner. Uncanny American Fiction: Medusa's Face. New York: St. Martin's Press, 1989.

Lovecraft, Howard Phillips. Supernatural Horror in Literature. New York: Ben Abramson, 1945; New York: Dover Publications, 1973.

Malin, Irving. New American Gothic. Carbondale, IL: Southern Illinois UP, 1962.

_____. "American Gothic Images." Mosaic: A Journal of the Interdisciplinary Study of Literature, 6 (1973): 145-171.

Phillips, George L. "The Gothic Element in the American Novel Before 1830." West Virginia University Bulletin Philological Studies, 3 (1939): 37-45.

Pribek, Thomas R. "Utility and Invention in American Gothic Literature." Dissertation Abstracts International, 47 (1987): 3429A-3430A (University of Wisconsin).

Quinn, Arthur Hobson. "Some Phases of the Supernatural in American Literature." Publications of the Modern Language Association, 25 (1910): 114-133.

Redden, Sister Mary Mauritia. The Gothic Fiction in the American Magazines (1765-1800). Washington, DC: Catholic UP, 1939.

Ringe, Donald A. American Gothic: Imagination and Reason in Nineteenth Century Fiction. Lexington, KY: Kentucky UP, 1982.

Russ, Joanna. "Somebody's Trying to Kill Me and I Think it's My Husband: The Modern Gothic." Journal of Popular Culture, 6 (1973): 666-691.

Schweitzer, Darrell. Discovering Modern Horror Fiction. Mercer Island, WA: Starmont House, 1985.

_____. Discovering Modern Horror Fiction: II. Mercer Island, WA: Starmont House, 1988.

Shelden, Pamela J. "American Gothicism: The Evolution of a Mode." Dissertation Abstracts International, 35 (1974): 1634A-1635A (Kent State University).

Simpson, Lewis. 3 by 3: Masterworks of Southern Gothic. Atlanta, GA: Peachtree Press, 1985.

Skarda, Patricia L. and Nora Crow Jaffe. The Evil Image: Two Centuries of Gothic Short Fiction and Poetry. New York: New American Library, 1981.

Sloan, De Villo. "Influences of Industrialization on the Origins and Development of American Gothic Fiction." Dissertation Abstracts International, 43 (1982): 1548A (SUNY at Buffalo).

Stewart, Susan. "The Epistemology of the Horror Story." Journal of American Folklore, 95 (1982): 33-50.

Thompson, G.R. "Gothic Fiction and the Romantic Age." Romantic Gothic Tales, 1790-1840. New York: Harper & Row, 1979.

Tucker, Amy. "America's Gothic Landscape." Dissertation Abstracts International, 40 (1980): 5868A (New York University).

Twitchell, James B. Dreadful Pleasures: An Anatomy of Modern Horror. New York: Oxford UP, 1985.

Weinberg, Robert. The Weird Tales Story. West Linn, OR: FAX Collector's Edition, 1977.

Williamson, J.N. <u>Masques: All New Works of Horror and the Supernatural</u>. Baltimore: Maclay, 1984.

Yates, Jo Anne. "American Gothic: Sources of Terror in American Fiction Before the Civil War." <u>Dissertation Abstracts International</u>, 41 (1980): 1602A (University of North Carolina).

Author and Critic Index

Numbers refer to entry numbers, not page numbers. <u>Underlined numbers</u> indicate primary entries.

Title Index

Numbers refer to entry numbers, not page numbers. Underlined numbers indicate primary entries.

Numbers refer to entry numbers, not page numbers. <u>Underlined numbers</u> indicate primary entries.

Index of Gothic Themes, Motifs, Events, Character Names, and Settings

Numbers refer to entry numbers, not page numbers.

ABBEY: haunted; 009, 122, 377, 383, 410
Abbot Boniface, 009
ABDUCTION OF HEROINE: 049, 060, 162, 224, 252
Abeles, Simon, 103
Addams, Frankie, 319
Addams, Jarvis, 319
Adeppi, 174
Ah Ben, 032
Albert, Sir, 451
Aldarin, 287
Alderling, Mrs., 219
Alençon, Antoinette, 002
ALIENATION: see ISOLATION
Almodham, Henry, 494
Amador, 048
Ambrose, Father, 069
Amelia, 504
Aminadab, 190
Anderson, Lydia, 142
Anderville, 215
Andrews, Emily, 429
Andrews, Phaeton Howard, 346
Andros, Sir Edmund, 181
ANIMAL: see BEAST
Animula, 360
Ansley, Edward, 482
Ansley, Matilda, 482
ANTI-CATHOLICISM: abuse of nuns, 070, 339, 420, 434; attack on convent, 252, 317, 339; secrecy, treachery, conspiracy, atrocity, 258, 409, 486; see

ANTI-CATHOLICISM (continued) also MONK, PRIEST, NUN, INQUISITION
ANTI-CHRIST: see ANTI-GOD
ANTI-GOD, ANTI-CHRIST: 115, 304; blasphemous portrait, 262
Antrim, Mary, 244
APOCALYPSE: see END OF WORLD
Apollinax, Mr., 276
APPARITION: see SPECTRE
Arabian, Keyork, 103
Arcane, Manfred, 276
Archer, Isabel, 241
ARCHITECTURAL SENTIENCE OR ALIVENESS: 232, 379, 427, 492; see also CHAMBER OF HORRORS
Armand, Jean, 435
Armand [the vampire], 400
Armina, 438
Armitage, Dr., 298
Arnold, Henry, 505
ARTIST: as maniac, 013; as violator of subject's soul, 017, 184; power to destroy, 008, 109; reduction of humans to material, 008; reordering of nature, 017; see also FAUSTIAN HERO, STUDIO
Ashley Family, 430
ASSASSINATION: see MURDER
Atlantes, 113
ATOMIC SHADOW OR THREAT: 051, 300
ATROCITY: by Indians, 050; by whites, 172;
Aun' Peggy, 092
Aunt Keziah, 205

MIRROR, LOOKING GLASS: container of secret self, 193, 337, 399; horror of self or monstrous reflection, 296, 313; spectral manifestation in, 144; obsession with, 284; see also DOPPELGÄNGER, CONFRONTATION

Misfit, 362

Miss Alice, 005

Miss Wisteria, 078

Missouri [Zoo], 078

MOAN: see SCREAM

Mobley, Alma, 461

Molineux, Robin, 202

Monaldi, 013

Monchell, Mr. 033

Mondelli, 407

Mondrick, Dr., 499

Mondrick, Rowena, 499

MONASTERY: see CONVENT

Moneypenny, Shadrach, 369

MONK: see PRIEST

MONSTER, CREATURE, THING: 301; 031, 463; beast of forest, 036, 497; cosmic, 298; creature from watery depths, 091, 222, 273, 324, 331, 345; invisible, 039; mechanical, 264, 266; unaware of hideousness, 102; see also VAMPIRISM, WEREWOLFERY, MUTILATION

Montfort, Captain Barral de, 128

Montgomery, Alice-Marie, 461

Montresor, 389

MOON AND MOONLIGHT: eerie lunar lighting, 042;

Montague, Dr., 232

Montalia, Madelaine de, 509

Morcell, 482

More, Dr. Thomas, 373

Morella, 375

Morely, Aurelia, 503

Morgan, Sir Henry, 255, 321

Morgan, Hugh, 039

Morgan, Michael, 030

Morton, Martha, 467

Moss, Rose, 445

Mostyn, Anna, 461

MOTHER: cruel and nefarious, 031; slaughtered, 038; see also FEMME FATALE

Munn, Percy, 480

Munson, Buford, 365

MURDER, HOMICIDE, ASSASSINATION: mass killing, 056, 128, 137; mob or lynch gang, 133, 202, 252; of child, 320, 339, 425, 460, 469; of entire family, 063, 261; of husband, 485; of lover, 119; of twin, 380; of wife, 041, 042,

MURDER, HOMICIDE (continued) 347, 352, 384, 403, 467; racial, 507; thrill killing, 082; see also DEATH, MUTILATION, REVENGE, SUICIDE

Murdock, Sue, 481

MUSIC: eerie, 112; from magic instrument, 325; hideous and dissonant, 088; raising dead, 126; see also HAUNTED OBJECT

MUTILATION, DISFIGUREMENT, DISMEMBERMENT: 039; 083, 102, 265, 287, 330, 376, 384, 386, 425, 469, 497; by machine, 264, 327; by whipping, 484; symbolic, 361; see also MURDER, HEADLESSNESS

Mysterio, Professor, 396

Naldi, Cora, 394

Nantauquas, 251

NARCOTIC, OPIATE, DRUG: 377; hashish eating; 010

Nast, Father, 108

NATURAL SUPERNATURALISM: 049, 084; see also WILDERNESS

NECKLACE: as Satanic charm, 112; see also HAUNTED OBJECT

NECROMANCY: see RESURRECTION

NECROPHILIA, CORPSE LOVE: 131, 186, 227, 320, 394, 406, 473; with dead wife, 288; see also CHAMBER OF HORRORS, CORPSE

Nefandor, Giles, 284

Neuvorne, Clarence, 401

NEVER-ENDING LIFE: see WANDERING JEW, ENTRAPMENT IN TIME

Neville, Robert, 311

NIGHTMARE: see DREAM, SLEEPWALKING

Nightshade, James, 061

NOBLEMAN: renegade or false, 023; sadistic, tyrannical, 023; see also VILLAIN

Norma, Maria of, 129

Norman, Jim, 265

Norman, Sir, 320

Norrys, Captain, 296

Nowell, Alice, 491

NUDITY: 090; as assertion of self, 014; sadistic, 318

NUN: as victim, 070, 317, 420, 434; bleeding or spectral, 456; escaped from convent, 070; walled up alive, 101, 409; see also ANTI-CATHOLICISM, PRIEST, MAIDEN MENACED

Nyarlathotep, 304

Oberon, 198

VILLAIN (continued)
  maniacal, 324; member of secret
  society, 065, 502; political,
  267, 268; scheming, 220, 241,
  255, 445; sexual, 013, 023; see
  also DEVIL, FAUSTIAN HERO
VILLAINESS: see FEMME FATALE;
Villaneuva, Sebastian of, 111
Vince, William, 067
Viney, Aunt, 170
Violante, 424
VIRGIN IN DISTRESS: see MAIDEN
  MENACED
Vironaldi, Marquese di, 058
VISION: see DREAM, CONFRONTATION,
  SPECTRE
Vivea, 138
VOICE: cadaverous, 094; from be-
  yond grave, 219; mysterious,
  023, 365; of the Almighty, 063;
  supernatural, 080, 109, 451,
  462; see also CEMETERY, COFFIN,
  LAUGHTER
Von Starkenfaust, Herman, 224
VORTEX: see WHIRLPOOL
VOYAGE: see JOURNEY, DESCENT

Waite, Asenath, 301
Waite, Ephraim, 301
Waite, Natalie, 229
Walcott, Edward, 178
Waldegrave, Mary, 066
Walsingworth, Foresetta, 401
Walter, Nurse, 332
Walters, Vincent, 079
WANDERING: denial of homecoming,
  022; eternal, futile, 400, 419;
  quest for lost beloved, 103,
  113; see also JOURNEY, DESCENT,
  WANDERING JEW
WANDERING JEW, CURSE OF CAIN, FLY-
  ING DUTCHMAN, NEVER-ENDING LIFE:
  021; 063; 097, 199, 281, 289,
  398, 417, 419, 487; see also
  FAUSTIAN HERO, IMMORTALITY, UN-
  PARDONABLE SIN
Wanderley, Donald, 461
WAR: as Gothic background, 212,
  220, 281, 480; embodiment of,
  202; see also BATTLEFIELD AS
  GOTHIC ENVIRONMENT, WOUND, HAUN-
  TED OBJECT, WEAPON
Ward, Charles Dexter, 302
Ware, Thereon, 051
Warfield, Capitola, 447
Warfield, Major, 447
Waring, Esther, 109
WARLOCK: see WITCH
Warner, Jacqueline, 154

Warren, Captain Charles, 161
Warrenger, Melany, 405
WATER: as home of spirits, 025;
  see also RIVER, LAKE, MONSTER,
  WHIRLPOOL
Watt, John, 445
Watts, Laverne, 364
Waugh, Commodore Nikolas, 443
WEAPON: hair-trigger rifle, 044,
  484; see also HAUNTED OBJECT
Weasel, Dr. E. Willamot, 485
WEDDING, MARRIAGE: enforced, 058,
  407; interrupted by violence,
  049, 254; missing bride, groom,
  138; spectral bridegroom or
  spectre at, 185, 468; see also
  CONFRONTATION, SPECTRE
Weigall, 020
Welbeck, 064
Wendall, Jules, 355
Wendall, Loretta, 355
Wendall, Maureen, 355
Wenonga, 050
WEREWOLFERY, LYCANTHROPY: 031,
  128, 159, 277, 330, 347, 353,
  497, 499; see also BEAST, TRANS-
  FORMATION
Werner, Carl, 428, 433
Wesley, John, 362
Westcott Family, 156
Westen, Franz, 282
Western Barbarian, 169
Wharton Family, 097
Whateley, Abner, 306
Whateley, Luther, 306
Whateley, Wilbur, 298
Wheatcroft, George, 141
WHIRLPOOL, MAELSTRÖM, VORTEX: 382;
  as image of Gothic experience,
  082, 324, 508; see also ENCLO-
  SURE, EXTRAORDINARY POSITION,
  UNDERGROUND
White, Carrie, 259
WHOREHOUSE: see BROTHEL
WICKED WOMAN: see FEMME FATALE
Wieland, Clara, 063
Wieland, Theodore, 063
WILDERNESS, WOODS, FOREST, FRON-
  TIER: as dark and bloody ground,
  036, 049, 050, 123, 349, 484; as
  version of haunted castle, 066,
  196, 408, 451; deserted cabin
  in, 109, 168; lost in, 045; see
  also INDIAN, JOURNEY
Wilkins, Abraham, 321
Willett, Dr., 302
Williams, Private Elgee, 318
Willieblud, 330
Willoughby, Georgiana [Yone], 449

About the Author

FREDERICK S. FRANK is Professor of English and Holder of the National Endowment for the Humanities Chair at Allegheny College. He has taught at Boston University, and is the author of many published articles and three books—*Guide to the Gothic: An Annotated Bibliography of Criticism, The First Gothics: A Critical Guide to the English Novel,* and *Montague Summers: A Bibliographical Portrait.*